GOOD NEWS YOU MAY HAVE MISSED

by Michael Joseph Halm, OFS, MI

CONTENTS

All of these articles previously appeared in *My People* newspaper published by Presentation Ministries (presentationministries.com) and were written by Michael Joseph Halm. The monthly newspaper was started in 1987 in response to St. Pope John Paul the Great's call to permeate the secular culture with the gospel. (*The Lay Members of Christ's Faithful People*, 23) I thank God that He guided me to *My People*, where I could write what He wanted me to write, the good things that His people needed to heard for over thirty years under editor-in-chief Judy Grogan, OFS. Many other good news stories by other contributors can be found in the archives (http://presentationministries.com/mypeople/MyPeople.asp).

Shaped History (November 2012), **Heroes Teach Us To Live** (October 2012), **Book Shares Healings At Lourdes** (September 2012), **Patriotic Rosary Offers Prayers For Nation** (July 2012), **Visit To Heaven Reaches Millions** (May 2012), **Videos Can Be Teaching Tools** (April 2012), **Games Have Religious Themes** (January 2012), **Priest Uses Media To Evangelize** (December 2011), **World Youth Day: A Life-Changing Event** (October 2011), **Christians Called To Evangelize** (September 2011), **Pope's Book Hits Bestseller List** (May 2011), **Martyrs Continue To Enrich Church** (April 2011), **Did Jehosophat Really Jump?** (March 2011), **Heritage Girls Provide Faith-Based Scouting** (February 2011), **Book Shares How To Be A Saint, Not A Dummy** (January 2011), **Book Shares Christmas Customs** (December 2010), **Creation Museum Provides Unique Experience** (September 2010), **Stop Cheating God And Yourself** (August 2010), **Microfinance Programs Aid Poor** (July 2010), **Travel Show Goes On Pilgrimages** (June 2010), **Book Reports On Resurrections** (April 2010), **Haiti Quake Produces "Miracles"** (March 2010), **Christians Unite To Affirm Principles** (February 2010), **Priest Uses Cooking To Encourage Community** (November 2009), **Pro-Life Decisions Have Great Impact** (October 2009), **Battle The Culture Of Death** (September 2009), **Miss California USA Defends Marriage** (June 2009), **Screenwriter Shares Conversion Experience** (May 2009), **Debt Continues To Enslave** (March 2009), **Mary Continues To Call For Conversions** (January 2009), **Books Focus On God** (November 2008), **Conversions Continue** (October 2008), **Chinese Church Built On Martyrs** (July 2008), **Faith-Building DVDs Are Increasing** (April 2008), **Iraqi Refugees Need Assistance** (October 2007), **TV Show Is Modern Morality Play** (April 2007), **Passion Play Continues To Proclaim Jesus** (March 2007), **Singer Evangelizes With New Lyrics To Old Songs** (February 2007), **Experience The Nativity Story** (January 2007), **Family Theater Lives** (November 2006), **Holy Families Are Possible With God** (October 2006), **God Cares About Your Finances** (September 2006), **Bishops Decode Jesus** (July 2006), **The Military Tells Their Side** (May 2006), **Decent Films Do Exist** (February 2006), **The Chronicles of Narnia Movies Begin** (December 2005), **Successful Marriage "Secrets" Revealed** (October 2005), **Interest In Papal Prophecies Increases** (July 2005), *The DaVinci Code* **Turned To Good** (June 2005), **Eucharistic Congress Builds Faith** (April 2005), **The Holy Eucharist Is Still Miraculous** (March 2005), **Men Called to Fight for Freedom** (May 2004), **The Greatest Gift: The Incarnation** (December 2003), **God Stars in New Series** (November 2003), **Year of Rosary Ends, But Rosary Power Continues** (October 2003), **Men Challenged to Change the World** (May 2003), **Ethic Saints Enrich Universal Church** (April 2003), **Year of the Rosary Begins** (December 2002), **Men In Black Delivers Message With Humor** (September 2002), **Miracles Are Happening In Mexico** (August 2002), **Jesus Is the Light** (July 2002), **Authors Make Case for Marriage** (June 2002), **Men Answer the Call Again** (May 2002), **The Gates of Hell Do Not Prevail** (April 2002), **The St. John Passion Play: A Cincinnati Tradition** (March 2002), **This Christmas Is Different** (December 2001), **The Net Is Being Mended** (October 2001), **Men Called to Change** (May 2001), **Christ Came at Christmas** (February 2001), **2000 Was A Year of God's Favor** (January 2001), **Christmas Is Miraculous** (December 2000), **The Signs of the Times Are Hopeful** (May 2000), **Sherlock Holmes Finds God** (January 2000), **Jubilee Means Debtfree** (December 1999), **Blessed Are the Persecuted** (September 1999), **Pope Challenges Youth, World** (March 1999), **Holidays Not Only Happy, But Holy** (December 1998), **Christians Bear One Another's Burdens** (September 1998), **Men Are Answering the Call** (August 1998), **Book Prepares for End of Millennium** (March 1998), **Play Together, Stay Together** (December 1997), **Ex-homosexuals Persecuted** (August

1997), **In God We Still Trust** (May 1997), **Jesus Is Alive** (March 1997), **Vitamins Are Pro-Life** (August 1996), **Film List Aids Viewers** (July 1996), **Astronomical Discoveries Glorify God** (April 1996), **Only Jesus Is The True Light** (December 1995), **The Truth About Pocahontas** (October 1995), **Stars Should Lead Us To Jesus** (December 1994), **Praise God For Jupiter's Comet** (September 1994), **Christians Produce Alternative Comics** (February 1994), **Angels Impact People's Lives** (December 1993), **Oldest Scripture Is Discovered** (March 1992), **Share Jesus This Christmas** (December 1990), **Celebrate A True Christmas: Adore Jesus** (December 1989), **Voyager Reveals Glory of God** (September 1989), **Jesus Cures "Holidaze"** (December 1988), **"Colors" Deglorifies Gang Warfare** (June 1988), **Prodigals Meet the Father** (February 1988), **Videos Tell the Good News** (December 1987), **Local Churches Fund Poverty Fight in Haiti** (March 1987)

College Program Impacts Many (August 2018)

The University of Kansas had a great books program in 1970s. After more than a hundred students decided to join the Catholic Church in ten years, the Kansas City *Times* depicted a hippie evolving into a monk. The three professors, all H. Bernard Fink Teacher of the Year award winners, Frank Nelick, Dennis Quinn and John Senior, were accused of proselytizing, found not guilty and it was closed down.

Quinn says, "You teach what you are. Well, we were Catholic, and it came out without us talking about it at all." He specialized in Renaissance literature, but taught a wide range of courses, including Greek, Roman and Medieval classics until he retired in 2006. He had numerous honors, including the and the 1969 HOPE Award from KU. His book, *Isis Exiled: A Synoptic History of Wonder* was published in 2002. Nelick was cited from 1951 to 1960 in "Our Outstanding Teachers" at KU and was nominated for the HOPE Award several times.

Senior won the Amoco Award and citation by *Esquire* magazine as one of America's fifty best teachers. Senior published several books, including, *The Way Down and Out*, *The Death of Christian Culture*, *The Restoration of Christian Culture* and *Pale Horse, Easy Rider*. Fr. Francis Bethel wrote *John Senior and the Restoration of Realism*. He converted to Catholicism in the Sixties, the Lefebvre schismatics.

One alumni of the program is Paul Coakley, now archbishop of Oklahoma City. He remembers, "It was an extraordinary experience, it was an extraordinary time and it was unquestionably the most significant educational experience of my life. Our professors taught as if they believed there was a truth and that that truth was knowable.

"In a certain sense, the focus was on educating the person, forming the person, not so much on training for a career," he points out. "It was a very good foundation for life, whether one entered a trade or a career or a religious vocation. Many people found their life's vocation as a result of that program." Some of these religious vocations were discerned at the Abbey of Notre Dame de Fontgombault in France, a popular student destination. While most enjoyed a sojourn at the Benedictine monastery's guesthouse before returning to Kansas, six stayed behind and took vows."

In 1999, those six graduates returned to their homeland to establish a new Benedictine monastery, Annunciation Priory of Clear Creek in Oklahoma (clearcreekmonks.org). Dom Philip Anderson is now the abbot of Our Lady of the Annunciation of Clear Creek Abbey, OK. In ten years it grew to about 50. "The average age is a little over 40 years. We have many young monks, but some of us are beginning to be not so young!," Abbot Dom says.

James Conley, now bishop of Lincoln, a convert from Presbyterianism, also graduated in 1977. He gave the eulogy for Quinn, which can be read or heard at adraughtofvintage.com.

Yet another alumni, Dr. Robert Carlson, is one of the three founders of Wyoming Catholic College. He told the story in *Truth on Trial: Liberal Education Be Hanged.* Reviewer Scott W. Dorsey wrote he had "never read an account that better exposes the dogma of political correctness and multiculturalism for what it is: a despicable incarnation of the worst sort of academic barbarism."

David Whalen, now associate provost of Hillsdale College in Michigan, calls the program "absolutely determinative" for their path in life. Specifically, says Whalen, the professors' focus on the three transcendentals -- the true, the good and the beautiful -- made an impact on his view on life. "I give credit to that experience," he adds, "for opening my eyes to permanent truth."

Talks by Faculty and Students of the Pearson Integrated Humanities Program are also on line at calliopemuse.wordpress.com. Erin Doom founded the Eighth Institute, inspired by IHP. Some Catholic grade schools and home-schools have tried to incorporate facets of the program, often intermingling the educational philosophy with the Great Books, as has the Thomas More College of Liberal Arts, Merrimack, NH. A scholarship and a memorial is planned (https://fundihpmemorial.org/) at the St. Lawrence Center near campus. It will proclaim the program's emblem and motto, "Nascantur in Admiratione" ("Let us grow in admiration.").

Contest Focuses on Peace (July 2018)

The Maryknoll Fathers and Brothers selected the topic for their annual student essay contest from Pope Francis. Six-to-eight-graders were asked to respond to his call "to take a clear stand for creative and active nonviolence and against all forms of violence."

The topic became even more relevant with new school shootings since then in Florida, Texas and Indiana. Not all students responded as well as eighth-grader Riva Maendel.

Riva begins her prize-winning essay "It Starts with Us" by sharing about her own relationship with her sister, but then applies what she learned from it.

"Our world is full of violence. There are people dying from drug overdoses, shootings, gang-related issues and war. I can't even begin to take a stand on these bigger issues if I fight my sister. So my first small step is to apologize, and I realize what an amazing power two small words, 'I'm sorry', can have.

"Almost everyone in the world wants peace, but we don't know how to find it. One way to bring peace is by praying. We need to pray every day for peace -- in our hearts, in our families, in our schools, communities, churches and the entire world. I think of all the Christians in the Middle Eastern countries who are dying for their faith. These Christians risk their lives to bring the message of peace and nonviolence to those in the Middle East. I also worry about the nuclear standoff that we have with North Korea. I pray that our country will find a peaceful solution to this issue. Another thing that bothers me is the escalation of shootings in our country. We need to pray for all those mourning the loss of loved ones. They are in desperate need of prayer.

"Before we can achieve peace on an international level, we must work toward attaining peace in our daily relationships with those closest to us. I will probably never get a chance to put my life on the line like the Christians in the Middle East. I pray that my school never experiences a school shooting, but nonetheless, I can take a stand for peace and nonviolence every day. I can show my convictions in the small things I do each day. Respecting my parents is promoting peace. Helping out with chores in my house and avoiding conflict with my sister are definite ways to promote peace. at school, the way I interact with my peers will influence the younger students in our school. I can also show interest and support the local organizations in my community that work for peace, our local police officers, AA and other organizations tat work towards bringing peace to those who are trapped in a cycle of violence. Even though our efforts might seem small and insignificant, we are actually working for peace.

"As we strive for peace, we must remember how important forgiveness is. When we forgive, we can learn to trust. Every little brick of peace will help build the foundation for future generations."

The full essays of the ninth-to-twelfth grade division, as well as the second- and third-place winners, can be found at www.MaryknollSociety.org/winners. The webpage includes not only the winning essays from 2017, but also 2016's on the theme "Caring for Our Common Home" and 2015's "real-life, inspirational stories of mercy". The 2014 contest asked students to describe how young people are following the Pope's personal message for them, "Have courage. Go forward. Make noise."

Highschooler Tasnim Islam won with "Voice Against Violence". In the previous years, Grace Smith won with "Respecting Earth, Through Myself and My Government", Meenu Johnkutty with "Saving Our Earth", Grace Wilson with "Someone Special Needs You" and Anna Brest with "A Journey Toward Mercy".

Are Quotes True? (June 2018)

Trent Horn says, "Writing [*What the Saints Never Said*] has shown me ... that it is easier to prove an authentic quote than disprove an inauthentic quote." He subtitles it "Pious Misquotes and the Subtle Heresies They Teach You".

"When it comes to famous saint quotes, some of them may not appear in any of the saint's extent writings or in any early secondary sources, or may contain ... anachronisms or may contradict something in the saints authentic writings, thus showing the quote in question is not authentic. An allegedly original saying found in the earlier writing of another person becomes proof of the quote's true origin."

The most well-know misquote by a saint is St. Francis of Assisi's "Preach the gospel always; if necessary use words." Pope Francis recently quoted it in a homily.

Horn however could find no reference to the statement with or without attributing it to St. Francis before 1990 in Daisy Osborn's *Woman Without Limits*. He also points out the problem with "if necessary".

Another quote attributed to St. Francis is "All the darkness in the world cannot extinguish the light of one candle." This Horn found in a prayer by Rev. Wilbur C. Christmas from 1972. It sounds like the motto of the Christophers theme song "One Little Candle" from 1952.

The Serenity Prayer prayed in Anonymous groups since 1941 has also been misattributed to St. Francis. Horn found a slightly different version attributed to Reinhold Neibuhr in 1927.

Yet another is "Start by doing what's necessary, then do what's possible and then suddenly you are doing the impossible." Horn writes that this "fails the 'sounds right' test" and is "probably fake."

The Prayer for Peace attributed to St. Francis does not come from him. It traces back to the French devotional magazine *La Clomesse* from 1912. Christian Renoux, author of "The Origin of the Peace Prayer of Saint Francis", traced the association of this French prayer to a holy card from 1918. Fr. Ètienne Benoît, a Franciscan, printed St. Francis on one side and the prayer on the other. It was translated into English in 1936 in *Living Courageously* by Kirby Page, a Disciple of Christ minister, misattributing it to St. Francis.

Saint-in-progress Pope Francis also has been misquoted. He did not say "You don't need to believe in God to be a good person." What he actually said was "The Lord has redeemed all of us, all of us, with the Blood of Christ, all of us, not just Catholics, Everyone! Even the atheists." and "We all have a duty to do good." In other words, it is by the grace of God that any person does any good.

Another Pope Francis misquote, one among many, is "Jesus Christ, Mohammed, Jehovah, Allah, these are all names employed to describe an entity that is distinctly the same across the world." It was traced back to anonymous fake news.

Horn investigates quotes allegedly from St. Augustine, St. Catherine of Sienna, St. Ignatius of Loyola, St. Francis de Sales, St. John Chrysostom, St. Theresa of Avila, St. Theresa of Calcutta, St. Thomas Aquinas and Ven. Fulton J, Sheen. He even includes what non-saints didn't say like Bishop Josip Strossmayer, C. K, Chesterton, Cardinal Ercole Consalvi, Galileo, Martin Luther, Tertullian

According to George Barna, author of *The Second Coming of Christ*, "God helps those who help themselves" is the most quoted verse thought to be in the Bible. St. Paul's "Money is the root of all evil" however is also much "quoted".

Horn also sprinkles "better quotes" from St. Cyprian, St. John, St. Paul. He also includes a section called What the Saints DID Say. These help tune the reader's 'sounds right' tester. A couple from St. Francis are "All this reverence which is paid to me I never take to myself, but simply pass it on to God." and "What are the servants of God if not His minstrels, who must move people's hearts and lift them up to spiritual joy."

Horn concludes his introduction appropriately with a true quote from Pope St. Clement, "Cleave to the holy [saints], for those that cleave to them shall [themselves] be made holy saints]."

[In St. Francis' Rule of 1221 he did write: "All the Friars … should preach by their deeds.", but without preaching with words also."]

Book Focuses On Mary (May 2018)

Lent and Easter with Mary by Thomas J. Craughwell is certainly different than his previous book. That book was *Saints Behaving Badly*, subtitled The Cutthroats, Crooks, Trollops, Con Men and Evil-Worshipers Who Became Saints. Just in the Easter part of this book are many little-known faith-building stories featuring Jesus' and our blessed mother.

Craughwell tells of the small painting of Mary and the Child Jesus on a thin piece of plaster found in Genazzano, Italy, in 1467, called Our Lady of Good Counsel. The town notary noted no less than a hundred seventy-one miracles within four months of its discovery. Several popes from Urban VIII to St. John XXIII have visited the shrine seeking good counsel.

He notes that St. Pope John Paul II added the title "Mother of the Church" in 1981 to the traditional Litany of the Blessed Virgin Mary. Pius XII added "Queen assumed into heaven" in 1950. Pope Benedict XV added Queen of Peace in 1917. Leo XIII added "Queen of the most holy rosary" in 1883. Pius IX added "Queen conceived without original sin" in 1846.

In 1874 at the shrine of Our Lady of Quito, the secular and Church leaders of Ecuador consecrated the country to Mary. In 1906 a copy of the cathedral's painting at the Jesuit College was witnessed by forty-two people to open and close her eyes. It toured the country before returning to the college church.

In 1873 a dark-skinned statue of Mary as Our Lady of Africa was brought to Algiers by Bishop Charles-Martial-Allermand Lavigerie. The bishop asked for her intercession for the conversion of Moslems and the end of slavery.

In 1640 Miguel Juan Pellicer prayed yet again to Our Lady of the Pillar. Mary is honored as such in the basilica of Saragosa with a statue on a pillar said to have come from St. James. Miguel had lost his leg to gangrene three years before. This time Mary responded miraculously, regrowing his leg overnight.

In 1630 a terra-cotta statue of Mary sculpted in Brazil was on its way to Argentina when the oxen stopped at the Lugan River. She became known as Our Lady of Lujan. For forty years the Rosendo housed the statue in their family shrine before moving to a large shrine church.

In 1502 Alfonzo and Antonio Trejo emigrated to what is now known as Higuey in the Dominican Republic. With them they brought a painting of Mary and Joseph with Jesus in the manger called Our Lady of Altagracia "High Grace"). In 1979 St. John Paul II called her under that title "the first evangelizer of the Americans."

The shrine of Our Lady of Willesden, near London, traces back to 938 when it was founded by King Athelstan. The future saint Thomas More visited there in 1537 just before he was arrested and martyred. Three years later Henry VIII burned the statue along with many others, but a replica was made in 1892.

In 1370 while throwing cargo overboard during a storm the storm suddenly stopped when a certain crate went into the water. When it came ashore in Sardinia it was found to be a sculpture of Mary and the Child Jesus. The Mercy Fathers there took it as the fulfillment of a forty-year-old prophesy of "a great lady" who would stop a plague of malaria ("bad air"). She became known as Our Lady of Bonaria ("Good Air"), patron of Sardinia.

Mary with the Child Jesus is honored in Moscow in an icon called Eleousa or Mother of Kindness. She is credited with saving the Russian capital from the Mongols in 1365, when she gained the additional title The Lady Who Saves Russia.

In 1204 the icon called the Virgin Nicopeia ("Bringer of Victory") was rescued during the siege of Constantinople. Pilgrims continue pray in Mary's chapel in St. Mark's in Venice for victory in both physical and spiritual battles.

[Other of Craughwell's books are: *101 Places to Pray Before You Die, Bad Kids from the Bible, Patron Saints, Pope Francis: The Pope from the End of the Earth, Popes Who Resigned, St. Peter's Bones, Saints or Every Occasion, Saints Preserved: An Encyclopedia of Relics, The Wisdom of the Popes, This Saint Will Change Your Life, This Saint's for You.*]

John Paul II Had Mission Of Mercy (April 2018)

"The future St. Pope John Paul II worked during the Nazi occupation of Poland in a chemical factory. It just happened to be just a few hundred yards from the convent chapel and the grave of Sr. Faustina Kowalska, the messenger of Divine Mercy. It was not until shortly before his elevation to pope that the mistranslation of her diary was re-translated and so removed from the Index of Forbidden books. His first canonization as pope was hers and he declared the Sunday after Easter Mercy Sunday, when Jesus' first words were "Peace be with you."

"Right from the beginning of my ministry in St. Peter's See in Rome," Pope St. John Paul II said, "I consider this message my special task. Providence has assigned it to me In the present situation of man, the Church, and the world."

"It is a message that is clear and understandable for everyone. Anyone can come here, look at this image of the merciful Jesus. His heart radiating grace and hear in the depths of his own heart what Blessed Faustina heard: 'I AM with you always,' and if this person responds with a sincere heart: 'Jesus, I trust in You!' he [or she] will find comfort in all his anxieties and fears."

"Fr. Michael Gaitley, the director of the Association of Marian Helpers, tells of his confirmation of his priestly and ministerial vocations. It was when he was one of many of the young people at Easter vigil in Rome in 1997. He prayed silently, "I want to be a priest like you." Just then Pope John Paul turned and looked right at him and give him a look as if to say, "This is serious." When he repeated the prayer he got what he took as a confirmation when the pope turned to him again.

"There are now many resources explaining this message for our age. Marian Helpers offers many DVDs on Divine Mercy. "The Doors of Mercy" set is called "an 8-week journey through salvation history." "Divine Mercy in the Second Greatest Story," in response to the book by Fr. Gaitley, is on Poland's salvation story and Our Lady's role in it. "Divine Mercy and Mary" from Franciscan University with Regis Martin and Scott Hahn also connect to two.

"Fr. Gaitley's series "You Did It To Me:" Putting Mercy into Action, shown on EWTN, is also on DVD. There is also "Divine Mercy Essentials" by Robert Stackpole and the booklet and ebook Divine Mercy Explained by Fr. Gaitley. A Journey to Healing through Divine Mercy by Teresa Bonopaktis is subtitled "mercy after abortion." For beginners there is "Divine Mercy 101" kit.

"They have A Year of Mercy with Pope Francis. The diary of St. Faustina comes in both print and audio versions. *Mercy's Gaze* by Vinny Flynn is a collection of parallel passages from Scripture and the Diary. *Divine Mercy: A Guide from Genesis to Benedict XVI* by Robert Stackpole makes an even more in depth connection. "Divine Mercy -- No Escape" is St. Faustina's story as told by Helen Hayes.

Loved, Lost and Found: 17 Divine Mercy Conversions edited by Felix Carroll tells of how Mercy saved an abortionist, an atheist, and adulterer, a cult member, a rape victim, and others. *Come to My Mercy* is called "a step-by-step manual on how to give and receive mercy." *Divine Mercy Minutes* by Fr. George Kosicki is excepts from St. Faustina's diary, "daily gems ... to transform your prayer life."

"More than one version of the divine mercy chaplet is sung on DVDs and CDs. The sisters of our Lady of Mercy have one, as do Trish Short and Michael Bethea. "Endless Mercy" contains songs of Vinny Flynn.

"Ignatius Press has "The Face of Mercy" documentary with Jim Cavieval, that shares true stories of mercy. Their *Disciple of Mercy Journal* is a twelve-week guide using Scripture as inspiration for acts of corporal and spiritual works of mercy. Christoph Cardinal Schoenborn does the same in *We Have Found Mercy*. The DVD "Fautina: apostle of Divine Mercy" is in Polish with English or Spanish subtitles. Their booklet *Divine Mercy and Faustina* briefly instructs.

"For other conversation starters there's Divine Mercy pens, bookmarks, tote bags, luggage tags, elastic bracelets, tapestries, pocket statues, lapel pins, prayer cards, key chains, and even dog tags.

Former Muslims Share Experiences (March 2018)

Former Muslims United is a program of the American Freedom Defense Initiative. It was formed in September 2009 by a group of leading American apostates from Islam, Nonie Darwish, Mohammed Asghar, Amil Imani, Wafa Sultan, and Ibn Warraq, to educate the American public and policymakers about the need for Muslims to repudiate the threat from authoritative Shariah to the religious freedom and safety of former Muslims.

Director Nonie Darwish puts it bluntly, "If you convert, you die," and explains, "Few Americans know what is going o inside the Muslim world and what it portends for them. The fact is that most Americans are subjected to much of the same misinformation with regard to Islam that I grew up with inside the Muslim world. Thus Americans are in the dark attempting to formulate their strategy to defend themselves against the threat of terror, domestic jihad, and Sharia. While they get ridiculed for being 'Islamophobes,' the Muslim world itself is undergoing a huge and painful awakening.'

She gives the example of Egyptian lawyer and women's rights activist Nagla Al Imam who announced her conversion to Christianity in Cairo, Egypt. It sent shock waves in and beyond Egypt, as perhaps the first case ever of its kind where a Muslim woman, who is also a Sharia expert, has openly challenged Islamic apostasy laws.

On an internet chat room she announced that she was not afraid to stand up for the human rights of apostates and refused to leave her homeland, Egypt. This was immediately followed by death threats. Upon arrival at an alleged interview, she was taken forcibly to a room and held against her will for hours, assaulted, threatened, and insulted by several people.

Darwish presents an insider's look at Sharia in *Cruel and Usual Punishment*. "This is Allah's law," she was told, and she knew what awaited those who questioned Allah's law. But she doesn't believe the lies anymore, and now she wants to share her experiences with the Western world.

Her book, *Now They Call Me Infidel*, is subtitled Why I Renounced Jihad for American, Israel, and the War on Terror. When she was a girl of eight, her father died while leading covert attacks on Israel. A high-ranking Egyptian military officer stationed with his family in Gaza, he was considered a "shahid," a martyr for jihad. Yet Darwish questioned the love of violence and hatred of Jews and Christians, the tolerance of glaring social injustices, and the blame America and Israel for everything. Today she thrives as an American citizen, a Christian, a conservative Republican, and an advocate for Israel.

Abdallah Saleed has written similar books, *Freedom of Religion, Apostasy and Islam* with Hassan Saleed and *The Dark Side of Islam* with R. C Sproul. In the second he focuses on four basic areas in which Islam rejects the very foundations on which Christianity is built. In addition to discussing the differences between Islam and Christianity, Saleeb gives his own perspective on the "dark side" of Islam in light of violence perpetrated b Jihadists.

Ibn Warraq's books, *Why I am Not a Moslem* and *Leaving Islam: Apostates Speak Out*, tell the same story again and again. "No quick portrait of the typical apostate is likely to appear," he writes, "some are young (students in their teens), some are middle-aged with children; some are scientists, while others are economists, business people, or journalists. Our witnesses, nonetheless, do have certain moral and intellectual qualities in common: for instance, they are all comparatively well educated, computer literate with access to the Internet, and rational, with the ability to think for themselves. However, what is most striking is their fearlessness, their moral courage, and their moral commitment to telling the truth. They all face social ostracism, the loss of friends and family, a deep inner spiritual anguish and loneliness -- and occasionally the death penalty if discovered."

Florida Martyrs Witness To Truth (February 2018)

The PBS special "The Secrets of Spanish Florida" made public some little-known and newly discovered history of the southeastern United States, the Spanish colony of La Florida. The documentary told of how St. Augustine, the oldest still-inhabited city in our nation, was founded in 1565. It started with a Mass of thanksgiving for having survived the monster storm that had driven them off course, on the very day Irma would later strike.

It told based on archeology and rediscovered manuscripts of how Europeans, free Africans, Messianic Jews and Native Americans worked together to build community and rebuilt the city more than once. It told of the runaway slaves who fled to Spanish Florida and the "Black Yamasee" and of how the fourteenth and fifteenth colonies, Florida and West Florida, were forced to accept slavery.

Liz Stiles and Michael Marcinowski commented that the show did not cover the Minorcan slaves who escaped to St. Augustine in 1777. The show mentioned but didn't tell the whole story of the martyrs of Spanish Florida.

Franciscan missionaries were more successful than Jesuits had been in establishing missions in what are now Florida, Georgia, and South Carolina. In 1573, nine Franciscan friars arrived. Fr. Maynard Geiger, a prominent Franciscan historian, notes that "at the height of activity there were fifty friars in forty-four mission centers working for the welfare of thirty thousand converted Indians."

Dr. Paul Thigpen, coordinator of the Friends of the Georgia Martyrs, says, "In our day, when the sanctity of marriage is so severely challenged, we desperately need the example, the courage, and the help of these heroic Christians. Because of their love for God, they gave their lives for the truth about marriage."

Some ministered to the Guale tribe who lived along what is now the Georgia coast. Their names were Pedro de Corpa, Blas Rodriguez, Miguel de non, Antonio de Badajez, Francisco de Verascola, and Francisco de Avila. De Avila lived to tell of the other missionaries' martyrdoms in September of 1597.

Life in the American mission field was harsh. Worse yet, the closest Spanish soldiers were far away in St. Augustine, so the friars had no protection from natives who might turn hostile.

Among the difficulties faced by the missionaries, perhaps the greatest was that of sharing Christ's teaching on marriage that marriage is a lifetime union of one man and one woman.

Juanillo, living in one of the missions, broke his promise of monogamy and took a second wife. Fray Pedro admonished Juanillo to repent. Instead he sought to rid himself of the "troublesome" friars.

When Fray Pedro was about to leave his cabin to celebrate Sunday morning Mass on the feast of the Exaltation of the Holy Cross he was killed, his body desecrated and left unburied for days. Fray Blas was permitted to celebrate Mass and to preach is last sermon. He said, "We, all of us, have to die someday. But what does pain me is that the Evil One has persuaded you to do this offensive thing against your God and Creator." He was clubbed to death and his body exposed.

Fray Miguel and Fray Antonio were warned and offered escape by other Indians, but stayed. Fray Miguel offered Mass on the feast of the Stigmata of St. Francis. The Gospel reading of the day contained Jesus' words: "Whoever loses his life for My sake will find it" (Matthew 16:25).

Fray Francisco was returning by canoe from St. Augustine with needed supplies and gifts for his Guale flock. He was attacked as he landed and his body was never found.

[Some of Thigpen's books are: *A Dictionary of Quotes from the Saints; A Reason for Joy; Be Merry in God; Blood of the Martyrs, Seed of the Church; Celebrate the Third Millennium; Jesus We Adore You; Last Words: Final Thoughts of Catholic Saints and Sinners; Restless Till We Rest in You; Saints Who Battled Satan; Turning Your Heart Toward God.*]

Fun Web Site Spreads Gospel (January 2018)

Church Pop is a creative way that the Catholic Church is reaching out to internet users with the motto "Make all things holy" in a fun, informative, and inspirational way. Its logo is a popsicle with a halo. It offers a daily feed of information on how to become a saint to your email, via facebook, instagram, snapchat, or twitter. It has passed a half a million followers. At the website one can interact and share, play games, take quizzes, watch videos, read articles, infographics, or comics. It comes in English, Portuguese, Spanish, and Italian.

An infographic is an eye-catching chart that graphically presents information rather than a list or article that presents it sequentially. "The Meaning of the Miraculous Medal," for example, points to the inscription and translates the Latin as "O, Mary, conceived without sin, pray for us who have recourse to thee." It points to the twelve stars and their connection to the twelve apostles, to the intertwined M for Mary and the cross of her Son, Jesus, and serpent, Satan, under her feet.

The infograph on the apostles connects them each to Jesus and includes fourteen, with Judas, Matthias, and Paul. It gives at a glance where they spread the Good News, how they died, and where their remains are.

They are not merely to be viewed, but interactive. Among the comments was the correction to the place of St. Thomas' relics, which have been moved from India to Italy, as most of the apostles had been.

At Church Pop Live on Wednesday features the rosary, on Thursdays "Live with Caroline," and on Fridays the Divine Mercy chaplet.

"The Spiritual Power of Holy Water" similarly points out that it erases venial sin, removes distractions, dispels evil powers, influences people and places toward holiness, including ourselves.

In the lists section "the Five Hidden Blessings from Having to Wait in a Long Line for confession" Laura Hudgens lists time for prayer, solidarity with other penitents, a sense of gratitude, pamphlet reading time, and pre-penance before the confessor-given penance.

"Seven Reasons to Pray the Rosary" comes from St. Louis de Monfort, "The Twelve Promises of Jesus for Those Who Practice the Devotion to the Sacred Heart" from St. Margaret Mary Alacoque.

"Ten Holy Married Couples," of course, includes the Blessed Virgin Mary and St. Joseph, Sts. Joachim and Anne, her parents, Sts. Zecharia and Elizabeth, parents of St. John the Baptist, and Sts. Aquila and Priscilla. It demonstrates that saints beget saints. Others not so well known are Sts. Louis and Zelie Martin, parents of St. Therese of Lisieux, Sts. Gregory and Nonna, parents of Sts. Gregory of Nazlanzus, Gorgonia and Caesarius, Sts. Vincent and Waldetrdis, parents of Sts. Landericus, Madalberta, Adeltrudis, and Dentelia, and Sts. Gordianus and Silvia, parents of St. Gregrory.

Also included are Sts. Isidore the Farmer and Bl. Luigi Betrame and their wives, both named Maria.

Some articles correct misinformation on St. Francis of Assisi, the crusades, Sola Scriptura, demons.

A tablold-like headline offers "Signs You Might Be a Zombie Catholic -- and How to Be Cured."

Another shares singer Stephani "Lady Gaga" Germanotta's photo of her praying the rosary and asking for prayers for her health. It shares actress Patricia Heaton's tweet on being brought to tears by the Eucharist after what she judged a "lame sermon."

Pop star videos are on Church Pop. One video shows NASCAR winner Johnny Sauter asking for prayers for the poor souls in Purgatory. Another has Bishop Andrew Cozzens leading the all-priest band "The Second Collection." Yet another shows NFL star kicker Justin Tucker singing "Ave Maria."

The games include two different spiritualities, the Franciscan "Friar Dude" and the Dominican "Passiontide." To reach Passiontide the player must collect candles and copies of the Summas, while jumping over holes and lava and jumping on Albigensians to convert them.

Explore Treasures From Bishop Sheen (December 2017)

Archbishop Fulton J. Sheen would make a good gift for those who herd him live or those who have never heard of him. Amazon has twenty pages of books by or about him. they also have several DVDs. The most valuable treasure, however, may be the Complete Fulton Sheen Audio Library.

He starts the lesson on "Persevering Prayer" in the section "A Retreat for Everyone" with two Christmas stories. One tells of a young boy from New York and an atheist friend of his theatrical parents. The boy said that he wanted snow for Christmas and the atheist asked, "Who's going to give you snow?" "I'm going to ask Jesus." When snow did come on Christmas the boy saw it and said, "Attaboy Jesus!"

In the other a girl asked for a thousand dolls for Christmas. When she didn't get them, her unbelieving father taunted, "Well, God didn't answer your prayers, did He?" To which she responded, "Oh, yes He did. He said 'No.' "

The whole disc contains a wealth of Catholic teachings, more than thirteen dozen, about fifty hours worth. They do overlap in content, but since he did not read from a prepared text each of them is unique. Sheen talks about topics still very relevant today, busyness, Communism, abortion, justice, sprinkled with anecdotes from his pastoral experiences and quotes from poetry. Throughout he promotes a daily Holy Hour, listening for God's word for the day from God's Word.

"Life Is Worth Living" includes fifty-six lessons with such intriguing titles as "Cure for Selfishness," "How to Improve Your Mind," "Meet a Perfect Stranger -- Yourself," "the Infinity of Littleness," and "The Value of Incompatibility."

"The Radio Addresses of Archbishop Sheen" are Sheen's words read by another from the transcript. In "Charity" from 1945, for example, he said, "America's greatest enemy is not from without but from within and that enemy is hate." And "If America ever dies it will not be through conquest but through suicide." He points out that there will be neither faith or hope in either heaven or hell, but true love will only be in heaven and advises, "Where you do not find love, put it there."

"What a Priest Should Be" applies not only to ordained Catholic priests, but also to the lay priesthood, all the Baptized. In the lesson "Reflecting Christ in Society," he notes, "there is less respect for the official Church," and "Manifest evangelism has less appeal then it once had." But he adds, "What does affect the world is the surprise, those characters that come along, that seem to be out of the ordinary, shock us into goodness, John XXIII, Malcolm Muggeridge, Solstinchen, and Mother Teresa. There's absolutely no reason for despair," concluding "the world will look to us, come to us only as we reflect Christ."

In "First the Spiritual, and then Take Action," he draws lessons from the Incarnation, Mary, Martha, and Peter at the Transfiguration to correct the supposed division between the faith and social action.

In "Getting to the People" Sheen says, "God is always recycling human garbage," and "the Resurrection continues." He advises reading the life stories of the fallible, but imitate-able, saints of the Scriptures, Jacob the deceiver, Moses the Murdered, Paul the persecutor. He advises, "Do not say 'I gotta to be me;' say 'I've got to be His.' "

Patrick Moore wrote, "Great teachings! I love Bishop Sheen. He is a modern day saint and I think his wisdom is one of the greatest in Church history. I could listen to him for hours."

Martin J. Cote said, "I love this guy!", Pax "Love it!" and Joaquin J. A. Olendzki just "Excellent!" R. V. wrote, "The collection is thorough and terrific," but added, "the sound quality of the recordings is seriously lacking but that is because the recordings themselves are very old and digital restoration can only do so much. This is nearly a lifetime of Fulton Sheen's work and his words are almost poetic. The talks themselves carry a lifetime of spiritual lessons and I find myself listening to them every day."

Even a non-Catholic such as B. Everett gave it five stars, writing, "I was very impressed by the depth and knowledge of the collection. I am not Catholic but I am Christian. I quite enjoyed every homily given by the bishop."

Museum Celebrates Bible (November 2017)

The Museum of the Bible opens this November in Washington, D. C. Museum president Gary Summers says, "Our mission is to invite all people to engage with the Bible. We can think of no more fundamental way to give people access to the treasures and experiences inside this museum than to offer public admission coupled with the ability to reserve timed entry tickets." For those who cannot visit in person the museum also has a traveling exhibits and a virtual on-line. The importance of the Bible was not so long ago an integral part of Western civilization.

As D. James Kennedy and Jerry Newcombe wrote in What If the Bible Had Never Been Written?, "We feel like strangers in a strange land, even though it was the Bible that shaped our nation, our culture, and our institutions from the start. What we need as a culture is to get back to the Bible."

Answering their question, they write "There would be no salvation, ... virtually no charity, no modern science, ... likely no hospitals, ... no universities, ... no capitalism, no accounting, no free enterprise. Literacy and education might well be the exclusive domain of the elite."

Judge Joseph Wapner points out the trial by jury, "taken for granted in America and Great Britain, one of the strongest safeguards against government's arbitrary authority, remains a rare privilege in much of the rest of the world." This comes from the Bible, specifically Leviticus 19:15.

The Supreme Court in 1892 declared, "We find everywhere a clear recognition of the same truth ... This is a Christian nation." In 1983 the U. S. Congress declared a year of the Bible saying, "The Bible, the Word of God, has made a unique contribution in shaping the United States as a distinctive and blessed nation." Deeply held religious convictions springing from the Holy Scriptures led to the early settlements of our Nation. In 1986 U S District Judge Frank McGarr concurred, "the truth is that America's origins are Christian and that our founding fathers intended and achieved full religious freedom for all within the context of a Christian nation in the first amendment as it was adopted," but added, "rather than as we have rewritten it"

Ulysses S. Grant said, "Hold fast to the Bible as the anchor of your liberty; write its precepts in your hearts and practice them in your life." Theodore Roosevelt said, "If a man is not familiar with the Bible, he has suffered the loss which he had better make all possible haste to correct." Ronald Reagan said, "Inside the Bible's pages lie all of the answers to all the problems man has ever known. I hope Americans will read and study the Bible."

Scientist Robert Oppenheimer wrote that the origins of the scientific revolution "took something that was not present in Chinese civilization, that was wholly absent in Indian civilization, and absent from Greco-Roman civilization. It took an idea of progress which has more to do with the human condition, which is well expressed by the second half of the famous Christian dichotomy -- faith and works."

Galileo wrote, "Holy Scripture could never lie or err, but its decrees are of absolute and inviolable truth. I should only have added that although Scripture can indeed not err, nevertheless some of its interpreters and expositors may sometimes err in various ways, one of which may be very serious and quite frequent, when they would base themselves always on the literal meaning of words."

Isaac Newton wrote, "There is a double revelation of God the one contained in His words found in Scripture, the other to be found in nature and its general laws."

In literature, Shakespeare, for example, had Polonius quote Ecclesiaticus 37:13 in Hamlet. Dostoevsky begins The Brothers Karamazov with John 12:24. Charles Dickens wrote, "The New Testament is the best book the world has ever known or will know."

Ernest Von Dobschultz in The Influence of the Bible on Civilization wrote, "There is a small book -- one can put it in your pocket, and yet all the libraries of America, numerous as they are, would hardly be large enough to hold all the books which have been inspired by this one little volume."

Both Leif Erickson and Christopher Columbus sought to spread the Good News and discovered the New World. Missionaries like Patrick and Boniface changed barbarous Europe into Christendom and may do so again.

Disaster Can Lead To Goodness (October 2017)

Hurricane Harvey may be an "act of God," but it can bring out godly acts in others. Courtney Kiolbass, for example, tells of a friend who spoke of her dad, who has back problems and the way his neighbors knocked on his door to help him move furniture upstairs.

She writes, "There are stories of civilians with boats rowing down the streets that have turned into rivers in order to rescue complete strangers. Emergency officials put their life on the line to do their job. I see photos of people transporting children and the elderly alike, crossing the water to get others to safety. A priest got in his kayak and went to check on parishioners."

Tens of thousands of people were displaced due to Katrina, including the Rojas family now of Robstown, Texas. Jesus Rojas says, "I want to thank the Fire Department of Robstown for courage to show up in the storm while the tremendous power, the wind, the rain were going and they were still out here trying their best, it was incredible!"

"Appreciate what you have, listen to the warnings, hug your children and thank God for today and yesterday," Natali Rojas advises, "and pray for a better tomorrow. Some may blame God, and some may blame the hurricane, but the only thing standing were holy things, as you can see this statue is the only thing that survived. I dug in there for things and all I found is a Virgin Mary."

Jude McFarland and Candace also relocated after Katrina. Then McFarland carried his expectant wife through neck-deep water for hours until he found an Army vehicle to take them to a hospital across the Mississippi. They named their daughter Miracle. Now in Corpus Christi with two sons added to the family they had to endure Harvey. "I'm just trying to be strong for my family," said McFarland.

Isabel Pena gave birth to Kataleya Rose by the light of cell phones as Harvey pelted Corpus Christi. She wasn't breathing for the long two minutes before the paramedics came. "She wanted to make her entrance; she made it!" Pena remarked.

Loralynn was born by Caesarean to Danielle Weeks in Corpus Christi after their home in Port Arkansas and their car were destroyed and their RV flipped over. Her husband Will called the little bundle their miracle and said, "as long as she is safe nothing else matters."

Brian Greene, who once headed the New Orleans food bank, also moved after Katrina, and is now president of the Houston Food Bank. Greene housed half a dozen of his neighbors in single-story homes, until volunteers came by on a boat Sunday night, took them out his second-story window and ferried them to emergency shelters.

"We are trying to wait it out. We have water and ham sandwiches," Destiny Wilson said. "I learned at a young age to value family and not material things, because we lost everything in Katrina."

Houston Police SWAT officer Daryl Hudeck carried both thirteen-month-old Aiden Pham and his mother. Alexandre Jourde with wet suit and paddle-board was also photographed paddling through rising flood waters four-year-old Ethan Colman. Dr. Stephen Kimmel canoed to the hospital through flood waters to a teen who need emergency surgery.

Dean Mize drove to Houston from his home in Chandler, almost two hundred miles away, to lend a hand with his boat and truck. Mize spent the night trying to rescue Shardea Harrison and her three-week-old daughter Sarai baby girl from their home. Jason Legnon from Louisiana's propeller boat took all to safety.

Houston Texan star JJ Watt, among other, put together a Hurricane Harvey fundraiser. Watt promoted it on "Good Morning America" explaining, "What's happening right now is so much bigger than football."

Vatican Astronomer Addresses Faith, Science (September 2017)

Br. Guy Consolmagno, S. J., the new director of the Vatican Observatory, says, "The hardest thing I have to deal with is trying to figure out where people are coming from when they don't see [science and religion] as a natural fit. Both science and religion are taking what we thought we knew and trying to understand it."

A native of Detroit, Consolmagno got his Ph. D. in astronomy at MIT before joining the Jesuits. Connecting the alleged conflict between astronomy and theology specifically, he explains, "It had nothing to do with Galileo. It had nothing to do with Giordano Bruno. It was a political invention to serve the secular interests of the [late 19th century].

He came to the answer himself only after teaching astronomy for the Peace Corps at the University of Nairobi and out in the field. As Christians he explains, "We believe in a God Who decided to create and the first thing He creates is light, so He's doing nothing hidden, nothing in the dark. God says everything He has created is good. He invites us, His creation, to enjoy it, and one way of enjoying it is learning how it works."

Consolmagno now practices "science evangelization," having appeared on "The Colbert Report," "On Being" with Krista Tippett at several science fiction conventions and in "A Brief History of the End of Everything" series for the BBC. He urges his audiences, especially Catholics, to cherish science as a part of their birthright, born out of the work of medieval clerics trying to understand both the Creator and His creation. He quotes Albert Einstein's observation, "The amazing thing about the universe is that it can be understood."

Many are surprised to learn that the Big Bang Theory came from a Belgian priest, who had to convince Einstein of the implications of his Relativity Theory. Consolmagno's specialty is meteors and asteroids. Asteroid 4597 is named for him and nicknamed "Little Guy" and he has received the Carl Sagan medal for outstanding communication by as astronomer to the general public.

His collection of dialogues with Fr. Paul Mueller, *Would You Baptize an Extraterrestrial?* was in response to the question posed by Pope Francis, "Imagine if a Martian showed up, all big ears and big nose like a child's drawing, and he asked to be baptized. How would you react?" It's subtitled "... and Other Questions from the Astronomers' In-box at the Vatican Observatory."

In it they answer other such questions as "How do you reconcile The Big Bang with Genesis?", "Was the Star of Bethlehem just a pious religious story or an actual description of astronomical events?", "What really went down between Galileo and the Catholic Church and why do the effects of that confrontation still reverberate to this day?", and "Will the Universe came to an end?"

"The fact that people kept asking such questions," Br. Guy says, "made me realize that there must be something serious and real behind them, if only I could put my finger on what that was. Maybe those questions had hidden assumptions that weren't quite right, but how could we tease out those assumptions?"

One of the strangest questions was when someone wanted to know if he was really in touch with aliens. When he told him he was not, he replied, "Ha! I knew you wouldn't tell me the truth!" What's sad are all the people like him who don't ask questions but who are sure they already know the answers. Unfortunately, the more certain they are, the more likely it's nonsense. Over the years, some people have e-mailed me offering long, detailed proofs that everything we know about religion is wrong, or everything we know about science is wrong. Others have sent me detailed descriptions of their own interactions with aliens. I really feel for those people; they are in need of the sort of help that no one can give them over the internet."

Ann Ferro commented "This is THE PERFECT stepping stone to a better understanding of my faith. Yes, the initial chapters that use references to quantum and traditional physics as if they were M & M's were a bit daunting, but I persisted and fell in love with the repartee and the elegant way in which the authors explained the relationship between science and religion." Robert G. Rich, Jr., wrote, "This small book by two Jesuit astronomers at the Vatican Observatory is a gem of a discussion on science and the Bible. It is hard to find such a responsible discussion of these issues in an accessible and entertaining package of modest length, but the two Jesuit authors have done it."

Consolmagno has also written *The Heavens Proclaim: Astronomy and the Vatican, God's Mechanics: How Scientists and Engineers Make Sense of Religion, Brother Astronomer: Adventure of a Vatican Scientist, Turn Left at Orion: A Hundred Night Sky Objects to See in a Small Telescope -- and How to Find Them*, and the audio book, *Meaning: Exploring the Big Questions of the Cosmos with a Vatican Scientist*.

Author Looks At Pivotal Players (August 2017)

Praying with the Pivotal Players by Amy Welborn has a rare five-star rating on Amazon. All the reviews gave it the maximum. Sunshine Alexander wrote, she "really loved this workbook. It is the perfect companion to the video series," while Lisa Rae called the book an "excellent supplement ... [that] can be enjoyed separately from the DVD series."

Both Welborn's book and Bishop Robert Barron's DVD series from Word on Fire tell the true story behind the Church's most influential people. The DVDs journeys through France, Italy, Spain, England, while the book moved toward a deeper intimacy with the Lord with insights about Jesus, prayer, the Church, and virtue from Sts. Francis of Assisi, the Reformer, Thomas Aquinas, the Theologian, and Catherine of Siena, the Mystic, Michelangelo Buonarroti, the Artist, G. K. Chesterton, the Evangelist, and Blessed John Henry Newman, the Convert.

George Weigel in his review tries to categorize them, "Two are doctors of the Church -- and a third may be one day. Several of them inspired successors of St. Peter; another told a pope off in no uncertain terms. Two were Englishmen and converts from Anglicanism: one, will-o-the-wisp slight and the other gargantuan; one the quintessential Oxford don, the other, the quintessential Anglo-eccentric genius. One grew up a wannabe knight errant before his abrupt turn into radical evangelicalism. Each of them was the human analogue to what astrophysicists call a 'singularity.' "

Welborn herself says, "I wrote the book last fall and really enjoyed the process. It gave me an opportunity to immerse myself in the writing of these figures and I learned quite a bit.

The five segments on Frances include the very relevant "Drawing Closer to Christ," "Not an Impossible Ideal," "Living in a Culture of Corruption," "Perfect Joy" and "Francis and Creation."

Aquinas's include the more thoughtful "Theology and Spirituality," "The Existence of God," "The Nature of God," "The Human Person," and "Christ," while Catherine of Siena's look both interiorly and exteriorly, "Self-knowledge," "Holy Desire," and "Charity."

At Word on fire a thirteen-page sample lesson on Catherine is available. It begins by identifying her as the only lay woman ever declared a doctor of the Church and reports that she died just after her thirty-third birthday. Welborn them quotes from her elegy by Neri dei Pagliaresi.

"Tell me, who will save me now from an evil end?
Who will preserve me from delusions?
Who will guide me when I try to climb?
Who will console me now in my distress?
Who will ask me now: 'Are you now well?'
Who will persuade me that I shall not be damned?"

The Questions for Understanding are: "What evidence do we have that God loved us first, and loves us unconditionally?", "How should we love God?", "In what ways did St. Catherine follow the commandment to 'love one another' during her life on earth?", "What re the characteristics of this type of love?"

Among the Questions for Application are "How can you be sure that you are doing the works that God wants you to do and not those that, in your own ego, you believe are necessary?", "What mission is Christ asking of you now and in the near future?"

Michelangelo's sections move from "Incarnation and Creativity" and "The Life of an Artist" to his art, "David," "the Pietá," and "the Sistine Chapel." Chesterton and Newman's have sections on Joy, sanity, and reason, the ethics of Elfland, the strangeness of man and of Christ, conversion and its price, the development of doctrine, the idea of the university and the grammar of assent.

[Wellborn's books include: *A Catholic Woman's Book of Days; Daybreaks; De-coding Da Vinci, De-coding Mary Magdalene, Friendship with Jesus, Here Now: A Catholic Guide to the Good Life; Loyola Kid's Book of Bible Stories, Mary and the Christian Life; Parables: Stories of the Kingdom, Prayerful Pauses*; the Prove It! series on Church, God, Jesus, Prayer, *The Da Vinci Code Mysteries; The Words We Pray; You; Wish You Were Here*.]

Book Explores Secret Archives (July 2017)

The first chapter of Maria Luisa Ambrosini's *The Secret Archives of the Vatican* sets the mood of the book, the exploration of "The Caves of the Time-Stream." She says, "These ancient papers, these writings of men dead for centuries, but still alive in their words and thoughts, make history seem no longer history but humanity," with issues like abortion, contraception, fake news, religious rights, sainthood.

Some documents publicly displayed for the archives centennial in 1981 were the excommunication of Luther, Henry VIII divorce petition, letters from both Lincoln and Jefferson Davis, from Mary the Queen of Scots, from Empress Helena Wong's letter, and Alexander VI's splitting of the New World.

Ambrosini begins at the beginning with the Ignatian exercise, "It may be that a fisherman's basket of papers was the very first of the papal secret archives." It is now twenty-five miles of bookshelves.

What comes through is a miracle as great as the survival of the Jewish people is that anything of the archives have survived. "Between Charlemagne's time and that of Innocent III in the late Twelfth Century" she says, "only a few important documents have survived."

There is a chapter on Napoleon's aspiration for a "world library." Librarian Gaetano Martini writes, "First to be packed were the volumes of bulls. Fr. Altieri and I were in charge of supervising this operation, and our eyes melted in tears. Many documents were specially requested at this time: the bull of excommunication against Napoleon, the trial of the Templars, the process of Galileo." With Napoleon's defeat many "unimportant" papers were sold by weight.

"Some documents, or copies of documents, were fortunate enough to be elsewhere than in Rome, like the letters of Pope Leo that had been sent to the provincial cities. Others ceased to be archives and became literature or history, like the writing of Augustine or Ambrose."

Sts. Flavius Clemens, brother of Emperor Vespasian, and his wife Flavia Domitilla donated what is now St. Clement's to the Church before they were martyred. It was where the list of Christians was hidden during the persecutions. It also preserved the story of Marcia, mistress of Emperor Commudus, inserted names on the list of pardons.

Ambrosini retells the story of the beautiful Pelagia who was converted by Bishop Nonnus of Edessa about 450 and lived the rest of her life on the Mount of Olives as Pelagius. She writes of the modern-day impediments to the canonization of the saintly Padre Pio or Pope John XXIII.

In the archives is Gregory II's letter to iconoclasts, "Go to the elementary schools and tell the children that you are the persecutor of images. They will throw their little tables at your head, and what you will not learn from the scholars you will learn from the ignorant."

Benedict VIII told Phillip the Fair, "There are two swords, one spiritual and one secular; the secular sword is to be used for the church, the spiritual one by the church. One is in the hands of the priest, the other in the hands of kings and warriors, but is to be used according to the priest's orders." The king promptly imprisoned the pope, who was freed after three days by relatives. A witness write, "Everyone shouted, 'Long live the Holy Father!' Everyone was able to talk to the pope as to another poor man."

Innocent VIII wrote against witches in 1484, "They have made to perish, suffocate, and die the deliveries of many women. They have kept men from impregnating and women from conceiving, so that men cannot give the due of marriage to their wives, nor wives to their husbands."

From the archives we learn that Pius IV made his nephew Charles Borromeo cardinal at twenty-one, advocated Communion under both species and marriage for ex-Lutheran priests.

Soon after the printing press, Pius V wrote "against those who write news, disclose secrets, and write of the faults of others, all mixed with many lies." His successor, Gregory XIII, wrote, "There has recently appeared a new sect of men illicitly curious, who write every kind of information of which they have knowledge, or which they make up out of their own libidinous imaginations, mixing the false, the true and the uncertain with no restraint whatsoever."

Entertainer Witnesses (June 2017)

Paulina Cerrilla lives out her Catholic faith while starting a multifaceted career. Although a redhead and fair-skinned, both her parents were immigrants from Mexico, and became citizens last November.

Her favorite saints are St. Jude, a good patron for an aspiring actress, and Mexico's Our Lady of Guadalupe. Having visited the shrine in Mexico City several times, the faith of the other pilgrims has inspired her.

Because her first language was Spanish, teachers mistook her accent for a speech impediment. "I do a lot of my praying in Spanish. My grandmas are so intensely Catholic, like let's-have-ten-children Catholic, Catholic-Catholic."

"Cerrilla began singing at three and began acting at nine. "I've known what I've wanted since day one. It's one of those childhood dreams I never let go."

Since she sang on "The Voice," she has gotten more than twenty-eight million views of her music videos. Her debut single "Homebody" can be found on iTunes. Her Christmas song "Melting Waters" got translated into Korean and sung by Girl Generation.

She has played Rachel in the zombi apocalypse web-series "Paul and Adam Save the Whole, Entire Apartment Complex" and songwriter Aurora in "String Theory." After playing the title role in "Narcissa," an updated retelling of the Greek myth, she became CoverGirl's "beauty guru."

Working with Family Theater Productions on faith-based projects, however, was different than her other acting jobs because of Fr. David. As national director, Holy Cross Fr. David Guffey is responsible for Family Theater, including both media production and spiritual out reach activities. His "Hollywood Prays" ministry includes monthly Prayer and Pasta gatherings, RCIA classes, Going Deeper, Faith & Film Bible Study, and Theology of the Body workshops, daily Rosary and Mass and the weekly Eucharistic Holy Hour.

"We wanted ... to create a truly wonderful, impactful project." Cerrilla says, "That's what made working on this series of films so special, because it wasn't necessarily for us." Before working there she says, "I didn't understand what it was like to have a day-in, day-out relationship [with Jesus]. Whatever I end up doing or being portrayed as in the media, I'm going to fight very hard to maintain my integrity. I want people to know that there can be a person just like them fighting the fight and trying to be a good person."

In "Family Dinner" she plays dark-haired Christina, a young Christian woman, whose parents won't let her go out with a potential boyfriend until they can meet him at the family dinner. She has to work with both family members and the boy to make it work.

"40 Hours" has Christina turning faith into good works at a soup kitchen, based on André House in Phoenix, started by the Holy Cross fathers. She makes friends with fellow volunteer Kat, who soon become a friend in need.

In "Down from the Mountain" Cristina befriends aspiring musician Adam McGlin. Adam renews his relationship with God and the Church, but finds his new faith challenged after the retreat.

Family Theater administrator Tony Sands says, "No one ever knows, but some people kind of have 'it.' And I would say she does."

"As long as I've been in the business," her manager Richard Ellis says, "I've never been as excited to work with an artist ... a really good kid who happens to have a lot of talent."

"I decided, after thirty-plus years in the music industry," Ellis continues, "that putting my expertise to good use to create the pathway for her to become a world-wide music star was well worth my time and effort."

She plays Ally Martin in the yet-to-be-released "Tell Me I Love You," a love story set in the electronic music industry and Brittany Crowder in "Hail the Apple Blossom Queen." Paulina wa selected for this latest role after auditioning via nationwide online casting call to which thousands responded.

Children's Books Aid Faith (May 2017)

Lisa Hendey is the founder and editor of CatholicMom.com and the bestselling author of *The Handbook for Catholic Moms*. Her Chime Travelers series is a retelling of the lives of the saints for children. Sr. Grace Dateno is a daughter of St. Paul and the author the Gospel Trekkers series. All the books in both series rate nearly five stars by Amazon reviewers. Christine Johnson's comment could apply to all eleven of these books. "It reminds me of the Ignatian spiritual exercises, but for kids! What a terrific way for children to engage in the faith and in the bible more deeply!"

Henley's first book *The Secret of the Shamrock* starts with Patrick reluctantly working on his church's cleaning team on a Saturday, but when the old church bells chime, he and his pet frog, Francis, find themselves in Ireland in 432. Barb Gilman's third graders said, "The book was 'Saint-tastic' and give if five snaps and Jazz Hands!"

In *The Sign of the Carved Cross* Katie, Patrick's twin sister, joins her friends in being mean to the new girl, Lily. Suddenly, when the bells chime, she becomes the new girl in a Native American village in 1675. She's befriended by Tekakwitha, a quiet girl with scars on her face, and together they run away in the middle of the night. Sarah Reinhard commented, "This isn't just a fun read: it's a chance to walk with a great saint."

In *The Whisper in the Ruins* the mystery of a broken stain glassed window triggers Patrick's trip to 1205 to fix and even more damaged church by a young Francis of Assisi and in *The Mystery of Midnight* Kate accompanies runaway Clare through the Door of the Dead in 1212.

It's Christmas time at St. Anne parish in *The Strangers at the Manger*, when the bell rings the twins are sent back and meet Mary and Joseph on their way to Bethlehem. When the Magi arrive, Katie asks Mary, "Are you sure you want all of these strangers around the baby?" Mary smiles and tells them, "Strangers are simply new friends, just waiting to be loved." Katie and Patrick think of five-year-old Mateo Perez and his family new to St. Ann's. Michele

Faehnie says, "This book will help you and your children see Mary, Joseph, and Jesus as real people who lived, worked, and prayed with simple and humble faith."

Sr. Grace's series starts with *Shepherds to the Rescue* in which three siblings, Hannah, Cleb, and Noah suddenly find themselves without bikes or cellphones near Bethlehem. There they meet a shepherd boy named Benjamin whose grandfather was one of the shepherds who heard the message of the angels at the first Christmas.

In the second book, *Braving the Storm*, the three children find themselves in Sogane where they hear Levi's tale of Jesus' multiplication of his five loaves and two fish. They set off with him to find Jesus, only to get lost in Cana in the middle of a raging storm!

In the third book, *Danger at Sea*, they meet Rebecca of Gennesaret, the child who was welcomed by Jesus when His disciples squabbled. Caleb offers to take her brother Seth's, who has a broken leg, at fishing but gets into trouble with both.

In the fourth book, *The Mystery of the Missing Jars*, the children meet Sarah of Capernaum, who Jesus raised from the dead. Caleb accidentally breaks the handle off of her father Jairus's pot, but is accused of stealing four missing jars.

In the fifth book, *Courageous Quest*, the three plus toddler Garret who they're babysitting meet Leah of Jericho and her son Daniel, who tells them of Jesus healing of Bartimaeus of blindness and his encounter with the tax collector Zacchaeus.

In the sixth book, *Discovery at Dawn*, the siblings are gathering canned goods for a food drive at their church, but only wanting to give away what they don't like, when all of a sudden they end up in Jerusalem. Stuart Dunn wrote this "is hands down my favorite of the six!" After sending Mary Magdalene away, the resurrected Jesus addresses the children by names and gives them a mission to go tell people in their own time His message.

[Hendey's other books include: *A Book of Saints for Catholic Moms, As Morning Breaks, O Radiant Dawn, The Catholic Mom's Prayer Companion, The Grace of Yes, The Handbook for Catholic Moms.*]

Muslims Find Christianity Is Religion Of Freedom (April 2017)

Fr. Felix Goldinger, a Catholic priest in Speyer, Germany, says many of the refugees he has baptized come from Iran and Afghanistan, as well as from Syria or Eritrea.

"A lot of [the Moslem refugees] come to Germany and think, 'Here I can choose my religion and I want to choose a religion of freedom,'" says Pastor Matthais Linke of the Evangelical-Freikirchlichen Gemeinde in Berlin. "For many Iranians that I've baptized, Christianity is the religion of freedom."

Adel, a twenty-five-year-old Iraqi refugee, said he did not feel free. He feared the reaction of other Muslim refugees and said his own brother attempted to prevent him from contacting Christian friends. Converting to Christianity in Spandau he says was the "happiest day of my life."

Former Muslims United is a program of the American Freedom Defense Initiative formed in 2009 by a group of leading infidels who have left Islam. Nonie Darwish, Mohammed Asghar, Amil Imani, Wafa Sultan, and Ibn Warraq occk to educate the American public and policymakers about the threat to the religious freedom and safety of former Muslims. Many are telling their stories.

Director Nonie Darwish puts it simply, "If you convert you die. Most Americans are subjected to much of the same misinformation with regard to Islam that I grew up with inside the Muslim world. Thus Americans are in the dark attempting to formulate their strategy to defend themselves against the threat of terror, domestic jihad and Sharia. While they get ridiculed for being 'Islamophobes,' the Muslim world itself is undergoing a huge and painful awakening.

"Sharia states that the killers of apostates and adulterers are not to be punished as murderers. That is why, for Islam to achieve four hundred percent compliance to Sharia enforcement, Muslim individuals were told they must be Allah's enforcers of Sharia on earth if the government fails to do so. That is the reason honor killing and killing of apostates happen in the West."

When prominent Egyptian lawyer and women's rights activist Nagla Al Imam announced her conversion to Christianity in Cairo, Egypt, she was lured by a TV station 'Al Mihwar' with the pretext of an interview. Upon arrival to the studio she was told the show had been canceled. She was then held against her will for hours assaulted, threatened, and insulted by several people. She was able to escape and told her story on her internet chat room.

Now Christians, respected evangelical scholars, and theologians, the Caner brothers, Ergun and Emil, have updated *Unveiling Islam: An Insiders Look at Muslim Life and Beliefs*. It offers a both sympathetic and realistic analysis of Islam's practices, ethics, and beliefs, and outlines the principle differences between Islam and Christianity.

When Nonie Darwish was a girl of eight, her father died a "shahid," a martyr for jihad. Today Darwish thrives as an American citizen, a Christian, a conservative Republican, and the author of *Now They Call Me Infidel: Why I Renounce Jihad for America, Israel, and the War on Terror.*

In converting from Islam to Christianity, Abdual Saleeb spent many years studying both. With Dr. R. C. Sproul he focuses in the Dark Side of Islam on four basic areas in which Islam rejects the very foundations of Christianity.

After writing *Why I Am Not a Muslim*, Ibn Warraq wrote about other converts in the introduction of his book, *Leaving Islam: Apostates Speak Out*. "No quick portrait of the typical apostate is likely to appear -- some are young (students in their teens), some are middle-aged with children; some are scientists, while others are economists, business people, or journalists; some are from Bangladesh, others are from Pakistan, India, Morocco, Egypt, Malaysia, Saudi Arabia, or Iran. Our witnesses, nonetheless, do have certain moral and intellectual qualities in common: for instance, they are all comparatively well educated, computer literate with access to the Internet, and rational, with the ability to think for themselves. However, what is most striking is their fearlessness, their moral courage, and their moral commitment to telling the truth."

Susan Crimp and Joel Richardson have also collected together many personal testimonies in *Why We Left Islam: Former Muslims Speak Out.*

Podcasts Spread Faith (February 2018)

Ascension Presents is a central location for entertaining faith-filled Catholic podcasts collected by Ascension Press. It is yet another way of permeating the culture's newest media. It also gives links to the contributors' more extensive websites.

Fr. Mike Schmitz, for example, ministers to students at the Newman Center in Duluth, MN diocese and posts as "the Bulldog Catholic." His recent short videos give answers to the many questions young people ask him, like "Will God Heal My Wounds?," "What Is Sin?," "Do We Deserve God's Love?," "Can I Get a Tattoo?," "Are all Catholics Hypocrites?," "Does God Love Some People More?," "Venting or Gossiping?," "Why Does God Let Bad Things

Happen?," "What constitutes a Practicing Catholic?," "Can I Go to Confession on the Phone?," "Will My Pet Be In Heaven?"

Fr. Josh Johnson is a young priest from LaSalle University, Baton Rouge, LA, and host of the hip-hop radio show "Tell the World." "I was raised Catholic," he says, "but I just never liked the Catholic Church growing up. I thought it was boring and I didn't understand it." He now explains "an old-school form of prayer that is pretty epic" in "What is Lexio Divina?" and answers questions like "Does God Always Show Us the Fruits of Our Prayers?" and asks "Who Do You Listen To?"

Fr. José Robles-Sanchez is a priest of the diocese of Alexandria, LA. In "The Light Shines in the Darkness" he talks about the light and darkness of family life, telling the teens at the Ascension Cafe that they can bring light into their family and all of their relationships. He challenges them to pray for their mothers and fathers, and help save families.

Maria Mitchell produces the "Caffeniated Conversations" series in which she literally converses over coffee with Spirit-led Catholics, like Lea Darrow with her young daughter Violet. Darrow shared that her new podcast, "Do Something Beautiful," was inspired by St. Teresa of Calcutta. After leaving behind her career as a model, Leah felt called to share with others that inner beauty is better and more lasting, that true modesty is not restrictive, but instead liberates by highlighting our God-given dignity.

Jackie and Bobby Angel shared with Mitchell about their faith, their baby Abigail, and the ins and outs of married life. At their website they blog on such things as "Our Lady of Fatima and Evangelization" and "Learning Accountability from Sam and Frodo."

Jeff Cavins talked about his favorite subjects, biking, bull-riding, and spreading the gospel through "Great Adventure" and "Bible Timeline," and "Encountering the Word" series. Church artist Anthonly Visco talked about the many aspects of religious art that have inspired him to make it his vocation. He encouraged young artists to always imitate their Creator in their work and never let themselves get dissuaded from their call.

Jason Evert explained the story behind Pope St. John Paul II's letters to Anna-Teresa Tymieniecka, so misreported by the secular media. Anna-Teresa was a married Polish philosopher and friend of the pope before and during his papacy. As Pope St. John Paul II himself said, "God uses human friendship to lead hearts to the source of divine charity." Jason and his wife Crystalina founded The Chastity Project.

Together they discussed with Mitchell how practicing chastity frees us to discover what love is really about. They answer the tough question, "Why is sex in marriage good and sex outside of marriage bad?" from both the husband's and wife's perspective in "YOU: Life, Love, and the Theology of the Body."

The musicians of His Own, Kara Klein, Maria Spears, and Christine Simpson, shared about their mission to inspire women to become all that God has created them to be. Pro-life speaker Megan Mastroianni shared her story about how God brought her down an unexpected path, and how she's loving every bit of it.

Catholic apologist and speaker Matt Fradd talked about fighting what he calls "the enemy of real love." Fradd founded The Porn Effect, a ministry that helps individuals end their pornography addiction. Maura Preszler, founded a similar ministry, Made in His Image, to teach women their dignity as Human. Women are telling stories of deliverance from their own enslavement to abuse, eating disorders, and negative self-images, while sharing their true identity sisters in Christ. Preszler also was inspired by St. John Paul II's Theology of the Body.

Sr. Miriam James Heidland was in her Society of Our Lady of the Most Holy Trinity habit in line at Sam's Club when a little girl asked, "Who are you supposed to be?" Answering the question, she shared from the wisdom of Pope Benedict XVI, C. S. Lewis, and Michelangelo to explain how each and every one of us are supposed to be a unique masterpiece made in the image of God.

[Fr. Schmitz has written *Beautiful Hope* and *Beautiful Mercy*, Frs. Schmitz and Johnson have a DVD "I Will Follow". Cavins has: *Catholicism 101, I'm Not Being Fed, My Life on the Rock, Praise God and Thank Him, The Bible Timeline Chart, The Rosary* and "15 Things to do in the midst of suffering" CD. The Everts have: *Answering Jehovah's Witnesses, How to Find Your Soulmate without Losing Your Soul, How to Talk to Your Teens about Chastity, If You Really Loved Me, Pure Faith A Prayer Book for Teens, Pure Love, Pure Manhood, Pure Womanhood, Puring 365, Raising Pure Teens, Theology of the Body in One Hour*. His Own's website is *behisown.com*. Fradd wrote *The Porn Myth*.]

Film Focuses On Christmas (January 2017)

This year's Christmas film "Believe" has a bit of "Christmas Carol" in it. Matthew Peyton is the most hated man in town, not like Scrooge for being miserly, but because he believes he has to cut back on the family business's employees and that he can no longer afford to sponsor the tradition christmas pageant as his father and grandfather had before him.

Then, of course, it gets worse. He's injured in an auto "accident," something like George Bailey in "It's a Wonderful Life." It's not an angel, however, that helps turn his life around, but the faith of a boy named Clarence and the faith expressed in works of the boy's mother.

It's not the 2013 film of the same name about soccer in 1984. This "Believe" premiered in Bristol and Grundy, Virginia, where it was filmed, in October during the PUSH! Film Festival and hit theaters in December.

It stars Southwest Virginia native Ryan O'Quinn and was co-produced by Matthew Pickett and Katy Bunn-Davidson also from the region. It was written and directed by Billy Dickson who with O'Quinn was executive producer.

Harry Smith of Smith Global Media brother of Will Smith, told Variety, "I picked 'Believe' as our first release because it's a great way to set the tone for what our company is about, filling the demand for top-quality family entertainment. We are extremely excited to bring wholesome family entertainment appealing to every genre, to audiences everywhere this holiday season."

O'Quinn is known for memorable roles in television shows and feature films such as "Starship Troopers" and "That Thing You Do." O'Quinn is also the author of Parenting Rules! The Hilarious Handbook for Surviving Parenthood and Marriage Rules! The Hilarious Handbook for Surviving Marriage. Coming soon he will appear in "A Horse from Heaven," another story of faith and healing about a girl and her horse.

Pickett worked on "Restitution" and on yet-to-be-released "Public Affairs." Dickson is known for "Babylon5: "The Gathering," "Ally McBeal" and "One Tree Hill."

Danielle Nicolet plays C. J.'s mother Sharon Joseph. She played a regular in the "Flash" and in several other TV series. She began acting in "The Jacksons: An American Dream" in 1992. The Internet Movie Data Base says, "She competed through her teenage years [in gymnastics], but finally admitted that acting was her dream. She has always played unpredictable characters, whether they be dramatic or comedic."

Isaac Ryan Brown plays Clarence Joseph, or C. J. as he prefers to be called. He has appeared in three movies already this year, in "Batman v. Superman: Dawn of Justice" as squatter boy, in "Dreams My Master" as Damien and in "the Land Before time XIV: Journey of the Brave" as the voice of Chomper. He started as Goby in "The Urban Odyssey of

Washington D.C.: A Bicentennial Celebration of Washington D.C.'s Heritate 1791-1991" a year before Nicolet.

The film's facebook page has encouraging quotes from Scripture, "Be strong and courageous. Do not be afraid, do not be discouraged, for the Lord your God will be with you wherever you go." (Joshua 1:9) and "The Lord will fight for you; you need only to be still." (Exodus 14:14) The site also has postings by the Salvation Army, long associated with Christmas giving, with the message, "We believe giving hope is priceless."

Julie Rowe Saleda's comment was a prayer, "Dear Lord, bless this movie and those who produced it. Inspire everyone who sees it."

Gunnar Sizemore tweeted, "Good seeing 'Believe' ... at the west coast premier! Isaac ... was awesome!" and Tess McClaine wrote, "I'm quite excited to see 'Believe' this Christmas season! Sending the TRUE message of Christmas ... Christ!"

[Smith Global Media has signed with Sony Pictures to distribute ten more films before 2020.]

EWTN Offers Inspiring Videos (December 2016)

EWTN offers a number of biographical DVDs. Some of the subjects are canonized, some blessed and all inspiring. All of them are inspirational.

Fr. Vincent Capodanno's film is called "The Grunt Padre in Vietnam," based on the book *The Grunt Padre* by Fr. Daniel Mode. It retells of his life as a chaplain during the Vietnam War. He died ministering to hopelessly out numbered marines. It features the personal stories of several veterans who remember him.

Ray Lowry writes, "I was the last Catholic priest to see Vince alive and the first to see him dead. On December 6, 1966, Vince and I changed jobs; I went out to 1/7 on the Batangan Peninsula and Vince replaced me at first Med. Within weeks of arriving in Vietnam I had heard stories about Vince and he indeed 'became a legend in his own time.' His CO at 1/7, Lt. Col. Buzz Lubka, told me that Fr. Capodanno 'could walk on water.' He was an inspiration to me and made me a better chaplain for knowing him. I'll never forget the night he died, but that is a story in itself. Fr. Mode has indeed captured the essence of the man. I still think of Vince daily. I am honored to have known him and to have shared my life with him as a Chaplain with the Marines in Vietnam. May God grant his noble soul eternal rest."

St. Junipero Serra has been quite misunderstood. "Serra: Ever Forward, Never Back" was filmed on location in the places he traveled, Spain, Mexico, and California. It shows his perseverance despite many trials in both the Old and New Worlds. Carolyn Williams gave this mini-series five stars. "I watch EWTN nightly for the daily Mass," she wrote, "and when this series ran for a week, I enjoyed it so much that I decided it was something I would like to watch again."

Archbishop Fulton Sheen is well known to those who are old enough to remember his Emmy-winning television show, "List Is Worth Living." He is virtually unknown, however, to many others. Some of the show's memorable episodes are included on the "Servant of All" DVD set. Interviews with those who knew him, including Regis Philbin and Cardinal Timothy Dolan, are also included. Some of these timeless episodes are "Ages of Man," "False Compassion," "Love is a Many Splendored Thing," "The Divine Sense of Humor," and "Angels." Other Sheen DVDs available at Amazon include "Sheen Gems," "His Irish Wit and Wisdom," "Faith Hope, and Love with Archbishop Sheen" and "His Last Words."

"Jerzy Popieluszko is called "Messenger of Truth" in the subtitle of his DVD. Another is simply called "The Making of a Martyr." He was the chaplain of the Solidarity movement in

Poland, that eventually helped topple the Soviet Union. He was martyred for speaking the truth. Cardinal Dolan called it, "A must-see documentary for all who believe in the rights of religious liberty and those who are lovers of freedom and defenders of truth."

St. Bakhita's story goes from life of slavery in Africa, eventually to a whole new life in a convent in Italy. Throughout her often harsh life Bakita was ever kind and generous, blessing hundreds even after her death. It is aptly subtitled, "From Slave to Saint." Another DVD of her life is called "Two Suitcases" which tells the story through another Canossian sister to her spiritually searching brother.

"The Healing Prophet" is the title of one of Solanus Casey's DVDs. Another is "Solanus Casey: Priest, Porter, Prophet." He too had difficulties living out his vocation. He was a simple priest, not allowed to preach or hear Confession. What he did do was pray through the intercession of St. Joseph and many were healed. He also just loved those who came to monastery, sometimes counseling them, but always simply loving them.

Of the second, John F. Oldani, Jr. summarizes, "Very interesting. Very interesting. I really enjoyed it. Need to watch it again. Very interesting! Farm boy grows up, works hard, stays humble, works miracles, suffers, dies, and is found casket under water, body expected to be completely deteriorated but is completely intact, even in better shape than when he died! Very interesting!"

"Media Apostle" tells of Fr. James Alberione's boyhood, of the vision as a seminarian that changed his live and finally to his founding what became a worldwide Catholic media empire and the Pauline Family of ten congregations and institutes under the patronage of St. Paul.

The life of "St. Gianna Beretta Molla" was that of an exemplary wife, mother, and physician, a saint. It includes many photographs and home videos from the Molla family. It also features the story of the St. Gianna Physicians guild, founded to promote Christian medical ethics.

Authors Look At Heaven (November 2016)

Writers who have never been there are writing about Heaven. Anthony DeStefano's is titled *A Travel Guide to Heaven*. Teresa Tomeo's is *God's Bucket List*, subtitled Heaven's Surefire Way to Happiness in This Life and Beyond.

DeStefano's is organized like a guidebook referring to fellow Christians as fellow travelers, saints and angels as our guides, our new glorified bodies as our luxury accommodations. He recommends leaving behind gloominess, stuffiness, cynicism, pessimism, intellectual snobbery, close-mindedness, self-righteousness, and prejudice against God or religion. That is because, as he emphasizes in the book, "if we know anything about Heaven, it's fun."

"It's a place of unlimited pleasure, unlimited happiness, and unlimited joy." It's the ultimate destination, "Disney World, Hawaii, Paris, Rome, and New York all rolled into one." He recalls C. S. Lewis's statement that the serious business of Heaven is joy. This tour would also add that much of the fun is getting there.

He does include Scriptural and theological references, of course, but looking at Heaven in this new way might help the reader break out of misconceived ideas about Heaven. For one thing those who already passed on are not angels. They are anxiously awaiting a new glorified body, like the one they had in life, but much better.

He notes, "Eye has not seen, nor ear has heard, what God has prepared for those who love Him," is all the Scriptures really tell us. He also compares Heaven to Dorothy's backyard, rather than far-off OZ. The things and people we love here is this life will be there in the next. The difference is that in Heaven they will never end. As he puts it "Ten billion years from today, your mom will still be your mom."

DeStefano writes that "As I've learned more about Heaven, my willingness to endure more suffering in this life has also increased." His belief in the eternal helped him, he says, accept many of the sacrifices and hardships of the temporal.

Tomeo looks at Heaven in a different way through her grandfather's eyes and her own life experiences as a revert. He taught her "l'arte di non fare nien," the art of doing nothing, of relaxing and enjoying the life and glory of God about you, in other words, preparing for life with Him in eternity.

She quotes Pope Emeritus Benedict XVI on the problem in our day, "Put simply, we are no longer able to hear God; there are too many frequencies filling our ears." She also reminds of St. Teresa of Calcutta's observation, "We cannot find God in noises and agitation."

We listen to hear our calling, our vocation. Tomeo mentions Nick Syko's "Careers Through Faith" seminars as a help here. His SAINT process includes examining one's Skills, Abilities, Interests, Nature, and Talents, and building on them.

Listening for God what God wants from us, however, takes many forms. She also encourages reading the *Bible*, the *Catechism of the Catholic Church*, the papal encyclicals, particularly Pope Paul VI's *Humanae Vitae* and St. John Paul II's *Evangelium Vitae*, and other Church writings.

She notes a Pew Center "U.S. Religious Knowledge Survey" found that Jews, Mormons, and even atheists scored higher than Christians. About 45 percent of Catholics had no idea what happens at Communion. A Kaiser Family Foundation study also found that teens and tweens spend fifty-three hours a week watching a screen, mostly television.

Getting disconnected from what the consumeristic world wants from us and reconnected to God is getting easier. As aids she recommends several daily devotionals: *The Magnificat, the Word Among Us, Living Faith*, and Presentation Ministries' own *One Bread, One Body.*

The Corporation for Nation and Community Service reported in The Health Benefits of Volunteering that all kinds of giving are more blessed than receiving. Volunteers reported greater longevity, lower rates of depression, higher functional ability, and fewer incidences of heart disease. Tomeo includes many more resources in an appendix.

[DeStephao has also written: *A Travel Guide to Heaven for Kids; A Travel Guide to Life; Angels All Around Us; Inside the Atheist Mind; I Just Can't Take It Anymore!; OK, I Admit It, I'm Afraid; Ten Prayers God Always Says Yes To; The Invisible World, The Love Book: A Simple Guide to the Most Abused and Misused Word in the English Language; Why Am I Here, Anyway?* Tomeo has: *Beyond Me, My Selfie, and I; Beyond Sunday; Extreme Makeover; Newsflash!; Noise; Walk Softly and Carry a Great Bag*]

Martyrs Continue To Witness (October 2016)

Elderly Fr. Jacques Hamel of Saint-Etienne-du-Rouvray, France, had his throat slit by an Islamic terrorist in July. Both the *Catholic Herald* and the *American Conservative* quickly labeled him a martyr. The president of Lombardy, Roberto Maroni, publicly called for him to be made a saint. Catholic Answers, however, explains that it takes more than a Christian being killed for being Christian to become a martyr officially recognized by the Church. The candidate must have the opportunity to witness to Christ before being killed. The world "martyr" means "witness." The official beatification process normally would not begin for Fr. Hamel until 2021.

How a person lived their life before their death, any signs of heroic virtue, also are important. Dominique Lebrun, the archbishop of Rouen, told the nearly two thousand attending Fr. Hamel's funeral in Rouen cathedral, some of them Muslims, his last words were:

"Get away, Satan," perhaps a reference to Jesus' words to Peter in Matthew 16:23. The archbishop praised Fr. Hamel for his fifty-eight years of loyal service to the Church saying, "Jacques, you were a loyal disciple of Jesus. Where you went you did good."

Adel Kermiche and Abdel Malik Petitjean, both nineteen, did talk about the incredibility of God becoming man, according to a surviving witness, but they also talked of politics. Sorting out the cases for other recent possible martyrs is taking some time already.

Jesuit Fr. Frans van der Lugt established a community center and farm near the city of Homs, Syria, and worked to reconcile Christians and Muslims. He was gunned down in the center's garden in 2014.

Clement Shahbaz Bhatti's killing in Islamabad, Pakistan, in 2001 might more accurately be called an assassination since he was a member of the National Assembly, but he was the only one who was a Roman Catholic. He spoke out against the country's blasphemy laws. the Taliban claimed it was for this he was killed. His cause for beatification was open in the usual five years.

Fr. Andrea Santoro was shot from behind while kneeling in Santa Maria Church, Trabzon, Turkey, in 2006. Oguzhan Akdin, 16, was sentenced to over 18 years for the crime. According to Msgr. Luigi Padovese, Akdin's mother compared her son to Mehmet Ali Agca, would-be assassin of St. Pope John Paul II in 1981. At Fr. Santoro's funeral at the St. John Lateran basilica, Cardinal Camillo Ruini already was suggesting in his homily that the beatification process for Fr. Santoro may be opened in five years.

Sr. Leonella (Rosa Maria) Sgorbati 2006 was shot in the back in Mogadishu, Somolia, in 2006 outside her children's hospital along with her bodyguard, Mohamed Osman Mahamud. Her last words were reported to be "Perdono. Perdono," Italian for "I forgive. I forgive." Fellow Italian Bishop Salvatore Colombo had previously been shot dead while celebrating Mass there in 1989.

Fabianus Tibo was a Catholic layman shot by firing squad with Dominggus da Silva and Marinus Riwu in Poso, Sulawesi, Indonesia, in 2006. Religious leaders of Christianity and Islam, including Pope emeritus Benedict XVI and former Indonesian president Abdurrahman Wahid protested the suspicious "execution" of Tibo and his companions.

[Fr. Jacques cause for canonization was opened several years early in 2017.]

Author Focuses On Transformation (September 2016)

Bear Wozniak, the author of the best seller *A Surfing Guide to the Soul*, has a new book. He was a world champion surfer, a ninja black belt, a Benedictine oblate, and now hosts "Deep Adventure Radio," which has over three million listeners on three hundred stations. Guests have included filmmaker Jason Jones and martial artist Jesse Romeo. The website invites visitors to share their own stories of how Christ has transformed their lives.

"Join us on this quest," it challenges. "Abandoning yourself to God's will takes every ounce of your courage and dedication. You will be tested, but Jesus is the one calling and He will empower you in ways you've never even imagined."

The new book, *Deep Adventure*, is subtitled "The Way of Heroic Virtue." Its chapters make their way from virtue to virtue, as Wozniak describes it toward "a life lived in pursuit of God's will in the boldest, most rewarding way possible to live." As Peter was asked by Christ on his way away from Rome, Wozniak asks, "Where are you going?" and then adds, "Are you ready to enter into Deep Adventure? Are you ready to take up your cross and follow Him? Are you ready to let virtue propel you into the wild adventure of God's will? Are you ready to walk the Way of Heroic Virtue?"

"True heroism," he explains, "the kind that saves lives, preserves dignity, and protects the most vulnerable, is a determined, steadfast power, under control, and directed toward the good with the clarity of purpose that comes with humility."

"A hero," he continues, "is cultivated by countless -- often unnoticed -- actions. They are ordinary humans -- you and me -- who direct their decisions and actions to be strengthened by goodness, compassion, integrity, and righteousness."

The chapters are connected by the adventure story "The Rescue" that works on its own. The chapters are also accompanied by commentaries from a variety of others on the virtues. He refers to the four virtues of Socrates, justice, prudence, temperance, and fortitude. He contrasts Socrates' misunderstanding of our fallen nature with St. Paul's understanding that we cannot become virtuous without a Savior.

He quotes St. Augustine on temperance, Friar Antonio de Montesino on justice, and Bl. Jose Luis Sanchez del Rio on fortitude. Mother Angelica comments on faith and Sts. Damien and Marianna of Molokai on hope.

Wozniak also shares his own "Scuba Tank Theology." He tells of being so overwhelmed by the sensation of flying underwater, of seeing all the sea life in its natural environment, that he forgot to conserve his oxygen. His diving instructor exchanged his fuller oxygen tank for his nearly empty one.

"In that moment," he writes, "holding my tank in my hands and my last breath in my lungs, I realized that if the transition did not go smoothly, I would have no air at 120 beet below the surface."

Anthony De Stefano, author of *A Travel Guide to Heaven*, calls Wozniak's new book "not a book to read and put away, but rather to read and keep referring to it."

"Men," he says emphatically, "this book will bring you closer to God and help you to become the man God intended you to be."

Reviewer Jeffrey Miller warns the reader that the book does contain many sports metaphors. He does, however, nevertheless call it "solid spiritual reading."

Sheila Liaugminas, author of *Non-Negotiable*, writes, "Take the spiritual classics of the desert fathers, put them in the hands of a modern ocean master and champion surfer, reintroduce them to modern culture with lost words like heroism and virtue ... and you have this powerful blast of clarity and pull of gravity toward the greatest force of nature: God Who is love."

Bishop Michael Byrnes of Detroit says, "I can affirm wholeheartedly with Bear the deep conviction that is at the heart of his book: 'The most radical thing that you can do in life is to abandon yourself to the wild adventure of God's will.' "

Besides the TV and radio shows and the blogs DeepInTheWave and BearsWave, Wozniak Deep Adventure Ministry also offers two-minute podcasts on living the virtues, retreats for both men and women, and the Renegade Rosary Run for everyone. The three 'laps' around the rosary are for the deeper conversion of friends and family, for the blessing of Deep Adventure and for your own personal intention, fifteen decades in all.

[Wozniak now is on on-line radio at blogtalkradio.com/deepadventure.]

Author Explores Miracles (August 2016)

Michael O'Neill is the author of *Exploring the Miraculous* and *365 Days with Mary*. He hosts "The Miracle Hunter" show in Revenant radio and has appeared on EWTN News. His Miracle Hunter's website includes several types of miracles, including apparitions, miraculous images, Eucharistic miracles, stigmata, and incorruptibles, all arranged chronologically.

The earliest known apparition was from St. James the Greater who saw the Virgin Mary while he was in preaching on the banks of the Ebro River in Saragosa, Spain, in 40 AD. Today, apparition reports occur more frequently. Some scholars estimate the total number of apparition claims throughout history to be approximately twenty-five hundred (with about five hundred of those coming in the Twentieth century alone). According to the Dictionary of Apparitions of the Virgin Mary, throughout history, 308 apparitions are attributed to saints and blesseds. Seven popes throughout history have witnessed Marian apparitions.

The most famous apparitions have been those reported in Guadalupe, Mexico (1531), Rue du Bac (1830), and Lourdes, Frances (1858), and Fatima, Portugal (1917). The most recently Vatican recognized apparitions are those from and Kibeho, Rwanda (1989) and Le Laus, France (1664). Those in Itapirange, Brazil (1994), Lipa, Phillipines (1948), and Robinson, WI (1859) were declared supernatural by the local bishop.

The appearance of Our Lady of Guadalupe to St. Juan Diego Cuauthtlantzin is well-known. The one to Juan Diego Bernadino is not. This Juan Diego was a young convert a few years after Mary's appearance to his namesake. This native Tlaxcalan was going to a river believed to have healing propeties when sickness had overtaken his family when he also encountered a lady. The lady told him, "I will give you another water with which you will extinguish the contagion and cure not only your family but all who drink of it, for my heart is always inclined toward the lowly and will not suffer to see such things without remedying them. When the server lead Franciscans there, they found also the lady's image in a pine tree and took it to the San Lorenzo monastery. She became known as Our Lady of Ocotlan. Many notable pilgrims visited her shrine, including Christopher Columbus. It was expanded into a monastery by Juan 1, but was besieged in 1835.

Bishop Juan de Zaumarraga mistakenly gave the name Our Lady of Guadalupe to the second appearance in Mexico, when St. Juan Diego called Coatlaxopeuh, meaning "one who crushes the head of the snake."

The original Lady of Guadalupe appeared near the Guadalupe River, at Caceres, Spain, in 1326 to reveal to Gil Cordano who was looking for a lost cow. She guided him to the cave where the statue of Seville had been hidden since 850. It was protected by a church bell and accompanied by the relics of St. Fulgentius and St. Forentina.

Pope Gregory the Great had given the miraculous statue from the basilica of Mary Major to St. Leander the bishop of Seville. It had lead a procession in Rome during which an angel appeared and a plague ended in 542.

In 1134 Our Lady of Liesse appeared to Ismenia, the daughter of the sultan of Egypt. Her father had sent her to seduce three captive knights from Laon, France. She, however, was converted and requested an image of Mary. The next day dazzling light and a delicious perfume accompanied their carving. On the next day she heard, "Trust me, Ismenia! I have prayed to my Son for you. You will be His faithful servant. You will free my three beloved knights. You will be baptized and through you France will be enriched by countless graces. Through you my name will become famous and later I will receive you forever in paradise."

The miracles are certainly not all ancient, though the Miracle Hunteer's are mostly associated with apparitions. The categories overlap. The painting and statues remind of the saints, particularly Mary, as do the saints' incorrupt bodies and relics. Their stigmata and Eucharistic miracles remind us of Jesus Himself through Whom all the miracles ultimately come.

On Christmas in 2013 a consecrated Host fell and was put into a container of water. Red stains then appeared on the Host and the bishop of Legnica had the Host investigated by the

Department of Forensic Medicine, Wroclaw, and the Pomeranian Medical University, Szczecin. They concluded that it was cross striated muscle, similar to heart muscle, of human origin and bearing signs of stress.

In 1936 Blessed Maria Pierina De Micheli of Milan, Italy, promoted a devotion and medal, which was approved by Pope Piux XII. He set the Feast of the Holy Face of Jesus for Shrove Tuesday.

In 1982 Myrna Nazzour's stigmata was approved by papal nuncio Luigi Accogli, the Melkite prelate Isidore Battikha and an Orthodox patriarch.

The body of St. Isadore, who died in 1172, was exhumed five times and found intact, though darkened and rigid. So too was Blessed George Preca of Malta, who died in 1962. St. John XXIII, who died in 1963, was exhumed in 2001 and found incorrupt.

[Neill's other books include *Mater Misericordiae*, *Exploring the Miraculous* and *20 Answers: Apparitions and Revelations*.]

Christianity Growing In Nepal (July 2016)

The World Christian Database identifies Nepal as having the fastest-growing Christian population of any nation. In 1951 there were no Christians in the country, then mountain-climbing opened Nepal up to the outside world. By 1961 there were four hundred fifty-eight, by 2001 over ten thousand. By 2008 the Hindu-dominated monarchy ended. By 2011 nearly four times than that, over ten thousand of them Catholics.

Bishwa Mani Pokharel of the newspaper *Nagarik* is of the opinion there are very many more Christians.

Most recently the Christian relief efforts in the wake of last year's earthquake near Katmandu has lead to conversions. This quake was sixteen times stronger than Haiti's 2010 quake, affecting eight million and killing nine thousand.

Gary Fallesen of Climbing for Christ says new Christians are coming from the lower castes, "It's the only way out. Socially there's nothing they can do to change that and then we come along and share about Jesus and the love He has for them."

Jo Ann Lyon, founder of World Hope International, concurs, "It's love like this that helps to propel the Christian faith in countries like Nepal. It's also why countries with greater religious freedoms are generally more peaceful, have greater degrees of gender equality, and also have more stable economies."

In 1990 Jesuit Anthony Francis Sharma founded Caritas Nepal, the Catholic service organization. In 2007 he was appointed Nepal's first Catholic bishop. He had taught both King Gyanendra and his brother, King Birendra Shah, at St. Joseph's College in Darjeeling, and established twenty-three schools.

"The Jesuits of Jawalakhel came to Nepal not to preach," he explained, "but to serve the nation by acting as an educational institution."

About 1760 he says Capuchin "priests were given full authority to preach Christianity and even build a church called Our Lady's Assumption somewhere in Lalitpur District." In 1996 a new Church of the Assumption was completed at Dhobighat.

"With twenty-five percent of the population of Nepal already in extreme poverty before the earthquake and eighty-three percent of Nepal's people living in rural areas, the impact of the earthquake on people's lives, and all that they had built over a lifetime was immense," said Jennifer Poidatz, director of Catholic Relief Services' Humanitarian Response Department.

Jyam Bahadur Thapa Magar, fifty-five, had been building homes in Bungkot, Gorkha district, since he was a teenager.

"I learned how to build houses from the elders," he says. "I went with them to work and I learned by seeing them working. I made houses that same way my whole life until I took a training from CRS."

"I think the houses built with the new techniques will not fall at once if a very strong earthquake happens," he says. "And it will take some time to fall if it is going to fall. So people can escape during the earthquake and aftershocks and be safe. And if it is a smaller earthquake, the house will stand strong."

Kalpana Shrestha, a seasonal farm worker, says, "I'm planning to work making houses after I finish the training. I want to earn more and have more regular work. It's not guaranteed that I will get work, but I think I can go to different places in walking distance and find jobs."

Kumari Gurung says, "I had a hotel with twenty-two beds. It was large and beautiful. When the earthquake happened it fully collapsed. My small granddaughter was trapped and we couldn't get to her until my son game to dig her out."She and her son now have an eight-room hotel, built with aid from CRS, though they still owe on the loan for the former hotel. She estimates it will take another five years for the market to reach its pre-earthquake level of economic activity.

[In 2017 Nepal assigned the "crime" of evangelization five years imprisonment.]

Is New Film True To Life? (May 2016)

Many are asking how true to life the new film "Miracles from Heaven." It is based upon the book, *Miracles From Heaven: A Little Girl, Her Journey to Heaven and Her Amazing Story of Healing* by Christy Wilson Beam, published last year. The Beam family have worked with the making of the film and have seen the final film and can best answer this question. they had to re-live the experience during the writing of the book and now again with the movie.

Kevin Beam says that real life was a bit different than portrayed in "Miracles from Heaven." He is portrayed in the movie as the calm parent who keeps faith throughout everything and does whatever he can to support his family. It also misportrays Heaven.

"It was a daily reset for me," he says, "and I feel like on the surface I had to be incredibly strong, first off for Anna because she was going through so much physically on a daily basis, that I need to be strong for her and then for the entire family."

"It doesn't come across in the movie, but they were there for me way more than I was there for them and our family. We just fed off of each other. Christy would be right there for me, Abby, Addeline, even Anna! There's times when she's comforting me when I was trying to comfort her."

"It doesn't mean that I wasn't challenged, it doesn't mean that I didn't question why things were happening, but I ultimately didn't question the source. I knew that God was ultimately in control. Never did I imagine that the outcome would be as beautiful as it was, but I knew that God knew."

"That whole time period was just so hard." Abby agrees. "In the movie it happens a lot quicker than it actually did in our lives. It actually went on for a period of a few years of when she was sick. So it was such a large section of my life that I don't really think about as much because it was so hard. Seeing it on screen was hard.

She does add however, "I just left feeling my faith so reassured. I'm just so excited for other people to see it and hopefully leave with that same sense of just faith that God is real and God is there."

"She was on 10 medications a day ... she just lived on the sofa in the fetal position with a heating pad on her stomach. That was her life."

Christy shares that she has heard from many people around the world who told her that her daughter's story has affected them deeply. All of the positive response have been a confirmation for her that writing the book was the correct thing to do. "So grateful," she says. "So grateful."

Annabel herself related that when she was stuck in the tree for five house before firefighters could extract her, she visited heaven, where she asked Jesus if she could stay. And he said, "No, Annabel, I have plans for you on Earth that you cannot complete in heaven."

According to the Beams, Jesus sent Annabel back with a guardian angel who looks over her. Christy says, they couldn't be happier about the way things turned out.

Keen Green's simple comment was, "This precious family's grief and struggles are deeper than most could endure, yet Divine Providence steps in to rescue more than just a little girl ... but all who partake of her witness of Him."

Mothers, who can identify with the author, write especially enthusiastically about the book, which rates near five out of five on Amazon. Those who already know that miracles are part of everyday life also welcomed the Beam's witness.

Becky Jackoby wrote of the book, "While she speaks of her faith, she does not dramatize it nor does she discount it. It is integral to the family's personal experience and is related with realistic dialogue of a believer's heart. For the most part, the family's story is related in enough detail to understand both the severity of the child's condition as well as the impending healing. The miracle is subtly described and almost downplayed, which was a bit disappointing until I thought more about the story.

"Being a mother and grandmother myself, I found myself sympathizing with Christy's substantial emotional, financial, and sacrificial investment in the care of Annabel's serious illness as well as the commitment of each family member to quality of life. In fact, Christy devotes the first half of the story to Annabel's care.

Kristin Plausky commented, "As a mom, I couldn't put this book down. I can't even imagine the heartbreak, pain, and stress it must be in your life to have a child so chronically ill that they must take the cocktail of medications that this poor child was taking just to keep a somewhat reasonable quality of life. As a mother it broke my heart. And then there was the terror of having that same child in such a nightmare situation, I can't even comprehend.

"The author did a fantastic job of keeping the reader engaged and pulling at our heartstrings. The tension in the storyline kept the book glued to my hands, there was no way I could put it down until I finished it."

Jennifer Rainey wrote, "I could not put this book down! It is always amazing to see God work and perform miracles! Annabel stole my heart from the beginning as did the rest of the family and kept it until the end! It warmed my heart that she wants to have the same career in life as the one person who was by her side during her darkest days in the hospital!"

Author Shares Tips On Evangelization (April 2016)

Steve Dawson met his wife in pro-life work but says that it was Fr. Robert's "Catholicism" series that inspired him to found St. Paul Street Evangelism (SPSE). He and his fellow Catholic evangelists offered miraculous medals, like those of Maximilian Kolbe. Within the year the new apostolate had expanded to twenty-five cities. Since their humble beginning in 2012 they have added many teachings explaining Catholicism in pamphlets and on-line.

After reading Evengeli nuntiandi he says, "I saw more clearly that abortion, monstrous as it is, is just a symptom. It is a symptom of the disease of Godlessness."

In his new book, *Catholic Street Evangelization: Stories of Conversion and Witness*, he shares tips on how Catholics can evangelize. He also shares encouraging stories from other evangelists and those they have evangelized. Many are lapsed Catholics who, like Dawson, have now taken their call to evangelize seriously after being evangelized themselves.

At first Dawson simply told inquirers, "Find like-minded Catholics and a public place, take a few sacramentals, and go to it." Their Basic Evangelization Training and Teen Encounter Workshop now include how to talk enthusiastically about the Faith, how to identify where people are at, how to share your own journey, how to pray with other, how to point people to more information.

Dawson concludes the book by quoting Pope Francis, "When the Church summons Christians to take up the task of evangelization, she is simply pointing to the source of authentic personal fulfillment."

Prisoner Karl Strunk was overwhelmed by the information from St. Paul Street Evangelization when he posted a comment on-line. He says, "I am now able to provide a small library for any and all who wish to become more intimate with our Lord, as well as for those who wish to become more intimate with our Lord, as well as those who desire to learn more about our doctrine and theology."

Fellow prisoner Gordon asked questions of Strunk after watching EWTN. Together they studied "Praying to the Saints" and "Confession" and the *Catechism of the Catholic Church*.

George Fisher prayed with and gave contact information to a man, who had been shaken up by crashing into a guard railing. A week later he called to say he wanted to come back into the Catholic Church.

Former Baptist Father Ed Graveline says, "By far the greatest work we can do on the street is simply to listen, to pray with people who stop, and to tell them about God's love and mercy." This is especially true in this Jubilee year of Mercy. "Being a street evangelist has been both humbling and rewarding," Fr. Graveline says. "Every day we reach hundreds of people. Many walk right by us, yet even they might be touched simply by our presence. I know that our evangelists and the evangelized alike are pleased with the non-confrontational approach that SPSE promotes."

Fr. Michael Mayer learned the differences of evangelizing in the inner city and the suburbs. In this he and his new parishioners were helped by SPSE. "Most people welcome our interactions," he says, "and some even give their own witnesses. This helps team members to see how important their presence is in facilitating and encouraging people to look at their faith and their walk with the Lord."

Edwin "Uzi" Mendez, formerly a Chicago gang leader says, "Like St. Ignatius Loyola, I had a near-death experience followed by a long recovery which brought me back to God." Now he says, "The most powerful tools of evangelization for any Catholic wherever they may be are prayer and the sacraments."

Lucy Stamm was away from confession for just months rather than decades like Mendez. ow as an evangelist she concurs, "I, too, have found that commitment to prayer and spiritual growth are keys to evangelization. Whether you are a 'natural' like [my partner] Val, or a 'not God's first choice' like me, God is calling you by name and can work wonders through you."

David the Jehovah Witness came into the Church, sponsored by his Catholic uncle, who was also praying for him. Tanya, a Subway sandwich maker, received a miraculous medal. Later she shared that her father was healing extraordinarily after his operation.

Pete was dying. A non-Catholic friend of his received a rosary from one of the Catholic evangelists at the farmers market, where Pete had worked. The friend's son prayed the rosary and Pete's daughter wore the rosary at the funeral. Pete's friend attributed the family's peace to it.

[The website streetevangelization.com now includes "Stories from the Street" podcasts.]

Book Promotes Spiritual Growth (February 2016)

"Fr. Spitzer is a Jedi master who can train you in the ways of the Force," reviewer C. S. Morissey of the Adler-Aquinas Institute wrote. Referencing the new resurgence of the Star Wars phenomena he explained, "By this I mean he can tutor you in how to see the evidence for the universe's transcendent dimension. He will open your mind's eye to look beyond scientific materialism."

The Soul's Upward Yearning by Jesuit Robert J. Spitzer, published just before the release of Star Wars VII, Morissey continues, "teaches us that the presence of God within us is the Source of our attraction to myths." Its subtitle describes the book as "Clues to Our Transcendent Nature from Experience and Reason (Happiness, Suffering, and Transcendence).

The publisher Ignatius Press notes that many from many fields have noted the "loss of confidence in our ability to soar upward," such as Carl Jung, Mircea Eliade, Gabriel Marcel, C. S. Lewis, and J. R. R. Tolkien. They cite the American Journal of Psychiatry study that linked the lack of religion with a marked increase of suicide, meaninglessness, substance abuse, and family separation.

Miochael Augros, author of *Who Designed the Designer*, also calls Spitzer "a master." His "brilliant use of physics, cosmology, psychology, NDE studies, and contemporary philosophy," Augros says, "reveals how all disciplines and shared human experiences converge on the truth."

Best-selling author Dean Koontz calls it "an intellectual triumph." "Those who think that faith is a matter of emotion and self-delusion could not intelligently defend that position," he continued, "if they read this book with an open mind and comprehend its arguments."

Fr. Spitzer is a Jesuit, the president of the Magis Center of Reason and Faith and the Spitzer Center. Both produce curriculum to strengthen faith in this very secularized culture. He has worked in many ways to correct this loss by making the abundant evidence for transcendence more available.

He has appeared on "Larry King Live" debating Stephen Hawking, Leonard Mlodinow, and Deepak Chopra, and on "The Today Show" debating on euthanasia. He has taken part in the History Channel's "God and the Universe" and PBS's "Closer to Truth."

He has produced several series for the Eternal Word Television Network. They include "Healing the Culture," "The Spirit of Catholic Leadership," "Suffering and the Love of God," "Finding God Through Faith and Reason," and "The Heavens Proclaim the Glory of God."

His *Finding True Happiness: Satisfying Our Restless Hearts* also published last year and his previous books also teach the Way. Others have been *New Proofs for the Existence of God: Contributions of Contemporary Physics and Philosophy*, and *From Mother to Cosmos, Five Pillars of the Spiritual Life*, and *Ten Universal Principles: A Brief Philosophy of the Life Issues*.

"We are transcendent beings," Fr. Spitzer writes, "with transphysical souls that survive bodily death, who are in search of perfect love truth, goodness, and beauty. The objective of myths is to express ultimate truth and meaning and in order to do this they must reach beyond the contingent barriers of this world and universe and reveal the source of truth and meaning -- that is ultimate reality."

On-line at the Magis Center site Spitzer has a searchable 500-page encyclopedia covering the answers to major questions on God and Jesus Christ. Part one covers God, physics, creation, philosophy, atheism, and suffering. Part two gets more specific, dealing with Jesus, historicity, resurrection, miracles, divinity, and unconditional love.

Fr. Spitzer is currently working on three books, *Personal Happiness, Jesus-Emmanuel: A Philosopher Examines the Evidence for Jesus* and with James Sinclair and Bruce Gordon, *The Grand Designer: The Evidence for Creation in Modern Physics*.

[His newest books are: *The Light Shines on in the Darkness* and *God So Loved the World*, previous ones: *Healing the Culture, Ten Universal Principles* and *The Spirit of Leadership*.]

Nun Witnesses Through Cooking (January 2016)

Sr. Anita Torres won the "Thanksgiving Souper Stars" episode on the show "Chopped" on the Food Network. All four of the contestants were soup kitchen cooks. Thirty-year-old Sr. Anita is a member of the Franciscans of the Eucharist, having only professed in October.

Fr. Bob Lombardo, the director of Our Lady of the Angels mission in the Humboldt Park neighborhood on Chicago's Westside, suggested she apply. It is located in what is considered a "food desert" with only convenience stores for the residents to choose from, rather that fresh food markets or grocery stores.

"This is an opportunity to highlight a major problem in our country," he says, "the fact that people are hungry and that there is food anxiety."

Fr. Bob was brought in by Cardinal Francis George in 2005 to help rebuild the Catholic presence in the neighborhood that had its church destroyed by fire. In 2010 he founded the Franciscans of the Eucharist as the support community for the mission.

"I think when you put in enough time and that famous "secret" ingredient, love," like St. Anita, he adds, "you put out a really good meal that people will enjoy."

Sr. Anita explains, "The Lord gave me this talent. I believe the kitchen is my canvas where I get to express myself creatively. When I cook, I want to share that love and I try to put care into everything that I make for every person that I serve."

"I am really grateful to the Food Network for making it a priority to have a show that highlights the work that people who work to serve the poor do. I wanted to do it for Jesus, to be a witness to how fulfilling a life surrendered to God can be. I also wanted to represent the least among us, the very poor, who are so dear to Jesus."

"The daily challenge to grow in holiness and serve my brothers and sisters in need," she says is a great blessing.

Being on the show was, she says, "a really good opportunity for all of those who are on the show, myself included, to kind of be a face or a witness or kind of spokesperson for the people that we serve and that we love."

"It's been a very humbling experience to share the freedom and joy of religious life on the show," she adds. "If we come together, brothers and sisters of people of good will, we can make a big difference."

"What it really is about is 'How can I be a good steward of everything coming in and make the most delicious meal possible with the ingredients we have right now?' "

"Not only is it an opportunity to be artistic, but even more importantly to show our deep gratitude to God and our benefactors for their generosity that sustains our life and our work."

Sr. Anita credited her spouse. "I felt His help and guidance. Perhaps being on national television and winning this competition will bring some attention to the issue of hunger and to the reality that God's love is so strong and so big. He can take this little nun from Chicago who never went to culinary school to compete. Literally nothing is impossible with God!"

As usual for the show they were all given an unusual collection of ingredients with which to work with and had to come up with servings in three different categories. One contestant was eliminated with each category.

For the appetizer category Sr. Anita created Mexican-style quesadillas. For the main entré she made a Mediterranean-style curry turkey, sweet potato-cranberry hash with goat cheese and green bean sauce. She won with her dessert entry, pancakes with dark chocolate sauce and cranberry salsa.

"I've been told," she admits, "my out-side-the-box pesto, moving beyond the boundaries of pine-nuts to other, more economical nuts, and my picadillo, Spanish beef dish, are well done."

She also loves to bake strawberry-rhubarb pie, which was a favorite of Cardinal Francis George, who died earlier this year. The prize of ten thousand dollars was used to restock Our Lady of the Angel's pantry for the holidays. For Christmas they expect to serve fifteen hundred and distribute twelve hundred Christmas gifts.

"We have an emphasis on satisfying not only physical hunger, but also spiritual hunger," she explains. "We begin any meal with a prayer service with a Liturgy of the Word format, as most of our neighbors are not Catholic, but Baptist. Keeping God's Word at the center helps us to stay united. I think, many people are attracted by the joy the sisters have and it makes them wonder if that joy is possible for them too."

The mission also serves nine hundred youth in their after-school program and summer Bible school. They serve thirty or more seniors with computer class, Bible study, lunch, and exercise. Another Franciscan of the Eucharist Sr. Stephanie's recent Olympic trial was covered in the *Wall St. Journal* and *Runner's World*.

[Their website franciscansoftheeucharistofchicago.com says they now have over a hundred discerning the call to their community.]

Book Focuses On Christianity In China (November 2015)

A Star in the East by Rodney Stark and Xiuhua Wang is subtitled "The Rise of Christianity in China." Stark comes at the topic as a sociologist researching both Christianity and Chinese history, while Wang provides an more modern inside look at both.

Together their book refutes the theories that China is invulnerable to religion or that past efforts of missionaries have failed or that the Cultural Revolution extinguished any chance for Christianity in China. They claim that just considering the visible Christians, those not part of underground Church, thousands still convert to Christianity each day, and forty new churches open each week. If the current rate of growth were to hold until 2030, there would be more Christians in China, about two hundred ninety-five million, than any other nation on Earth. By 2040 there could be twice that many.

A Chinese friend of Joann Pittman of the Gospel Coalition told her, "What we need is more persecution. It is way too easy to be Christian in China today." Pittman herself notes in her review of the book, "As hostility to Christianity and the gospel grows in the West, I suspect that we have much to learn about standing firm from the historical experience of our brothers and sisters in China."

"Persecution served as a potent selection mechanism," the authors write. "Lukewarm liberalism could not generate the level of commitment needed to hold onto one's faith in the face of considerable persecution risk." The Protestant missions were more successful in the long run than Catholic missions, although starting three centuries earlier and initially growing much faster. The pope connection and the need for priests for the sacraments made persecution easier.

But they add "Without the conviction that they were bringing priceless truths to those in need, the mission spirit quickly dissipated in liberal Protestant circles." Christianity has been legal since 1979. Today Catholic Christians in China are outnumbered by Protestant Christians by at least ten-to-one.

Not all of the converts were "rice Christians," as The Keys of the Kingdom by A. J. Cronin pointed out. A remnant survived both the Nationalists and the Communists. "Conversion," Start and Wang's analysis of surveys says,"is the result of coming to agree with others to whom one is attached via family of friendship," not through media, even the Bible, or through preaching. They even found that more of the affluent and well-educated than the poor convert and have a chapter devoted to each.

Catholics were severely persecuted. About four thousand Catholic schools were closed, as well as all the Catholic hospitals and orphanages and printing presses. Many priests and bishops were killed. "By 1954 three hundred Chinese priests were in prison ... and then ... there was a mass arrest of more than two hundred clergy" (p 53) and other Catholics.

"Ironically, the persecution of Protestants [under Mao] may have been the single most beneficial event for the success of Christianity," the author conclude. "The continuing growth of Christianity in China during the years of the Cultural Revolution was truly an underground activity."

David Aikman, author of *Jesus in Beijing*, wrote, "Readers who enjoyed [Stark's] earlier works on the Crusades, the rise of Christianity in the Roman Empire, and Christianity's role in ending slavery will be grateful that he has now applied his brilliance to China." Fellow Baylor professor Phillip Jenkins noted, "What makes *A Star in the East* wholly distinctive though -- and so very valuable -- is its reliance on credible and strictly current quantitative evidence."

Reader Lemas Mitchel commented on Amazon that although "Baylor University is known to be a Baptist university, yet the authors were very even handed in their treatments." She also liked that the book was wonderfully brief, a hundred sixty pages, that took her about three hours. She asks, "If people who are well-fed, who have time to ponder existential questions, such as "values" and the "meaning of life." Why should we not be surprised that as China gets richer there are more people who have time to find such needs?"

Many Chinese practice fold religion, based on ancestral worship with some Confucianism and Buddhism thrown in, and yet will nevertheless say that they don't practice a religion, meaning an organized religion. Even many who will admit to believing in Jesus Christ, do not identify as Christians. Estimates on Christians in China vary widely between 16 million and 200 million.

In his review of *Jesus in Beijing* Louis F. DeBoer asks a question that applies also to *A Star in the East*, "Is Christ extinguishing His Church in the West? Is Christ replanting His Church in other parts of the globe?" He continues to explain, "As we look around us we see a Post-Christian America and an apostate West that has not only forsaken its spiritual heritage, but actively hates Christianity."

"According to Aikman," DeBoer says, Christianity is growing by leaps and bounds in China and is on a course to become not only the dominant religion in China, but also the dominant cultural force in the great nation."

DeBoer notes that "classes in Christianity at secular Chinese universities are packed. Many intellectuals ... have a very favorable attitude towards Christianity. They have seen the kind of societies that Buddhism, Hinduism, and Islam have produced and are not impressed. They have seen what Christianity ... has historically produced and they believe that this is an example to emulate."

An example given in the book was Jiang Zeming, President of China and leader of the Chinese Communist party, who when asked in 2002 before leaving office if he could make one last decree that would be obeyed in China, what would it be? He replied, "I would make Christianity the official religion of China." The Chinese Christians are not crusading to overthrow communism, only to advance Christianity. They are already sending out missionaries to neighboring nations with a zeal to convert the Islamic world.

Pope Francis in his recent visit to the United Nations, speaking for all Christians, emphasized the same, avoiding the political divisions. "The hour has indeed struck for conversion, for personal transformation, for interior renewal," he told the General Assembly. "The hour has come for a halt, a moment of contemplation, of reflection, almost a prayer, a moment to think anew of our common origin, our history, our common destiny."

[Stark's books include: *America's Blessings, Bearing False Witness: Debunking Centuries of Anti-Catholic History, Cities of God, Discovering God, Exploring Religious Life, For the Glory of God, God's Battalion: The Case for the Crusades, One True God, Reformation Myths, Religious Movements, The Rise of Christianity, The Triumph of Christianity, The Triumph of the Faith, The Victory of Reason, What Americans Really Believe*.]

Books Look At Pope Francis' Vatican (October 2015)

Pope Francis and the New Vatican is primarily a coffee table book, full of impressive photos by Dave Yoder of Pope Francis, the Vatican, and the people who are the Church. The accompanying text by Robert Draper explaining this "newness" is an added bonus. It is a companion piece to the best selling August 2015 issue of the *National Geographic magazine*'s "Pope Francis Remakes the Vatican" and *National Geographic Traveller's* August/September "Inside Vatican City." The book and these issues are timed to coincide with Pope Francis' historic first visit to the U. S.

National Geographic has long been known for its excellent photography. This book is more, describing "the interaction between place and culture -- the never-ending story to which National Geographic is dedicated."

Although St. John Paul II and Pope Emeritus Benedict XVI were the first non-Italian popes in centuries, Pope Francis is the first from the New World. Although John Paul II was the most globally mobile pope ever, Pope Francis has been called the most accessible. He is the first Jesuit pope, the first to choose to name himself after Francis of Assisi, lover of the poor and of all creation.

Yoder spent six months following Pope Francis throughout photogenic Vatican. He captured many touching scenes, the first photo of the current pope with his predecessor, the pope emeritus, Francis with parents and children, newlyweds, laity, clergy and religious, the handicapped, the old and young. He shares a photo of Pope Francis alone in the Sistine chapel on Christmas.

Draper draws his insight into the new pope from interviews around the world with many who had never spoken publicly before. It also includes the life story of Jorge Mario Bergoglio, "Padre Jorge." Sprinkled throughout the book are nuggets of the pope's wit and wisdom.

Pope Francis is a humble porteno, a life-long resident of Buenos Aires. He, however, has accepted that the Lord has put him in this position and has chosen to enjoy the experience. He has taken on the task of dealing with "the sickness," the worldliness, both within and outside of the old Vatican.

Although he appears spontaneous, Franciscan Ramiro de la Serna says, "He's true to himself, but he understands the consequences of what he says and does." He himself has said, he seldom acts on impulse because "the first answer that comes to me is usually wrong."

It was his behind-the-scenes negotiations that led to the new more open relations between the United States and Cuba. He has continued St. John Paul II's emphasis on Divine Mercy by scheduling a Year of Mercy.

As Nancy Gibbs of *Time* put it, "He has placed himself at the very center of the conversations of our time: about wealth and poverty, fairness and justice, transparency, modernity, globalization, the role of women, the nature of marriage, the temptations of power." He became *Time*'s Man of the Year because he has resisted that temptation to appropriate the power of Christ's vicar to himself.

The National Geographic Society thanks readers "for sharing our belief in the power of science, exploration, and storytelling to change the world." This is especially true when the story is the Greatest Story Ever Told, how God is still working in the world through the Church and working the world out of the Church.

The back of the book includes a timeline making significant events in the papacy. It color codes the popes by nationality, showing a hundred four Italians, the last Fifth Century African pope (Gelasius), the last Eighth Century Asian pope (Gregory III).

There is also, of course, geography, a global map illustrating the shift in the Church southward. Subsaharan Africa and the Philippines have grown greatly in the past century. In 1900 two-thirds of Catholics were Europeans. That is now less than a quarter. American has grown to fifteen percent, the United States from nearly eleven million to nearly seventy-five million. Brazil increased from six percent to thirteen percent, while Italy fell from twelve percent to five percent and France from fifteen percent to seven percent. This is the reason for the New Evangelization.

Much of *Pope Francis and the New Vatican*, naturally, is very similar to Rodolfo Felici's *Pope Francis: A Photographic Portrait of the People's Pope*. It is even more of a "picture book" with a minimal of editing by Fr. Michael Collins. It includes images from his historic trips to Brazil, Israel, South Korea, Turkey, the Philippines, and Sri Lanka.

Felici, from the family of papal photographers, says, "The picture of the Pope releasing a dove in the sky over St. Peter's Square is one of my personal favorites. It is an image that I was lucky enough to shoot at the beginning of his pontificate and I think it catches well the enthusiasm and joy that Pope Francis communicates."

C. William Anderson comments, "Some may wonder why a photo journal of the Pope is important. Any leader who can claim a following of twelve hundred million people commands attention. I believe only China and, perhaps, India's leaders can make such a claim." Pope Francis seems to claim a following by much of the rest of the world as well.

John Chancellor wrote, "If you appreciate the good that Pope Francis has done for the Catholic Church and the world, then you will really enjoy this book. It is both beautiful and informative. A real treasure tat captures the essence of Pope Francis." The same could apply to National Geographic's.

As a non-Catholic Elisa wrote, "From the beginning, Pope Francis ... was different. To the surprise of many, he has continued to take inspiration from Jesus' humble work with the poor, and to seek out those who are marginalized in society, reaching out to the poor and ill, but also to Rome's prisoners and even to convicted Mafiosa as part of his effort to remind people

-- Christians and non-Christians alike -- of the love that Jesus had for His fellow men and women, no matter how 'slowly' society may feel they are."

Karie Hoskins shared, "Even though I am not a Catholic (anymore) -- I still think he is an inspiration for the world -- and a force for good and for much needed and LONG overdue change. This pope seems to have connected with Catholics and non-Catholics alike in his care for the poor, the environment, and peace programs internationally."

[Draper has also written the pamphlets, *Called to the Holy Mountain* and *The Search for King David*.]

Celebrities Promote Chastity (September 2015)

The Centers for Disease Control and prevention recently reported the proportion of fifteen-to-twenty-four-year-olds who have had some kind of sex dropped in the past decade from seventy-eight percent to about seventy-two percent. The study found that forty-four percent of females and forty-seven percent of males in the fifteen-to-nineteen-year-old age group reported having had sex between 2011 and 2013, much lower than in 1988 when fifty-one percent of females and sixty percent of males in this age group reported having had sex.

Experts think an emphasis on abstinence in sex education or concern about sexually transmitted diseases may have played a role in the decrease. it may, however, quite possibly be celebrity endorsement of waiting until marriage for sex.

Waiting Till Marriage's stated mission is "to help those who wait through the unique challenges and hurdles that come with this path." Although the ratio of women-to-men is about two-to-one, they have "waiters" from all the major faiths and even some "nones" (those with no religious affiliation). They have WTMers from every English-speaking country.

The site, waitingtillmarriage,org, currently gets about fifty-six thousand unique visitors a month, and that is growing at a rate of about five percent per month. It has articles on the advantages of waiting, The *Waiting Till Marriage Survival Guide*, WTM wristbands, videos, songs, a forum, and even "Sexless in the City" and links to other abstinence sites. It devotes a whole section of the website to the witnesses of such celebrities who have or are still waiting until marriage for the marital embrace.

Several are known from television, Megan Alexander, the host of "Inside Edition," who recently "came out" as a virgin, produced a special segment on herself and her decision to wait until marriage. Reality star Angela Zatopek says, "I am hoping to break the stereotype that just because you are waiting until marriage, it doesn't mean you can't have a passionate relationship that's not sexy. You can still have that type of relationship and still wait for the right person."

In the third grade, Chelsie Hightower started as the worst dancer in the class, and the slowest learner. Today she's the star of shows like "Dancing with the Stars" and "so You Think You Can Dance." Meagan Good started her acting career at age four as an extra on Doogie Howser M.D. She waiting until finding her perfect match in DeVon Franklin, a studio executive and preacher. Tamera Mowry appeared in the hit TV shows "Sister Sister" and "Tia & Tamera." Several years before their wedding, Tamera Mowry and her husband Adam Housley decided as a couple to wait until marriage.

Best known as simply "The Doritos Girl," former Miss USA Ali Landry made Mexican Director Alejandro Monteverde wait. They are now happily married with two beautiful children.

On "Grey's Anatomy," Sara Drew played Dr. April Kepner, a highly religious character who fails at being a born-again virgin. In real life she and her husband, a UCLA professor, did wait until marriage.

From the sports world, there has been Prince Amukamara, a real Nigerian prince whose first name actually is "Prince." He's also the top cornerback for the New York Giants and waiting until marriage. Collin Klein, the starting quarterback for the Kansas State Wildcats, and his wife Shalin are devout Christians. They didn't date formally until they were engaged, and didn't kiss until they were at the altar.

Philip Rivers has proven himself in both basketball and football. Throughout his athletic career, Rivers has been outspoken about his faith and his decision to wait until marriage. Pro basketball player "Iron Man" A. C. Green took up the cause of waiting until marriage. He waited until he married at thirty-eight.

Contemporary Christian singer Jamie Grace has released several albums and EPs, won the Dove Award for New Artist of the Year, and starred in the movie "Grace Unplugged." Beginning her singing career at thirteen, Rebecca St. James waiting until her wedding at thirty-three. The Christian Rock band Barlow Girl, sisters Becca, Alyssa and Lauren Barlow, decided not to date until courted for marriage.

Pattie Mallette decided, after two decades of sexual abuse, rape, drugs, and petty crime, to turn her life around the day she gave birth to her son Justin Bieber. She promised herself that she would not date again until her son turned eighteen, and would not have sex again until she was married.

From film there is Cheryl McKay, an accomplished Hollywood screenwriter and Christian novelist. She shares about waiting till marriage, writing, and her latest book, Finally the Bride. Nick Vujicic, the motivational speaker who happens to have no arms and no legs doesn't stop him from achieving his dreams. He stars in the award-winning short film "The Butterfly Circus," and directs his own non-profit organization. Nick is also a successful waiter-till-marriage.

Julia Carolyn McWilliams, better known as Julia Child, was a beloved wife, chef, author, Emmy award winning television personality and research operative within an international spy ring. She waited until thirty-six when she married her husband Paul.

Legendary inventor Nikola Telsa was also a lifelong virgin. He is an inspiring example of what people can accomplish when they dedicate themselves fully to their creative pursuits and ignore everything else.

Adande Thorne, "Swoozie", is a professional gamer and creator of an extremely popular YouTube channel, where he dramatizes stories from his life. He's waiting till marriage, and frequently applies his storytelling talents to talk about waiting. Shay Butler and his wife Collete, nicknamed "Katilette," run one of the largest video blogs on the web and waiting until marriage.

For nearly a decade Lakita Garth has been promoting abstinence, including as a regular guest on "Politically Incorrect" with Bill Maher. She also practiced what she preached, kissing her husband for the first time at their wedding.

Kirk Cameron started as a young atheist on the hit show "Growing Pains," but now creates movies about faith and family. He waited until he married his wife at age twenty.

Adrina Lima is such a popular supermodel, the Urban Dictionary defines the term "adriana lima" as "someone beyond perfection." She waited until her marriage at twenty-seven.

[The debate continues even as more young celebrities come out as virgins.]

Catholic Answers Addresses Gender Issues (August 2015)

With the national legalization of gay marriage replacing "bride" and "groom" with "spouse 1" and "spouse 2," "father" and "mother" with "parent 1" and "parent 2," and by extrapolation "spouse 3" and "parent 3" etc., Catholic Answers is answering questions on the ever more confusing subject of gender.

Trent Horn recently responded to the question, "What does it mean to be a man or woman?" He rephrases it as, "What is the difference between a gender-non-conforming man (a biological male who enjoys looking and acting like a woman but wants to be called a man) and a transgender woman (a biological male who enjoys looking and acting like a woman and wants to be called a woman)?" Then he continues, "If the only difference is the terms themselves, then modern 'gender ideology' is guilty of eviscerating the concepts of male and female of any objective meaning beyond 'what I want to be called.' "

In answer to the question of the Intersex, those with indeterminate sex at birth, Horn admits this "requires unique pastoral and medical considerations." He adds, "I understand there are conditions, such as hermaphroditism or Turner and Klinefelter syndromes, where sex determination is not exact. However, cases where determining someone's sex is difficult do not obviate the vast number of cases where people's sex is clear and it is their mental states that are disordered with reality."

In 2013 Gender Identity Disorder was reclassified as Gender Dysphoria by the American Psychiatric Association. Their recommended treatment now is to physically change the person's anatomy in order to match the sex they identify as. The *Catechism of the Catholic Church*'s warning against body mutilation (*Catechism of the Catholic Church* 2297) would apply here as well. So too would Christ's own words, "There are eunuchs who were born that way from their mother's womb; and there are eunuchs who were made eunuchs by men; and there are also eunuchs who made themselves eunuchs for the sake of the kingdom of heaven. He who is able to accept this, let him accept it." (Matthew 19:12)

Pope Francis has spoken out on "gender ideology" recently when visiting Puerto Rico. "The complementarity of man and woman," he said, "the summit of divine creation -- is being questioned by what is called 'gender ideology' in the name of a society that is freer and more just."

"The differences between man and woman are not of the order of opposition or subordination, but rather of communion and generation," he said, and "without mutual commitment, neither of the two will be able to understand the other in depth."

Previously Pope Francis elaborated, "The biblical story [of Adam and Eve], with the grand symbolic fresco of the earthly paradise and original sin, precisely tells us that the communion with God is reflected in the communion of the human couple and the loss of trust in the Heavenly Father generates division and conflict between man and woman. To solve their relationship problems, man and the woman should instead talk more, listen more, know more, [and] love each other more. They must treat each other with respect and cooperate with friendship."

Austrian Bishop Andreas Laun says that Pope Francis spoke even more strongly on the subject in a private conversation earlier this year as a "profound falsehood" and "demonic." He recommended Gabriele Kuby's *The Global Sexual Revolution: Destruction of Freedom in the Name of Freedom*.

Todd Aglialoro quotes Pope Benedict XVI on this "new philosophy of sexuality." "People dispute the idea that they have a nature, given by their bodily identity, that serves as a defining element of the human being. They deny their nature and decide that it is not something previously given to them, but that they make it for themselves."

Aglialoro adds, "When we deny our nature we deny our dignity, and thus destroy justice: law, morality, human rights, all of it." He also quotes Pope John Paul II's Theology of the

Body, "The relation between 'us' and our flesh is never accidental or incidental. Our souls and our bodies are partners, never -- as gender theory asserts -- strangers or even enemies."

Horn points out that studies confirm the Church's teachings, that "When children who reported transgender feelings were tracked without medical or surgical treatment at both Vanderbilt University and London's Portman Clinic, seventy-to-eighty percent of them spontaneously lost those feelings." A long-term Karolinska Institute study in Sweden, he writes, "revealed that beginning about ten years after having the surgery, the transgendered began to experience increasing mental difficulties. Most shockingly, their suicide mortality rose almost twenty-fold above the comparable non-transgender population."

Matt Fradd points out that the word "gender" until late last century, referred exclusively to language (most languages apart from English assign male, female, or neuter genders to nouns)." Until 1974 the American Psychiatric Association classified homosexuality as a mental disorder.

Catholic Answers now must answer the charge that the Catholic Church is homophobic? "While the Church does recognize homosexuality as disordered," the website explains, "this does not mean that the Church is uncompassionate to those who suffer from the disorder. The *Catechism of the Catholic Church* states: "Men and women who have deep-seated homosexual tendencies ... must be accepted with respect, compassion, and sensitivity. Every sign of unjust discrimination in their regard should be avoided."

Study after study in archives of General Psychiatry have shown that both male and female homosexuals have much higher rates of interpersonal maladjustment, depression, conduct disorder, childhood abuse (both sexual and violent), domestic violence, alcohol or drug abuse, anxiety, and dependency on psychiatric care than heterosexuals.

Stanley Kurtz of the Hudson Institute quotes radical homosexuals who state that their goal is not personally to be married, nor to achieve domestic equality with heterosexuals, nor even to attain social respectability, but rather to empty the institution of marriage of its meaning. The Church's defense of the traditional meaning of marriage must be opposed to this.

Catholic Answers even advises, "We must not recognize homosexual activity as legitimate, and we must not give public approval to homosexual marriage because of the harm that will do to the institution of marriage and because of the social harm that will result from emptying marriage of its meaning."

[Kuby has written in German, *Gender: Eine neue Ideologie zerstört die Familie* and *Harry Potter -- gut oder böse?*]

Church History Portrays Saints And Sinners (July 2015)

Saints and Sinners by Eamon Duffy is a different sort of Church history. Duffy focuses in on the popes, both the holy and the unholy. He also ties these vicars of Christ to their place in His story, how God has worked through them with anecdotes from their lives.

Reviewer Peter Stanford called it an "outstanding work of popular scholarship." T. F. X. Noble went even further and called it "the best one-volume history of the papacy ever written." The reader can judge for himself.

"[Pope] Stephen's invocation of Matthew 16 is the first known claim by a pope to an authority derived exclusively from Peter," Duffy writes. This was, he explains, in response to Cyprian editing out such references from his book *Unity of the Catholic Church*, and so dividing it.

Gregory was an example of one of the saints. He was the great-grandson of Pope Felix III and a relative of Pope Agapitus I. His father was a Church regionary, a lay official responsible for temporal affairs for the Roman See. His mother became a nun when widowed, living in retirement on her own property, where two aunts reported having visions of "St." Felix. He retired himself from his secular career, donated his wealth to the Church and became a hermit. He missed that simple, prayerful life as a "Great" pope.

Charlemagne is said to have cried "as if he had lost a brother" upon hearing of Pope Hadrian's death. In 799 his nephew Paschalis had incited a mob to blind and rip out the tongue of Hadrian to make him unfit to serve as pope. A year later after receiving protection from Charlemagne Hadrian crowned him emperor.

Dunn even includes Popess Joan, not because there actually was or could ever be a popess, but because it figured in the story of John XXII and the Franciscans. William of Ockham, the famous Franciscan philosopher, argued that one false pope proved there could be another.

The papacy of holy Celestine only lasted six months. Unlike Gregory, he did go back to his hermitage. He was the last pope to resign before Benedict XVI.

Although the book does not cover the papacy of Pope Benedict XVI or Pope Francis by name, Duffy does write about the post-Vatican Church and the future. He ties the Bolshivik Revolution to Fatima and to the failed assassination of Pope John Paul II. He explains that the then Cardinal Ratizinger's Congregation of the Doctrine of Faith, "generalized the meaning of the 'Third Secret' into an unexceptional meditation on the difficulties of the Christian life in the modern world."

In talking about John Paul II and especially his vision of the Church of the Third Millennium, Duffy writes of "a spiritual status and prestige greater than at any time since the high Middle Ages. This standing was based in large part on the personality and patent Christian goodness of so many of the recent popes, and on the manifest greatness of Wojtyla himself."

He begins the last section of the book, "The Oracles of God," with Pius X in 1903. The son of a postman and a seamstress, Giuseppe Sarto's papacy was marked by simplification of Canon Law, improved seminaries, the breviary and missal, and more frequent Eucharist. He was a people's pope like John XXIII, John Paul I, and now Francis. He chose the name Pius X as successor to Pius IX, with whom he identified.

Over a hundred years ago as Patriarch of Venice, Sarto wrote, "God has been driven out of public life by the separation of Church and State; He has been driven out of science now that doubt has been raised to a system ... He has been driven out of the family which no longer considered sacred in its origins and shorn of the grace of the sacraments.

He continues, "the abilities and inclinations of the last pope of the twentieth century and the first of the twenty-first, point elsewhere, to a more exalted, lonely, and hierarchic vision of the papal office and the Church it serves ... towards a recovery of balance, a restoration of order, and true faith in the flux of time."

The Church certainly has survived the flux of time in the past. On his return to Rome from the Avignon papacy, Martin V found it "so dilapidated and deserted that it bore hardly any resemblance to a city." When Leo X tried to raise funds for rebuilding, the abuses of indulgences prompted an even greater schism started by Luther.

By the 18th Century, despite all the historical evidence to the contrary, relics and other devotions too had become considered superstitions and monasteries useless. The French Revolution was horrible, yet Dunn comments, "it was hard to maintain that the new arrangements were much worse than those which had produced unbelievable bishops like Tallyrand or the Cardinal of Toulouse."

Duffy connects the past and the future with the revolutionary Vatican II council, particularly its documents *Lumen Gentium* and *Gaudium et Spes*. Ecumenism, though in Pius XI's Mortalium Annos was given a boost.

"The persecution of heresy and enforcement of Catholicism had been reality since the days of Constantine, and since the French Revolution pope after pope had repeatedly and explictly denounced the notion that non-Catholics had a right to religious freedom."

This movement toward reconciliation with other Catholicism too prompted schism by Archbishop Marchel Fefebvre. Mercifully now many of the schismatics have been reconciled. As Protestant denomination become more and more secularized, and the persecution by anti-Christian terrorists continues, so too does the story of the Church's saints and sinners.

The note on the third edition (2006) says that it includes an updated bibliography, an extensively revised and extend account on Pius XII, the death of John Paul II and the election of Benedict XVI.

[Duffy has written: *Faith of Our Fathers; Fires of Faith; Marking the Hours; Reformation Divided; Saints, Sacrilege and Sedition; Ten Popes Who Shook the World; The Creek in the Catechism; The Heart in Pilgrimage; The Stripping of the Altars; Walking to Emmaus; What Catholics Believe About Mary.*]

Learn From Martyrs (June 2015)

Brian O'Neel's book, *150 North American Martyrs You Should Know*, is both informative and entertaining. The canonized North American martyrs, Isaac Jogues and companions Kateri Tekakitha and chaplain Fr. Emil Kapaun are somewhat known. The rest may not be so familiar, but their lives certainly are relevant today.

Fr. Sébastian Rale was inspired by the earlier North American martyrs and had more success. He converted the Wabanaki of Maine and defended their rights to practice their religion and to property, making them all enemies to the English. He stayed with those who did not flee to New France. When the English attacked in 1724 he and his twenty companions died for the Faith. Neel nicknames him "the Mama Bear Father."

Fr. José Antonio Diaz de Leon also fought for the rights of the Karankawa and Coahuiltec Indians' rights in Texas. Although a Franciscan, he was made pastor of Nacogdoches when the missions were confiscated. Fr. de Leon was shot in 1834, as O'Neel puts it, "He was not only the last Franciscan in Texas, he was the last priest in the state for several years." The church was burned and he was not replaced until 1847.

Neel's chapter on the martyrs of Georgia is subtitled "The Sanctity of Marriage Was Their 'Old Sweet Song.'" Fr. Pedor de Corpa and his companions were martyred by the son of the chief of the Guales in Georgia in 1597. Juanillo had been baptized, but hated Fr. de Corpa for rebuking him for marrying a second wife.

He then led twenty-four others to kill the other Georgian missionaries, first Fr. Blas Rodriguez de Montes. Fr. Miguel de Aunon and Br. Antonio de Badajoz were warned and so Fr. de Aunon was able to say Mass before the war party arrived. The Gospel for the day included, "Whoever loses his life for My sake will find it." (Matthew 16:25) A few days later they caught up with the rest, Fr. Francisco de Berascola and Fr. Francisco de Avila.

Melchor Jayme took the name Luis as a Franciscan. He was sent to San Diego. When 600 Indians led by two apostate converts attacked the mission in 1775, he was killed as he greeted them. St. Junipero Serra thanked God saying, "Now that the terrain has been watered by blood, the conversion of the San Diego Indians will take place."

Fr. Luis Cancer de Barbastro said much the same thing. He returned to where Dominican Fr. Diego Tolosa and Br. Fuentes were martyred near Tampa Bay, Florida, in 1549. He died just as them.

Fr. Juan de Padilla's chapter is called "Don Quixote Comes to Kansas." He was a Franciscan accompanying Coronado's quest for El Dorado. He chose to stay behind and minister to the Native Americans. He was martyred in 1542 by Quivira Indians who did not go along with his outreach to their mortal enemies and neighbors, the Guas.

Neel calls Ann "Goody" Glover "The Witch Who Wasn't." Her husband had been killed for being "a Roman Catholic and obstinate in idolatry." She was tried for witchcraft just four months after William of Orange had defeated Catholic James II in 1680. Like Joan of Arc she weakened after three months imprisonment and confessed and then repented of her lapse of faith. At the end, like Jesus, she prayed for her accusers. Her last words before she was hung, holding a crucifix to her chest, were, "I die a Catholic."

Neel also includes information you should know about the history of persecution of Catholics in America. He tells about such little known things as the Québec Act that threatened Protestants and fueled the Revolutionary War, the Know-Nothings and the Klu Klux Klan.

For example, Fr. James Coyle was shot by Rev. Edwin Stephenson in 1921 after the priest had blessed the marriage of the Methodist Klansman's daughter to a dark-skinned Puerto Rican. He was defended by future Supreme Court justice and fellow Klansman Hugo Black and acquitted.

Robert J. "Sandy" Cairns was born in Scotland, but his parents settled in Massachusetts. He choose to become a missionary to China. When the invading Japanese threatened in 1941 he spent more than an hour before the Blessed Sacrament. Then he wrote, "It is my duty to stay at [Shangehaun] with the people and administer the Sacraments."

Bishop Patrick J. Byrne was captured when the Korean War began in 1959. March Till They Die by Fr. Phillip Crosbie says, "Byrne never claimed his fair share of anything except work; and of that he always claimed more than was his due." The day before he was martyred he told Bishop Thomas Quinlan, "Tom, don't be sad. I have always wanted to lay down for our Faith and the good Lord has given me this privilege."

Besides many other saints the book includes two appendices. The first is a calendar of the North American martyrs with the place and year of their deaths. The second answers the question, "Did George Washington die a Catholic?"

Although Neel concentrates on martyrs from or martyrs in the United States and Canada, he explains North American begins at Greenland and ends as Panama. It even includes islands in the Caribbean. The last chapter briefly mentions many more Mexican martyrs, so there may be a sequel.

[Neels has also written: 39 New Saints You Should Know and Saint Who? 39 Holy Unknowns.]

Pope Francis Tweets (May 2015)

Pope Francis recently tweeted, "A credible witness to truth and to the values of the Gospel is urgently needed." He is showing the world by being a good example of such a witness to truth.

His predecessor Pope Benedict XVI set up a Twitter account in 2012. At that time it was considered a positive step toward evangelizing the world through modern technology. However, Archbishop Claudio Maria Celli, the head of the Vatican's pontifical council for social communications, explains that offensive replies soon become a "crisis." They were, however, more easy to ignore on Twitter than they would have been on other social media.

Celli explains that the Vatican already spends too much hours "cleaning" the Facebook page of its official news website News.va, while leaving "educational debates."

The offensive replies are almost always from respondents not using their right names. Many are the usual rants against the Church. They sometime prompt more tweets they likely do not expect, like Mary Piro's recent, "Lord, bless all this negativity -- if they are commenting here, they are definitely searching for You. Thank You God." And her, "Funny that an Atheist is following a Christian site. Please stay on ... and you will find Him." Or Katie Dieringer Kahr's, "I am praying for you, sounds like you could use a lot. God Bless."

Tens of thousands of others all over the world share the Pope's tweets, sometimes adding like Elissa Bogos Merzaei, "Wise words from the Pope." Others just add a one-word comment since tweets are limited as to number of characters like Tiffany Elyse's, "Inspiration." or Laura Pastrana's and William Taylor's, Amen!"

In the second year of papal tweeting Monsignor Paolo Luca Braida was named coordinator of the preparation of the pope's speeches and homilies. The pope selects tweets from extracts of these speeches and homilies proposed by the monsignor, not just a few a month but nearly every day.

Last year Pope Francis was identified as the most influential world leader on Twitter in the annual Twiplomacy survey. He then had fourteen million followers in nine languages.

"It's not the number of followers which is really important," Matthias Luefkens says, "but the reach, the engagement, the real benchmark is tweets re-tweeted by followers to their own network."

That is where Pope Francis wins hands down, with his Spanish-language tweets re-tweeted more than ten thousand times on average, and his English-language tweets over 6,400 times. Luefkens says that while television remains the key channel to hit the widest audience, Twitter is an increasingly-powerful tool.

"It helps you to broadcast, and if you broadcast to the right audience, that has huge impact," he said. "The social network enables politicians to create a sense of intimacy and even to interact with one another in public."

During the Pope's visit to the Philippines earlier this year, one tweet in Filipino had nearly seventy-six thousand re-tweets. The English version, "The Philippines bear witness to the youthfulness and vitality of the Church," had nearly thirty-seven thousand. Other tweets were nearly as popular, "The family is the greatest treasure of any country. Let us all work to protect and strengthen this, the cornerstone of society." and "How often we forget to dedicate ourselves to that which truly matters! We forget that we are children of God." and "The compassion of God, his suffering-with-us, gives meaning and worth to our struggles and our sufferings."

Before reaching the Philippines, he tweeted, "Please pray with me for everyone in Sri Lanka and the Philippines as I begin my trip," and again got nearly thirty-seven thousand retweets. To my friends in Sri Lanka and the Philippines: May God bless you all! Please pray for me."

The number one English language Pope tweet was, "Every Life is a Gift," on the occasion of the Roe v. Wade anniversary at over twenty-four thousand.

For those not on Twitter the tweets are also available illustrated and sharable on Facebook's Pope Tweets produced by Ed Vizenor.

"The laity are called to become a leaven of Christian living within society," prompted Andy Doherty to write "lucky to be laity." Adoration Servants commented, "Establishing Perpetual Eucharistic Adoration everywhere as John Paul II hoped for will do this." David Rhodes added, "The whole people of God are called to be leaven. In fact the whole of humanity."

To "Suffering is a call to conversion: it reminds us of our frailty and vulnerability." Allen V. Harris responded with, "This accents last Sunday's sermon." Cindy Mercurio suggested, "Sent this tweet to a friend who is suffering with depression. Struggling to find her way. Pray it may lead her back to the Church."

George Wilson called the pope's prayer, "May every Church and Christian community be a place of mercy amid so much indifference" an excellent message.

To "Humility saves man: pride makes him lose his way." Shafiq Pontoh responded with, "Soooo TRUE." L. M. Sawyer had a more general comment, "Daily goodness from the pope." Scott Gower shared, "I'm not Catholic, but Pope Francis has authored some solid tweets."

Lee Llewellyn sent a message unrelated to any individual tweet, "Many congratulations to your Papal anniversary and thank you for trying to modernize, unify and welcome ALL to faith/church."

[Pope Francis now has 17.9 million followers on twitter, Papa Francisco 16.8 million, Papa Francesco 4.9 million, Pape François 1.26 million, Papa Franciscus 895 thousand, nearly 42 million in just five languages.]

Series Focuses On The Birth Of The Church (April 2015)

"A. D.: the Bible Continues" is, as its title says, the continuation of the story begun in the miniseries "The Bible" (2013) and its film adaptation "Son of God" (2014). "The Bible" had a hundred million viewers and "Son of God" grossed over 70 million dollars, but as their tagline for this series says, "The crucifixion was only the beginning." Although the first installment is not coming until Easter Sunday, there have been several sneak previews made available.

Some of these feature the accompanying sings "By Our Love" by For King and Country and "We Believe" by the Newsboys. Lorne Balfe, who composed the music for both "The Bible" and "Son of God" also composed for "A. D."

Some fans of the cast in "The Bible," however, are upset about the many new cast members replaying the ending scenes of the first series in the beginning of the new one. Others consider the recastings an improvement. Perhaps most confusing is recasting Francis Magee who previously played Saul now playing Levi.

Cardinal Donald Wuerl of Washington, D. C., says, " 'A. D.' is a triumph! It tells the riveting story of the very beginning of the Church with reverence, excitement, and brilliance. This series not only captures our attention but also our hearts as we trace the steps of those who first walked in the way of Jesus.

"While 'A. D.' dazzles the eye" he continues, "it also engages the imagination. The narrative recounts how, with the guidance of the Holy Spirit, a small band of men and women witnesses to the Risen Lord and set out to change the world. The mission endures today and people everywhere can find both drama and inspiration in this telling of the story of the Church, her origins, mission, and timeless challenge. 'A. D.' helps us recover the wonder of the ongoing Christian adventure."

Several best-selling Christian writers also praise the film. Wilfredo De Jesus, author of *Amazing Faith*, says, "Finally someone has told the story of the birth of the Church in all of its power, drama, and glory. 'A. D.' masterfully shows why it is that Christianity emerged from nowhere to become the largest and most diverse religious movement in history."

Max Lucado, author of *You'll Get Through This*, says " 'A. D.' shows us how a deep faith results in raw courage. The key players in this story -- the earliest Christians, stunned by the brutal execution of Jesus, were pathfinders for today's believers. Their compelling story gives hope for the modern-day faithful, who face brutality and persecution simply for believing ... even today."

Christine Caine, founder of the A21 Campaign, says, "'A. D.' shows us in living color how that movement changed the world -- and why it is still changing the world today. This television series is historic."

Karen Kingsbury, author of *A Treasury of Miracles for Friends* and *A Treasury of Miracles for Teens*, says, "This epic real-life story that will take you back to the beginning and leave you with tears on your face and Jerusalem dust on your feet. 'A. D.' is going to capture the nation. Get ready America!"

Francis Chan, author with his wife of *You and Me Forever*, just says, "Pray with us that God would use this series to lead many people to Himself."

The *Study* and *Guidebook* included in the Church Kit is "to help viewers learn more about how the stories they're watching apply to their lives and faith today."

The first episode, "Hope for a New Beginning" retells the passion. Episode 2, "What for It" covers the ascension, with "it" being the descent of the Holy Spirit in "Pentecost Power." Episode 4 illustrates "What Matters Most" with Barnabas. With the martyrdom of Stephen we get "A Bigger Picture" and the real persecutions begin. The Christians flee Jerusalem and are pursued by Saul in "Scattered Seeds." Then in "A Wider Circle" Saul the persecutor becomes Paul the apostle.

In the eighth week after Easter, Pentecost, "Respond to God" has Paul visiting the other apostles in Jerusalem. In "Let It Go" Paul leaves Jerusalem. In "Life Moments" ordinary Christianity is shown in the conversion of the Ethiopian eunuch and the raising of Tabitha. In "Credit the Source" Peter proclaims Jesus as the Healer, and the series finally concludes with the baptism of the Gentiles in "Unstoppable," chapters ten and eleven of Acts.

Many of the early comments at the Internet Movie Database are from unbelievers who dismiss the Bible itself as myth or fiction and who obviously do not know either Christ or the Bible. One commenter, however, did know that Acts does have twenty-eight chapters and expects the series to continue for at least another season.

Someone else asked if there was any connection to the 1985 miniseries "A. D.," the sequel to "Jesus of Nazareth," which continued the story through to the reign of Nero. There will undoubtedly be comparisons between the two. The first was six hundred minutes, the new one will be nearly as long. IMDb says people who liked the first one will also like the second.

Executive directors Mark Burnett and Roma Downey, however, seem not yet working on a trilogy, but on a new version of "Ben Hur" for 2016.

[De Jesus has also written *In the Gap*. Lucado's books include: A Gentle Thunder, A Love Worth Giving; *Anxious for Nothing; Before Amen; Care for the Common Life; Come Thirsty; Experiencing the Heart of Jesus; Experiencing the Words of Jesus; Facing Your Giants; Fearless; For the Tough Times; Give It All to Him; Glory Days; God Is With You Every Day; God Will Carry You Through; God Will Use This for Good; Grace: More Than We Deserve, God's Promises for You; Greater Than We Imagine; Grace for the Moment; He Choose the Nails; He Fights for You; He Still Moves Stones; In the Eye of the Storm; In the Grip of Grace; It's Not About Me; Just Like Jesus; Less Fret, More Faith; Let the Journey Begin; Life*

Lessons; Make Every Day Count; No Wonder They Call Him Savior; One God, One Plan, One Life; Pocket Prayers; Outlive Your Life; Safe in the Shepherd's Arms; Ten Men of the Bible; Thank You, God, for Loving Me; The Applause of Heaven; The Crippled Lamb; The Great House of God; The Oak Inside the Acorn; Trade Your Cares for Calm; Traveling Light; Unshakable Hope; When God Whispers Your Name; You Were Made to Make a Difference; You'll Get Though This, etc.]

Book Challenges Christians (March 2015)

Brian Fisher's new book *Deliver Us From Abortion* challenges Christians who are not fighting to end the killing of the most innocent, the unborn, and encourages those who are. Its subtitle is "Awakening the Church to End the Killing of America's Children." He dedicated the book to a Korean girl who could have been aborted, but was left at an orphanage and then adopted by an American Christian couple. "To my wife," he writes, "and best friend, whose very presence at my side is a constant reminder that God is the author of every life, and every life has priceless value and unlimited potential."

Brian Fisher is co-founder and president of Online for Life. He has written books on other aspects of the subject, such as, *Abortion: The Ultimate Exploitation of Women*. In his "Personal Note to Parents and Relatives of Aborted Children" he writes, "My hope and prayer is that you finish this book with a renewed sense of Christ's work in your life and a passionate desire to stop this unspeakable tragedy."

The book is aimed particularly at Protestants, but many Catholics need to hear the message as well. Julie Klose wrote, "Last week I had the privilege of attending the 2015 March for Life conference and walking in my first March. At the conference there was the first ever evangelical worship gathering called One Voice DC. One of the leaders prayed about the church's sin of apathy over abortion.' His words hit me with such great conviction. That was once me, but tragically that is the state of the evangelical church in America.

"The Catholic Church has often been outspoken warriors for life," she points out, "and they are without a doubt a strong presence within the anti-abortion movement. But unfortunately, even a recent study by the Guttmacher Institute (a pro-abortion research group) reports that twenty-seven percent of Catholic women and thirty-seven percent of Protestant women received abortions."

Fr. Frank Pavone of Priests for Life shares that "Dr. Bernard Nathanson, whom I knew personally, and who was a key architect of the abortion industry, said he succeeded only because the Church was asleep. To end abortion, the Church must awaken, and that's why this book is so important."

The first section, called Abortion 101, is an overview of abortion in America, pointing out for example that ours is one of just four countries, with North Korea, China, and Canada, that permit abortion at any stage of pregnancy for any reason. Chapter two deals with the Dr. Kermis Gosnell scandal and others. Chapter three is unabashedly entitled "Child Sacrifice in Church."

The next three chapters are a Bible study on the value of human life and the role the Church to protect it. Fisher quotes passages like, "Rescue those being led away to death; hold back those staggering toward slaughter" (Proverbs 24:11) and "And he will answer, â€˜I tell you the truth, when you refused to help the least of these my brothers and sisters, you were refusing to help me' " (Matthew 25:45).

Proving the authority of God over all human life, Fisher refers to Psalm 24:1, "The Earth is the Lord's and all it contains, the world and all who dwell in it," and Matthew 10:31, "You are more valuable than many sparrows," among other verses. "God is the author of all life," he tells the reader, "regardless of how he or she is conceived, has priceless value, uniqueness, and purpose."

Going through the Scripture pointing out God's concern for every human conception, every human life. Then he writes, "I can think of no better reason to equate the value of life in the womb the same as life outside. God Himself came to earth as a zygote."

He quotes other verses to demonstrate that the good news is not "fire insurance," a way to avoid hell. It is much, much more. "The kingdom of God is at hand." He describes some of this in his previous book, *Media Revolution: a battle Plan to defeat Mass Deception in American*.

In another chapter, "Deadly Doctrines," Fisher deals with individual Protestant churches, particularly with their leadership. As he puts it, "what a few pro-life are (or are not) doing from the top down."

In the back of this book fisher includes "a partial list of post-abortive recovery sites, curricula, and resources." These include books, organizations, and websites. He invites the reader to search for others.

The book seems to be getting very favorable reviews. This is perhaps mostly because of the final practical chapter. In it Fisher describes seven obstacles to ending abortion. Some think the issue too political or too offensive or too accusatory. Others think it is not a core issue or not evangelical enough. Still others are put off by thinking it is too challenging a task.

He also lists seven areas in which the Church must act, in the church itself, in business, education, government, the arts and entertainment, family, and the media. These are just the areas that Pope John Paul II's *Toward the Third Millenium* directed us.

He ends by describing seven ways in which the Church can act. We can learn about the issue from others, pray for and assist in the healing of the aborting parents. We can rescue babies in danger of being aborted. We can teach others the truth about abortion and the abortion industry. We can give our time and finances to the cause, and perhaps most importantly we can disciple others to do likewise.

Dr. Alveda King prays, "May [this book] challenge and equip the Church to end the abortion holocaust in America." Shadia Hrichi joins her, writing, "I pray it will stir the hearts of our church leaders and laypeople to embrace the call to defend -- through both word and deed -- God's most vulnerable image-bearers."

Josh McDowell wrote, "The author provides a powerful defense for the children who can't speak for themselves."

Delivering the world from the evil of abortion "will only happen," John Stonestreet of the Colson Center for Christian Worldview says, "when the church addresses abortion with all the fervor, clarity, love, and compassion it can muster by God's grace and power."

Book Presents Life's Greatest Lessons (February 2015)

Archbishop Dennis Schnurr gave parishioners in Cincinnati a Christmas present of the book, *Life's Greatest Lessons* by Allen R. Hunt. He must have thought it worthwhile. Its prologue rather grandly describes it as "the cure for selfishness, for anxiety, for sluggishness, and even for anger." Sarah Anne Carter at GoodReads says she was handed the book as she left Christmas Eve Mass, also a gift from her archbishop.

"I honestly thought it would be a cheesy religious story with an overemphasis on some point of religious life. I was pleasantly surprised," she wrote, describing it as "a good, modern-day parable ... a story that captures your attention and teaches you a lesson along the way."

It is more than just the coming-of-age story of Lavish Grace's ten-year-old grandson Christopher. These are obviously allegorical names like Bunyan's Christian. Mercifully unlike Bunyan's classic it is only a hundred fifty-four pages. Fr. Frank Cascia and Christopher's wife Rita, immediately brings to mind St. Rita of Cascia, the patroness of the impossible, and Lake Bobola the martyr St. Andrew Bobola. Hunt says, however, that "while the names and details have all been changed, most of the stories are true."

Hunt's story can be found in his book, *Confessions of a Mega-Church Pastor: How I Discovered the Hidden Treasures of the Catholic Church.* After fifteen years he converted to Catholicism, very likely thanks to the prayers of the Dominican sisters at Monastery of Our Lady of Grace in North Guilford, Connecticut, where he lectured in 1992.

In his *Confessions* there are some very similar life lessons, "When you suffer, you are being conformed to the image of Jesus. When you pray, you are being made holy in the image of Jesus. When you quietly serve a person in need, you are being shaped into the image of Jesus," and "When you generously give, your heart is being remade into the image of Jesus, our Lord and Savior."

Tracey Axnick wrote, "I was a big fan of Allen Hunt's radio show here on WSB radio in Atlanta (and rarely miss the show!). Most talk radio is about politics ("right and left"), but Allen's show was about morals ("right and wrong"). His radio show was always fascinating, frequently moving, and right on the money. This is the first of his books that I've read. The story line is simple, sweet, and meaningful. I look forward to reading his other books as well."

D. Anstrey wrote, "I loved this book. Great message and engrossing story. I am buying copies for every member of my family and will certainly include it in our study group."

Don Womick wrote, "I just finished reading this book by Dr. Hunt, and it is simply amazing, as in, I needed to read this book at this time in my life ... that kind of amazing. I won't give the plot away, except to say that the book is a parable about learning how to give. If you are concerned that you could be doing better in your stewardship, read it and then pass it on."

Billo Breen simply wrote, "Great, inspiring little book."

Although Luke Paul DelVecchio wrote, "I'm a huge Matthew Kelly fan. And I love Dynamic Catholic," he found the book hard to follow because of the nesting of the narrative of the ten-year-old narrator. He does, however, "give the author credit for attempting to convey this message through characters in a story" and thinks "this is such an important message."

The book is aimed at those like the adult Christopher Grace of the postscript, prompted to remember the forgotten wisdom of his grandparents. It is an attempt to re-evangelize as three popes now have been encouraging Catholics to do.

Some of the other books featured in the 2014 Dynamic Catholic Parish book Program are Allen Hunt's *Everybody Needs to Forgive Somebody* and *Nine Words on Galatians*, Matthew Kelly's *Rediscovering Catholicism*, *The Seven Pillars of Catholic Spirituality and Becoming the Best Version of Yourself*, and John R. Wood's *Ordinary Lives, Extraordinary Mission*.

Their growing list of books also include both old, *Finding True Happiness* by Fulton J. Sheen, and new, *The Joy of the Gospel* by Pope Francis and *Pope Francis: A Living Legacy* by James Campbell. Their CDs include "Five Things Women Need to Know About Men," "What's Weighing You Down" by Allen Hunt, and "The Best Way to Live" and "My Spiritual Journey" by Matthew Kelly.

They also offer the DVDs, "What Science Says About God" by the Magi Center and the music CDs, "Rediscover" and "A Collection of Christmas Songs" by Elliot Morris, and "Hold My Hand" by George Mower.

Dynamic Catholic promotes these books, DVDs, and CDs because the founders noticed in 2008 that only one percent of Catholics read a Catholic book, while the average Evangelical-Christian read four. Over the past five years they have changed that providing more than four thousand parishes and five million Catholics with such books. The program has the advantage that it can fit into anyone's busy schedule. Books can be passed on, especially to those not at Christmas Mass, changing lives exponentially.

The goal of Dynamic Catholic is impressively stated as: to "invite and inspire people of all ages to rediscover Catholicism; re-engage disengaged Catholics and increase the overall level of engagement among Catholics; develop the most dynamic and engaging Catholic learning systems to educate Catholics about the modern relevance and timeless genius of Catholicism; equip modern Catholics to live their faith in this every-changing world; give Catholics a reason to feel good about being Catholic again; energize Catholics to participate more fully in their faith and in their lives; ignite a desire for continuous learning and best practices among all Catholics."

[Hunt also authored *The Turning Point* and *The 21 Undeniable Secrets of Marriage*.]

Martyrs Offer Great Witness (December 2014)

Martyrs are not easily identified until their deaths, but they are certainly a crowd of witnesses throughout history, throughout the world. In *Faces of Holiness* Ann Ball tells of Fr. David Galvan, who dropped out of the seminary and even got drunk and jailed for hitting his girlfriend. After a year's probation he was allowed to return and ordained in 1909. He was arrested for aiding the wounded and dying when persecutions started in Guadalajara. Going to his execution by firing squad he said, "What greater glory is there than to die saving a soul?"

Jacque Fesch was an atheist like his father. After being separated from a wife he married when she became pregnant, he tried armed robbery After being wounded himself when the gun discharged when he hit the shopkeeper, he then killed a policeman, before his blood trail led other police to him.

His Catholic mother offered her suffering from terminal cancer that he might die well. His awaiting his execution by beheading in 1959 he wrote, "Now, He is all that matters ... I am amazed and surprised at the change grace has affected in me.

"Above all I have wanted to make you understand the Cross. Crucified love! Was there ever a greater crime? It is this sacrifice which saves us and it is through it that Jesus continues to live here below."

In *Letters from the Saints* (Hawthorn Books, Inc.) we have a wonderful glimpse into Fr. Theophane Venard's last days.

"Adieu, dearest father and sister, bothers, do not mourn, do not shed tears over me, live the years that lie ahead in unity and love. One day we shall meet one another again in Heaven.

"The mandarin treated me with every consideration. His brother came at least ten times to try to persuade me to trample the cross under foot rather than see me die young. When the judges asked again for the last time, he said, "What! I have preached the religion of the cross all my life until this very hour, and you can expect me to objure it now? I do not set so high a price upon this world's pleasures as to want to purchase them by apostasy."

To his family he wrote, "Adieu, dearest father, sister, brother ... , do not mourn ... One day we shall meet one another again in Heaven.

"Within a few short hours my soul will quit this Earth, exile over, and battle won. I shall mount upwards and enter into our true home. There among God's elect I shall gaze upon what eye of man cannot imagine, hear undreamt -- of harmonies, enjoy a happiness the heart cannot remotely comprehend."

He had been fortified by his cooks who smuggled the Eucharist to him during his imprisonment and another priest in disguise heard his last confession. On the way to his beheading he sang the "Magnificat".

The persecution of Christians in Viet Nam began in 1630. By 1864 an estimated 300,000 were martyred, many by beheading, often after horrible tortures, reminiscent of Maccabees or the daily news. In *St. John Paul's Book of Saints* by Matthew, Margaret, and Stephen Bunson are listed man of these martyrs of which very little is known.

Fr. John Charles Cornay was framed with weapons planted in his garden. He was tortured and forced to watch other Christians being tortured, but kept the faith. Before his beheading in 1837, he wrote his parents, "Be comforted; soon it will all be over and I shall be waiting for you in Heaven."

Agnes Thanh Thi Le was sentenced to be trampled by an elephant in 1841. When going to her death she requested beautiful clothes and ebony fan. When asked why, she answered, "I go to meet the Divine Husband."

Bishop Melchior Garcia Sampedes watched as his two servers were beheaded. When he would not abandon the Faith, he was executed with a dull blade. For twelve blows he repeated the name "Jesus!" and received another fifteen before it as over. When he was buried, elephants refuse to walk on his grave.

Francis Igleby and his companions were martyred in the persecutions in England in 1586. Jesuit Roch Gonzalez was martyred by a hatchet in the back in Paraquay in 1628. Maria Pilar of St. Francis Borgia and her companion Carmelite sisters of Guadalajara were shot in 1936. Fr. Peter Chang Wen Chao was martyred in 1948 and Bishop Vincent Eugene Bossilkov in 1952.

Bishop Lawrence Imbert, called "Bom" ("Good"), gave himself up rather than have others die trying to save him. After severe beatings he was beheaded with Frs. Philibert Maubant and James Honore Chastan in 1839 Korea.

Bishop Valentine Berriochora knew he risked his life by accepting the assignment to the Philippines. After two years of torture he was beheaded with Bishop Jerome Hermosilla in 1861. In 1940 Philip Siphong and Srs. Agnes Phila, Bibiana Khamphai, Maria Phon, and Cecilia Butsi were martyred in Thailand.

Marek Krizin, a Croat, Stephan Pongracz, a Hungarian, and Melchior Grodecz, a Czech, were martyred together in Slovakia in 1619. Sr. Rosalie du Verdier de la Sorinire and her twenty-six companions were killed in France 1794. Fr. Felipe de Jesus Munarriz and fifth companions were martyred in Barbastro, Spain, in 1936. There is even a St. Casanova, Ignazio Casanova, martyred with the Scalopian martyrs in 1936.

[Hunt has also written: *A Litany of Mary, ... of Saints, Blessed Miguel Pro,* Catholic Book of the Dead, *Catholic Traditions in Cooking, ... Crafts, ... the Garden, ... the Home and Classroom, Crafty Catholic Kids, Encyclopedia of Catholic Devotions and Practices, Holy Names of Jesus, How to Book of Sacramentals, Jose Finds the King, Modern Saints, Stations of the Cross/Stations of Light, The Other Face of Mary, The Saints' Guide to Joy That Never Fades, Viva Cristo Rey!.*]

Nuns Return Home (October 2014)

Sr. Mary Eucharista, a member of the Sisters of Mary, Mother of the Church, will never forget Pope Benedict XVI. As she and her community watched his installation in 2005, some of the sisters objected and insisted the radio be turned off, others were confused, while she and a few others recognized him as the Pope.

"We knew we needed to go," she says. "But it wasn't easy. We had to leave the other sisters and a home we loved; a place many of us had been part of since we were kids. In the minds of the sisters we had left behind, we had become part of the 'enemy' Church."

They were at that time sisters in the schismatic sedevacantist Congregation of Mary Immaculate Queen, where they had believed that the popes since Vatican II were invalid. The name comes from the Latin for "empty seat" (sede vacante). With the blessing of Bishop William Skylstad, the sisters now teach and work at the Immaculate Heart Retreat center in Spokane. The Association's name includes their long-held devotion to the Blessed Mother, but also their desire to be in communion with the Catholic Church.

While retaining their dark navy blue full habits, the sisters now wear white veils trimmed in blue to honor the Blessed Mother as well as Mother Teresa's Missionaries of Charity, whose visit in 2006 also contributed to in their reversion.

"As a diocese, we welcome the Sisters of Mary, Mother of the Church to our Catholic family here in Eastern Washington," said Bishop Skylstad. "Their discernment, which has led them back to the Church, their courage, and their deep faith have truly been inspiring to me personally."

For Mother Kathryn Joseph, it was a conversation she had with her brother, Mike Duddy, that changed her mind. He had taught philosophy at St. Michael's Academy and secretly made the journey back to the Church, until he was later fired.

"There are many small, independent sedevantist groups like the Religious Congregation of Mary Immaculate Queen and the better known Society of Pius X," Duddy says. The groups are not in any way unified, however, and fight amongst themselves

Mother Kathryn Joseph says honestly, "I had an epiphany. I realized that I had been wrong for thirty-five years. But I was happy to have been proven wrong." We have been forty years in the desert, another sister said.

"It's been painful for all the sisters, for those who felt the need to leave and those who remain here," said Sr. Mary Dominica. "We've been a family for so many years," she said. "We feel like they are still our sisters."

Sr. Marie Vianney, one of the nuns who has remained with the congregation, explains, "It's inconceivable that I could think ill of them. This isn't an 'us against them' things." "We all have different ways in dealing with the current crisis in the church."

When some visited Rome it "was not what we had been told," explains St. Francis Marie. "Every church was full. There was modesty, Confessions, Masses. We saw an extraordinary pilgrimage of holiness."

They had been taught that the Church had changed her doctrines. "That's very troubling, when you're told that truth is unchanging. Christ is the unchanging truth," she said.

"I feel great joy in knowing I'm a part of the Church," said Mother de Lourdes. "I was not willfully outside."

"We did this because of the promises of Christ to his Church: that it was founded on Peter, and that Christ would be with them for all days," said Mother de Lourdes. " 'The Promises of Christ:' I could not get that out of my mind. Christ is eternal truth. Upon that rock (Peter) He built His Church, and the gates of hell will not prevail ... The Church has gone through so many stormy periods, but it cannot be destroyed because Christ is with His Church."

The reconciliation ironically flows directly from the true ecumenical spirit of Vatican II says Father Connal. "We didn't compromise our principles as Catholics. We made certain demands of them in light of our Faith. They fulfilled those requirements. We approached our separated brethren through honey rather than vinegar. We aren't changing our teaching, we're changing our approach."

Since their return to full communion with the Church in 2008 they have had a few sisters join other orders and some novices join theirs. There is an Adopt-a-nun program and Project Joseph for the building of a convent. "As the reality of new members joining us grows every day, the necessity of a convent follows," the site sistersofmarymc.org says.

Their apostolate includes Religious education as they themselves catch up on decades of papal documents, Youth and Retreat Ministry. "With Mary, the Mother of the Church, [they] communicate the knowledge, love, and hope of the Risen Christ and His Church through communal charity and joyful evangelization."

The connection with EWTN continues. St. Joanna and her mother, Esther Ranelli, an Amish convert, were interviewed by Dr. Ray Guarendi on "Living Right with Dr. Ray" earlier this year. Sr. Mary Eucharista appeared on an Al Kresta's "Kresta in the Afternoon" and Teresa Tomeo's "Catholic Connection."

[The Sisters of Mary, Mother of the Church, are the beneficiaries this year of the Third annual Holy-in-One Golf Tournament.]

Films Build Faith (September 2015)

Ignatius Press now has many of its best selling films dramatizing the lives of the saints and saintly available via streaming as well as its usual DVDs. The streamed films are available for viewing for just seven days, rather like a movie rental. These popular DVDs can be watched and re-watched, though they are often "temporarily out of stock."

"Pius XII, Under the Roman Sky" tells the "often hidden struggle waged by the pope and many others with him to save the Jews from the Nazis." It refutes the widespread lie that the Holy Father was one of their greatest enemies.

As Bently Donegal commented, the film is "finally setting the record straight on Pius XII. The revisionist history propagated by the Soviets on Pius VII is rampant today. History was actually very different. At Pius' funeral Israel sent the largest delegation and the New York Times twice on December 25, 1941, and in 1942 editorial sections claimed the Pope stands alone in his opposition to Hitler and people can look that up for themselves and see it with their own two eyes.

There are films chronicling the lives of our most newly canonized popes and the first pope. Of "John XXIII, The Pope of Peace" starring Ed Asner Sr., Beth Ann Dillion wrote, "I am happy to say that this film is great and more authentic than I expected. It depicts so well the human journey of a 'simple' Italian priest who left Sotto de Monte, Italy, to rise to the Chair of St. Peter!"

Jon Voight was nominated for an Emmy Award for his performance in "Pope John Paul II," one that Variety called "remarkable," and of which USA Today said "Voight stands out as he closely mirrors our image of the Pope ... with a mix of majesty and humility, humor and steel."

"St. Peter," stars Omar Sharif, a Lebanese Christian convert to Islam. After shooting the made-for-TV movie, he claimed he could "hear voices" and that it "will be difficult ... to play other roles from now on." He is said to have received a number of death threats on a website popular with al-Quaida members, but this is nothing new to him. He had previously portrayed a Muslim who befriends a Jewish boy in "Monsieur Ibrahim."

Marcina Kukuczka called it a "brilliant movie filled with Christian joy ad love," and says, "seldom have I seen such a purely faithful movie where almost each moment is an experience."

Ignatius also offers "Peter: Keeper of the Keys," the series, "The Footprints of God" by Stephen K. Ray, "Paul: Contending for the Faith," and "The Apostolic Fathers: Handing On the Faith" continue the series to Ignatius of Antioch, Clermont of Rome, Polycarp of Smyrna, Irenaeus of Lyons, and Justin Martyr and shows the continuity of the faith from the apostles to us. The series is described as an "entertaining biography, travel documentary, Bible study, apologetics course and Church history study rolled into one."

Some of the newest saints also have streaming videos. "Seelos: Tireless Intercessor" portrays the heroic and miraculous life of a young immigrant priest, Bl. Francis Xavier Seelos. "Love Is A Choice" tells the story of St. Gianna Beretta Molla, the mother and medical doctor who sacrificed her life to save her unborn baby.

Andre Z. T. Queiroz says, "Love Is A Choice" "... portrays the love abounding from a modern Saint such as Gianna Molla that it is hard, in my opinion, not to get moved by it. Gianna's self-giving sacrifice to her child makes us ponder what love really is." He and others, however, did prefer the original Italian to the English translation.

"Archbishop Fulton J. Sheen, Servant of All" is a two-DVD set that includes five episodes of possible future saint Archbishop Sheen's "Life Is Worth Living" series: "Ages of Man," "False Compassion," "Love is a Many Splendored Thing," and "The Divine Sense of Humor" and "Angels." It also has an hour-long documentary with interviews of his biographers, his surviving relatives, and friends.

"Ocean of Mercy," subtitled "Three Lives, One Vision, No Limits," shows the connection between the three Polish saints, Faustina Kowalska, Maximillian Kolbe, and Pope John II. It includes never before seen film, photos, and interviews, to explain their common mission of promoting Divine Mercy.

"Faith of Our Fathers" takes the viewer to the time of the English martyrs, Thomas More, Edmund Campion, Margaret Clitherow, and others. They were heroes for our times.

"St. Barbara, Convert and Martyr of the Early Church" tells of her conversion to Christianity because of the example of her friend Giuliana. As T. E. Salapatek commented, "It is a movie about love, a mother's, a friend's, and eventually about God's love. This movie showed how, initially, it was Christian love and sacrifice which made Barbara a convert."

"Mother Teresa" includes her childhood in Albania through her call to become a nun and then the founder of the Missionaries of Charity in India and the world,

"The Reluctant Saint," orignally on video, tells the story of St. Joseph of Cupertino. It is described by Thomas Zabiega as "a true gem of a movie. It has amazing performances from great actors such as Maximilian Schell and Ricardo Montalban, and would suit anyone who likes a good movie. If anyone is Catholic, this is especially a great movie, orthodox to its core and accurate with the life of this amazing saint."

"Padre Pio, Miracle Man" shows the man behind the miracles. As Frank G. Ramirez puts it, "This movie on the life of St. Pio is excellent! This movie shows people the life of St. Pio from his human perspective. The viewer will see St. Pio get angry, laugh, love, and suffer."

"God's Doorkeeper" tells of St. Andre Bessette of Montreal, the first male Canadian-born saint and the first saint for the Congregation of Holy Cross. It tells of this simple man's devotion to St. Joseph and miracles God worked through his intercession.

"Lourdes: A Story of Faith, Science, and Miracles" is not a documentary or a fictionalized biography. It is rather the story of Bernard Guillaumet, a non-Christian French journalist who in the 1990s finds his ancestor Henri Guillaumet's account of his visit to Lourdes in 1858. Henri's wife Claire's miraculous healing from tuberculosis changes both Henri and Bernard.

Author Urges Change (August 2014)

His book, *Complex Craniofacial Problems: A Guide to Analysis and Treatment*, is not a best seller, but his newest book is. *One Nation, What We Can All Do To Save America's Future* by Ben Carson continues his diagnosis and treatment for what ails America shared in his other books and is co-authored with his wife, Candy.

"We each need to take an active role in changing the course of our nation," he writes, "if we are to live up to the motto 'one nation under God, indivisible, with liberty and justice for all.' We are the pinnacle nation in the world right now, but if the examples of Egypt, Greece, Rome, and Great Britain teach us anything, it is that pinnacle nations are not guaranteed their place forever. If we fail to rediscover the basic principles of common sense, manners, and morality, we will go the same way they did."

"Knowing that the future of my grandchildren is in jeopardy because of reckless spending, godless government, and mean-spirited attempts to silence critics left me no choice but to write this book," he says. I have endeavored to propose a road out of our decline, appealing to every American's decency and common sense."

Common sense, manners, and morality, however, are not common. The Carsons see as logical not redefining of marriage, a proportional tithe-like taxation, creation rather than evolution, personal rather than national health care.

Denis Vukosav wrote, "If you share the opinion of the author, his book will make you even more convinced, and if you were against it, you will oppose even harder." The Wall Street Journal's review rather put it as, "The Johns Hopkins neurosurgeon may not be politically correct, but he's closer to correct than we've heard in years."

As Abe Krieger explains it, "[This book]'s one hundred percent common sense, nothing that any sane person can disagree with. Live within your means. Say what you mean and mean what you say. Play hard but fair. Get educated. Read." Given the insane dependance on government handouts, however, Krieger considers it "too late," definitely not Carson's message.

Vanessa Bush notes that Carson intersperses his argument for change with his own inspirational life story and biblical passages. Dr. Miguel Faria, also a retired neurosurgeon, agrees, "He has done a great job putting his thoughts and ideas into words that every American can read and understand."

L. F. Lettier adds some advice to those understand, but may not like what the doctor says, "We would do well to listen to the Doctor and heed his prescription. A valuable read for all persuasions."

Rosalie Chaplet expressed her hope, "If only the leaders of this country would listen and read this book, we could save the USA from the path we are on." Robert McNutt added, "It should be required in grade school." Ann Parker even includes a prayer with her review, "It is so refreshing to hear solutions; opinions are a dime a dozen. Thank you, Dr. Carson, I am praying for you."

Gifted Hands: The Ben Carson Story, which was made into a film, told of his personal and medical successes, how God and a belt buckle changed his life. After his keynote address at the National Prayer Breakfast last year he has focused more on national issues. When asked afterward about running for president, Carson responded: "If the Lord grabbed me by the collar and made me do it, I would."

He has said, "I believe it is a very good idea for physicians, scientists, engineers, and others trained to make decisions based on facts and empirical data to get involved in the political arena and help guide our country," and has done so in several previous books.

In *America the Beautiful: Rediscovering What Made This Nation Great* Carson looked back on American history and at its present and future. He points out too that at one time our leaders were not exclusively politicians and lawyers. Once upon a time our populous was well-read, rather than spoon-fed. "In 1931, [when] Alexis de Toequeville came to our country ...anybody finishing the second grade was completely literate."

In *Think Big: Unleashing Your Potential for Excellence*, he gave a prescription for both individual and national excellence. The acronym "think big" points out the principles to live by: T for your gifts of talents and time, H for hope for good and honesty, I for insight from people, N for being nice to all people, K for knowledge, the key to living, B for good books, I for in-depth learning skills, and last but not least, G for God. These are the remedies for the epidemic of wasted time and talents, hopelessness and dishonesty, ignorance and godlessness.

Take the Risk is subtitled "Learning to Identify, Choose, and Live with Acceptable Risk." First comes a four-part method of identifying the risk, the Best/Worst Analysis (B/WA). It means simply asking yourself what is the best and worst that could happen if taking or not taking a risk and basing your choices on the honest answer. It also includes "a short review of risk-taking in history."

His book, *The Big Picture* is about why you should take risks. It is based on asking ourselves three questions, "When my life is over, what do I want to be remembered for?", What do I want to be doing five, ten, and twenty years from now?" and "What do I want to be sure I am not doing five, ten, and twenty years from now." By honestly answering these questions we can choose to take the risks to broaden our perspectives, find our life vision, changing our priorities, energizing your efforts, and being inspired as he has been to change the world for the better.

[Ben Carson accepted to position of HUD secretary after running against Trump. He's also written *My Life*, based on *Gifted Hands, A More Perfect Union, One Vote, You Have a Brain*.]

Film Generates Strong Reactions (July 2014)

Blackstone Films "The Third Way" seems to have generated strong reactions from both sides. There are no actors, just homosexuals telling their story of finding their way back into the Catholic Church, that accepts them, but not their former lifestyle.

The film was given its name, rather than the alternative, "Unnatural Law?," because it focuses on the Church's teaching of accepting the homosexual as a child of God and yet not accepting the homosexual lifestyle. "You belong here with us," says Fr. Michael Schmitz at the end. "You can share with us your struggle. You can share with us your attraction and we're still going to love you."

Ironically, or perhaps intentionally, "The Third Way" also refers to a political action group that, among other issues, promotes marriage. They, however, mean other than the marriage between one man and one woman under God, a re-definition which they have pushed through teachers, politicians, and the media.

Frank Weathers at "Why I Am A Catholic" says, "This may be the best 38 minutes and 14 seconds you'll spend on the subject of the Theology of the Body."

As Stephanie Block of Spero News wrote, "The viewier feels tremendous compassion for struggles that are not particularly 'homosexual' but common to everyone under the weight of original sin. Purity, in a broken world, is no easy achievement."

David tells how as the child of an alcoholic father everything masculine terrified him. He first identified himself as gay after a teenage friendship became sexualized. A priest "made himself available to me in a way no one else ever has. He was truly a father to me." Now he says, "I know I am a Catholic man; that's my identity. I used to think I was gay. I'm not gay; I'm David, a Catholic man." He learned to get affirmation from men who were non-homosexual and can say, "That's what I was really looking for, in all my acting out. Now I experience true, authentic love."

Julie was sexually molested as a child. She felt lost and broken, unwelcome in her church and ashamed of herself out of it. "I knew I needed God and I knew the Catholic Church was the true Church."

Melinda identified herself as bi-sexual, but eventually learned to replace her unsatisfying relationships with more perfect one with God. Richard knew that his attraction to men rather than women was not "just a phase." It was not something that would go away, that he had to deal with it the rest of his life. As many of the interviewees would agree, Sr. Helena Burns, F. S. P. notes that "We can have lots of sex with no intimacy and lots of intimacy with no sex."

In his plea for funds, John-Andrew O'Rourke explained, "The hearts and minds of countless individuals are being turned against the Church everyday. It's time for us to reverse that trend."

"Prodigal Son" who identifies himself as "a Catholic with same-sex attraction" commented on-line, "They, at least, realize that our failure to pastor gay people well is the single greatest obstacle facing the growth of the Church in America. Young people "gay or straight" care far more about this issue than any other issue. And rightly so, a Church without compassion is a Church without Christ," he commented on-line, "but a Church without truth is a Church without Christ, too. Hence: the THIRD way."

Tom Hoopes who referred to the *Catechism*, with the comment, "It seems that for one part of the culture, the Church's teaching (*Catechism of the Catholic Church* 2357) that homosexual sexual acts are 'intrinsically disordered' and 'contrary to the natural law' is unthinkable. For another the church's teaching a few sentences later is unthinkable. 'These persons are called to fulfill God's will in their lives and, if they are Christians, to unite to the sacrifice of the Lord's Cross the difficulties they may encounter from their condition."

Sue McGlone, however, wrote, "These men and women were claiming to have found a sense of peace, acceptance, and belonging within the church. Fantastic. 'How positive,' I thought." She seems to have gotten the message, "You are suffering from a pathological condition. If you opt for a lifelong commitment to celibacy you can be happy like these people despite this flaw," but saw this as "emotional and spiritual blackmail."

Similarly J. Patrick Redmond of the *Huffington Post* quotes from the film, "Those with same-sex attraction aren't being asked to do anything different than a heterosexual. We're all called to chastity, every single one of us." But he rejects that as unrealistic.

He sees Catholic position as conditional, "One must deny their biology in order to receive the love." rather than as accepting both our fallen human nature and the Love Incarnate that redeemed it. He should have read Matthew 19:26, "Such a thing is impossible to man's powers, but to God all things are possible," and "Go and sin no more." (John 8:11)

David Romero on the other hand commented on his own re-identification. "The word 'gay' carries certain baggage," he explains, "a specific lifestyle and political agenda. It assumes I'm dating and/or sexually active. It assumes I'm out of the closet and participating in a specific community. And yes, it means I likely support specific political agendas, such as the ruling from the Third Circuit which just declared Pennsylvania's Defense of Marriage Act unconstitutional."

He does not identify either with "people who struggle with same-sex attraction." He has, however, "made the decision to live in accordance with Catholic teaching and live as a celibate and chaste man. Forgetting all those things which used to define me, and looking forward instead of backwards. I'm not rejecting my orientation, but the baggage which comes from identifying with it."

In another posting Romero answered why he stayed Catholic. "There's a call on our hearts which goes so much deeper than, 'Oh, crap, if I'm gay, I must be disordered and better stay single because homosexuality is a mortal sin.' We see the beauty in God's natural design and nature, and we follow His law because it brings us into that beauty."

He passes on several encouraging "wow moments" from *Supernatural Fatherhood Through Priestly Celibacy* by Carter Griffin. One was simply, "Jesus was celibate. His masculinity s completely separate from his sexuality or sexual activity. Jesus, as an image of the Father, is in its highest form, totally separate from sex and sexuality."

[Other films from Blackstone Films on Vimeo are: "40 Years for Life", "A Call to Battle", "A Foundation in Truth", "A Nation Rises", "A Prayer for the President", "A Promise for Life", "A Vision for Excellence", "Aid for Women", "Celebrating All Mothers", "Easter Invitation", "Into the Breach", "Legacy for the Holy Land", "National Organization for Marriage", "Roman March for Life", "Stand Up for Religious Freedom", and "They Opened They Doors". Fr. Gordon tells his conversion story at Why I'm Catholic (whyimcatholic.com).]

Ask Angels For Help (June 2014)

Preciosa S. Soliven recently wrote a series of articles called "Angels Are Real" in the *Philippine Star* (philstar.com). She notes that interest in these supernatural beings continues as does the confusion about them. She counts about twenty-one books about angels at the bookstore. *TIME* magazine reported that sixty-nine percent of Americans believe in angels while thirty-two percent have felt an angelic presence. Ten percent of all popular songs are estimated to reference angels.

Malcolm Godwin in *Angels, An Endangered Species*, comes at the subject from several directions. "On one level angels still manage to retain their magical popularity and power, while on the other no one quite believes in them any more." His book includes the history of angels in many cultures and modern theories that try to explain them away as a delusions or extraterrestrials.

Soliven quotes Mortimer J. Adler in *The Angels and Us*, "Angels and angels alone are minds without bodies, when they assume bodies, they do so only for the sake of engaging in their earthly ministry." She notes "rules" from G. Don Gilmore's *Angels, Angels Everywhere*, "unless people revive their childhood wonder and imagination, they may never experience such things." And from Joan Wester Anderson's *Where Angels Walk*, "unless we deliberately invoke their aid, angels can help only in a limited way."

Eileen Elias Freeman, author of *Touched by Angels: True Cases of Close Encounters of the Celestial Kind*, adds that discernment of spirits is very important. We should ask ourselves "does the suspected angelic messenger confuse or clarify, order, or invite? Does its message bear good fruit in your life and others?" She warns, "any being you can summon at will ... is probably not an angel," that is, an unfallen one.

Those who are open to and pray for angelic help from their guardian angel or the archangels Michael, Raphael, and Gabriel have some wonderful and surprising experiences. Rev. Fr. Antonio M. Rosales, OFM, wrote her, "I also have a special devotion to my guardian Angel that has inspired me to write a book *Jesus: The Story of Jesus of Nazareth as Told by His Guardian Angel.*

"I was recovering from the life-threatening experiences of an irregular heartbeat, remedied with a pacemaker implant," he says. "After my stroke in 2007, my seizures became more regular and even violent. I prayed hard to my guardian angel. I asked myself what the guardian angel of the God-made man, Jesus of Nazareth, would have done while Jesus was going through His passion, and how would he have told the story of the Lord.

"In this context I took my mind away from my fears about my health. I thought that this telling of the life of Jesus Christ from the point of view of His guardian angel will be a humble contribution to this Year of Faith, and could be part of the long-term preparation for the 500th anniversary of Christ in the Philippines."

Laura Leigh tells of watching her son Danny hurtle head-first toward the sharp corner of the table and stop in midair. Later he told her, "Mommy? I saw a beautiful lady with wings. She caught me yesterday so I didn't hit my head against the table."

Jean Biltz had a similar experience when expecting her fifth child in a few months. She slipped on her icy porch and two strong arms caught Jean and stood her up straight against the door. It wasn't her husband, however. There was no one there at all.

Elaine Elias Freeman's guardian angel spoke to her one night when she was young to ease her fears about her deceased grandmother. The angel spoke tin a voice that Elaine describes as "like pure crystal." The experience prompted her to become Catholic and found the Angel Watch Network.

She retells the James DiBello's story, "The Angel Who Saved My Marriage." He got angry at God when his brother died when he was eight and stopped praying. He got so angry when his wife left him that he wanted to begin breaking his mother's old dishes. But he couldn't pick up the last dish and remembered the words "make room for your guardian angel at the table." As soon as he prayed to his guardian angel again, he heard the sound of his wife Marie returning.

Margaret Ann Guiterrez was just starting school and frightened by a thunderstorm when her guardian angel appeared to her. "She was the most exquisite, holy, beautiful being I have ever seen," she says, over thirty years later. "She was surrounded with a blue-white light, brighter than the lightning. Her face was so peaceful, so quiet and confident, and I felt some of that peacefulness come into me."

Andy Lakey was twenty-seven when he had a near-death experience. "I felt my angel reach out to me and wrap his (or maybe hers or its) arms around me in a gesture that was so protective and loving and crying and understanding," he says, "I have no words to describe it."

He remembered other times when his angel intervened in his life. When he was young he and his father had moved out of the path of an out-of-control car. Another time a mysterious stranger returned him hime when he'd gotten separated from his parents in Japan. He began a new career painting angels.

Freeman asks some questions to increase your awareness of angels. "How many Michaels do you know? How many pizza parlors named Angelo's?" Be more aware of being protected, inspired, and encouraged. Most importantly she writes, "We must also commit to seeking God and to becoming the most loving person we can be toward ourselves and others. And as we grow in this commitment, our own wavelength will more closely match that of our angels, who live for love and for love and we will be able to understand their guidance and follow it, and we will know when they intervene in our lives for good."

[Gilmore also wrote *No Matter How Dark the Valley,* Freeman *Angelic Healing* and *Mary's Little Instruction Book.*]

Faithful Experience Marvels Of God (May 2014)

Joan Carroll Cruz has chronicled many miracles in her books on *The Incorruptibles, Eucharistic Miracles* and *Miraculous Images of Our Lady and Miraculous Images of Our Lord.* In *Mysteries, Marvels, Miracles in the Live of the Saint*s, however, she includes the most unclassifiable in the chapter "Marvels of Every Sort."

On the title page she quotes Acts 2:19, "I will show wonders in the heavens above and signs on the earth beneath." God, Who does not change, has and will continue to answer spoken and unspoken prayers.

A pilgrim to the Holy Land was forced to abandon his journey and so left his gift, a ivory ship at Our Lady of Monaria in Cagliari on Sardinia. The ship was hung by a string behind the high altar. The mysterious tunings of the ship in the narrow stairway corresponds to the winds on the sea outside.

Catherine dei Ricci and Philip Neri shared the marvelous gift of conversing at long distance with each other. Although the two saints never met and never wrote each other, five people swore that they had witnessed such communications.

Uneducated Bl. Anne of St. Bartholomew of St. Theresa of Avila's community, learned to write from copying Theresa's letters as her secretary. She later wrote her own autobiography. Catherine of Siena had difficulty learning to read the breviary. She prayed and the "Divine Novice Master" enabled her to read.

Carbel Markhouf is reported to have prayed his breviary by the light of a lamp that a brother monk had deliberately filled with water.

Several saints made use of lamp oil for their purposes. Theresa Margaret Redi used the oil from before a Marian shrine to anoint her fellow sisters and heal them. Bl. Gerald Cagnoli used oil from a St. Louis shrine. Clelia Barbieri used his community's patron Francis of Paola's. Bl. André used oil from a St. Joseph shrine for healing.

Bl. Peter Geremia was such a sought-out preacher that he had to preach in the public square of Bologna. One of his monastic brothers said that his voice was heard more than a mile away.

Fr. Francisco di Lucia was distributing a pamphlet on St. Philomena. He had done so for several months before he noticed that he had been taking them from just the one uncovered stack. Then one evening he found booklets scattered all over the floor and the original stacks still undisturbed. His original two hundred twenty-one copies had been nearly tripled.

Another miracle involves the stonecutter Giovanni Cimaforte. While working on an altar for chapel to Philomena, the marble slab developed a long, jagged crack. His repair attempts made it worse. His patching made it even more noticeable. He prayed and the crack's patch blended together with the natural stone.

Both Benedict and Francis of Paola are said to have miraculously moved boulders that were hindering construction. Benedict prayed, blessed the stone, and then moved it as if it were weightless. Francis kneeled, then prayed with his arms raised, and the stone rose up out of the ground.

Catherine of Bologna had just put her loaves into the oven when the bell rang for a sermon by her Franciscan provincial, Br. Albert. She prayed for protection for the bread and when she returned five hours later it was not only not burnt, but a beautiful brown. The oven is said to emit a wonderfully sweet perfume on the novena before her feast day and several days after.

Gerard Majella was the instrument of a similar miracle. He noticed that teams of oxen could not move the large chestnut trees needed for the construction of a church. He tied a rope to one of the largest, ordered it to follow him, and dragged it to its destination. The workmen followed his examples and easily removed the other trees.

The custom of writing the prayer SAG for "St. Anthony Guide" or pasting stamps with the initials on envelopes traces back to 1729. The wife of Antonio Dante in Spain had not heard from him since he went off on a business venture to Peru. To ensure that her letter reached him she prayed to his patron St. Anthony of Padua and placed it in the hand of the church's statue. When she returned the next day the parish priest said he had noticed the letter but could not remove it. She, however, removed it easily, but discovered it was not her letter. It was the answering one from Lima.

Antonio had gotten her letter from a Franciscan. He had not written because he had not gotten her letters and thought her dead. Included in the envelope was 300 gold coins, enough to provide for her until his return.

Gemma Galgani asked her guardian angel to deliver letters to the Giannini family. To test this a letter was locked in a chest by Fr. Lorenzo Agrimonti, but was delivered to her confessor nevertheless. "Angelic letters" from him to her were delivered in the same way.

Bl. Mary Fortunata Viti and his sister Benedictines were filling a wine cask when it began leaking. When sealing the leaks failed, Sr. Fortunata made the sign of the cross with her St. Benedict medal and prayed. The cracks in the cask closed and the wine stopped flowing.

When Phillip Neri and his community were trying to decide whether to repair or replace an old church donated to them, he had a vision. He ordered the roof of the corner of the church near an image of the Madonna and Child be torn down immediately. He had seen the Madonna supporting the roof with one hand. The workman discovered that the main beam that had been supporting the roof had come out of the wall.

Alphonsus Liguori was buried wearing the Scapular of Our Lady of Mt. Carmel that he had worn during his lifetime. Forty years later his scapular was found incorrupt, even though everything else in his tomb had turned to dust.

[Cruz died at 81, having been a member of the Discalced Carmelite Secular Order for 50 years.]

John XXIII And Francis Share Positive Qualities (April 2014)

It is quite fitting that Pope Francis will be canonizing Pope John XXIII on Divine Mercy Sunday. They share many of the same qualities, humility, love of the poor, and disregard for formalities. *The Wit and Wisdom of Good Popo John* by Henri Fesquet (1965) is well worth a re-reading.

There are many other, newer books and e-books on Pope John XXIII, such as *Pope John XXIII: the Good Pope* by Wyatt North (2014), *The Good Pope* by Greg Tobin (2012), and *Pope John XXIII* by Peter Hebblethwaite (1985, 2000). There are also DVDs like "The Good Pope: John XXIII" (2003). There is, of course, his own autobiography, *Journal of a Soul*, and his *Prayers and Devotions* as well. Fesquet's paperback, however, is a very easy read.

Just before his death, Fesquet notes, Good Pope John wrote of the Second Vatican council, "May He grant me enough time to finish it? May He be praised if He does not grant it. I shall see the happy conclusion from Heaven where I hope, and am even certain, Divine Mercy will allow me to enter."

The devotions which he carried on since childhood were to Jesus, Joseph, and the three Francises, Francis of Assisi, Francis Xavier, and Francis de Sales. At the end of his life, like Francis of Assisi, he welcomed Sister Death. "I await the arrival of Sister Death calmly and gladly," he wrote and died the morning after Pentecost, 1963, just as Mass im the next room ended.

While walking through Rome, he heard a woman remark, "God, but he's fat!" He responded with, "But Madam, you must know that the conclave is not exactly a beauty contest."

On another occasion a boy asked him in a letter, "My dear pope: I am undecided. I want to be a policeman or a pope. What do you think?" Pope John answered, "If you want my opinion, learn how to be a policeman, because that cannot be improved. As regards being pope, you will see later. Anybody can be pope; the proof of this is that I have become one."

One of thirteen children, he nevertheless says that his farming family had all that they needed. Yet Pope John wrote, "I thank God for this grace of poverty to which I vowed myself in my youth, poverty of spirit as a priest of the Sacred Heart and real poverty. It sustains me in my resolve never to ask for anything."

Pope John XXIII is said to have used only two missals to celebrate Mass. Both were gifts from prisoners he had visited. One had been presented to him by inmates of Melun and the other from Regina Coeli prison in Rome.

Pope John admitted that he had some difficulty sleeping on the night after he had announced the Vatican II council, the first in almost a century. He says he talked away his anxiety by putting on the mind of Christ. He told himself, "Giovanni, why don't you sleep? Is it the pope or the Holy Spirit Who governs the Church? It's the Holy Spirit, no? Well, then go to sleep, Giovanni!"

In the midst of the Cold War, and as a veteran of World War I, he wrote "What a response to *Pacem in Terris*! What there is of myself in this document is above all the humble example of the 'peace and patient man.' (*Imitation of Christ*, 2, 3) which I have tried to set during the whole of my poor life."

Pope John was uncomfortable with all the applause that followed his words. He, therefore, ordered the Credo be said as soon as he had finished speaking. Thus he re-focused the attention of his listeners on God and away from God's messenger.

Like Pope Francis he preferred informality to formality. When president Kennedy and the first lady visited him, he asked how he should address the president's wife, but then simply called her Jacqueline.

On another occasion while visiting the Hospital of the Holy Spirit in Rome, he met with the mother superior. She introduced herself as the Superior of the Holy Spirit. He replied, "I must say you're lucky. I'm only the Vicar of Jesus Christ."

He sometimes had to remind himself that he was now pope and not say, as he had as a cardinal, "I'll talk it over with the pope." He changed that to "I'll talk it over with our Lord."

Like Pope Francis Pope John caused unintentional distress among his staff. When he could not be found in his private apartment or the chapel, the cardinal, police, and Swiss guard were alerted and he was found reading in the park.

Fesquet also includes some of Pope John's favorite maxims. Several are trinitarian: "Listen to everything, forget much, correct little."; "Let us look at each other without mistrust, meet each other without fear, talk with each other without surrendering principle." and "Unity in necessary things, freedom in doubtful things, charity in all things."

"We are here on Earth," he explained in words of his own, "not to guard a museum, but to cultivate a garden flourishing with life and promised to a glorious future." Yet he also warned against keeping "hidden the treasure that is the truth handed down by our forefathers."

Pope John was pastorally concerned about modesty as well. When he was apostolic nuncio to France at banquet, he noticed one lady had a very low neckline. He offered her an apple, saying, "Do take it, madame, please do. It was only after Eve ate the apple that she became aware of how little she had on!"

Another time when asked if such dress embarrassed him he answered, "Why no, when there's a woman with a plunging neckline, the guests don't look at her. They look at the apostolic nuncio to see how he is taking it."

[Some other books on St. Pope John XXIII are: *A Pope Laughs* by Kurt Klinger, *A Retreat with Pope John XXIII* by Alfred McBride, *"I Love Life!" Said Pope John XXIII* by Frederick Franck, *I Will Be Called John* by Lawrence Elliot, *Meet John XXIII* by Patricia Treece, *Overlook Much, Correct Little* by Rothlin Hans-Peter, *Praying the Stations with St. John XXIII* and *Praying with Pope John XXIII* by Bill Huebach, *Praying with St. Pope John XXIII* by Fr. Jean-Yves Garneau, *Secret to Happiness: Wisdom from John XXIII* by Donna Giaimo, *The Good Pope* by Greg Tobin, *The Humor and Warmth of Pope John XXIII* by Louis Michaels, The Stories of Pope John XXIII by Louis Michaels, The Vision of St. Pope John XXIII by Randell S. Rosenberg, Walking with St. John XXIII by Gwen Costello.]

Deathbed Conversions Inspire (March 2014)

In her new book, *Deathbed Conversions: Finding Faith at the Finish Line*, Karen Edmisten tells of the famous and not so famous who came to God when near death. The stories show that such late conversions usually "don't track in straight lines," but are full of twists and turns.

"An honest-to-goodness deathbed conversion," she says, "offers everything good storytelling demands: drama, pathos and sin, despair, chaos, confusion, love, enlightenment, and finally, redemption."

As a convert herself from atheism at thirty-five, she now says, "We Christians might discover a host of other feelings when we take a long, hard look [at deathbed conversions]: pity for people's squandered lives, compassion for their black holes of despair, sorrow for the changes they missed, and happiness that could have been theirs had they submitted to God sooner."

Mike Aquilina wrote, "I love this book. It has all the attractive power of the supermarket tabloids -- big celebrity names, sex, violence, everything but aliens -- but with the grace, eloquence, and profundity of Augustines' *Confessions*."

Carol Earls wrote, "It was so 'good' I simply could not put it down. It made me realize how fortunate I am to be a Catholic."

She tells of Oscar Wilde, poet, writer, and out-of-control hedonist, whose deathbed conversion to Catholicism is just about completely ignored.

Arthur Simon Flegenheimer is a deathbed convert few have heard. He was better known as Public Enemy Number One "Dutch Shultz." His parents were both German Jews who attempted to raise their son in their faith. As he lay dying in the hospital from gunshot wounds, he registered as a Jew. But early the next morning he unexpectedly called for a Catholic priest. Fr. Cornelius McInerney baptized him and gave him the last rites. He was later buried in a Catholic cemetery.

Actor Frank James "Gary" Cooper had a long-running affair with actress Patricia Neal that helped break up his marriage. He talked her into having an abortion, but two years before he died he converted to Catholicism. Within a month of Jimmy Stewart's emotional speech for him at the Academy Awards he was dead from cancer, just after his 60th birthday. He was buried at Sacred Heart Cemetery, Southampton, NY.

Patricia Neal also died of cancer, but converted four months before her death, largely because of the surprising forgiveness she eventually received from Cooper's wife and daughter. She was buried in the Abbey of of Regina Landis, Bethlehem, CT, where her friend Dolores Hart had become a nun.

Fr. Matthew Munoz says that his grandmother Josephine Saenz never stopped praying for her ex-husband, Marion Michael Morrison's conversion. He was better known as "John Wayne".

Fr. Munoz also said that his grandfather expressed a degree of regret about not becoming a Catholic earlier in life, explaining "that was one of the sentiments he expressed before he passed on, blaming "a busy life."

His son, Patrick Wayne, tells how he called the chaplain and left them alone for fifteen minutes and could hear them talking. When the chaplain came out, he told me he had baptized Dad.

Alexis Carrel, the Nobel Prize winner, was an avowed atheist but he witnessed a miracle in Lourdes when Marie Bailly didn't die of tuberculosis. He promoted eugenics for decades, but early the next morning she got up on her own and was already dressed when Carrel saw her again. She was healed. Later he saw a child regain its sight. Carrel refused to accept the possibility of a miracle for years and promoted eugenics. Nearing the end of his life, however, Carrel finally called his friend Trappist monk Alexis Presse and returned to the Catholic Church of his youth.

King Charles II suffered a sudden apoplectic fit and died four days later. On the last evening of his life he also was received back into the Catholic Church.

William Frederick "Buffalo Bill" Cody is one of the most iconic figures of the Wild West. He because a Catholic the day before his death. It is believed that he was inspired to do so by his friend Sitting Bull, himself a Catholic convert, being instructed by Bishop Marty of Dakota.

Pulitzer Prize winner Wallace Stevens was baptized a Catholic by Fr. Arthur Hanley, chaplain of St. Francis Hospital in Hartford, Connecticut, where Stevens spent his last days suffering from cancer. In the same year, 1955, mathematician John von Neumann was diagnosed with cancer and died a year and a half later. On his death bed he told Fr. Anselm Strittmatter that Pascal had a point, referring to Pascal's wager.

After artist Aubrey Beardsley converted to Catholicism he begged his publisher to "destroy all copies of Lysistrata and bad drawings ... by all this is holy all obscene drawings." Smithers, however, ignored Beardsley's wishes and actually continued to sell reproductions as well as forgeries of Beardsley's work. He died at just 25 from tuberculosis and was buried at Menton Cathedral cemetery.

Seven months before his death, agnostic journalist Heywood Broun converted to Catholicism after discussion with Archbishop Fulton Sheen. More than 3,000 mourners attended his funeral at St. Patrick's Cathedral.

Many other little known celebrity conversion stories can be found on the internet. Although not deathbed conversions those of Newt Guingrich, Jeb Bush, Vincent Prince, and Norma "Jane Doe" McCorvey are interesting. John Henry "Doc" Holiday is said to have been a deathbed convert because of Fr. Edward Downey and cousin Sr. Martha Anne "Mattie" Holiday.

Actor Alec Guinness, an Anglican, was filming "Father Brown" when he was mistaken for a real priest by a local child. Later when their eleven-year-old son was ill with polio, Guinness began visiting a church to pray and a few years later converted to the Catholic Church. A few years after that his wife also converted, only telling him afterward.

Black Elk, the Oglala medicine man, married his first wife, Katie War Bonnet. She and all three of their children became Catholic. After her death, he was baptized Catholic as Nicholas.

[Other books by Edmisten are: *A Little Way of Homeschooling, After Miscarriage, Word by Word: Slowing Down with the Hail Mary, Atheist to Catholic, Through the Year with Mary* and *You Can Share the Faith.*]

Author Discusses Benefits Of Religion (February 2014)

Rodney Stark, Baylor University sociology professor, has written a new book, *America's Blessings: How Religion Benefits Everyone, Including Atheists*. He has counted our blessings for us, referencing three hundred and fifty wide-ranging though little-known studies.

In 2004 Stark became co-director of the Institute for Studies of Religion at Baylor University, whose motto is "Treating religion with the respect that sacred matters require and deserve." He has authored more than a hundred fifty scholarly articles and thirty-two books, including best-selling titles like *The Triumph of Christianity: How the Jesus Movement Became the World's Largest Religion, God's Battalions: The Case for the Crusades*, and *The Victory of Reason: How Christianity Led to Freedom, Capitalism, and Western Success*.

Simon Smart at Mercatornet describes Stark "as correcting false perceptions and challenging the ignorance and prejudice of influential but misinformed commentators and writers who he says are often contemptuous of faith and religious people. Stark is reacting to not only the outright hostility of a media unenlightened in spiritual matters, but also the neglect of well-attested studies that highlight the positive impacts of faith."

Although many surveys have noted the increase of the "nones," those who answer "none" to the religion question, Start has found that religious practice is now more prevalent than it ever has been in America. He devotes whole chapters to unpacking the latest research on how religion affects different facets of modern American life, including crime, family life, sexuality, mental and physical health, sophistication, charity, and overall prosperity.

Stark explains, "Contrary to the popular wisdom, more affluent and better educated people are more likely to belong to a local church. Hence, the bias in completion rates easily could account for the rise in the percent who say they have 'no religion.' "

"These people are not really saying they have no religion," he claims, "but merely that they have no church membership. That is very different and is consistent with the fact that the majority of them are quite religious in terms of belief, prayer, and the like."

Mark L. Movsesian of St. John's University similarly notes, "About seventy percent of Americans now belong to religious congregations, the highest percentage in our history. One possible explanation [is that] some Evangelical Christians who are members of free-standing congregations, without denominational ties, do not think they belong to a 'religion.' "

Compared with western European nations, he finds that the United States comes out on top again and again. Our country, founded on religious freedom has far lower crime rates, much higher levels of charitable giving, better health, stronger marriages, and less suicide.

The biggest [benefit] by far has to do with the criminal justice system. If all Americans committed crimes at the same level as those who do not attend religious services, the costs of the criminal justice system would about double to, perhaps, two trillion dollars annually.

Second is health costs. The more often people attend religious services, the healthier they are. However, the net savings involved is reduced somewhat by the fact that religious Americans live, on average, seven years longer than those who never attend religious services.

Jamey Brown at Catholic Stand wrote: "Uproariously Good News: Religion Is Good For You!" and gives a Catholic twist on the news. Seventy percent of Americans belong to a local parish. Of the twenty percent "unaffiliated" most "pray regularly," just not in church. He notes Christianity's "growth [in] Sub-Saharan Africa and Latin America has been phenomenal. It is important to note that Islam is not growing nearly as fast worldwide and the Muslim birthrate in Europe is declining significantly due to modernization."

Brown also notes that Professor Stark found that religious people rank lowest among believers in Bigfoot, psychics, and astrology, etc. and says, "if you want to find believers in those things, you'll find them in the faculty lounge."

Greg Smith quotes some other benefits from the book: "Religious Americans are more successful, obtaining better jobs, and far less subject to be on unemployment or welfare" (p. 5). "Religious Americans have more children than others making American one of few developed nations not facing real peril due to declining population" (p. 57-58). "Religious Americans are more likely to 'delay premarital sex' and to have 'superior sex lives' within the context of marriage" (p. 90-91). "Religiousness 'provides substantial protection against mental illness' and can 'even make people happier' " (p. 95). "Religious Americans are generous citizens who display 'higher levels of generosity with their money and their time' " (p. 131). "Religious students have a superior level of academic achievement however it is measured" (p. 134).

Charles Reed wrote, "In a time when the less-than-helpful actions of central governments and political manipulation are obvious to many, being well informed as to dynamics which shape life, such as the leadership/influence of the Messiah, and having the opportunity for respectful, patient, well-conceived dialogue together will give us a better chance for positive change than our continued frustrating reliance on the federal government to help us."

Markku Ojanen writes, "Though I have written about this research in three books (in Finnish) there is much new for me, too. The data I do have point to very similar direction: religiousness is related to many good things from the point of [view of] society.

Ojanen does, however, express his own opinion on our mixed blessings, Stark does not mention our low voting (though high political activity), poor social security (though a lot of volunteer work), and quite poor basic schools (though many great universities). As a European he found the statement, "the average person in 'irreligious' Sweden is three-and-a half times as likely as the average American to be criminally assaulted, and twice as likely to be the victim of theft" hard to believe.

[Stark has more recently written *Bearing False Witness: Debunking Centuries of Anti-Catholic History, The Triumph of Faith: Why the World Is More Religious Than Ever,* and *Reformation Myths: Five Centuries of Misconceptions and (Some) Misfortunes.* Catholic Stand (catholicstand.org) has links to many Vatican, news and Catholic sites.]

Holmes Tackles Biblical Mysteries (January 2014)

Len Bailey's novel, *Sherlock Holmes and the Needle's Eye* is better explained by its subtitle, "The World's Greatest Detective Tackles the Bible's Ultimate Mysteries." It doesn't, of course, cover all of the Bible's mysteries, but it does come up with plausible solutions to ten of them. Presumably -- or hopefully -- there will be many more such mysteries coming.

Diane Lawrence pleads in her review, "Please write more in this genre." Pamela Jane Sutton comments, "The words 'riveting' and 'Bible study guide' have never been used in the same sentence, until now. This is a must read!"

Nancy Famolari wrote, "I enjoyed each one, although some, like "The Hanging Man," were particularly well done. The Biblical puzzles are all fascinating. The author has done a considerable amount of research and all his facts seem to be accurate."

Bob Hostetler puts it a bit less enthusiastically, and with different favorites, "As can be expected, some were more convincing than others and some were highly speculative -- especially for the world's first and greatest consulting detective. My personal favorites were the chapters on the raising of Lazarus and the woman caught in adultery."

"Don't be fooled like me," Kenneth G. Campbell III warns. "These are mysteries, not contradictions. I thought this would be an apologetics book, but to my surprise Holmes and Watson get assigned to go back in time to find answers to interesting and helpful Bible questions."

Bailey, a history major from Trinity College, pits Holmes's hyperrationalism against Dr. Watson's simple faith, all the time using Biblical and historical references, both Victorian and Biblical. By the end the reader is perhaps a bit more convinced that the truth, and the Truth, can be reached via either. Mrs. Hudson, their landlady, even takes part in a couple of the adventures.

"In truth, Holmes and Watson are the halves of one man, any man, sliced down the middle into a head-half and a heart-half," Bailey explains. "Every person harbors rebellion toward God: we want to go our own way, to act in accordance with our wisdom and reasoning. But every person possesses a faith part, no matter how small: we want to believe that God (the real God) is a Father in Whose arms we find forgiveness and in Whose arms we can rest. This is the real beauty of Sherlock Holmes and Dr. Watson: They represent every man."

Amber Godman says, "Having just read an original Sherlock Holmes, I picked up this new version with much skepticism. However, within the first few paragraphs I was not disappointed ... I was intrigued by the author's use of very familiar stories from Sunday school and the nuances of mystery that they held."

After Holmes constructs a time machine from Moriarty's design, a mysterious client poses unsolved mysteries to solve using it. Sometimes it makes them mere observers of the past, other times they take an active role in the events. Why the machine behaves the way it does is an on-going mystery itself.

It is more than just a mystery novel or a series of mystery stories, however. Bailey also provides Investigative Study Questions to help the reader ponder these mysteries and connect them to their own lives. It is a Bible Study Guide like none other.

The Needle's Eye refers to the time machine that takes Holmes and Watson to Giloh in Judea to discover why Ahithophel hung himself. Finding out involves investigating both his and David's families, and quite a lot of political intrigue in 2 Samuel. This investigation uncovers envy, jealousy, revenge, lust, despair in the royal family.

They go back to answer the question of why young David chose five stones when confronting Goliath. Could it be his faith in the Lord was weak? Did it have to do with the sacred *Penteuch*? They wonder with the disciples why Jesus waited to visit the dying Lazarus.

The reader is invited to ponder "Why does God delay answering prayer? Why does He seem to always answer them in the most unexpected ways? Or is all history just 'co-incidence' and 'change?' "

Another mystery lies in what Jesus wrote in the sand when the woman caught in adultery was accused. They could not see for the crowd. Watson proposes that Jesus wrote the Pharisees' past sins, but Holmes disposes of the hypothesis. Watson, as usual however, does intentionally lead Holmes to the most logical solution by scrutinizing in Mark, John, and Philippians.

The investigation of Matthew 23:25, leads to unexpected discoveries about all of the prophets from Abel to Jesus Himself. Investigating the Temptation in the Desert, Holmes is led on the trail of the Devil himself. The quest is "just when was the 'more opportune time' for the last temptation? It proves not to involve Mary Magdalene.

They follow Paul in his travels to learn why he went where he did. They are confronted by the Romans more than once and by the London police as well. They reconcile Luke and Matthew's genealogies by tying it into a previous mystery. They sort out the confusing variety of Herods and find out why when Jesus was born when He was.' At the Battle of Jericho and again back in London, Mrs. Watson proves herself more that merely a good cook and a long-suffering landlady. She also adds much of the comic relief in a very tense situation.

This book may even encourage the reader to read some of the reference books Bailey lists. These include *Thirty Days in the Land with Jesus* by Charles H. Dyer, *Matters and Customs in the Bible* by Victor H. Matthews, and *The Annotated Sherlock Holmes* by William S. Baring-Gould. It might even encourage someone as apparently irreligious as Sherlock Holmes to read the Bible.

Mary Lavers, for example, wrote, "I may not be a Christian, but the Sherlockian in me LOVED [her emphasis] it!"

[My own *Sherlock Holmes and the Mad Doctor* continues where Bailey's story leaves off with the Lord of lords still trying to get Holmes not to trust in his own understanding, as will the sequel *The Curse of Sherlock Holmes*.]

Website Promotes Faith (December 2013)

Faithit.com is a place to find faith-building videos on the usually faith-challenging internet. This one site collects thousands of testimonies from many sources.

Heath White's story, for example, from "The Best Stories in Sports" has a seemingly perfect beginning. He was a 4.0 student and winning long distance runner. He became Air Force pilot and married his middle school sweetheart, Jennifer. Then they learned their baby had Down syndrome.

"I did everything I could to try to force her into having an abortion," he says on his video. When Paisley was born White quit running and made himself absent from his family.

Jennifer says, "I felt like I had a broken baby, that I had lost a baby," and still breaking up at the memory, "I thought he would leave."

When he tickled his little daughter and she laughed and pushed away his hands, "Paisley was able to change me," he explains.

He began running again this time pushing Paisley's baby carriage. By their ninth marathon they came in first together.

"I'll never be perfect," White now proclaims, "but my love for Paisley is perfect. If I can keep one family, one person, from having to live with the guilt and almost making the mistake I almost made, it's going to be worth it, the pain that Paisley will feel later in life knowing the way I felt."

Scott Hamilton's story doesn't start out perfect. An unknown disease stunted his growth, but his mother strengthened him. He was a world champ skater 16 years in a row. Then she died of cancer and he got testicular cancer. He found Tracy who took him to church and his life seemed to be getting better. God blessed them with a child just nine months and two days after their marriage.

Fourteen months later when the doctors found a tumor in his brain, they prayed, "Whatever it is, whatever it takes, we're going to face it."

It turned out to be a pituitary tumor he was born with, the reason he was only 5 foot 4, the reason he got into skating. He thanked God. "I changed the way I pray now," he says, after the tumor re-grew. "I ask uninhibitedly. I asked for strength. I ask for courage." He asked for another child and they were blessed with "Miracle Max."

God changed Eric Metaxas's life with a dream. His grew up in a culturally Greek Orthodox family, but by the time he had graduated from Yale, he says, "I didn't know what to believe. He got a job at Union Carbide and was encouraged by a co-worker to "pray that God reveals Himself to you."

He was put off, however, because he did not have faith in a God who actually cared, like his co-worker, but in a distant, impersonal God, if he existed at all.

God did reveal Himself using Eric's own "secret vocabulary of the heart." In his dream he was ice fishing, when a shining, golden fish came up out of the hole. His father had explained to him that the ICHTYOS symbol meant Christ. Jung had used ice and water as symbols for the conscious and subconscious mind.

"It was life-changing and mind-blowing," Eric says. "It was transcendental."

"To think that I could grow up in a church and go to one of the finest universities and never encounter any credible witness of this kind of faith says a lot about this culture we live in."

Metaxas's video comes from "I Am Second," with the implication that God is First, or as John put it, "He must increase and I must decrease" (John 3:30).

From "On The Road" by Steve Hartman comes a Secret Santa story, where one recipient was more than usually surprised by the gift of hundred dollar bills.

Thomas Coates was an atheist, a drug addict, living off his girlfriend. The night before she encouraged him to pray and he did for the first time since childhood.

Coates says, "It was God saying 'Have you had enough yet now?' "

He re-entered rehab yet again, but this time relying on a higher power.

Katie Davis writes her story in "Kisses for Katie". She felt called to volunteer in Uganda against the advice of her parents. When she took in an orphan girl, just until she could be adopted, it lead her to take in another and another. Then one little one called her "Mom." She now is in Uganda for good and found what God has called her to be, the adoptive mother of fourteen children.

When asked why she does it, Davies answers, "Jesus said 'Love your neighbor as yourself.' Myself doesn't want to be starving, so I don't want anyone to be starving."

Allison Vesterfeld's book Packing Light is actually a collection of stories like her own. She went on a road trip finding other people who had re-directed their lives by simplifying their lives in different ways.

Carlos Whittaker had his family put everything they really needed into one room and then had an estate sale of all the stuff they didn't really need. Bryan Allain quit his job of 14 years to start his own business. "It was a leap of faith," he says, "but I don't regret it." Matt Appling unloaded himself of his prayer requests. "It's when I empty out my prayer life," he says, "that's when God does surprising things."

Marissa Cope starts her story with the puzzling statement, "When I was born my parents were at the circus." That was true because her adoptive parents didn't get her from her teenage biological parents until five days later. Although she had a head indentation from being birthed with forceps, her new brother commented, "Isn't she pretty? Doesn't she look just like me?"

Cope says she thinks of this as how Jesus presents us to His and our adoptive Father. She didn't learn about Jesus, however, until she got a Christian babysitter. Eventually Marissa's family became adopted into God's family too. She now tells her story for Heroic Media, which encourages adoption rather than abortion.

"We see that God intervenes in almost flagrant ways in our lives," she says. "He took me from being an unwanted pregnancy to a pined after, inordinately loved child, who has had a life defined by hope."

Bible Is Focus Of Game Show (October 2013)

The cable network GSN's (Game Show Network) religious game show, "The American Bible Challenge", premiered last summer to the GSN's highest ratings for any show in their 18-year history. Now it has been renewed for a third season.

It is no wonder with the climax of the second season ending with the winning Dominican Sisters of Mary, Mother of the Eucharist, out of Ann Arbor. They were winning in more than one way, with their smiles and their answers.

The three young nuns say that they got on the show because they want to provide support for the Sisters in their order, especially the older Sisters, who have been sources of inspiration to them and because they love a challenge -- from soccer to Scrabble.

The contestants were allowed a quickie Bible study of the Old Testament before the final round on the final show. It did not start out so well with Sr. Evangeline passing on the first question of ten questions, "What animal in the Book of Daniel had its mouth closed?" They continued on one by one to answer more questions correctly than did their opponents.

Network executive Amy Introcaso-Davis says, "We are proud of the breakthrough success of this atypical series."

"Sometimes a show perfectly hits that sweet spot of exciting competition blended with real heart, and that's the story of 'The American Bible Challenge'," added Tom Forman, CEO of Relatively Television. "Our TV and online fans can look forward to another fantastic ride in our third season."

The "real heart" part is in the Faith Moments, where authors and celebrities share their faith, challenging viewers to live the Bible. Rev. Randy Frazee tells how he chose his future wife when she said grace. Karen Kingsbury tells how tearing up her boyfriend's Bible got her to finally get and read one. Max Lucado spoke of God's mercy, Sherry Surratt of security in God, and Rabbi Joshua Stanton of the power of prayer.

Faith Moments has a Facebook fan page as well as an app on iTunes, iPhone, and Android. There is also an associated Bible quiz at www.beliefnet.com. (It did, however, incorrectly give the number of books in the Bible as sixty-six.)

Jonna Infield Piece, one of the Faith Fans, says about the show, "It is wonderful to see something worthy of watching on television! I have always had a profound appreciation of your clean humor. Thank you for proving funny doesn't need to be vile. God bless!"

Jonathan Mosebach agrees, "[It is wonderful] that there is a Christian, Bible-based trivia game show on TV! I wish there were more." So does Gwendolyn Cason, who says, "Love the show and thrilled that there's something wholesome on TV to watch!"

The Facebook page also poses such uplifting questions for Faithful Fans as: "What was your favorite moment from either season one or two?"

Michelle Parrish answered, "Who can pick a favorite moment when every show rocked!" Rose Marie-Miranda even most simply added, "Everything!" Martha Sterling, Nicholas Limon, and Cindi Bond, however, unanimously said the nuns.

Jenny Lynn Shumate pleaded, "Loved it all, but the first and second seasons were too short. [Only nine episodes each.] Please don't be away too long for season three (but I heard it would not be back on till the year 2014). Please hurry back -- surely it cannot take that long to have more contestants and wonderful questions."

Past contestants included the brothers Daniel Wagner, Joshua Wagner, and Jesse Wagner of the Wagner Warriors, and Anointed Ink playing for Inner Cry Ministries, that help rehabilitate former gang members by covering gang tattoos with uplifting substitutes.

Still others were the Rocking Rabbis, Philip Weintraub, Jeffrey Abraham, and student rabbi Eve Eichenholtz from New York, and the Redeemed Rednecks from Georgia, the Men of Motor City, and Holy Rollers from California.

The only thing the contestants and fans all have in common is their love of God's Word: This can be seen on the fan page which also asks non-trivial questions such as, "What is your favorite part of having Faith?" and got answers like "Watching God do things in ways I never in my wildest dreams could have imagined." (Theresa Little) and "Knowing that He is there for me." (Pearl Dass)

Gary Robets shared, "I just sit back and watch how the Lord helps me deal with this cruel and unpredictable world." Ed Bundas said his favorite thing was, "Seeing God come through."

Judy Campbell testified, "My favorite part is where Jesus stands next to me through the difficult times in my life. My dad died, three months later, my husband died, and two years later my fourteen-year-old grandson died. Without faith I would not have made it."

Others quoted Scripture. "Knowing whatever happens, Abba Father has me covered!" (Jeremiah 29:11, Sandy McCabe) "Just being able to leave everything in the hands of my Savior and know He will not allow me to go through more than I can bear as Paul tells us in Corinthians 10:13." (Joycelyn Winans)

Susan Ballard, Audrey Ann Casper, and Erica Stewart all simply said, "Peace."

[The show only lasted until 2014.]

Pope Francis Names New Saints And Blesseds (September 2013)

The approved canonizations of the beloved Popes John XXIII and John Paul II have been well publicized. Perhaps less well known, however, are the stories of the hundreds of saints Pope Francis has already canonized. He has already broken, almost doubled Pope Benedict XVI's canonization record.

In his book *Their First Two Thousand Years*, Ted Byfield retells the story of the Church, including the eight hundred men near Otranto, on Italy's "heel," who were told after a two-week siege to convert to Islam or die on August 14, 1480.

A tailor named Antonio Primaldi is said to have responded, "Now it is time for us to fight to save our souls for the Lord. And since he died on the cross for us, it is fitting that we should die for him."

His companions cheered. They were all led to the Hill of Minerva, later renamed the Hill of Martyrs. Primaldi was the first to be beheaded, but his headless body stood, "remaining stubbornly and astonishing upright on its feet. Not until all had been decapitated could the aghast executioners force Primaldi's corpse to lie prone." An Ottoman officer named Bersabei who witnessed their courageous faith and this miracle is said to have converted on the spot and been impaled for doing so. Thousands of others of the townspeople were sold into slavery.

St. Francis of Paula who had prophesied the capture of the city, however, had also prophesied its recapture. That happened the next year, after the sudden death of Sultan Mehmet "the Conqueror" under King Ferdinand's son Alfonso of Aragon. Francis was found to be incorrupt in 1562 as were those of the Otrantines.

These men naturally became the patron saints of the city of and whole archdiocese of Otranto. They have been credited, by delaying the invasion for that crucial two weeks, with saving "the Eternal City" from a similar fate to Constantinople.

The miracle necessary for their formal canonization involved the Poor Clare Sister Francesca Levote. She suffered from a serious form of cancer but was healed after a pilgrimage to pray before the martyrs' relics in Otranto, a few months before Pope John Paul II's visit in October, 1980, on the occasion of their five-hundredth anniversary.

At their canonization Pope Francis said, "As we venerate the martyrs of Otranto, let us ask God to sustain those many Christians who, in these times and in many parts of the world, right now, still suffer violence, and give them the courage and fidelity to respond to evil with good."

Pope Francis also canonized with them two contemporary women from Latin America. One was Laura of St. Catherine of Siena Montoya y Upegui (April 27, 1897 to June 24, 1963). She journeyed with five other women by horseback in 1914 into the forests of Columbia to be a teacher and spiritual guide to the indigenous people.

The other, Maria Guadalupe Garcia Zavala (May 26, 1874 to October 21, 1949), co-founded the Congregation of the Handmaids of St. Margaret Mary Alacoque and the Poor. They dedicated themselves to nursing the sick in Mexico, during the persecutions of the 1920s. Known as "Mother Lupita," she hid the Guadalajara archbishop in an eye clinic for more than a year.

Other Blesseds still in the process toward canonization under Pope Francis came from Brazil, Spain, Italy, Poland, and Switzerland. Men and women, clergy, religious, and laity, they lived in the Sixteenth through Twentieth centuries.

Bl. Francisca de Paula de Jesus Isabel (1810 to June 14, 1895), also known as Nhá Chica of Baependi, was a laywoman of the diocese of Campanha, Brazil. She dedicated herself to the Blessed Mother when her own mother died when she was 10. Although she never learned to read or write, she was noted for her heroic virtue. She built a church next to her house that became the Sanctuary of Our Lady de Conceicao.

Bl. Cristóbal López de Valladolid Orea (July 7, 1683 to July 21, 1690), known as "Fr. Christopher," was a hermit, a priest, and a member of the Third Order Regular of Saint Francis. He founded the Congregation of the Franciscan Hospitallers of Jesus the Nazarene in Córdoba, Spain. He died while tending to cholera victims there and miracles soon followed.

Bl. Luca Passi (Jan. 22, 1789 to April 18, 1866) was a priest and founder of the Institute of the Teaching Sisters and the Pious Society of Saint Dorothy most successfully in Frassinetti and Venezia, Italy. The second Italian, Bl. Luigi Novaese (July 29, 1914 to July 7, 1984), was the youngest of nine children and healed of tuberculosis at 17 by the prayers of Don Bosco and his boys. He dedicated the rest of his life to serving the sick and in 1962 Pope John XXIII appointed him to take care of religious assistance in hospitals in all Italy.

Bl. Odoardo Focherin (June 6, 1907 to December 12, 1944), the third blessed from Italy, was a father martyred for his association with Italian Catholic Action. He died at the Hersbruck concentration camp, Germany.

Bl. Zofia Czeska neé Maciejowska (1584 to April 4, 1650) became a childless widow at 23. In 1625 she founded the first school for girls in Poland and the teaching Congregation of the Virgins of the Presentation of the Blessed Virgin Mary.

The second Polish blessed, Bl. Malgorzata Lucia Szewczyk (c. 1828 to June 5, 1905), was born in the Ukraine, but founded the Congregation of the Daughters of the Sorrowful Mother of God or Seraphic Sisters in Poland. It now has outposts also in France, Sweden, the United States, and Italy as well.

Bl. Nicoló Rusca (April 20, 1956 to September 4, 1618) was a priest tortured and martyred in Thussis, Switzerland. A Vatican official responsible has also reported that for the sainthood cause of Archbishop Oscar Romero of El Salvador has been "unblocked" by Pope Francis.

[Edward Bartlett "Ted" Byfield's history of the Church, *The Christians: Their First Two Thousand Years*, is actually twelve volumes. He is also the president and chairman of SEARCH (The Society to Explore and Record Christian History).]

Film Touches Hearts (August 2013)

Catholic Underground described "Crescendo" as "a short, period film that celebrates the incredible potential of every single human life." Dr. Ted Baehr of Movieguide called it "a beautiful, powerful, transformational short movie that reveals an important deeper truth." Hannah Welch at the International Movie Database (imdb.com) wrote, "Wonderful film, truly a masterpiece. Was inspired by the acting. All those involved, kudos. Overall a great film. The adult actors were full of imagination and portrayed their characters with great skill and feeling. The child actors were joyful and inspiring to watch as they filled the screen with their sweet faces and awesome expressive portrayal of their characters. I would recommend seeing this when you are able as you will not be disappointed."

Based on her diary, it's the story of Maria Magdalena, pregnant by her abusive, alcoholic, and adulterous husband, a short story, told in just fifteen minutes. She tries to take her own life, but doesn't and so changes the world. The child she did not kill along with herself the baby named Lodewijk, now known to the world as Ludwig van Beethoven.

The film has won more than eleven international awards, including the Rochester International Film Festival's Best of fest award. It has, however, been attracting more national attention in the politically-divided United States, because Pattie Mallette is its executive producer.

Mallette is better known as the author of *Nowhere But Up: The Story of Justin Bieber's Mom*. Justin attracted the same controversial attention when he told Rolling Stone, "I really don't believe in abortion ... It's like killing a baby." In 2011, he donated proceeds from one of his songs to help save the Bethesda Center in Lonton, Ont., where his mother stayed while pregnant with him.

"I am involved with this project to tell my story and to encourage young women and to give them hope," Mallette explains, "not to make a controversial statement or to promote what I think other women should do."

"When I became pregnant," she says, "I knew for myself that I had to keep my baby and I want other women in the same situation to know that there is a place for them to go if they find themselves with nowhere to turn."

"I don't know where we would be without that [crisis pregnancy] center," Mallette says, adding, "I would hope that anyone, whether for or against abortion, would always want any young woman who may need a place to be cared for, loved, and helped, to have what she would need."

The other executive producer, Eduardo Verastegui, was the star in "Bella," produced by his own production company, Metanoia Films, and in "For Greater Glory."

The co-producer of the film, Jason Jones, was co-executive producer of "Bella." That film made ten million dollars at the box office and, more importantly, is credited with saving lives.

"Over five hundred eighty-one women chose life after seeing 'Bella,'" he notes, "and we know that 'Crescendo' will continue to inspire a global movement that transcends time and cultures to communicate the dignity and worth of the human being."

Jason is the founder of HERO (Human-Rights Education and Relief Organization), a non-profit for promoting human dignity outside of film. In 2009, despite the government's warning of unsafe travel, he visited Darfur distributing two million dollars in food, medicine, and other aid.

As the president and founder of Movie to Movement, he headed the grassroots campaign for the political documentary "2016: Obama's America." Movie to Movement teamed up with Heartbeat International, the world's largest network of pregnancy help ministries, to raise money for local CPCs through private and public showings and the sale of DVDs at cpcmovie.com. For every DVD bought they will donate a copy to a Crisis Pregnancy Center.

Peggy Hartshom, Heartbeat International's president, says, "This film is riveting and its powerful and life affirming finale will stay in your heart. What a unique, enjoyable, and beautiful way to raise a much needed million dollars to save and change lives in our pregnancy help centers, clinics, and housing ministries!"

"This film serves our cause to defend life," explained Jones, whose personal story has propelled him to work in support of crisis pregnancy centers all over the world.

Jones' own story is that when he was seventeen, his pregnant girlfriend's father pressured her to have an abortion at six months. "Crescendo" is dedicated to Jessica Jones, their aborted baby, who would now have been twenty-three years old.

Miss USA 1996, Ali Ladry, played in both "Bella" and "Crescendo." More recently she gave birth to her and her husband Alejandro Monteverde's third child.

Casey Vroman of Students for Life of America saw the film at the Los Angeles Regional Leadership Summit. "I was so impressed with the way the team brought the injustice of our day to a time and place many of us are removed from. It left me feeling more passionate to fight the injustice than before."

Dr. Alveda King of Priests for Life said, "'Crescendo' touches the heart and soul of life's bittersweet song with a powerful promise that if the notes are left in God's hand, He will create a masterpiece."

[Mallette is also was executive director of "To Write Love on Her Arm" about Renee Yohe and the founding of the organization of the same name started by Jamie Tworkowski on DVD in 2015.]

Abortion Survivors Tell Their Stories (July 2013)

Melissa Ohden recognized the need for both support for and among abortion survivors, and for better information about abortion survivors to the public and so created The Abortion Survivor Network. It is just one of the many ways that abortion survivors are now telling their side of the story.

"The reality is that abortion doesn't just impact a woman's life," she says. "It ends a child's life and it forever changes the lives of everyone it touches, including women, men, extended family members, friends, and our communities."

Melissa's mother was a nineteen-year-old college student when she underwent a saline infusion abortion in 1977. After she survived, the doctor estimated her at thirty-one weeks gestation. She was adopted, but didn't learn she was an abortion survivor until fourteen. She is the subject of the award-winning documentary, "A Voice for Life".

Sarah Smith's mother, Betty, tried to abort her in Los Angeles in 1970. At the time, Betty did not know she was pregnant with twins. Sarah's twin brother, Andrew, was aborted, but weeks later she felt Sarah's kick. She went back to the doctor and told him she was still pregnant, that she had made a big mistake and wanted to keep this second baby.

She did have to have leg casts from nine days and a body cast from six weeks and still requires corrective surgeries. For five years, however, mother and daughter have traveled the world speaking together about the pain and suffering caused by abortion.

Sarah says, "The protective hand of Almighty God saved my life. God's hand covered and hid me in her womb and protected me from the scalpel of death. Please share our story with others so the tragedy of abortion stops hurting babies and families. Everyone needs to know the truth about abortion. Thank you."

Dr. Imre Téglásy learned that he was an abortion survivor at 11. "My father told some relatives the story," he says, "and I just had a very sad feeling because at once I was able to see clearly why my relationship with my mother was so complicated."

He is now the president of Alpha Alliance for Life, Human Life International's affiliate in Hungary. His documentary "Central and Eastern Europe: A Return to Life" was broadcast on EWTN in January.

Gianna Jessen survived a saline abortion at seven months to be born the next day to Tina, her seventeen-year-old mother. Tina sought a saline abortion at seven months pregnant. Gianna was, however, severely injured by the abortion attempt, was diagnosed with cerebral palsy, but surpassed all expectations. Today she is able to run, dance, and walk, even take up rock climbing. In 1996, she testified before the Constitution Subcommittee of the House Judiciary Committee on the issue of abortion.

Tina Huffman found herself a pregnant, unwed seventeen-year-old from a broken, dysfunctional home in 1978. Her parents and her boyfriend's parents both adamantly insisted she had to abort

After feeling her "insides being pulled out" by the suction machine and two months of sickness, she learned from her own physician that the abortion had failed. Her daughter Heidi was born by C-section at twenty-eight weeks, surviving with minimal placenta and minimal amniotic fluid.

Clare Culwell's mother became pregnant at just thirteen. After the abortion she too found she had been pregnant with twins. Claire was adopted at birth by a loving, stable family. She now counsels at the Coalition for Life in Bryan College Station.

"If my life can touch just one person who has had an abortion or considering an abortion or adoption," Culwell says, "then I am fulfilling my purpose in the pro-life movement. I will not be silent because each mother and child are in the same place my biological mother, my twin, and I were in twenty-two years ago, and I am here to say there is hope and there are options!"

James Wilkins did not learn of his survival from abortion until after his mother died, having held in the secret for thirty years. He tells his story in his book *Survivor*, which he describes as exposing the struggle of two great powers, the father of abortion who is the literal Devil and the Father of life, the True God of love and Heaven.

Laura Tedder survived several abortion attempts before her birth in 1948 and was adopted by her aunt and uncle. At two she was diagnosed with retinoblastoma, a cancer of the eye, and her right eye was removed. She later survived a brain tumor.

"I'm a walking miracle," she says. "I'm lucky to be alive. God put me here for a reason. No matter how you get pregnant, it's a miracle baby. No matter what the circumstances, it's not the baby's fault. They were meant to live. Everyone needs a chance for life, you don't get many shots at it."

Sarah Brown was thirty-six weeks old when she was injected with poison in her brain three times. Yet two days later she was born with visible puncture wounds above her left eyebrow and at the base of her skull. She was adopted by Bill and Marykay Brown who wanted a "special-needs child."

At about five or six months Sarah suffered a stroke from which she never fully recovered. "She learned that if she held her breath the monitor would go off," Brown said. "We would jump out of bed and she would be grinning at us. That was how she got attention."

Sarah had progressive airway disease, and although blind, when she died at the age of five, her corneas were donated to other children to see. Marykay, however, speaks not only of Sarah's survival but also about the abortion of her own biological child when she was 19 and her own long road to healing.

"It has come full circle for me," Brown said. "I talk about what it's like to be post-abortive and about the forgiveness God gives and also about abortion from the child's point of view. I've watched Sarah change people's lives."

One-month-old Jacob would not be alive today if not for little Sarah Brown. Jacob's mother had scheduled an abortion, but then heard Sarah's remarkable story of having survived an abortion attempt. When she saw the precious little girl, instead of keeping the appointment, Jacob Alan's mother gave him the gift of life.

[Both the Network at theabortionsurvivors.com and Heartbeat International at heartbeatinternational.org continues to post testimonies, support and news.]

Saintly Army Chaplain Receives Medal Of Honor (June 2013)

Chaplain Emil Kapaun has been declared a Servant of God, the first step for formal canonization. He also recently was awarded the Medal of Honor, over 60 years after his death.

He has long been remembered by those who knew him however. Fr. Arthur Tonne wrote *Chaplain Kapaun: Patriot Priest of the Korean Conflict*. The "Crossroads" TV episode "The Good Thief" told of him in 1955. More recently his story has been retold in *The Miracle of Fr. Kapaun: Priest, Soldier, and Korean War Hero*, a book by Roy Wenzl and Travis Heying as well as an eight-part mini-series and DVD.

"He has left us a stirring example of devotion to duty," Tonne wrote. "He has passed on to us a spirit of tolerance and understanding. He has given us a share of dauntless bravery -- of body and soul. He has transmitted to every one of us a new appreciation of America, and a keener, more realistic understanding of our country's greatest enemy -- godlessness, now stalking the world in the form of communism. He has bequeathed a picture of Christ-like life."

Kapaun became a chaplain in 1943 at Herington Army Airfield, Kansas. When the Korean War broke out, he served there on the Pusan perimeter. He was constantly on the move northward. His main complaint was lack of sleep for several weeks at a time.

Although a retreat had been ordered, the "Padre" showed heroic virtue by staying behind to tend the wounded and comfort the dying, and continuing to make his rounds even as hand-to-hand combat ensued. He convinced an injured Chinese officer to negotiate the safe surrender of American forces and then, when he saw a Chinese soldier about to execute a wounded GI, Kapaun calmly pushed aside the enemy and carried the U.S. soldier away.

He carried Sgt. Herbert Miller for four miles as the North Koreans marched the POWs 87 miles to Pyoktong prison camp. He picked up soldiers who stumbled and encouraged those who had almost given up to keep walking, for fear that they would be shot.

At the awards ceremony, President Obama said, "This is the valor we honor today, an American soldier who didn't fire a gun, but who wielded the mightiest weapon of all: a love for his brothers so pure that he is willing to die so that they might live."

"Without him, a lot of fellows would have never made it," Miller says. At the prison camp, in freezing temperatures, Kapaun offered fellow prisoners his own clothes. He dug latrines, snuck past guards to forage in the fields for extra food, convinced the POWs to share, pounded metal into pots to catch water to wash their clothes, and cleansed their wounds. He even led prisoners in acts of defiance and smuggled dysentery drugs to the doctor, Sidney Esensten.

Kapaun led night prayer, saying the rosary and administering sacraments, and even led Easter services. The Communist guards naturally ridiculed his devotion to the Savior. They took his clothes and made him stand in the freezing cold for hours. Yet, he never lost his faith. If anything, it only grew stronger.

"That faith, that they might be delivered from evil, that they could make it home, was perhaps the greatest gift to those men," Obama said. "That even amidst such hardship and despair, there could be home ... that even in such hell, there could be a touch of the divine," Obama said. "He offered three simple words· 'God bless you.' ... He could just for a moment, turn a mud hut into a cathedral."

He gave encouragement also in words, saying, "Start out with some little thing. Try to say your prayers with more devotion. Try to attend at Mass with greater devotion. Try to talk about the good things of others rather than talking about their faults. Try to treat others more kindly. Try to tell the truth always."

His "trying" eventually got him sent to what his comrades called a "death house" when he fell ill. There he died from a blood clot in his leg, dysentery, and pneumonia and was buried in a mass grave near the Yalu River.

The miracles submitted for the chaplain's cause for canonization include that of a 20-year-old Chase Kear. He survived a severe head injury last year, because his family petitioned Fr. Emil Kapaun to intercede. As a member of the Hutchison Community College track team, Kear fell on his head during pole vaulting practice in October 2008, and nearly died.

Fr. John Hotze, judical vicar of Wichita, has already spent eight years investigating the proposed sainthood of Kapaun. He is being considered for possible designation as a martyr, as were Maximilian Kolbe and Edith Stein, WWII?death camp prisoners.

In 2011, Nick Dellasega collapsed at a Get Busy Living 5K race in Pittsburg, KS. He seemed to be dead at the scene, but survived. His childhood friend, EMT Micah Ehling, said, "I know what a face looks like when the soul leaves the body and that's what Nick looked like." Other witnesses attribute Dellasega's survival to the prayers of Dellasega's cousin, Johah, to Kapaun. "Coincidentally" Dylan Meier, in whose memory the 5K was being held, planned to teach English in Korea at the time of his death.

The guild formed for the promotion of his cause encourages the Father Kapaun prayer: "Fr. Emil Kapaun gave glory to God by following his call to the priesthood and thus serving the people of Kansas and those in the military. Father Kapaun, I ask your intercession not only for these needs which I mention now ... but that I too may follow your example of service to God and my neighbor. For the gifts of courage in battle and perseverance of faith, we give you thanks, O Lord." Continue with one Our Father, one Hail Mary, and one Glory Be.

[The cause for the beatification of Fr. Kapaun continues.]

Media Campaign Focuses On Bible (May 2013)

"The Bible" is not just The Good Book any more. This year it has come to mean the media campaign by Mark Burnett and his wife Roma Downey. Burnett is best known for the popular shows "Survivor" and "The Celebrity Apprentice," and Downey for her role in "Touched by an Angel."

Downey suggested the idea to her husband over a cup of tea nearly four years ago, after they watched the classic "Ten Commandments," and it grew and grew. It now includes not only a mini-series on the History Channel, but a game on Facebook, on-line communities, companion study guides, books, DVDs, and even a Bible app.

"The most-read book of all time is the most watched TV event of our time!" Burnett said. "Roma and I can't thank the show's millions of fans enough for taking this passion project of ours and making it the breakout hit of the year."

Bishop Michael Sheridan, Diocese of Colorado Springs, CO, said, "What I saw impressed me a great deal. It's quite a challenge to get hold of both the Old and New Testaments in only 10 hours of film, but Mark and Roma did a fantastic job. May God bless them, and may many souls be led to Christ by their viewing 'The Bible.' "

Tom Peterson, of Catholics Come Home, was also favorable, saying, "We were extremely impressed by the production quality of Mark and Roma's mini-series 'The Bible,' and thankful for their personal testimonies and commitment to spreading the good news of Jesus to the world."

"We just wanted to breathe a little fresh visual life into the sacred text we both love," Downey explains. "The response has been more than we could have hoped for. The Bible says we love God, because He first loved us; the ratings show just how deeply people love God, and we pray the series makes clear just how deeply God loves us."

"Jesus is coming!" she said. "He's the 'leading man' of the Bible's grand story of God's love for us." He came back on the first Easter and has come back for many this Easter.

Timing the ending of the series with Jesus' passion and resurrection on Easter was certainly part of their strategy. There was, however, much more to the evangelical media blitz.

"We brought experts in once the scripts were created to take a look at the scripts to make sure we were accurate and true to the Bible," she says, "but obviously we're making a movie, and so we breathed creative expansion into that."

"The Bible" project advisers included: Leith Anderson (National Association of Evangelicals), Andrew Benton (Pepperdine University), Jim Daly (Focus on the Family), Paul Eshleman (Campus Crusade for Christ), Craig Groeschel (Life Church), Bobby Gruenewald (You Version Bible), Tom Peterson (Catholics Come Home), Sam Rodriguez (National Hispanic Christian Leadership Conference), Denny Rydberg (Young Life), Geoff Tunnicliffe (World Evangelical Alliance), George Wood (Assemblies of God), and Frank Wright (National Religious Broadcasters).

The mini-series has many supporters, but also some critics. "The characters are just as one-dimensional as the ones described in a Sunday school fable, only angrier," said *Businessweek*.

Downey countered such criticism by explaining Diogo Morgado's Jesus as "both tough and tender, exactly as Jesus is depicted in the Bible. Diogo is both the Lion and the Lamb, strong when it's called for and sensitive when it's called for."

The Portuguese actor himself explained, "When you grow up in a religious country, you take it for granted. [Playing Jesus] was a really personal journey. From now on I'm going to pay even more attention to stuff that will show even more of the human condition."

He also noted that following after "The Passion of the Christ," they did not want to repeat what had been done so well in that film. They tried to tell the larger story, focused on portraying Jesus' suffering through Mary's interior suffering.

Talking about the series, Downey also denied the mistaken idea that the actor playing Satan was cast to took like President Obama. Talking about the book, the Bible, she says, "It's something everybody should know. What God reveals about Himself through the Bible is our pathway to truly knowing Him."

"Light the Way: The Bible" is the associated hidden-object adventure game. Many are playing the game as they watch the mini-series. With the prophet Daniel as their guide, players follow Abraham, Moses, David, and others in their faith journeys. Although it takes a bit of patience to upload the images and music, they are worth it.

Brenda Angel Rose says, "I love this game." Barbara Starr Scott commented, "I love Jesus!!!" Hundred of others have "liked" the game with comments like "I [heart] Jesus. Share if you agree God is good," or "My heart belongs to Jesus," or "I want all my Facebook friends to know I love Jesus."

Both the game and the miniseries websites have grown into on-line communities. Many fans share favorite Bible quotes or personal praises. Jude Jorge, winner of the on-line contest, posted, "Watching 'The Bible' going into Holy Week has made me fall in love with Jesus all over again. I'm sure others will be inspired to know more about Him after seeing this." Still others have been prompted to ask and answer basic questions about Easter, Mary, Bible authority, etc.

There are also associated books. *A Story of God and All of Us; Reflections: 100 Daily Inspirations* includes a Bible verse, a personal reading, and a short prayer accompanied again by images from the mini-series. An abridged Young Readers edition is for children eight and up and a little 8-page pamphlet *Easter: an Epic Story of Love* is for mass distribution.

Regarding the Bible app by YouVersion, Downey and Burnet say, "We are thrilled to provide millions of people with an easy way to explore this sacred text." It does so with four hundred translations in two hundred languages.

[Roma Downey has also been the executive producer of "Women of the Bible", "Little Boy", "A. D. The Bible Continues", "Answered Prayers" series, "Ben-Hur" and the yet to be released series "Faithkeepers".]

Don't Forget God (March 2013)

In *Miracles in American History,* Bill Federer notes that he might very well say the same to Americans in this Lent, 2013. "It's in time of crisis," he says in the book and the DVD, "that we need to follow our leaders in the past and turn to the God our Creator that we acknowledge in our Declaration of Independence."

"It behooves us then," he quotes Lincoln, "to humble ourselves before the offended Power; to confess our national sins and to pray for cleansing and forgiveness." Within days after he prayed, General Stonewall Jackson had died, shot by his own soldiers and the tide of the war turned.

Mabel Kunkel notes in *Abraham Lincoln: Unforgettable American*, that on July 4, 1861, he prayed with Congress, "Having thus chosen our course, without guile, and with pure purpose, let us renew our trust in God."

It was not only during times of war that the country has prayed. When cholera threatened the country in 1849, President Zachery Taylor led prayer and the epidemic ended. Nixon encouraged the country to unite in prayer when *Apollo 13* was falling to Earth in 1970 and they returned safely.

In *Seven Miracles that Saved America*, Chris and Ted Stewart include the unlikely discovery of America by Christopher Columbus, the survival of the Jamestown colonists, the Constitution, and the breaking of the so-called curse of Tippecanoe with the preservation of Ronald Reagan's life. John Ferling's book, *Almost A Miracle: The American Victory in the War of Independence*, gets its title from Washington's calling America's providential survival, like that of the Jewish people, "little short of a standing miracle."

James Madison wrote, "Had the people, during the Revolution, had a suspicion of any attempt to war against Christianity, that Revolution would have been strangled in its cradle."

Before the American colonies became the United States, the country was founded on prayer from the first meeting of the Continental Congress. In 1746, colonial governor William Shirley's declared a fast when the British fleet threatened. Rev. Thomas Prince of Boston prayed, "Send Thy tempest, Lord, upon the water ... scatter the ships of our tormentors." The hurricane that came destroyed d'Anvilles' seventy-three ships and killed two thousand of the enemy.

During the French-Indian war, Col. George Washington wrote that Providence had saved him. Although he had four bullets passed through his coat and two horses were shot out from under him, he was not harmed. The Indian's medicine man call him "not born to be killed by a bullet."

In 1775 Gov. Jonathan Trumbull prayed, "make the land a mountain of holiness and habitation of righteousness forever." At the battle of Bunker Hill, where Americans were outnumbered two-to-one, the British brought the wrong sized cannonballs.

Washington's comment then was, "I shall rely, therefore, confidently on the Providence which has heretofore preserved and been bountiful to me."

After Henry Know brought forty-two cannons from Ticongaroga in 1776, Washington declared a fast day, asking Americans "to pay all the reverence and attention on that day to the sacred duties to the Lord of hosts for His mercies already received and for those blessings which our holiness and uprightness of life can alone encourage us to hope through His mercy obtain."

Yale president Ezra Stiles asked the rectorial question, "Who but a Washington, inspired by Heaven, could have conceived the surprise move upon the enemy at Princeton or that Christmas Eve when Washington and his army crossed the Delaware." Then he concluded, "The United States are under a peculiar obligation to become a holy people unto the Lord our God."

After the victory of Valley Forge, Washington wrote, "I most devoutly congratulate my country, and every well-wisher to the cause on this signal stroke of Providence." Elsewhere he added, "The Hand of Providence has been so conspicuous in all this -- the course of the war -- that he must be worse than an infidel that lacks faith, and more wicked that has not gratitude to acknowledge his obligation; but it shall be time enough for me to turn preacher when my present appointment ceases."

Speaking of Benedict Arnold's plot to betray the American forces at Annapolis, John André Stiles wrote, "The Providential train of circumstances which led to its discovery affords the most convincing proof that the liberties of America are the object of divine protection."

After the battle of Cowpen in 1781, in which three rivers flooding thwarted the pursuing British army, Washington wrote, "We have ... abundant reason to thank Providence for its many favorable interposition in our behalf. It has at times been my only dependence, for all other resources seemed to have failed us."

Washington was called out of retirement when the War of 1812 broke out. The city named after him was attacked, the White House, Capital building, and Library of Congress was burned. The residents prayed and tornadoes put out the fires and saved the city named for him.

William J. Federer has also written: *Backfired: A Nation Born for Religious Tolerance No Longer Tolerates Religion, St. Patrick,* and *The Ten Commandments and Their Influence on American Law.* Chris Stewart's also wrote *Redefining Joy in the Last Days and Ted Daniel* and *Solving the Exodus Mystery,*]

Economic Crisis Needs Creative Solutions (February 2013)

Many voices are agreeing with Pope Benedict XVI's message for this year's World Day of Peace, though perhaps without realizing it. In "Blessed Are The Peacemakers" the pope said, among other important things, "In order to emerge from the present financial and economic crisis -- which has engendered ever greater inequalities -- we need people, groups, and institutions which will promote life by fostering human creativity, in order to draw from the crisis itself an opportunity for discernment and for a new economic model."

In the introduction to his book, *Rediscovering Values,* Jim Wallis, editor-in-chief of Sojourners, credits the Pope. Benedict warned, as had other popes before him, "Once profit becomes the exclusive goal, if it is produced by improper means and without the common good as its ultimate end, it risks destroying wealth and creating poverty." (*Caritas in Veritate*)

He also quotes Gandhi's social sins, politics without principles, commerce without morality, pleasure without conscience, knowledge without character, science without humanity, worship without sacrifice, but particularly focuses on wealth without work. He also quotes Franklin Delano Roosevelt quoting the Bible, "When there is no vision the people perish." Many are now being involuntarily humbled, forced to make sacrifices, giving up homes and jobs.

Willis put the current situation in perspective with statistics. The lowest five percent of America's a hundred eighty-one million credit card holders account for twenty percent of the debt, much of it college debt. In 1800 eighty-five percent of Americans were "extremely poor," by 2007 just the opposite was true. So, as he points out, now eight-five percent are afraid of becoming poor.

"The current crisis was created by decades of social deregulation," he says, "... which ultimately compromises not only the common good, but [corporations' and banks'] own good in the long term." The crisis of shortsightedness must be countered by foresightedness, social services by social change.

"The opportunity this crisis offers now is the chance to rethink the important question of work." He recommends simplifying, buying less, buying locally, downsizing. He encourages sharing or doing without a car. This is much the same as the pope's, "True and lasting success is attained through the gift of ourselves, our intellectual abilities, and our entrepreneurial skills."

Mike Gerson, author of *Heroic Conservatism*, says, "One does not need to agree with Jim Wallis on everything to find Rediscovering Values insightful and timely."

Commenting on this "conservatism elevated by a radical concern for human rights and dignity," Wallis refers to what he calls New Old Values, Catholic social teaching. "While it affirms the principle of limited government -- asserting the existence of a world of families, congregations, and community institutions where government should rarely tread -- it also asserts that the justice of society is measured by its treatment of the helpless and poor. And this creates a positive obligation to order society in a way that protects and benefits the powerless and suffering."

Michael J. Sandel, professor of government at Harvard, says about *Rediscovering Values*, "Jim Wallis argues persuasively that the financial crisis is also a moral crisis ... and how repairing the economy requires a moral awakening and a new commitment to the common good."

His book, *What Money Can't Buy: The Moral Limits of Markets*, makes a similar point. "The problem with being able to buy and sell increasing numbers of things," he says, "is that we devalue the things we are buying and selling."

He notes many outrageous examples. A single mother in Utah got ten thousand dollars for tattooing a casino ad on her forehead. Others sell their bodies as human guinea pigs for pharmaceutical companies for up to seventy-five hundred dollars. Lobbyists pay others to stand in line for a congressional hearing twenty dollars an hour. School children are being paid two dollars for reading a book.

As he puts it, "It's hard to imagine a reasoned public debate about such controversial moral questions as the right way to value procreation, children, education, health, the environment, citizenship, and other goods. I believe such a debate is possible, but only if we are willing to broaden the terms of our public discourse and grapple more explicitly with competing notions of the good life."

His "Justice" course has become a PBS series and a book. They "try to model what public discourse would be like if it were morally ambitious than it is," Mr. Sandel said. "The title is 'Justice,' but in a way its subject is citizenship."

Rich Stearns, author of *The Hole in Our Gospel*, says Wallis "argues that the world can change when people of good faith make different choices and act collectively."

That is the same message he tells in his own book, the story of how an encounter with the poor in Kenya changed his life. He realized that the gospel was not "just me and Jesus" but was always meant to be a world changing social revolution. He is now president of World Vision.

Reader Scot McKnight called the book "a return to the themes and to the fire of his classical period of fighting for American Christians to cut back and help the poor and to take stock of how we live." Todd Bartholomew called it simply "challenging, yet also invigorating."

[Sandel has written *The Case against Perfection: Ethics in the Age of Genetic Engineering*. Sterns also wrote *He Walks Among Us* and *Unfinished*.]

Film Captures Fight For Religious Freedom (January 2013)

Who are you if you don't stand up for what you believe? There is no greater glory than to give your life for Christ." That question and its answer, spoken by Father Christopher, gives the film, "Cristeros," now on DVD, its English title, "For Greater Glory."

It begins with Fr. Christopher (played by Peter O'Toole) joining what would become the ninety thousand killed in the three-year war against religious freedom in Mexico in the late 1920s. He inspired the future martyr, fourteen-year-old Jose Luis Sanches del Rio (played by Mauricio Kuri), who in turn inspired General Corostieta and many others.

In three years of the Marxist Calles's presidency he reduced the total priestly population to some two hundred fifty among Mexico's fifteen million Catholics. Masses and Bibles were outlawed. After a boycott failed it turned to an armed people's rebellion.

Jack Kenny relates the situation then to ours now. "Catholics in the United States today, for example, face the prospect of either denying a tenet of their faith, namely to not practice or promote artificial contraception, or suffer sanctions from the federal government," he wrote.

"Your heart naturally goes out to the youngster, already beaten and tortured, who is told he can save his life by reciting some oath that ended with, "Long live the federal government." The youngster swallowed hard, shouted, "Viva Cristo Rey!" ("Long Live Christ the King!), and chose death.

Pablo Barroso said the timing for its early release in Mexico was providentially perfect. "Who would have thought back then that the pope would be going to Mexico, much less to Cubilete, home to the national Cristo Rey monument and patron of the Cristero War heroes, to say his first Mass there. This really came from Heaven."

Director Dean Wright shares similar experiences. "Something followed us the whole way, I'm telling you. We finished on schedule, to the day. We left this incredible place where the camp was; the next day, the hurricane went through. We were in Cuetzalan for two and one half weeks; the day after we left, the road collapsed and there was no way in or out."

If you watch or re-watch the film we shot, he says, "you'll see visual motifs that are repeated over and over again for specific reasons as specific times. Camera work is done that way too; it's symbolic. When we're on the Federalese or President Calles, it's solid, it's firm. We don't move; we're very slow. It's like a rock that's hard to push against.

"When we're with the Cristeros, it's free-flowing; it's pulling you into the war. You feel the kinetic energy that' happening there.

Wright shared how he met Gorostieta's daughter and relatives of Anacleto. "I traveled the country and saw -- in the middle of nowhere," he says, "a church with a shrine, with a little picture and some flowers in remembrance of the priest who wouldn't leave and was shot."

Eduardo Verastegui agreed to do the part of Anacleto Gonzalez Flores, because it required only about two weeks, since he was working on another movie at the time. The martyr's story however "inspired me," he says, "and touched my heart and made me want to live like them. That's what I tried to do, every day in my work, to try and imitate these Mexican heroes who have their very lives to defend their faith."

"Hopefully, many people will watch it, see it, and take the video home. On September 11, it's going to come in a combo packages where you are going to see scenes which weren't in the movie, there will be a documentary which is going to show you more of the history of Mexico in the 1920's so you can get the whole picture."

Jim Cichochi wrote that "This movie will be successful, not by the amount of dollars it makes, but by the number of people who will return to their faith. There are going to be future wars concerning our faith. I only hope that we can be half as brave and courageous as the Cristeros. Viva Cristo Rey!"

Like Kenny and others he sees the relevance of this historical film to our time. "Your right to practice your religion within your own institutions is regarded as an offense against the nation-state in America of 2012, as in England in the Sixteenth century or Mexico in the 1920s."

He does note that the film does not come out of Hollywood, but "has the advantage of being the work of Mexican producer Pablo José Barroso's Dos Corazones Films."

Edie J. Adler says, "Take my Jewish word: 'For Greater Glory' is a must-see, regardless of religious affiliation or non affiliation." It "is an important reminder of what could happen when a few godless are allowed to impose their views, all in the name of 'tolerance.' Religion is not the problem; fanatics on either side are."

Leticia Velasquez at CatholicMom.com advised, "Do not miss this remarkable salute to the little known heroes of the Cristeros rebellion. I give 'For Greater Glory' my highest recommendation." Although she notes that it is, like "The Passion of the Christ" rated R for its violence, she says, it is "suitable for ages thirteen and up." Like el Gibson's "The Passion," the screen violence is only a hint at what the real violence actually was.

As Verastegu explains, "the reason they did that was to make it more watchable for the people who are more sensitive to violence. They wanted to reach them too, and they wanted to bring the volume a little bit down so you can still see the essence of the film, and the message and the heroes."

The Mormons' *Meridan Magazine*, which also does not usually review R films, wrote "some characters who matter to the viewers don't end up with happily ever after stories. Yet the film is a powerful portrayal of the human heart and how tyranny seeks to trample religion. More important, it portrays characters who rise above themselves for a noble reason."

[Books on the Mexican persecutions include: *Blessed José* by Fr. Kevin William McKenzie, *For Greater Glory* by Ruben Quezada, *La Cristiado* and *The Cristero Rebellion* by Jean Meyer, *Mexican Martyrdom* by Wilfred Parsons, *Mexican Exodus* by Julia G. Young, *The Holy War in Los Altos* by Jim Tuck.]

Character Is Destiny (December 2012)

Character is Destiny is full of inspiring stories. Some of them may already be familiar to Catholics, that of saints, Thomas More, Joan of Arc, Maximilian Kolbe, or Mother Teresa. Some of those collected by authors John McCain and Mark Salter, however, might be less familiar. All are inspiring. Those on Faith, Cooperation, Courtesy, and Excellence, however, demonstrate the book's subtitle, "inspiring stories every young person should know and every adult should remember."

Under the heading "Faith" McCain tells of "the enemy who helped me understand the power of my faith." "This is war's greatest tragedy, but no matter how just or necessary your cause, a part of you must become less human to serve it on a battlefield."

To keep his human dignity McCain had to keep faith in his fellow POWs that some would survive to tell their story. They had to keep faith that America would do all it could to bring them back. They had to keep faith in "a God Whose love for [them] was ever present."

One Christmas when he was tied up in solitary, one of the guards quietly came in and loosened his ropes during the night, retying them in the morning. It was not until another Christmas came that he learned the reason, though he might have suspected. Then the guard made the sign of the cross in the dirt before rubbing it out.

"I have never forgotten him," McCain writes, "or the kindness he showed me as a testament to the faith we shared."

Under "Cooperation" they tell of John Wooden's character that led to his success as a coach. After World War II he was a basketball coach at Indiana State. He chose not to play in a national tournament because they would allow one of his players to play, an African-American. At UCLA his teams won eighty-eight consecutive games and ten championships.

Kareem Abdul-Jabbar says, "Coach taught us self-discipline, and he was always his own best example."

"[Basketball] is such a team sport. It's a beautiful game when it's played as a team." Wooden explains, "I tried to explain to my players that every person has a role and every role is important."

Under "Hopefulness" the authors tell of Puritan John Winthrop's journey to America. He hoped to find a better life there than in England with the Massachusetts Bay Company. He was selected its governor for "no other member of the company was considered a more just, wiser, more compassionate, or upright man."

Just three weeks after arriving at Salem, his son Henry drowned. Two hundred settlers returned to England when winter came.

The next year his wife Margaret came to him at what would become Boston, having lost two more of their children since he'd left, including the daughter he'd never seen. After sixteen years Margaret too died, but he remarried and had a son before he died.

The life inspiring the virtue of "Courtesy" is that of Aung San Suu Kyi. The authors explain, "In Burma, courtesy is a rebellious gesture to a ruling elite that has tried to terrorize such refined kindness from their culture."

Suu, as she prefers to be called, returned to Burma from Oxford, because Burma needed her, the daughter of Gen. Aung San, Burma's greatest hero. She ran, won against the military regime, and then got imprisoned.

She has shown courtesy fearlessly for many years in prison or house arrest, because, as she said in her Peace Prize letter, "It is not power that corrupts, but fear. Fear of losing power corrupts those who wield it, and fear of the scourge of power corrupts those who are subject to it."

The story of "the Black Gazelle," by Wilma Rudolph, comes under the title "Excellence." She was the twentieth child of railroad porter Eddie and Blanche Rudolph, born two months premature. She contracted measles, mumps, chicken pox, whooping cough, scarlet fever, and pneumonia by the age of five, when she got polio.

"The doctors told me I would never walk," she wrote, "but my mother told me I would, so I believed my mother."

By seven she could go to school with leg brace and crutches. She walked in the church without them just before her tenth birthday. At sixteen, she won a bronze in a four-hundred-meter relay in Melbourne and made being the fastest woman in the world her goal.

In the Rome Olympics nineteen-year-old Cassius Clay, the future Mohammed Ali, won gold in boxing. Rudolph won three. Back in Claryville, she won again when she forced the town to let other blacks to parade and awards ceremony.

Relics Shaped History (November 2012)

In *Holy Bones, Holy Dust: How Relics Shaped the History of Medieval Europe*, Charles Freeman takes the reader not only back in world history while reaching toward the otherworldly. He relates the saints and their relics to iconoclasts and reformers, peasants and kings, East and West, Romans and barbarians, witches and witch hunters, believers and non-believers.

Freeman is a historical consultant to the prestigious Blue Guides series and the author of numerous books, including the bestseller *The Closing of the Western Mind* and, most recently, *A New History of Early Christianity*.

For believers in the resurrection of the body and the communion of saints, they can link the natural and the supernatural, life, death, and the afterlife. Body parts and items like clothes that the saints had touched were connected to God Who worked and still works miracles through the saint.

Reader Michael McGreevy asks, "Is this a book for today's citizens of a secular society?" and answers, "I believe it is." He quotes Freeman, "A modern mind can become irritated with the belief in so many stories of resurrections, healings, and rescuing for which there is no 'scientific' explanation. Yet if the supernatural is treated as a 'real' world, on a different level, its events, or lack of them, can be accepted as easily as they were in the natural world we can see or touch."

Cynthia Hahn in *Catholic Historical Review* said, "Generally there are big themes -- politics, religion, conflict, and resolution -- but there also are many telling anecdotes and a sense of the personal and the tougheningly human." Andrew Butterfield at The New Republic agrees, saying "Freeman ... overflows with countless bizarre and fascinating deeds." Anastasia Fitzgerald-Beaumont adds, "A lot of [the book] is dryly amusing, the obvious fraud which must have been obvious even at the time, but Freeman tells his story without condescension."

Thomas McGonigle, in *ABC of Reading*, praises it as "a model for how history is to be written." Catholic News Service calls it "for anyone curious about [relics'] long history, *Holy Bones, Holy Dust* is essential reading."

Freeman's story begins long before the Middle Ages, with the pious legends of the early martyrs. Pionius, for example, was said to have rejuvenated as he was burned alive in 250, "like gold purified in fire." As the Church turned Arian, disbelieving in Christ's divinity, Jerome preached on how both celibacy and relics both relate to the holiness, otherworldliness of the saints.

Augustine opposed the excesses of the relics cult. He had a change of heart, however, after a dream of Gamaliel led the priest Lucian to Stephen's body in Jerusalem. By 418 even Augustine could not deny the miracles attributed to Stephen's "holy dust," though he gave the credit to the faith of believers. For more than a thousand years relics have shaped our history and still do.

Alleged relics began to be collected in Constantinople and Rome, like Christ's Manger or Blood. Other cities became competitive for prestige and profit. From England came stories of healings by the church buttress where Cuthbert died in 635. When Oswald of Northumbria was beheaded fighting pagans in 642, his arm was cut off, not as a war trophy, but as a relic.

The story of a white arc appearing over Wilfred's tomb prompted pilgrimages there. On the other hand, more well documented miracles continued as well. Nine years after she died Etheldreda was found incorrupt. Her doctor verified the jaw wound she died with was only a scar.

By the ninth century relics were used to stop wars in the Peace of God movement or as peace offerings. The Crusades flooded Europe with relics and their miraculous and incredible stories from the Holy Land and Constantinople. By the Twelfth century *The Life and Passion of St. William the Martyr of Norwich* popularized local "saints" and in the Thirteenth *The Golden Legend* popularized lives of other saints. Thirteen hundred was a record year for pilgrimages and in 1350 over a hundred of pilgrims were crush.

In the Sixteenth Martin Luther's *On the Slavery of the Will* rather orthodoxically calls love of neighbor greater than pilgrimages to any shrine. Others tried to teach of the primacy of the Eucharist. Henry VIII, however, looted Swithbert's and Thomas Becket shrines and by 1588 Diego of Alcalá was the first saint canonized in sixty-five years.

Perhaps most interestingly Freeman refers to *On Incantations* which proposed that interest in relics undergoes cycles. In 1520 the author noted the beginning of a trough in faith that seems to continue to our new millennium.

Aldo Matteucci says, "He writes with a sure, yet light and entertaining hand -- and through his words the power of true faith shimmers anew."

"It is fitting," he continues, "that the book end with the Council of Trent -- after Vatican I the most important Council of modernity -- where theology and mysticism found a new and rigorous synthesis, and the Church's new liturgy conflated all previous rites into a structured whole."

[Freeman also wrote *A. D. 381* and Cynthia Hahn *Portrayed on the Heart, Strange Beauty* and *The Reliquary Effect*.]

Heroes Teach Us To Live (October 2012)

Do you remember the names Blunk, Brooks, Larimer, McQuinn, or Teves? Some commenting on the Aurora, Colorado, movie theater shootings bemoaned that there are too many villains and too few heroes. Some people believe that it is rather that the heroes, the self-sacrificing first responders, are not as long remembered or as well as they ought to be.

Colorado Governor John Hickenlooper noted that the Aurora shooting prompted "many acts of heroism that can't even be described in a bright enough light to do the heroes justice." William Bennett of CNN generalized, "Good triumphs over evil, not just in movies, but also in reality." Even if we might have forgotten the first responders who were there at 9/11 or in more recent wild fires, we ought not soon forget their self-sacrifice.

Russell Simmons said, "These are the names that we must remember and carry with us as a source of inspiration." Kathee Alexander McCarl added, "We should be hearing the names of these men over and over and over again in the news, praising their heroic deeds and giving them the honor they deserve. Matt McQuinn, Alex Teves, Jon Blunk, and John Larimer should be the names we remember, not the name of an evil madman."

Jonathan Blunk shielded Jansen Young with his body. He had served five years in the Navy and planned to become a SEAL. He went to the theater with three other sailors from nearby Buckley Air Force Base.

"Jon just took a bullet for me," Young said. "He knew and threw me on the ground, and was like, 'We have to get down and stay down.' "

"He wanted the kids to look up to him," Blunk's wife, Chantel, back in Reno, said. "He always said, if he was ever going to die, he wanted to die as a hero."

Anna Soull shared about Jarrell Brooks who died protecting a woman whose boyfriend had fled. "If that wasn't what a hero is, I don't know what one is," was Gagnez Le Jeu's comment.

U. S. Navy Petty Officer third Class John Larimer saved Julia Vojtsek at the cost of his own life. "John immediately and instinctively covered me," she told reporters, "and brought me to the ground in order to protect me from any danger. Moments later, John knowingly shielded me from a spray of gunshots. It was then I believe John was hit with a bullet that would have very possibly struck me. I feel very strongly that I was saved by John and his ultimate kindness."

Matthew McQuinn used his body to shield both his girlfriend Samantha Yowler and her brother, Nick. He took three bullets, while she took a bullet in the knee, and her brother was uninjured.

Alex Teves was a recent University of Denver Masters graduate. His girlfriend, Amanda Lindgren, told of his last heroism, "I was really, really confused at first about what was going on, so confused, but, it's like Alex didn't even hesitate, because I sat there for a minute, not knowing what was going on and he held me down and he covered my head and he said, 'Shh, stay down. It's OK. Shh, just stay down.' "

"My other half was just ripped apart from me and so for me it's still unreal. I can't picture my life without him. How do you? When someone loves you that much and you love somebody that much how do you believe that this is real?"

Jon Miranda addressed his comment to the ladies who want their man to be a hero, "Make sure your lives were worth saving."

Much quoted Jessica Ghawi had survived another mass shooting at the Eaton Centre Mall, Toronto, before dying in Aurora. It was after the earlier experience that she wrote: "I was shown how fragile life was on Saturday. I saw the terror on bystanders' faces. I saw the victims of a senseless crime. I saw lives change. I was reminded that we don't know when or where our time on Earth will end. When or where we will breathe our last breath."

Although these men did not give their lives for their wives, we are reminded of "Love ... as Christ loved the Church. He gave Himself up for her." (Ephesians 5:25) and "There is no greater love than this: to lay down one's life for one's friends." (John 15:13)

Some just marveled that anyone could give their life for anyone else. ?Others, both men and women, commented on the meaning of true manliness, while praying for the families of the victims.

Ryan Carranza called these heroes "just awesome guys protecting what they love. Anyone who lives someone unconditionally will face danger for them."

"These men are truly heroic," was Paul Till's comment. "These were men, not the coward who took their's and many others' lives." Jeff Emanuel's comment was, "That's going out like a Man. RIP." Whitney Bittner had a similar comment, it "takes a real man to protect [who] he loves till the end."

Jacqueline L. Steinert wrote, I am "proud to call them men! Their friends, family, and acquaintances can take some comfort and honor in their last selfless act! Pretty awesome!"

Renee Gagne wrote, "I know that these men were raised to have honor and their parents should be very proud of them. I pray that everyone finds peace."

Missy Louise Tatro's prayers were for her own family, "All I can hope is that someday my girls find men like this. And that if I am every lucky enough to find a man like this that I cherish him and make sure he knows how thankful I am to have him."

You might remember Chesley "Sully" "Sully" is now known as the who became a hero when he safely landed a U. S. Airways jet in the Hudson River saving a hundred fifty-five lives. In recent appeals for St. Jude's Children's Hospital, he calls the children there who risk their lives to save other children "the real heroes."

You may not remember Lenny Skutnik who became a hero in 1982. He saved six people by handing the rescue helicopter's life ring to the other survivors before sinking into the icy Potomac back in 1982.

Some heroes same many lives. Some save a few or just one. One Hero gave His life to save us all.

["Sully" is now well-known from the portrayal of him by Tom Hanks in the 2016 movie of the same name.]

Book Shares Healings At Lourdes (September 2012)

The book, *The Wonders of Lourdes* edited by Gerald Korson, only chronicles a few of the miracles of Lourdes. As Dr. Theillier explains, however, "The miracles of Lourdes are all miracles of healing -- healings of the heart, of the soul, of life's wounds that hurt us. The graces of Lourdes are far more numerous than anyone knows, because they take place most often in people's hearts."

Another observation would be that, like Jesus healed while He was here during His earthly life, He still heals in many different ways. There are stories here of healings associated with the water, the prayers, the Eucharist. All are tied to the pilgrim's faith or sometimes to that of the person who got them there.

Many of the healings in the book are the official, highly investigated cases. One of the many more but unofficial healings in the book is that of John Traynor. His eight-year-old injuries were getting worse and worse. Already paralyzed, his damaged brain was causing epileptic seizures. His faith in a healing was so strong he bought shoes for the trip home to England.

Thea Angele had suffered with multiple sclerosis for six years. After visiting Lourdes as so many others "as a last request" in 1950, she was healed. She never did leave Lourdes, but stayed and entered the convent there. That same year Evasio Ganora, suffering from Hodgkin's disease, was put in the pool and then insisted on walking out unassisted. Paul Pellegria's wife insisted he try a second bath. His liver abscess was healed.

One of the most interesting miracles in the book took place long before Bernadette, in 778. After an eagle dropped a salmon before Mirat, Bishop Turpin, so the story goes, persuaded the Moslem to believe in greater wonders. He was baptized Lorus and the town that grew up around his Miranbelle citadel was named after him.

Another Lourdes miracle took place during World War II and not in Lourdes. When the Nazis invaded Oradour-sur-Glade they shot most of the men with machine guns and set fire to the church holding the women and children. Only about twenty-five survived. Six hundred forty-two were killed, but the statues of Our Lady of Lourdes and Bernadette survived. That was not the end of the miracle, however. As the pastor tried to remove Our Lady's statue during reconstruction, it disintegrated. As the story "The Virgin of Dust" describes it, her mission as "guardian of the dead and comfort of the living" was ended.

Edeltrand Fulda's was a war-time miracle too. She had had two-thirds of her stomach removed because of Addison's disease. By 1938 her kidneys were failing. She went to Lourdes, was healed, and "ate enough for four and rested for the first time in thirteen years."

Some of the official healings are miraculous, yet incomplete. Jeanne Gestas tells her story in "The Song of Hope". As a formerly non-practicing Catholic, she writes, "I have rediscovered the path to faith. My medical condition still isn't the best, but my heart has irresistibly turned to the Virgin."

In "Appetite for Life" Maddalena Carini tells how she was taken to Lourdes as "a woman's last whim." Her tuberculosis was critical. After being healed, she says, "I want to give thanks every day of my life."

The very first healing of Louis Bourriette, as shown in "The Song of Bernadette," brought back the sight in his injured eye after nineteen years without it being physically changed. In that same year, Croisine Bourhort took her crippled two-year-old son to Lourdes. His tuberculosis was healed when she dipped him in the water.

Julienne of Brine was allowed to make her profession in 1889 as a sister even though she was dying of tuberculosis. Then she went to Lourdes to prepare to die, but was healed instead.

Two years after a train accident paralyzed Gabriel Gargan, he went to Lourdes just to avoid yet another threatened surgery. He was healed at the consecration of the Eucharist. In that same year, 1901, Marie Savoye, twenty-four yet just fifty-five pounds, was healed as the Eucharist passed. Having been bedridden for six years she got up, walked, and shouted, "I am healed!" Her doctor's comment was, "This is no miracle, it's a resurrection."

Jean Frétel had suffered from appendicitis complications for ten years. After receiving a small piece of the Eucharist, she says that she had "the appetite of an ogre" and no morphine withdrawal.

Marie Bigot, blind and deaf, with skin disease and poor health went to Lourdes and got worse. She was diagnosed with severe meningitis and became paralyzed on one side. The next year she went back and was healed of paralysis, went again the next year in 1954 and regained her hearing, and then her sight on the way home. That same year Br. Leo Schager was healed of multiple sclerosis as the Eucharist passed.

Alice Couteault's niece tells the story, "The Miraculously Healed Woman and the Young Physician." Her aunt insisted that she take her to Lourdes to "see how, despite their illness, all these people are happy. It is that happiness, more than healing, that they will take back from here!" Yet her aunt was healed at the Eucharistic blessing.

Élisa Aloi was taken to Lourdes in a body cast in 1957 after suffering for 10 years with tuberculosis. She got worse, but went back again the next year. After asking her nurse to soak her dressings in Lourdes water, her wounds healed.

Juliette Tamurini just went to Lourdes, so she thought, for courage to face the amputation of her legs. Her nurse Isabelle injected her with Lourdes water when she was unable to make it to the grotto and she was healed. She was healed enough to then make it into the pool and be healed completely.

Maria-Thérése Canin, who was dying as her parents had from tuberculosis, never made it to the shrine. She became so ill that she was taken to the Lourdes hospital. She miraculously was healed there, got dressed, walked without help, and ate a normal meal.

Serge Perrin's inoperable blockage had paralyzed him and was causing him to go blind. His wife urged him to go to Lourdes and he was healed at the anointing of the sick.

Delizia Cirolli was an 11-year-old girl in 1976 who only weighed 50 pounds because of a leg tumor. The tumor suddenly disappeared four months after visiting Lourdes and then not all at once. First she could stand and later walk as she regained her strength.

[Other books on Lourdes include: *Bernadette of Lourdes* by Rene Laurentin, *Lourdes Diary* by James Martin, *Lourdes: A Modern Pilgrimage* by Patrick Marnham, *Lourdes Today* by Kerry Crawford, *Our Lady of Lourdes* by Rev. Lawrence G. Lovasik, *Our Lady of Lourdes*

Catholic Story Coloring Book by Mary Fabyan Windeatt and Gedge Harman, *Pilgrim's Guide to Lourdes* by David Houseley and Peter Latham, *The Lourdes Pilgrim* by Oliver Todd, *The Miracle of Lourdes* by John Lochran.]

Patriotic Rosary Offers Prayers For Nation (July 2012)

With the two hundred fiftieth anniversary of the Civil War and the life-or-death battle for our country, many in the United States of America are uniting in praying the Patriotic rosary. Like other versions of the rosary, the Scriptural rosary, etc., some additional passages for intentions and reflections are added. This version was composed by "a friend of Medjugorje," the funder of Caritas of Birmingham.

Each of the five mysteries begins with an apt, even prophetic, quote by a famous patriotic American. A fuller version of the rosary and other links can be found at the website, patriotic-rosary.com/patriotic-rosary.html.

There are other very similar versions out on the internet. Some versions also include patriotic songs for singing between the decades, such as "America," "America the Beautiful," "God Bless America," "The Battle Hymn of the Republic," and "The Star-Spangled Banner."

Each has its own special intention and each of the ten Hail Maries of the decade are prayed for ten of the states, as listed in alphabetical order, "We plead the Blood of Jesus over _____ and every soul in that state."

The first mystery prays for Alabama, Alaska, Arizona, Arkansas, California, Colorado, Connecticut, Delaware, Florida, and Georgia and quotes George Washington (6/29/1788), "The Great Governor of the Universe has led us too long and too far on the road to happiness and glory, to forsake us in the midst of it. By folly and improper conduct, proceeding from a variety of causes, we may now and then get bewildered; but I hope and trust that there is good sense and virtue enough to recover the right path before we shall be entirely lost."

The second mystery prays for the Supreme Court, the states of Hawaii, Idaho, Illinois, Indiana, Iowa, Kansas, Kentucky, Louisiana, Maine, and Maryland and quotes John Adams (7/3/1776), "The furnace of affliction produces refinement, in states as well as individuals and the new governments we are assuming, in every part, will require a purification from our vices, and an augmentation of our virtues or there will be no blessings ... But I must submit all my hopes and fears to an overruling Providence, in which, unfashionable as the faith may be, I firmly believe."

The third mystery prays for the Senators and Representatives and the states of Massachusetts, Michigan, Minnesota, Mississippi, Missouri, Montana, Nebraska, Nevada, New Hampshire, and New Jersey.

It quotes future Supreme Court Justice James Iredell (5/1/1778), "... the glorious effects of patriotism and virtue. These are the rewards annexed to the faithful discharge of that great and honorable duty, fidelity to our country ... I pray to God that the fair character I have described may be that of America to the last ages."

The fourth mystery is prayed for all the governors and the states of New Mexico, New York, North Carolina, North Dakota, Ohio, Oklahoma, Oregon, Pennsylvania, Rhode Island, and South Carolina. It quotes the pastor father of Samuel F. B. Morse, Jedediah Morse (1799), "All efforts to destroy the foundations of our holy religion ultimately tend to the subversion also of our political freedom and happiness. Whenever the pillars of Christianity shall be overthrown, our present republican forms of government, and all the blessings which flow from them, must fall with them."

page 98

The fifth mystery prays for all county and municipal offices and the states of South Dakota, Tennessee, Texas, Utah, Vermont, Virginia, Washington, West Virginia, Wisconsin, and Wyoming.

It quotes Robert E. Lee, "Knowing that intercessory prayer is our mightiest weapon and the supreme call for all Christians today, I pleadingly urge our people everywhere to pray. Believing that prayer is the greatest contribution that our people can make in this critical hour, I humbly urge that we take time to pray -- to really pray.

"Let there be prayer at sunup, at noonday, at sundown, at midnight -- all through the day. Let us pray for our children, our youth, our aged, our pastors, our homes. Let us pray for our churches.

"Let us pray for our nation. Let us pray for those who have never known Jesus Christ and His redeeming love, for moral forces everywhere, for our national leaders. Let prayer be our passion. Let prayer be our practice."

Lee prayed this prayer for "our nation" in 1863, the year of the tragedy at Gettysburg, while he was fighting not so much against the United States as for his state of Virginia. Lincoln, the nation's leader, always contended that Virginia and the other Southern states had really never left the Union, because they could not legally do so.

Visit To Heaven Reaches Millions (May 2012)

Colton Burpo's visit to heaven and back when he was four has now reached over six million people in various formats. *Heaven is for Real* has been a bestseller for adults and is again in an edition for children, *Heaven Is for Real for Kids*, illustrated by Wilson Ong.

From the comments of readers at its Facebook page, it is not surprising. Andre Landgraf wrote, "Every human being should read this book." Collette M. Imbeault's reaction was that of millions of other readers, "I loved this book! Totally awesome!"

Cyndi Benner Gray's comment was "You know you have a good book when you are telling someone about it and there are tears in your eyes."

Laura Minchew, Senior Vice President of Specialty Publishing at Thomas Nelson says, "It is a simple and pure message from the experience of a four-year-old child: 'Jesus really loves children. And He loves You!' "

The new book features a letter to parents and a section that answers questions kids frequently have when they finish Colton's story.

The "Heaven is for Real" DVD includes a Conversation Kit feature with footage of the Burpo family talking about their experiences while offering discussion questions and suggestions for participants.

It is even an interactive children's app through Apple. Among its features are Ong's artwork, sound effects, coloring pages, and jigsaw puzzles and the capability to gift the app to friends.

"This delightful app, with strong messages of faith, comfort, and hope makes a perfect gift for kids," Minchew says. "Parents and grandparents will enjoy the ability to record their own voice reading the story."

Basically the story is that while on a trip to Colorado, Colton complained of a stomach ache. After five days of being misdiagnosed, his appendix burst. Through the difficult surgery, his pastor father Todd Burpo and mother Sonja prayed.

Passing the hospital four months after his surgery, Colton said, "You know, Dad, the angels sang to me while I was there."

Colton went on to tell of the other things he saw including Pop, his great grandfather who died 30 years before Colton was born. But Colton says he didn't look like the photo in his house. He was a young man without glasses.

He told of the miscarried sister that his parents had never told him about, who was a young girl who wanted to be given a name, of sitting on Jesus' lap, and even of Armageddon.

When the folks in little Imperial, Nebraska, encouraged Todd to write Colton's story, he prayed, "God, if this is really You, if You want me to do this, You will have the publishing industry come to me."

God answered his prayers again and they did. "I don't know why God picked us," Todd says. "We are just normal people that God did a miracle for."

The story, however, has triggered many more miracles for other people, has gotten them to believe and pray. Jennie Belinsky writes, "This was certainly an eye opener for me. I laughed and cried and cried more. I have never been to Heaven but I cannot wait to go! I was just asking my husband about what happens to babies when a woman has a miscarriage -- I did last month -- and he wasn't sure; it was so comforting to read that they are in Heaven. It's as if God wanted me to read this just to find out."

Amanda Lynn Rugg wrote, "Thank you so much, little Colton. I lost my grandma and pappy. I love them so much and I couldn't get over the loss of them. I also lost my baby at 17 weeks pregnant and after reading your story it helps my heart to know that my loved ones are in such a beautiful place."

"I read the entire book from front to back today," Lisa Paone says. "I couldn't put it down. It's such a powerful and uplifting story!" and prays "May God continue to bless that precious child and his family."

[In 2011 Heaven Is For Real Ministries was founded (heavenlive.org). It now offers *God Is For Real, Heaven Changes Everything* and *Heaven is Real* for Little Ones. Colton sings on tour with Read You and Me. Although still Wesleyan, they they share the basic good news.]

Videos Can Be Teaching Tools (April 2012)

"If we obey the commands that God has given us, He will make us more than we ever dreamed possible." So says Willie Aames, former child star on "Eight Is Enough." He became a superhero called BibleMan in the series and in "BibleMan Live" performances.

"My own life is an example there, I think," he explains, having succumbed to the Hollywood lifestyle. "I think certainly there are plenty of Bible characters you can see that in. David would be one. Moses would be another one."

"What God really wants is for us to obey Him. First He wants us to love Him, because I don't think you can obey anyone you don't love. The word 'obey' has taken on such a negative connotation that we wanted to let people know [in "Breaking the Bonds of Disobedience"] that when we obey people it's a sign that we love them."

Tracy Henao plays Lia Martinez playing BibleGirl in a "BibleMan Live" performance in this story within a story. Her character chooses to obey God rather than her own desires for a career on Broadway

"I've always known," Henao says, "that God was preparing me for His work, but I must say that the exact direction of His plan was unexpected."

The videos and performances have many kid-friendly elements. The DVDs feature bloopers, deleted scenes, and a video game based on "A Fight for Faith." There are talking computers, light sabers, and other familiar science fictional gadgetry complete with technobabble. There is Bible Cave under Eaglegate manor where the heroes pray and a transporter-like Bible chamber where the armor of God from Ephesians 6:11 is put on.

It doesn't take itself too seriously, and especially not the foolish villains. The exception is when the Bible Trio, BibleMan, BibleGirl, and BibleBoy, fight evil by referencing Bible verses. Then the villain sometimes misapplies Bible verses.

When the villain in "Jesus Our Savior" misapplies a quote from Ecclesiastes, for example, BibleMan counters with another quote from Ecclesiastes. A quote from the prophet Amos is countered with another from Ephesians in the New Testament.

Although purposely childish and entertaining, this could provide an opening to getting parents and children to discuss how Scripture can apply to their own lives. Playing together with the action figures or the video game could get them to use Scripture in their play with each other. Although "Miles Peterson," the original BibleMan was replaced by Robert T. Schlipp's "Josh Carpenter," Aames says, "this is want He wants. It's awesome. I don't know where He's going to take it, but God is building this thing. We've been called and He has blessed."

Another DVD series also intended for kids, but with less emphasis on the Bible and more on fantastic animation, is called "Angel Wars." Extra features, however, do include the usual commentaries and music videos, as well as an interactive "How to Draw Angel Wars." Chris Waters compares his creation to C. S. Lewis' Chronicles of Narnia. "Someone who isn't a Christian can still appreciate the struggle and not feel like they are being preached to or being smacked over their head."

Michael leads other Angels in a futuristic world with hovercars and a moonbase to guard us Humans against the fallen Angels. The Humans re realistically portrayed as unaware of the great battle going on about them, as when a boy steals from a candy store, while a battle rages.

These Angels or Anawim also fight evil with cool armor and weapons, music videos, and action figures. There is even a board game and Redemption collector cards. There are also, however, interactive Bible studies for kids, at least in the later DVDs in the series.

The episode "Grace and Glory" deals with the theme of obedience when Morgan steals one of the Foundation Stones and becomes the demon Morg, the Angel of Death. Michael almost forgets that Morgan is his brother angel in the fight, but then gives Morgan one last chance to come back into God's family. He wouldn't give up his pride and literally falls from grace into the pit of hell.

The accompanying Bible study draws lessons from the Old and New Testaments and asks viewers to apply them to their own lives. The full length DVD, "The Messengers," is based on Michael's role in the book of Daniel.

["Bibleman: The Animated Adventures" began in 2016, continuing the fight against Dr. Fear and the Master of Maybe with Scripture. The fan website angelwars.wikia.com started in 2012 continues. The main character is, of course, the Maker.]

Games Have Religious Themes (January 2012)

Facebook games have recently turned to Bible-based and Church-based themes and so are perhaps not quite such a waste of time as they had been.

"With web-based games played on social networks drawing nearly half a billion people worldwide, we felt it was time for a Biblically-based game that showcases one of the greatest adventures of all time," said Brent Dusing, CEO of Hexify, creator of the first Biblically-based Facebook game.

"We were careful to adhere to the accounts in the Bible and the overarching spirit of the story, even vetting certain aspects with theological leaders," Dusing said.

The art style is meant to reflect "the casual social game" that it is, says Dusing. The Journey of Moses is the first game. "It's a fun, immersive, adventure game, so it's meant to be fun but respectful to the content and appropriate for the gravity of the story."

"It's an adventure quest game," or a "map exploration game," Dusing said. "A little bit like Zelda merged with the Moses story -- that kind of game play where you're exploring different areas and find different items and meet different people to propel the story."

"Whether you already play social games or you are interested in the story of Moses, we believe we have created a game that everyone can enjoy," said Dusing.

"It's a well-polished game with amusing visuals and a surprising amount of depth, much more so than Vatican Wars or Holy Town," wrote AOL Games Blog.

"The very fact that this game does a pretty good job of clearly relating these events [of Moses' life] in such a simple format like a Facebook games is pretty impressive ... Besides, if you're going to waste time on Facebook playing a game, why not play a well-made one that's about the Bible?" wrote Hollywood Jesus.

Cheyenne Ehrlich, founder of SGR Games (named for St. Genesius of Rome) makes the point that they "are not affiliated with the "Roman Catholic Church, the Vatican, or the Holy See". As a Buddhist, he had intended to make the priests Buddhists, but decided on the larger Catholic Church.

Ehrlich claims that playing Vatican Wars has increased people's desire to attend Mass and join the priesthood, based on a player survey. Rev. John Kita, a parish priest in Elkland, PA, wrote to a Knights of Columbus publication earlier this year praising the game as a "great tool to motivate more men to consider the priesthood."

Deacon Nick Donnelly wrote on his blog, Protect the Pope: "A pope could not change the Church's teaching on same-sex marriage, abortion, contraception, homosexuality, or the ordination of women. To change these doctrines would be to break with the apostolic faith."

Players build their diocese while taking stands on the controversial topics such as abortion, artificial birth control, clerical celibacy, the definition of marriage, and ordination of women.

The war started in earnest when ten dissenting cardinals elected Higgins pope last July. Since then there have been nineteen popes, thirteen Templars, and six Crusaders. As of this writing Pope Munificentissimus still heads the virtual Church. His rival, "Saint" Gemma, however, writes, "Come together, Crusaders, and join my quest to reclaim the Papacy from the judgmental Templars. Support my quest and I guarantee support of yours so that we can establish a chain of Crusader succession."

His successor will likely be Dodo 7 who is said to be leading in the vote so far two-to-one about the same as the pope ratio. That is likely the reason he had not made a counterstatement, since he does not need to do so.

The key to influencing the social agenda of the Church, according to the game rules, is to get as many Stature Points as possible, and to get as many people to play for your team as you can. The more Stature Points your team has, the more likely you or one of your teammates are to become Pope and control the game and thus ensure that the social agenda of the Church reflects Christ's true teachings.

"It attracts people to the game who perhaps used to be Catholic and who are not anymore, or who simply disagree with the Church's social positions," said Ehrlich.

Becoming a bishop requires, among other things, speaking out about clerical sex abuse. Players buy or donate religious goods, so the game is like a visit to a virtual Catholic store including vestments, religious texts, and relics. That the Shroud of Turin is for sale is not the only departure from the real Church. Here all players may vote in papal elections, not just cardinals.

There are a few other faith-based games. For the evangelical Protestant market there is Holy Town in which the player founds his own church and builds his/her congregation by preaching. In Soul Journey the player is the dying victim of a horrible accident trying to save his/her soul by solving Hidden Object mini-games.

[After the short-lived SGR Games, which Ehrlich describes as a hobby, he went on to found Perceptual Networks and SaferKid. Big Fish Games has a forum for players of Soul Journey.]

Priest Uses Media To Evangelize (December 2011)

The "Catholicism" series on eighty PBS stations and on EWTN is not all that Fr. Robert Barron is doing. The Word on Fire Ministries which he founded is doing much of what Blessed John Paul II called "the new evangelization." The series itself guides the viewer, particularly lapsed Catholics, through the wondrous breadth and depth of the Catholic Faith. The website has a virtual tour of the places Fr. Barron visited, a forum for questions and much more.

The series begins with "Amazed and Afraid" in the Holy Land where the Church was founded upon Peter at Caesarea Philippi and in Jerusalem where the Holy Spirit came to the Church and to Rome. It continues in "Happy Are We" showing how the Church still proclaims Jesus in France, Poland, Russia, and the United States.

In the third installment Fr. Barron become less the Church historian and more University of St. Mary of the Lake professor, when he talks on the "The Ineffable Mystery of God." There are, however, still visits to Sinai, Istanbul, Paris, and the Sistine Chapel. This followed by one of the most important elements of Catholicism, Mary. He does this by visiting some of the most visited Marian shrines, Lourdes and Guadalupe, as well as Nazareth and Ephesus.

"To the Ends of the Earth" tells of Peter" and Paul's missions to Jews and Gentiles. Other episodes focus on the Eucharist ("Word Made Flesh, True Bread of Heaven") and saints ("A Vast Company of Witnesses").

"The Fire of His Love" tells how the Holy Spirit still works through Catholics now, just as with Mary, Peter, Paul, and the other saints. The last of the ten-program series returns to Jerusalem, but emphasizes Jesus' second coming, "World without End -- The Last Things."

George Weigel has called it "the most important media project in the history of the Catholic Church in America." Brad Miner, the Catholic Thing blogger, says it is "the most vivid catechism every created, a high def, illustrated manuscript for the Twenty-first century."

It is not just an easily ignored or forgotten miniseries. With the DVDs are included study lessons by Carl Olson with commentary, and questions designed for both understanding and application. The book *Catholicism: Journey to the Heart of the Faith* also includes a facilitator's guide and answers and promotional materials.

There is a virtual tour following the production crew from Jerusalem in 2008 to Mt. Sinai in 2010, through fifty locations in fifteen countries. There is an interactive map with photo galleries, videos, crew blogs, and art and architectural factoids.

There are companion guides on Conversion and Eucharist. There are follow-up books: *Eucharist: Catholic Spirituality for Adults*, *The Strangest Way: Walking the Christian Path*, and *Now I See: A Theology of Transformation Bridging the Great Divide* and more.

On his YouTube video channel from All Saints Day, Fr. Barron explained: "The saints are like a burning bush. They're on fire with Christ, but they are not consumed; they're lit up; they become more radiant. That's what we admire about them. That's why the artists portray them with haloes, I think. They are the source of illumination to others."

Matt Nathan Lee's comment is typical, "Thanks Father for all your explanation. It has helped me to strengthen my faith."

Luishazong wrote, "I've only watched 2 of your videos, but I must say they are amazing. I want to thank you for expressing to the world all these ideas and concepts that many just don't know or understand. They sure bring people closer to God. Amazing Channel, I subscribed! :D" [The colon and capital D at the end is read sideways as the emotion for "with a big smile."]

His Sunday sermons going back to 2000 can be downloaded in MP3. Number 563 for example, lists the three tasks of the Church: "Christ calls us to worship the Father, teach and evangelize in His name, and serve and care for Him in the poor."

John commented by writing, "Wonderful lesson as usual. Funny that the hardest part for me is the evangelization calling. Worshiping God, easy; helping the poor, kind of easy; evangelizing, hard. As Fr. Barron states, it is difficult to get out of the secular norms regarding telling others about our faith in God. Thanks, Fr. Barron, to remind me that the three go together and don't have to be divisive! God bless.'"

Fr. Barron can also be found on Facebook, where we learn that he has such diverse interests as Gregorian Chant, Prince, "The Exorcist," "Ground Hog Day," preaching, and the harmonica. On the Word on Fire Facebook page he has commented on the saints of the day, Pope Benedict's Year of Faith initiative, on current movies, and on the culture and how to change it.

Most of the activity at the Word on Fire forum is questions and answers about the Faith from lay people who have been touched by this far-reaching new evangelical Catholic ministry.

[Fr. Barron became a bishop in 2015 and now has a million and a half facebook fans. His newest books are *To Light a Fire on the Earth* and *Catholicism: A Journey to the Heart of the Faith*.]

World Youth Day: A Life-Changing Event (October 2011)

Some of the pilgrims from Cincinnati to World Youth Day 2011 in Madrid made a side trip to Fatima, Portugal. Some even visited Rome, Assisi, and Lourdes as part of their pilgrimage.

Magnificat Travel (www.holytravels.org) which specializes in "taking pilgrims to holy places" took a group of sixteen from Cincinnati, among a hundred thirty pilgrims total, to Assisi on the feast of St. Clare and Lourdes on the feast of the Assumption.

"We were high on the Holy Spirit before we got there," said Pam Bettner, mother of three of the pilgrims. "It was one amazing God experience after another."

Taylor Marie Harbison, seventeen, one of the Bettner sisters' friends, describes the trip to Fatima as "gorgeous!!"

Along with hundreds of photos, she writes on Facebook, "It wasn't what I pictured it to look like, but it was still beautiful. People would crawl on their knees there for reparation of sins and it just moved you to tears, knowing that people really do care about their sins and really do want to be forgiven."

They saw a fireball while across the street from the basilica. They were awed also by the silent prayers of many penitents, and the candlelight procession.

"The Holy Spirit was palpable," Mrs. Bettner said.

Finally, after missing the plane, the pilgrims reached Madrid and "The Pope was there!!" as Miss Harbison writes.

"He talked to us. He had adoration with us, heck he stood in the pouring rain and lightning storm with us!! He was like our Father; he had our best interest at heart. He talked to us about Faith, and he gave us advice and his blessing."

Some of the eighty-four-year-old pope's more memorable quotes to the youth during the week-long "day" were: "The man can be happy being a man. Do not fear to imitate Jesus Christ! Do not live in fear, and give life!" and "The happiness that you seek has a name, a face: Jesus of Nazareth Who awaits you in the Eucharist," and "Only love guides and gives pain meaning. To suffer with others, for others, due to love is a sign of humanity."

Estimates of up to a million and a half million are said to have attended WYD 2011, but it wasn't the numbers that were important. Just in the Magnificat pilgrimage were pilgrims from Cuba, Ireland, and Korea as well as the U.S.

"People from around the world were there!" Miss Harbison explains. "We met people from Brazil, Ireland, Australia, Italy, Spain and those are just the people we talked to. You should have seen all the flags flying in the wind! The world was present that night in one place, without fighting. The world was united with Pope Benedict, even if it was just for a week. One day the whole world will be like that. You just have to have faith, sooner or later the world will realize that we need God, not just on Sundays but everyday!"

"Pope Benny really knows what he's talking about," Miss Harbison says.

Because of the storm, event organizers were recommending Pope Benedict cut short his planned speech on the sanctity of marriage, responding to Spain's recent legalization of so-called gay marriage.

Instead, as BBC's William Crawley wrote on his blog, "Pope Benedict stressed the value of spiritual friendships and encouraged young people -- both Catholics and non-Catholics -- to lead 'authentic lives, lives which are always worth living, in every circumstance, and which not even death can destroy.' "

At Guestview Jo-anne Rowley wrote, "Three hundred times more people traveled vast distances to celebrate their faith with the Pope than those who came to protest, but you wouldn't have known it. For us pilgrims, it was about unity, about remaining firm in the faith when faced with hardship."

"Leaving the stage briefly," she wrote, "the Pope returned with the Blessed Sacrament. Then amazingly the thunder, rain, and lightning stopped as if the Holy Father had pressed pause. 'Thank you for your joy and resistance. Your strength is bigger than the rain,' said the pope as the rain began to settle. 'The Lord sends you lots of blessings with the rain.'

"The pope thanks you," he said, "for your affection and sends you out as ambassadors of the joy that our world needs."

The pilgrims responded to the Pope's call. "What I experienced that night at the vigil," Rowley wrote, "was worth all of that because that night I fell in love with faith and God again."

As Mary Grace Strasser, eighteen, put it, "I don't really care if they label me a Jesus freak. There ain't no disguising the truth."

John Paul Hennessey, sixteen, could just simply say, "Awesome! I can't describe it."

Pam Bettner said, "It was a lightning show and a half." The young people she chaperoned were literally dancing in the rain in Spain, which cooled the unbearable 106° heat.

"His Church was there. Our Holy Father took care of us."

Although their group of pilgrims were among those who did not make it into their designated area, because of over-booking, they were able to make the Stations of the Cross with Pope Benedict via jumbotron. They did get back to their hotel in time to watch most of the Mass on

TV, when the Host tent collapsed, and had a Mass of their own celebrated by fellow pilgrim Fr. Marty Mannion.

The next international World Youth Day will be held in Rio de Janeiro, Brazil, in 2013 with the theme, "Go and make disciples of all peoples" (Matthew 28:19).

[Magnificat Travel continues to offer tours to Canada, France, the Holy Land, Ireland, Italy, Mexico, Portugal and Spain.]

Christians Called To Evangelize (September 2011)

Fr. Tom Forrest, a Redemptorist missionary priest, was a speaker at the 25th annual Presentation Ministries' Bible Institute. The missionary has served the poor in the Caribbean and the charismatic renewal. "Forget your excuses," he told his listeners. "You are in trouble with God if you aren't making an effort to bring about the Kingdom. We have been given the Superpower of Jesus' Spirit."

Quoting John 14, Fr. Forrest said, "This work is more than walking on water, multiplying loaves and fishes. We have the task of calming the storms of violence in our culture. We have to overcome the forces of evil, the fires of hell, Satan, and his minions."

Fr. Forrest makes no excuses. At eighty-four, he has evangelized to Mother Teresa and her sisters over 60 times. He is on Facebook, YouTube, and Vimeo, getting comments like "I bet nobody sleeps through his Masses" and "I agree nobody sleeps. He makes you feel so alive and strong." Or "I prayed for you at CBN one evening before you were to talk ... in winter of '87 or '88. I often think of you. You impacted my life greatly."

The priest has audio tapes not only on evangelization, but on John Paul II, Mother Teresa, "The Virtues of a Happy Home," and "Walking in the Footsteps of Jesus" available at My Catholic Faith.

"Mother Teresa was so small you couldn't have seen her behind this podium," he says. "Such a small woman, but a really powerful soul for God."

Mother Teresa's only request of him was to "please pray for me that I don't do damage to the work of God."

In his presentation, he told of others who prayed and who God worked through, including Moses, Paul, and Monica. Our Mother Mary asks us to pray.

"Pray through Mary's mediation, entrust your causes to her. Pray with confidence. Pray and believe that you have already received it, and it will be granted to you" – faith to move the mountains blocking us, wisdom, freedom from sin, holiness, patience, generosity, kindness, healing a broken heart.

Fr. Forrest has written that there are "many people in this world, perhaps countless millions, who live their whole lives in darkness because they are living without the Light Whose name is Jesus."

Evangelism, being light rather than darkness in the world, is "the supreme Christian service of teaching the spiritually blind to cry out like that man in the Gospel, 'Lord! That I might see!' (Mark 10:51).

"Every single one of you," Fr. Forrest writes, "should be doing what [Mother Teresa] did, shining with the light of Christ, letting in the light of His holiness, His goodness, love, His dependence upon the Heavenly Father to light the path for others. Be a people of light. Bring your light together and shine together."

The missionary said, "Our call is more important than rescuing a child from a well. It is greater than launching a man to the moon. It's an urgent call to you – not your aunt Josephine – and I'm trying to give you the knowledge of what to do, to let the Holy Spirit do it."

Fr. Forrest concluded by complimenting those in attendance: "You know I have been to 110 countries. I have met many people and I have to tell you, you are very special here. You are the best. Your faith is strong. I am very impressed. This is wonderful."

[In 2012 Fr. Forrest's prayer for Ireland was posted as a YouTube video, "Prepare the Way".]

Pope's Book Hits Bestseller List (May 2011)

The Italian and German first editions of Pope Benedict XVI's second volume of *Jesus of Nazareth* were sold out in one day. The U.S. edition was half sold out in a week. At this writing, it is climbing the New York Times top ten.

At Reading Pope Benedict (readingbenedictxvi.blogspot), his new book is described as a challenge to look at the evidence fairly for Jesus' claim of divinity. After looking at the life and teachings of Jesus in Part One, he addresses the most important evidence, Jesus' passion and resurrection.

Jeff Mirus at Catholic Culture (catholicculture.org) emphasizes "Ratzinger's gift," rejoining the traditional lectio divina, "reading Scripture prayerfully to seek the joy and nourishment of God's presence in His word" with "attention to the original languages, a study of what other great commentators have written, and the deliberate unraveling of obscure and possibly even disputed themes."

At Amazon it has a five out of five stars rating. Shanon Grice, for example, writes, "I'm not even Catholic, I guess you would say I'm charismatic or Pentecostal, and I've found myself just loving the Pope's books, and have encountered Jesus and the Holy Spirit afresh. Now I have such a fresh and new appreciation for the ancient Catholic faith also which is part of our Christian roots, just like our Jewish roots are part of our faith. I highly recommend this book to everyone."

Geza Vermes of the guardian explains, "The critics took exception to the book's rejection of the principal finding of the historical-critical school: the distinction between the Jesus of history and the Christ of faith.

In his own words, Pope Benedict identifies his intention as "to understand the figure of Jesus, His word and His actions." He understands well enough.

In the first chapter, "The entrance into Jerusalem," he begins bringing out the "failure to recognize Jesus through a combination of indifference and fear." The Pharisees recognized His authority and feared it, while people like Nathaniel dismissed Him as not what they expected as the Messiah.

The Pope takes us through Jesus' discourse on the last days, His words and actions at the Last Supper, at the garden, trial, and crucifixion. In answering "Who exactly were Jesus' accusers?" he notes John clearly identifies the Temple authorities with a few exceptions like Nicodemus. He analyzes the Greek word ochlos translated as "masses" or "mob" as meaning the organized supporters of Barabbas while the numerous "followers of Jesus remained hidden out of fear."

"The pope displays courage for a Christian leader of his disposition," Vermes writes, "and correctly concedes that what Matthew reports is not a 'historical fact': the whole Jewish people, he argues, could not have foregathered outside Pilate's residence. The exoneration of the Jews from the crime of deicide thus receives papal approval: the guilt lies."

Finally in chapter nine he guides the reader to "the Resurrection is the crucial point. Whether Jesus merely was or whether He also is -- this depends on the Resurrection [his emphasis].

He calls Jesus' Resurrection "an entirely new form of life," "a life that is no longer subject to the law of dying and becoming but lies beyond it -- a life that opens up a new dimension of human existence," "a dimension that affects us all, creating for all of us a new space of life, a new space of being in union with God." It is not something that should be feared or ignored.

His analysis in this chapter goes so far as to dissecting the punctuation in Acts 1:3-4 in the Jerusalem Bible. He makes the case that there should be a comma, not a period, in "He had continued to appear to them and tell them about the kingdom of God, when He had been at table with them."

The literal meaning of the word used by Luke is "eating salt" which points to preservation, covenant-making, and so the new covenant and the Eucharist.

There is also a surprising addition to the book, since its subtitle is Holy Week from the Entrance into Jerusalem to the Resurrection. That is the epilogue on Jesus' Ascension and present life as King of kings.

He uses non-scholarly explanation as well in making his point that Christian faith leads to the Christian's hope. "The Lord is 'on the mountain' of the Father. Therefore he sees us. Therefore he can get into the boat of our life at any moment. Therefore we can always call on Him."

He even occasionally gets personal, as when he explains how we are now living between Jesus' first and second coming.

"The Lord comes," he writes, "through His word; He comes in the sacraments, especially in the most Holy Eucharist"; and using "me" rather than the more usual "we" to add, "He comes into my life through words and events."

(Editor's note: L'Osservatore Romano English edition of 3/30/11 quoted a press release from Mark Brumley, president of Ignatius Press, a publisher of the book. Brumley stated: "We're delighted that Jesus of Nazareth: Holy Week is an instant New York Times best seller. It means that many people across the country are discovering Pope Benedict's insights into the life of Jesus Christ." And, he continued, "in this way, more and more people will encounter the real Jesus, which was the Holy Father's goal in writing the book.")

[In 2018 Pope Emeritus Benedict XVI wrote he was "on a pilgrimage toward Home." In 2017 Last Testament: In His Own Words was published.]

Martyrs Continue To Enrich Church (April 2011)

In his article "The New Martyrs" in The Catholic Thing, Robert Royal comments on the recent killings of Christians in Egypt, Philippines, Nigeria, and harassment in India.

"These religious conflicts are regrettable and Benedict XVI eloquently regretted them and several others earlier in the week," he writes, "but there's a whole other category of violence against religious people that is far worse and largely overlooked.

" 'New' in this context does not mean simply 'recent,'" he explains. "John Paul intended to call attention to a whole class of victims of various nefarious forces in the twentieth century and beyond -- victims whose absence from our consciousness gives a false picture even of the secular history of modern times."

Royal reminds us that "Hitler threatened in his table talk that he would 'crush the Church like a toad,'" "that the Soviets brutally suppressed the Ukrainian Catholic Church, making it the largest underground religious body in the world," and that during the Spanish Civil War "for the first time in Europe since ancient Rome, defenseless Christians (in this case, priests) were once again killed by wild animals, in Spanish bull rings."

In his book, *The Catholic Martyrs of the Twentieth Century*, Royal noted that in the twenty centuries of Church history, about 70 million Christians have given their lives for the faith, and of these, nearly two-thirds were in the last century. This is according to *The New Persecuted* by Antonio Socci, whose estimates are based on Oxford's *World Christian Encyclopedia*. Royal's new martyrology includes Catholic martyrs who died for their faith, on every continent but Antarctica and Australia. He includes Miguel Pro and the Mexican martyrs of the 1920s, saints like Edith Stein and Maximilian Kolbe under Nazis in the 1930s and '40s, Burundi and Rwanda in the 1990s, Archbishop Romero in El Salvador, and lesser-known martyrs of the Spanish Civil War, Romania, and Albania.

Socci includes especially the martyrs under Communist Cuba, Vietnam, China, and the former Soviet republics, and in fundamentalist Moslem countries like Saudi Arabia, Bangadesh, and Indonesia. He also estimates that about 160,000 Christians have been killed every year since 1990 in places like Algeria, Nigeria, Sudan, and Pakistan.

As such worldwide persecution threatened even our country, it seems appropriate then that Fr. Prentice Dean, a former Episcopal priest who is now a Catholic priest in Nashville, Tennessee, has recently founded Our Lady of the Martyrs Anglican Use Society. They remember martyrs, such as the Anglican companions of the Ugandan martyrs, who were united in death with Catholic martyrs.

Of particular interest is Mukasa Kiriwawanvu, who was baptized by blood and desire rather than by water. He was from the Muganda tribe, Ndiga (Sheep) clan, Kyaggwe county. He served as a page to both King Muteesa I and Mwanga II. He died in his early twenties by being burnt alive in the Namugongo furnace on the Ascension, Thursday, June 3, 1886. Mukasa is the patron of hotels, restaurants, bars, and all kinds of public recreations.

We know more about Chi Zhuze, who was also an unbaptized martyr, born four years later in the village of Dezhaoin Shen County, Hebei Province, China. Although illiterate, he made great efforts to learn the Catholic doctrine and attended Mass every Sunday. When the Boxer Rebellion raged, his parents objected saying, "If you want to remain a member of this family, stop going to church and wait until the rebellion has ended."

Chi Zhuze, however, remained firm, refusing to join them in worshiping the family idols on New Year's Eve and was banished from the family. However, he gladly endured all hardships in the name of God.

Since Zhuze was not yet baptized, he was not known among many of the Catholics of the village, but finally found one who knew him, took him in, and gave him a job as a servant in his house.

When his parents discovered his refuge, he returned home with them. On the way, however, he met some Boxers who ordered him to worship idols. When he refused, they cut off his arm and continued to mutilate him. Some of the villagers notified his parents but they took no measure to save him. After his death, they became Catholic, which was a sign of God's blessing on his sacrifice of life.

[In 2015 Royal wrote *A Deeper Vision: The Catholic Intellectual Tradition in the Twentieth Century*. He has also written *The God That Did Not Fail: How Religion Built and Sustains the West*.]

Did Jehosophat Really Jump? (March 2011)

The *Bible Archeology Review* contains many scholarly articles. Its website, however, also offers several free e-books, such as *Easter: Exploring the Resurrection of Jesus*; *The First*

Christmas: The Story of Jesus' Birth in History and Legend; James, Brother of Jesus: Forged Antiquities; and *the Trail of Oded and Robert Deutsch.*

It also offers a variety of free downloadable articles, two of which ask the intriguing questions, "Did Jehosophat Really Jump?" and "Is Hershel Doomed to the Lake of Fire?"

In the first Leonard J. Greenspoon begins by telling where the expression "jumping Jehosophat" comes from. The London *Daily Mail* says, "Around the middle of the Nineteenth century, his name was used in the United States as a mild oath, a euphemism for Jehovah or Jesus.

It first appeared in print in 1866 in *Headless Horseman*, "an adventure tale set in Texas by British author Mayne Reid." It was used as a euphemism for Jehovah or Jesus.

Then, however, he notes that the phrase may not be merely meaningless alliterative. He references Rev. Betty Peebles who claims that "praise dancers originated in the Bible with King Jehosophat under attack."

"God told Jehosophat," she says, " 'Don't carry any weapons into battle; just get yourself some praise dancers.' " (2 Chronicles 20)

"I will sprinkle clean water upon you to cleanse you from all your impurities, and from all your idols I will cleanse you. I will give you a new heart and place a new spirit within you, taking from your bodies your stony hearts and giving you natural hearts. I will put My spirit within you and make you live by My statutes, careful to observe My decrees." (Ezekiel 36:25-27)

He also notes contemporary use by The New York *Times* movie review that "probably left most fans of westerns longing for the days when the hero never even kissed the girl and when the raciest flight of language might be Walter Brennan shouting 'jumpin' Jehosophat!' "

This Biblically inspired phrase is sometimes combined with others, as in "Jumpin' Jehosophat, Land o' Goshen and saints preserve us, they've done it again" as in The Washington *Post's* description of NBC.

In the second article Adela Yarbro Collins, author of Cosmology and Eschatology in Jewish and Christian Apocalypticism, wrote on whether the Gideons' claim that Jew Hershel Shanks, and other non-Christians, is destined for the lake of fire of Revelation 20 is true.

"Is Hershel Doomed to the Lake of Fire?" They even suggested that the earthquakes in Chile and Haiti may be signs that the end of time was near.

Collins emphasized that Revelation is not on beliefs but on works. Those who will be vindicated in Revelation 6:9 are those who have been slaughtered on account of the word of God, both Jews and Christians. They are described primarily as those who break the Ten Commandments, no matter what they believe or claim to believe.

She includes in her article an explanation of the long list of those bound for hellfire for the evil they have done.

The answers to these two questions are therefore "Yes, Jehosophat probably did jump," and "No, Jews are not necessarily condemned."

One of the most popular articles, however, is Ehud Netezer's "In Search of Herod's Tomb," reprinted after Netzer's death from a fall while working at Herodium last October.

"Herod's luxurious desert retreat, this architectural masterpiece has yielded many treasures," he wrote, "but none more exciting than the 2007 discovery of Herod's tomb."

Netzer retells Josephus' story of how Herod died at 70 "consumed with uncontrolled anger." He explains that modern physicians suggest it was "age-related failure of the heart and kidneys, with terminal edema of the lungs."

Then he proceeds with his own story: "The precise spot where we ultimately found the mausoleum eluded us for decades. We excavated almost all of Lower Herodium without finding it. Time and time again over the years our hopes were dashed. Excavating on the northeastern slope of the hill was a last desperate effort after years of disappointment. But here it was!"

The nearly destroyed mausoleum and its sarcophagus were, Netzer believed, destroyed by Jewish rebels who occupied the site during the Great Jewish Revolt because of dated coins found in the garbage heaps.

[The July/August 2018 issue, for example, describes the discovery of the tomb of the vizier to two pharaohs, Amenhotep III and his son, Akhenaten, Abdiel ("'servant of God").]

Heritage Girls Provide Faith-Based Scouting (February 2011)

While the Boy Scouts of America celebrated their 100th anniversary last year, the American Heritage Girls celebrated their 15th. They were founded in Cincinnati with ten troops and 100 members and are now over 11,000 members in 40 states and three other countries.

Patti Garibay co-founded the new group after her beloved Girl Scouts voted to eliminate "God," allowed lesbian troop leaders, and prohibited singing "offensive" Christian songs. In 2004 the Girl Scouts' support of Planned Parenthood led to a Girl Scout cookie boycott in Texas initiated by Pro-Life Waco. Garibay and her staff have to answer 50 calls per day on such issues.

While those contacts are helping grow AHG's numbers, they are far from joyful, she says.

"I've never encouraged boycotting cookies or anything like that," Garibay says. "I just want to make it so parents can be aware of what's going on and make the best decision for their children."

"I started the organization to offer a faith-based alternative to the Girl Scouts for families who love scouting, but want their girls' program to complement their families' values."

The previous year the two groups allied with the Memorandum of Mutual Support uniting in their "desire to establish and maintain a collaborative relationship on behalf of youth, young adults, and families ... for the purpose of confirming a framework of cooperative relationship under which the American Heritage Girls, Inc. and the Boy Scouts of America will assist one another in areas of mutual objectives ..."

At the Centennial Boy Scout Jamboree last summer, AHG became the first all-girls organization to be represented at this quadrennial gathering, maintaining an exhibit throughout the week.

The girls in the AHG range from age 5 to 18 with a five-level program: Path- finder, Tenderheart (grades 1 to 3), Explorer (grades 4 to 6), Pioneer (grades 7 to 8), and Patriot (grades 9 to 12) and the highest grade, the Stars and Stripes Award.

Pursuit of religious emblems (such as the PRAY Program) is integral to the AHG experience. Each AHG Troop is led by a Troop Shepherd and must be sponsored by a church or private school which holds to the principles of AHG. "It's people who really want a wholesome program for their daughters," Garibay says.

The heart of the group is the American Heritage Girl's Oath, "I promise to love God, cherish my family, and honor my country and serve in my community," and promise "As an American Heritage Girl, I promise to be: compassionate, pure, helpful, resourceful, honest, respectful, loyal, responsible, perseverant, and reverent.

The theme of the convention last year is exemplified by Betsy Henry's song, "Be A Moon," which begins, "... wants me to shine His light everywhere I go and if I will reflect His Son His glory I will show and I will glow-ow-ow-ow-ow-ow-ow, Glow-ow-ow-ow-ow-ow-ow, I will glow-ow-ow-ow-ow-ow-ow!"

More than 340 attendees visited Cincinnati's Underground Railroad and a sneak peek at the AHG's new badge, the Freedom Seekers. Thus Sacajawea and Harriet Tubman were also at the organization's 15th birthday celebration. They were joined by Bob the Tomato and Larry the Cucumber promoting their latest Veggie Tale's movie, "Sweetpea Beauty."

Student Outdoor Experience, another AHG partner, provided archery, tent building, and other camping training. Community service, an essential component of the girl's activities, took the form "Scarf It Up," donating fleece and making it into scarves for inner-city children.

They can be contacted at 175 Tri-County Pkwy. #100, Cincinnati, OH 45246 and americanheritagegirls.com. The troops in the Cincinnati area include St. Ignatius of Loyola and St. James.

[The American Heritage Girls helped with the formation of the Christian boy's alternative to scouting, Trail Life USA (traillifeusa.com).]

Book Shares How To Be A Saint, Not A Dummy (January 2011)

Saints for Dummies by Fr. John Trigilio, Jr., and Fr. Kenneth Brighenti covers all the basics about saints. They begin with sharing what the word saint means.

"Saints are simply ordinary men and women who, through their faith, overcome weakness, failures, and shortcomings." They quote Blessed Teresa of Calcutta that a saint never quits trying to do better.

Trigilio has a doctorate in theology and is a retired Navy chaplain, while Brighenti, also a doctor of philosophy, has worked as a hospital chaplain. Together they co-host a weekly television program, "Crash Course on Catholicism" and have co-authored *Catholicism For Dummies, Women in the Bible For Dummies*, and *John Paul II For Dummies*.

This book, they explain, is written for those not already saints, those curious about saints, or curious about a particular saint, or anyone wanting to overcome his or her own shortcomings and become a saint rather than a dummy.

The book includes cartoons illustrating the more humorous aspects of trying to become more saint and less dummy.

It also includes optional sidebars like that answering "Are Christopher and Valentine still saints?" They are still saints. A saint cannot be "defrocked." They and other formerly honored saints have just been removed from the Church calendar of feasts to make room for newer, more reliably documented saints.

They give examples of saints who exemplify the saintly virtues -- Thomas More for prudence, Joseph for justice, Teresa of Calcutta for fortitude, and Josemaria Escriva for temperance.

Trigilio and Brighenti inform about some of the more notable saints, the Blessed Virgin Mary and the apostles, and some of the more notorious ones: Augustine who overcame a playboy lifestyle, Camillus de Lellis who overcame a gambling addiction, Dismas the thief, angry Jerome, falsely accused Padre Pio, and nearly despairing Monica.

They explain that saints, although reverenced, are not worshiped. They are not angels -- except for three exceptions, the archangels mentioned in the Bible, Michael, Gabriel, and Raphael.

Much of the book is lists including that of thirteen undecayed saints, thirty-two martyrs, plus the mentioning of hundreds more from Rome, Bethlehem, Mexico, North America, Korea, and Japan.

Saints come from all walks of life. They list eleven virgins, eleven founders of orders, and eleven nobility. They list nine Latin fathers of the Church, thirteen Greek fathers, and ten Orthodox saints.

They list the seventy-five popes (including Peter who was also an apostle) who have been canonized, thirty-two doctors of the Church, and only twenty-four pastors.

Their top ten list of lists, however, includes such saint-related things as favorite litanies or list-like prayers to saints, and novenas or nine days of prayers before a feast day, favorite shrines, families of saints, things saints are the patron of, places where saints lived and died, and saints' feast days.

All of the fathers' books can be found at dummies.com. At the site is also "a cheat sheet" which explains what it takes to become a saint, two verified miracles after death or a martyr's death and a virtuous life, then the process of canonization is explained.

Some "little known facts" about saints are collected like Pope Blessed John XXIII's answer when asked, "How many people work at the Vatican?" "About half of them."

Another fact is that St. Isidore of Seville became the patron of the internet because he compiled the first written database in the sixth century, a 20-volume encyclopedia on everything known at the time, from A to Z.

[Fr. Trigilio also has the books, *Thomasistic Renaissance, Essential Bible, The Everything Bible Book, 101 Things Everyone Should Know About the Bible* and the "Council of Faith: the Documents of Vatican II" DVD. Fr. Brighenti has *Marriage as Covenant*.]

Book Shares Christmas Customs (December 2010)

Reginald Holme, one of the authors of *Christmas Around the World*, gives many different ways in which to make the Christmas season more meaningful.

He shares about how a Sunday school in Japan thanked their policemen with flowers and cake at Christmas and told them the true meaning of Christmas.

Holme quotes one student who was also touched who said, "Before last Christmas I experienced Christmas only as enjoying myself and I held parties with my friends and feasted. Now I take delight in serving others."

The author also tells of Don Richardson, a Canadian missionary who converted the Sawi of New Guinea. They had a custom of exchanging children to ensure peace. When Richardson told them about God sending His Son as a Peace Child for all tribes they accepted it.

Holme starts his Christmas customs chapter by noting that even the date of the holiday varies between peoples. It is not just one day but a Christmas season. Catholics, since the 4th century, begin celebrating Christ's birth on Christmas Eve, December 24. Greeks, Syrians, and Ethiopians still celebrate on Epiphany, January 6, and the Armenians as late as January 18.

In pre-Communist Ukraine he tells his readers there was the tradition of fasting for thirty-nine days before Christmas. When the first star was seen, the twelve-course supper began, including fish, beet soup, stuffed cabbage, and cooked dried fruit.

During the first week of Advent in Bavaria St. Nicholas visits, but children receive gifts from the Christkind (Christ Child). In Westphalia is the custom of writing letters to the Christ Child.

When St. Nicholas (feast December 6) visits Holland, accompanied by Black Peter, gifts are given, and hot punch or chocolate served.

On December 13, in Sweden a daughter in the family dresses as St. Lucia and serves the rest of the family, escorted by her brothers, the "Star Boys."

On December 16 Mexicans begins a novena, a time of the pilgrimage to posadas (lodgings) imitating Joseph and Mary's journey to Bethlehem. After being turned away the procession ends that night with prayers followed by refreshments, music, and dancing.

In Norway a thaw after the first heavy snowfall is called the "biscuit thaw" because of the heat from all the Christmas biscuits being baked.

Sicilians fast from sunset to sunset the day before Christmas Eve. After carols and songs before the creché comes a feast of eels, fish, pasta, and sweet bread. Italians eat no meat for 24 hours before Christmas Eve, Holme writes, "But there follows a meal as big as the family can afford."

Christmas Eve is called "Dipping Day" in Sweden from the custom of dipping rye bread in the Christmas ham drippings. In Ireland the youngest child lights the window candle for the Holy Family on Christmas Eve and caraway seed cakes are baked.

Hungarians feast and give presents on Christmas Eve before the evening meal with seeded rolls, dumplings, or biscuits.

In Greece Mass starts before sunrise on Christmas. The meal afterward includes Christ's Bread decorated with nuts.

In Urdu and Punjabi Christmas Day is called Bara Din, "the Big Day." In Southern India "The host however poor," Holme writes, "will try to bring out a thali or tray filled with chunks of sweetmeat for the forty to fifty people crowded on his verandah," some even his non-Christian neighbors.

In Finland Christmas Day is celebrated with gingerbread in many shapes and spiced red wine with raisins. In Greenland the men serve the women coffee and cake, rather than the other way around. Everyone in the village gets a gift as children go from hut to hut singing carols.

The Venerable Bede wrote that the English began their year on December 25. Joseph of Arimathea is said to have planted his staff on Weary-All Hill, which grew into the Glastonbury Thorn which flowers at this season. In Dewsbury, Yorkshire, the Devil's Knell has been toll for seven centuries, once for every year since Jesus' birth.

In Rome a cannon at Castle of St. Angelo proclaims Christmas. In Alsace a goose is traditional, in Brittany buckwheat cakes and sour cream. In Burgundy it's turkey and chestnuts, in Paris oysters.

In Minho province, the Portuguese eat a Christmas banquet in the early hours of Christmas, praying for the dead and leaving the table spread to remember them.

New Year's Eve in Scotland is celebrated as Hogmanay with cheese and oat cakes. The first one to cross the threshold after midnight, whether family member or stranger, prompts the celebration of the First Foot. In Italy it's celebrated with raisin bread, turkey, chicken or rabbit, and of course, spaghetti. In France the New Year starts with champagne.

Puerto Ricans continue to celebrate Christmas on January 6, Three Kings Day, and the two following with house-to-house processions, fruit, and guitar music. Bethlehem Day, January 12, concludes the Christmas season.

Creation Museum Provides Unique Experience (September 2010)

The Creation Museum claims in its brochure to be "a unique and unparalleled experience" and many would say they believe it is so. Even on a weekday the museum is quite crowded with visitors from all across the country. Located near Petersburg, Kentucky, it succeeds in demonstrating the truths of both science and Christianity.

Upon entering the museum a visitor is offered the opportunity to be photographed with a dinosaur. Upon entering "The Walk through Time," two paleontologists, one Bible-believing and one unbelieving, present their differing points of view from the video display. Nearby visitors can find opportunities to learn about and hunt for fossils in the rock wall themselves.

The Walk then continues on through a presentation of the history of the Bible in tableau, from Isaiah's prophecies to Moses' history to David's psalms to John and Peter at the empty tomb and Paul writing his letters. From there it lists the opposition to the Bible through time, in Esther's and Daniel's time in Babylon, in the time of the Maccabeans and in Herod's and Diocletus. It even goes on to list opponents like modernists, even specifically The Da Vinci Code.

Despite all attempts to destroy the Scriptures past and present, it has survived. It is the most translated, and by far the most best-selling book ever.

The museum shows one of the most significant turning points in the history of the Bible, Gutenberg's print shop. Nearby, however, are shown a facsimile of the original Greek Codex Vaticanus and a portion of three-hundred-year-old sheepskin with Genesis in the original Hebrew from a Torah saved from the late Saddam's ban.

Next comes the worst part of the whole museum, the depiction of what the world would be like without faith, what it is becoming with growing disbelief. Belief in God's design makes all the difference in a world that otherwise is without purpose, without hope.

Continuing on to "The Wonders of Creation" the visitor is mercifully presented with countless examples of the Creator's handiwork in His creation. From botany, biology, astronomy, and genetics the diversity and unity imaging the Trinity is shown. The best image of God, it is pointed out, is man, created to oversee His creation. Unexpectedly we are made in God's image no matter how unintelligent or uncreative we may be.

The Walk through Time includes a walk through Eden with the Serpent in the tree and Adam and Eve below. Immediately after the Fall, however, the visitor is encouraged to contemplate the prophecies of a future when there will again be no death (Isaiah 11:8), not pain (Revelation 21:4), no conflict (Isaiah 11:6), no hard labor (Isaiah 65:23), before witnessing the murder of Abel by Cain.

A lively nine-hundred-sixty-nine-year-old Methuselah tells the visitor of the coming flood while Noah and his sons work on the Ark. Visitors can learn about the Ark, view the interior and the animals, and even (via an interactive game) help Noah build the Ark.

After watching the Flood from space, the visitor can ask Noah questions and watch as Noah's family makes their thanksgiving sacrifice on Mt. Ararat.

Possible causes and consequences of such Deluge are speculated on. Underwater volcanic eruptions could have caused hypercanes bringing nearly endless rain and then an ice age. Prehistoric lakes in the West and Southwest could have carved out canyons without leaving debris, including the Grand Canyon.

"The Last Adam" rounds out the Walk through Time with visits with Mary who touchingly recalls Joachim explaining the need for the sacrificial lamb -- and her understanding her Son was that Lamb. With her is the Centurian movingly describing Jesus' last words, "It is finished," as "like a receipt, 'paid in full.' "

The Stargazer's Planetarium shows include "Created Cosmos" and "Worlds of Creation." The first is a tour from Earth to the farthest reaches of the known universe and back again to the Creation Museum. Delightfully mixed with the up-to-date astronomy and high-definition special effects are appropriate quotes from Job, "The Earth hangs on nothing," and Isaiah's "The Earth was made to be lived in."

page 115

The second is "just" a tour of the planets of the solar system with a brief stop on Mars. Earth is, like the museum, proved to be unique.

Among other offerings available are a "Creative Adventure Workshop," "Creation Musical Adventure," "Men in White," and "Dino-mite Readers," even a petting zoo and camel and dinosaur rides for youngsters. For adults the Dragon Hall Bookstore and gift shop is stocked with books, DVDs, and other things both scientific and Christian.

Because the museum has so much to offer, two-day passes are available.

[The Creation Museum now has its "sister attraction" forty miles away, the life-sized Noah's Ark and on-line virtual tours of both.]

Stop Cheating God And Yourself (August 2010)

"Stop being niggardly," that is, stop cheating yourself and God, is what Karen Hunter says in her new book. The full title is *Stop Being Niggardly and Nine Other Things Black People Need to Stop Doing*, but many of the things apply to anyone.

The dictionary definition quoted on the front flap says, "niggardly (adj.) [nig'erd-le]

1. stingy, miserly; not generous
2. begrudgingly about spending or granting
3. provided in a meanly limited supply.

It continues with the warning: "You'd better know what the word means before you pour your energies into overreacting to it."

"Stop cheating yourself out of the blessings you are supposed to have," Hunter elaborates, "by focusing on the things you don't have, by looking at what others have and are doing instead of being excellent and following your own path and purpose."

She explains that the idea for the title of the book came in 1999 when the word made the headlines. It had been used in connection to the District of Columbia budget, but because of ignorance of the meaning of the word, its user was forced to resign.

It showed up again in 2002 when Stephanie Bell used the word in a spelling class. She was forced to write apologies to all the children's parents and promise to never use the word again.

"I wished I could just shake them and tell them how important it is to give your child a proper foundation -- a solid name, strong values, a strong sense of self, and the value of learning and obtaining a solid education." And so she did.

Hunter herself stopped being niggardly in 1996 by acting on Habakkuk 2:2 and making a list of her goals. At the top of the list she had "Get closer to God." To do so she read through the sayings of Jesus, in a red letter edition of the Gospels. By the next year the top thing on her list was "Have a really deep relationship with God."

Many of her other helpful advice also comes from Scripture. She quotes Ecclesiastes 5:10 on the consequences of loving money. She explains that this means being satisfied with the income you have, don't go into debt, don't play the lottery, tithe.

Much of her advice comes from another Black woman, Nannie Helen Burroughs, who wrote *Twelve Things the Negro Must Do* in the 1890s. Hunter quotes Burroughs in hers with commentary.

Burroughs in turn quotes John 5:8, advice "Taking up your own bed and walk," and not always remaining dependent on others or God. Hunter connects this Ecclesiastes 5:10 with not loving money, while throwing it away in the lottery or credit card debt. She advises tithing, living on ninety percent or less rather than a hundred ten percent.

Burroughs advised making "religion an everyday practice and not just a Sunday-go-to-meeting emotional affair."

In response Hunter tells about her own battles against atheists on CNN, speaks out against Richard Dawkins, defends Creationism. She told the atheists, "There's no need to say, 'hey, wait a minute, you people! I don't believe in God and I'm offended that you all are praying!' " and has received hate mail ever since.

"I realized that I must have struck a nerve. I also realized that this was war and I had to be really serious about which side I stood on," she writes, and "it became increasingly more important that I studied that word, that I knew that word, but more importantly that I lived that word."

"Church for me," she continues, "is not about getting up and going to a building on Sunday, but an everyday reflection and fellowship with other believers and working on my relationship with God."

She retells the story told by George Washington Carver. He asked the Creator "Why did You create the universe?" God said, "You ask too much for your small mind to understand. Ask for something smaller." Carver asked, "Why did You make the peanut?" and God showed him three hundred uses for the peanut.

Burroughs encourages an Ezekiel experience like in Ezekiel 3:14-19, a command to warn the wicked. Hunter refers to Hebrews 13:3 that commands remembering those in prison. She encourages reading Deuteronomy 24:18, "Remember you were once a slave."

[Hunter has published *Twelve Things the Negro Must Do: With Special Commentary By Karen Hunter* and *Revelations: There's a Light After the Lime*, the story of rapper Ma#&36;e's transformation into Pastor Mason Betha.]

Microfinance Programs Aid Poor (July 2010)

Microfinancing is nothing new. Catholic Relief Services has over thirty years experience at making small loans to the world's poorest communities. CRS's microfinance activities are an outgrowth of Catholic social teaching, which unlike traditional banking institutions, promotes the sacredness and dignity of the human person.

CRS's microfinance programs target the self-employed poor, seventy percent women, reaching more than a million clients in thirty-six countries, typically with loans as low as forty dollars.

They work, not relying on a client's collateral, but linking the loan to savings, repayment of past loans, and getting clients directly involved as is CRS, from start-up to sustainability.

In Gambia, for example, eighteen women formed Sutura to save money. Soon, however, they began to work to eradicate malaria from their village. They got nets and instructed neighbors in their proper use.

In Guatemala Fortaleza (Strength) brought together HIV patients. Catalina Gomez says for them all, "More than anything, I want to live, I want God to keep giving me life."

In Rwanda neighbors who barely talked joined SILC (Savings and Internal Lending Communities) and Yvonne and Francois, for example, found they enjoy each other's company as much as the loans. They found they shared more in the aftermath of the genocide than separated them.

The EnComun de la Frontera microfinance project helped Patricio and Guadalupe buy a car for their tortilla business in Sorona, Mexico. "It used to take about five hours, now it takes me a little less than an hour. That means I can cover a greater area and have more clients."

Haoua Mamoudou is president of a sesame seed union of two hundred fifty growers in Nigeria. "Before the program started," she says, "we used to go to bed hungry. Now we have enough money to eat rice regularly and meat once a week."

When Taheya's husband passed away, leaving her with an astonishing debt of over seven thousand dollars, six times Egypt's average annual salary, she started a grocery business with her aunt Taheya and Hana's families'. Their lives has improved tremendously. Hana's family can now afford to eat meat twice a week instead of only once. She has also been able to buy a bicycle, telephone, refrigerator, and other items.

Some other organizations, like Kiva (kiva.org), give more direct links between individual lenders and clients. It reports on each entrepreneur's progress, posts both lenders and lendees' photos, provides weekly statistics. It can be linked to the lenders' facebook pages. There is even a journal link with the clients' own stories, often in their own languages. Every week they report about a million dollars in loans to three thousand entrepreneurs by sixteen thousand lenders.

The Serigne Mansour group in Senegal, for example, is through the CRS partner, CAURIE (Caisse Autonome pour le Reinforcement des Initiatives Economique) which became independent of CRS in 2005. This added information, however, does increase costs and reduces the ninety-five percent efficiency rating that CRS rates.

The Josephina Yasay's group is seven women who raise pigs in San pedro, Philippines. They have thirty lenders and have six more months to pay back the one thousand, nine hundred twenty-five dollar loan through ASKI (Alalay sa Kaunlara, Inc.).

The Virgen de Fatima communal bank in Huancavelica, Peru, received six thousand, seven hundred fifteen dollars through FINCA to finance small animal sales. The twenty-ninety entrepreneurs were backed by fourteen individual lenders (four anonymous).

Jivan Baghasaryan has received three thousand dollars for barber shop expansion in Yerevan, Armenia, from ninety-seven lenders through SEF (Small Enterprise Foundation), a partner of World Vision International. Of this, three hundred dollars is still needed with repayments continuing until July 2012.

The thirteen-member Yesu Amala group in Kampala, Uganda, took a loan to finance charcoal sales. They have a hundred twenty-one lenders for their three thousand six hundred twenty-five dollar loan, an average of thirty dollars each.

In answering why he does this, one featured lender, Percy, quotes Mark Twain: "Broad, wholesome, charitable views cannot be acquired by vegetating in one little corner of the earth." Since 2007 he has helped back fifty loans in nineteen countries, and as Kiva says, "changed lives."

Travel Show Goes On Pilgrimages (June 2010)

Burt Wolf's shows, "Travel and Traditions" and "Taste of Freedom," are both entertaining and informative. He mixes food, history, and often theology. Since they have been translated into Russian, Polish, Mandarin, and Korean, they reach a worldwide audience of over 150 million people. He has written thousands of segments for cable and hundreds of half-hours for PBS. He's been nominated for two CableAce awards and an Emmy.

Transcripts are available to even more on-line at www.burtwolf.com. Many are pilgrimages to religious sites. For the associated cruises see www.wmfe.org/burtwolf. "I don't think of myself as a travel writer," he says. "I know very little about the 'business' of travel. I make programs about cultural history which began when Ted Turner invited me to report for CNN." This was after he appeared on the Johnny Carson Show.

"For years, I wrote for the Washington Post, but like most newspaper writers, I had very little control over what actually went to print."

In "On the Pilgrimage to Santiago de Compostella" and "Santiago de Compostella," he joined pilgrims Francis of Assisi and Shirley McLaine, in "a physical stress test, a place to grieve, a journey of spiritual awakening, and a unique vacation."

In "Assisi, Italy" he tells about Francis and Clare, but also about the origin of the Christmas cribs, admirers of Francis from Protestantism, Judaism, Hinduism, Islam. "But they all appreciate St. Francis and his message of love and respect for everything -- people, animals, and our natural environment."

"The Shine of Guadalupe, Mexico City" tells the story of our Lady of Guadalupe and Juan Diego. It also touches on the National Shrine in Washington, D. C., and the Knights of Columbus. He also includes his favorite subjects, food and drink, gordita (griddlecake), and goat with "drunken sauce."

In New Mexico he pilgrimaged to Chimayo, "the Lourdes of North America." It had been a sacred site to the local Indians for ten thousand years. In 1810 a sand pit was discovered which was recognized as sacred by Catholics. Wolf, however, also looks into other local specialities, the weaving and chili.

Wolf's trip to the Vatican "happened" to be just when John Paul II died and a new pope was chosen. "The first thing that I learned was that the history of the papacy is not just the history of the Catholic Church," he says, it's "actually an essential part of the history of the entire world."

"The Land of St. Patrick" has to do both with Ireland and St. Patrick's Day. It also involves another pilgrimage, this time to Patrick's Purgatory in Donegal. (www.loughderg.org)

"Austrian Monasteries" emphasizes especially Klosterneuberg and Melk with a stop at Land-haus Bacher restaurant between.

The Book of the Year: A Brief History of Our Seasonal Holidays corresponds to the "Taste of Freedom" series, emphasizing food and feasts. Of particular interest are the spring and winter feasts of Christians and Jews.

The Easter episode actually covers Holy Thursday through the whole Easter season. He had lamb with Count Ugo Contini Bonacossi near Florence. Pan de Ramerino (hot crossbuns), la Columbo (dove-shaped dessert). He explains egg decorating in Ukraine and Russia, and the annual White House egg hunt.

The Christmas episode includes the traditions that have accumulated around the holiday: Advent, the Christmas tree, the yule log, caroling, and Midnight Mass. Christmas foods include German Christollen (nut bread), Pfefferkuchen (spice cake), Lebcuchen (honey cake), gingerbread, and eggnog.

"I think it's essential to remember that the central theme of the story of God giving His only Son as a gift to humanity," he explains. "To me, Christmas is about rebirth during the darkest time but it is also about generosity and sharing."

The Passover episode covers not only the history of the eight-day holiday but also Italian Jews' macaroons, matzo ball soup, and American Jews' interfaith Seders, such as at Sammy's Rumanian Steakhouse.

The Hanukkah episode includes the deidel, the Northern European latke (potato pancake), Israeli soufganioth (jelly doughnuts), Spanish fritters, and American gift-giving and decorating.

He was filming on his seventieth birthday. "The whole idea of retirement makes no sense to me. Keep challenging your mind and you'll stay young."

When asked which was his most "entertaining" European trip, he quickly answered, "My honeymoon. Because I had just married the woman of my dreams and the dreams keep getting better."

He also has a series just on local foods, both in the U.S. and Europe, called "What We Eat." Knowing French, he says, "will not help you appreciate the food in Paris. Look around the room at what other people are eating and if it looks good to you, point it out to your waiter."

[Wolf also has episodes of pilgrimages to Czestockowa and Lourdes.]

Men Witness About Jesus (May 2010)

The first speaker at this year's Answer the Call Men's Conference, Jack McKeon was introduced with "Take Me Out to the Ball Game" because of his career in baseball. His message was never give up your dream. His boyhood dream was of beating the Yankees in the world series. When he didn't get into the majors as a player, he changed directions and became a manager. At seventy-two he became the oldest manager ever to win the world series for the 2003 Florida Marlins.

He joked that he was so old that he remembered Preparation A. He also joked that the Cincinnati Reds haven't had a winning season since he left.

More seriously he attributed his success to his prayers to St. Teresa. "God was with me," he says. "It was His plan so I could reach souls and spread His good word."

Even more so since then he meets people who tell him, "You got me going to church" or "You got me back to church."

"We have to practice our faith," he says. "It's something we have to do on a regular basis. We live in the greatest country in the world, have the freedom to practice our faith, and set a good example for others."

He told about one fellow who asked for a ride to the stadium back in the Canadian league. He told him he'd have to go with him to Mass first. That's all it took. The man converted and continues to thank McKeon for introducing him to Jesus.

He ended his witness with, "I hope some day -- through the power of prayer -- your dreams will come true."

Brian Rooney also talked about victory. Coming from a background as a lawyer and a marine, he spoke of victory over "a diabolical enemy who hates us and wants to destroy us." He wasn't talking about terrorists or socialists, against which he's fought, but of the forces of hell.

His story is all too common, the slow process of a second conversion after having fallen away from the faith in college. Receiving Communion in Biblical lands with a diabolical enemy two blocks away moved him. So did the martyrs dying for the faith there.

Reminding the men at the conference of the two miraculous victories of Christendom in 732 and 1683, he calls our time "the last hope of Western civilization." The enemy is not just the radical Muslims either.

He also learned about the enemy first hand when he discovered "the bias to get you to terminate your child's life." His son Blase was baptized before his five surgeries in his first three months in case he didn't survive. He had many including the Dominican nuns who appeared on "Oprah," praying for him, but through it all Rooney learned, "Never be afraid to be a Catholic."

Fr. Mark Berger prayed, asking the Lord what to say and got two strange visions, the bishop sawing a man in half lengthwise and snakes laughing. Only just before coming out to speak did he learn their meaning. The first meant "There is no divided life. It's either all or not at all." The second meant "Shed what's dead."

Jim Gruden was similarly guided by promptings of the Holy Spirit, beginning with one Lent when he began visiting church during lunch. "By the time Lent was over," he says, "an hour was not enough."

He was prompted in adoration to change jobs and within two years his old company not only had been sold, but had been torn down. He was also prompted to become a lay pastoral minister and to donate a kidney to a stranger. His wife wasn't so convinced until the Lord communicated to her through a bumper sticker that said, "Don't take your organs to heaven. We need them here." He introduced the kidney recipient who was no longer a stranger.

"If you think the enemy works against one marriage or one priest," he challenged the men, "think about how much he hates the Eucharist."

"Become a DAD," Gruden said. "Someone who Discerns, Accepts, and Does the will of God," adding that if God can work with an engineer who plays the accordion, there's hope for everyone.

The Most Rev. Roger J. Foys also shared a moving story about the necessity to practice the faith always. A convert in his former parish chose to cut off from his whole family rather than lose the precious gift he found in the Catholic Church. Within two years the rest of the family joined him because of his witness.

As Gruden summed up the seemingly impossible challenges the Church faces, "Nothing -- absolutely NOTHING, is impossible with God!"

Book Reports On Resurrections (April 2010)

Raised from the Dead by Fr. Alfred J. Hebert is a good book during Easter to increase one's faith in the power of the Resurrection. He retells stories of resurrections from the dead from Scripture and from the lives of the saints. He also relates resurrection miracles to "Visits to and from the Other World," "Miraculous Bodily Phenomena," and our own resurrections at the End of the World.

"Miracles are performed for the glory of God and the good of men," he explains. "Miracles also provide proof for the truth of the Catholic Christian Faith."

In October, 1370, he writes, Catherine of Siena's mother, Mona Lapa, suddenly died, and she was very concerned about the state of her soul. Catherine had been told by God that it would be better that her mother die soon for many misfortunes awaited her. Lapa, however, had refused to confess before she died. What happened next was witnessed by Catherine's sister-in-law and two other women.

"Lord, my God, are these promises You made to me?" Catherine cried out. "That none of my house should go to hell? ... I beg You not to let me be defrauded like this. As long as there is life in my body I shall not move from here until You have restored my mother to me."

Catherine's mother not only lived, she lived to be eighty-nine and endured many sorrows.

In early March, 1430, Joan of Arc arrived in Lagny-sur-Marn on her way to Paris. There some villagers told her of a mother in distress over the stillbirth of her son. The woman asked only that the child might be brought back to life to be baptized, so Joan went to the church where the child had been laid before the statue of Mary where several young girls were already praying. When Joan added her own prayers, the boy began to yawn. He was baptized and then died again.

One of the thirty miracles recorded soon after Bernadine of Siena's death in 1444 was the resurrection of eleven-year-old Blasio Massei of Cascia. His whole family had been praying to

Bernadine, when the boy rose up on the way to his gravesite. He said Bernadine had restored him to life to tell of the wonders he had seen in Heaven.

In November of 1561 Teresa of Avila's six-year-old nephew Gonzalo died. Keeping his death secret from his wife Juana, her brother-in-law Juan de Ovalles carried the boy's cold body to her. Teresa covered him with her veil when Juana came into the room asking what was wrong. He began to breathe again.

In Lima, Peru, on November 8, 1639, five-year-old Mary Monroy fell from a second story along with an iron lattice that had split her skull, smashed her face, and popped out one eye. The distraught mother asked for oil from the lamp at Francis Solanus' tomb. When it was applied, the girl was instantly healed.

Andrew Bobola was martyred in 1657. His body was found to be incorrupt in 1702, his wounds still fresh. On February 1, 1711, in Pinsk, nine-year-old Anne was found dead by the maid sent to awake her for school. Her father, Capt. Peter Gluszynski had once said, "Until Bobola performs a miracle I shall not believe in his power." The Roman rite priest was not available, so the Greek Orthodox priest was sent for. Peter prayed to Andrew and when the priest read "The child is not dead but sleeping," she moved her head and awoke.

In September, 1741, a boy fell out of a window watching those leaving church while Paul of the Cross was giving a mission in Orbetello. The boy's parents fetched the departing missionary who returned, prayed, and restored him to life.

When John Baptist Ramirez's son died of a fever in 1647 in Chelva, he placed an image of Louis Bertrand on his body and prayed. The boy opened his eyes and asked for food. Louis was canonized twenty-four years later.

In Turin in 1849, fifteen-year-old Charles, who was attending the Oratory of Don Bosco, died before the saint could get there. Before the boy's mother and aunt Don Bosco said, "Charles! Rise!" and he tore himself out of his shroud. He gave thanks that he could repair the bad confession he had made. He had gone to hell, but a beautiful Lady had told him, "There is still hope for you have not yet been judged." After making a complete confession, he leaned back, closed his eyes, and died again.

On a lighter note Fr. Hebert includes the resurrections of Antonella and Martinello. A visiting priest had caught and cooked Francis of Paola's pet trout Antonella. When Francis sent a messenger to retrieve it, the thief threw it to the ground shattering it. Nevertheless when given the pieces the saint prayed, "Antonella, in the name of Charity, return to life!" On another occasion some workmen had cooked and eaten his pet lamb, Martinello. Like Ezekiel, Francis raised the lamb back to life from bones and fleece.

Haiti Quake Produces "Miracles" (March 2010)

At least a hundred thirty-five people buried by Haiti's earthquake and its aftershocks were rescued by search teams. "'If you save one man,' we say in Hebrew," Col. Gili Shenhal said, "'you save the whole world,' and this is one of the main reasons that we are here." Some, however, consider the outpouring of charity from so many recession-hit nations to these very needy people the greater miracle.

Most were rescued within a few days. Reinhard Riedel's wife was pulled, dehydrated but otherwise uninjured, from a hotel's ruins on Saturday. "It's a little miracle," he said. That same day a baby boy was delivered aboard a U. S. Coast Guard vessel by medical rescue personnel who had rescued his mother.

Eight days afterward, seven-year-old Kiki and his sister Sabrina Joachim were rescued. Their aunt Denival Orana returned to salvage some possessions, and heard Kiki's faint cries. American firefighters were able to cut a hole in the floor and pass water down to them.

Describing his rescue, he said, "I smiled because I was free. I smiled because I was alive." He added, "I am sad for my brothers and sister but happy with my mama."

Although losing three of her five children, his mother Ena said, "When I saw them, I collapsed in tears and hugged them. We were all laughing and crying at the same time."

Also on the eighth day twenty-two-day-old Elizabeth Josaint was rescued in the devastated seaside town of Jacmel, where her mother Michelin Josaint's husband was killed. The baby's grandfather, Michellet Josaint, calls it a sign. "When I come here," he said, "I don't find the baby. The people tell me, 'Relax.' And I come here and I find my children with the baby ... fantastic!"

"At ninety degrees, you would die of dehydration in seven days," Dr. Kent Holtorf explains, "but if you add in the extra humidity, like in Haiti, you're not losing water through your skin as quickly, and you can survive for an extra three to five days."

Even so, twenty-one-year-old Emanuel Buteau survived ten days under the wreckage of his collapsed apartment building. He was saved by an Israeli rescue team and revived at an Israeli field hospital.

"It's a big miracle!" Buteau said through a translator. "I was praying to God and I was saying, 'God, if it's Your will, I will die. If its Your will, I will survive."

After being knocked unconscious, he woke up in a cramped, dark air pocket. He prayed a lot and cried a lot. Then Buteau's mother returned to try to find his body to bury. Hearing her speak of him in the past tense, he called her name, and she called the Israeli rescue team.

After 11 days Haitians turned out for an open-air funeral Mass for the archbishop of Port-au-Prince, Monsignor Joseph Serge Miot, who was buried at Lilavois Cemetery. Thousands of others, however, had to be buried in unmarked mass graves. From six in the morning to six at night, they prayed.

Pastor Gregory Toussaint of the Tabernacle of Glory Church in Miami, Florida, who helped organize the event, said that those who suffered when the Earth shook wanted to ask for God's forgiveness. Others came to openly give thanks.

That's when the Haitian government declared an end to searches for survivors. Wismond Exantus Jean-Pierre, twenty-four, was rescued eleven days after.

Dehydrated and exhausted, Wismond said he stayed alive by diving under a desk and drinking cola, beer, and eating cookies.

"I was hungry, but every night I thought about the revelation that I would survive." Scottish-born Carmen Michalska, thirty-six, from Sheffield, was attached to the Hellenic Rescue Team from Greece. After two and a half hours of digging, she volunteered to squeeze down a tiny hole to get to him under twenty feet of what had been the two-story Napoli Inn hotel.

"To save somebody's life was amazing," she said.

"He smiled and was so happy to see us. He held our light for us while we sawed the wood in front of him away. I couldn't talk to him because I don't speak French but he said 'Merci.'"

Wismond's brother Enso, twenty-three, who lost six relatives in the earthquake, shared: "I had a dream that my brother called to me and told me he was alive. He told me to come get him and I have been coming every day."

Later, at a French field hospital, Wismond told his own story. "I was hungry but every night I thought about the revelation that I would survive. I prayed. It's a big miracle for me. When I leave the hospital I will give my heart to the Lord because He saved my life."

Fourteen days after the original quake, thirty-five-year-old Rico Dibrivell was pulled out in just dusty underpants, likely buried in one of the aftershocks. After fifteen days, however, came yet another miracle. Near St. Gerard University, Darlene Etienne was found. Dr. Claude Fuilla of the French rescue team found the young woman, who was taken to the French Navy hospital ship Sirocco.

"We cannot really explain this because that's just [against] biological facts," Dr. Evelyne Lambert says. "We are very surprised by the fact that she's alive ... She's saying that she has been underground since the very beginning."

Christians Unite To Affirm Principles (February 2010)

Last November a "call of Christian Conscience" was written called the Manhattan Declaration. So far it has a third of a million signers, according to its website, www.manhattandecllaration.org.

Cardinal Justin Rigali explained its points "are not the unique preserve of any particular Christian community or of the Christian tradition as a whole ... They are principles that can be known and honored by men and women of goodwill even apart from Divine Revelation. They are principles of right reason and Natural Law."

Although the declaration itself is nearly five thousand words long, it can be easily summarized. In the preamble our debt to past Christians is acknowledged. The main body of the document deals with attacks by the culture of death against life, marriage, and religious freedom. Reminding readers of the forgotten reasons why these need to be defended are what takes so many more words.

"We claim the heritage of those Christians who defended innocent life by rescuing discarded babies from trash heaps in Roman cities and publicly denouncing the empire's sanctioning of infanticide." The authors declare, "We remember with reverence those believers who sacrificed their lives by remaining in Roman cities to tend the sick and dying during the plagues, and who died bravely in the coliseums rather than deny their Lord."

"The great civil rights crusades of the 1950s and '60s were led by Christians claiming the Scriptures and asserting the glory of the image of God in every human being regardless of race, religion, age, or class."

"This same devotion to human dignity has led Christians in the last decade to work to end the dehumanizing scourge of human trafficking and sexual slavery, bring compassionate care to AIDS sufferers in Africa, and assist in a myriad of other human rights causes."

Robert George, one of the declaration's authors, is a Princeton University professor of jurisprudence. He explains: "For too long, the historic traditions of Catholicism, Evangelical Protestantism, and Eastern Orthodoxy have failed to speak formally with a united voice, despite their deep agreement on fundamental questions of morality, justice, and the common good. The Manhattan Declaration provided leaders of these traditions with an opportunity to rectify that. It is gratifying that they were willing -- indeed eager -- to seize the opportunity."

The other authors are Timothy George, professor of Samford University, and Chuck Colson, founder, Center for Christian Worldview.

On their FAQ (frequently asked questions) page is the further explanation, "We are seeking to build a movement -- hundreds of thousands, perhaps millions, of Catholic, Evangelical, and Eastern Orthodox Christians who will stand together alongside other men and women of goodwill in defense of foundational principles of justice and the common good.

"We believe God is looking for good men and women who will pledge (as those who have done in signing the Manhattan Declaration), never to compromise the Gospel, and to become well-informed, effective advocates of true and godly principles."

In explaining the passage on "... the failure to take steps necessary to halt the spread of preventable diseases like AIDS, it defends the pope. "When Pope Benedict XVI was attacked for saying that the condom distribution in Africa is not the solution, he was supported not only by conservative Christians, but by Edward C. Green, Director of the AIDS Prevention Research Project at Harvard University's Center for Population and Development Studies."

The declaration is not just the facts, but a pledge for the future. By signing you would be agreeing with "We will be united and untiring in our efforts to roll back the license to kill that began with the abandonment of the unborn to abortion," and "We pledge to labor ceaselessly to preserve the legal definition of marriage as the union of one man and one woman and to rebuild the marriage culture."

It ends with the even stronger pledge of civil disobedience, "We will not comply with any edict that purports to compel our institutions to participate in abortions, embryo-destructive research, assisted suicide and euthanasia, or any other anti-life act; nor will we bend to any rule purporting to force us to bless immoral sexual partnerships, treat them as marriages or the equivalent, or refrain from proclaiming the truth, as we know it, about morality and immorality, and marriage and the family. We will fully and ungrudgingly render to Caesar what is Caesar's. But under no circumstances will we render to Caesar what is God's."

[In 2012 the Manhattan Document was cited in the case of a Nicaraguan mother's custody suit by her former Lesbian partner.]

Priest Uses Cooking To Encourage Community (November 2009)

Fr. Leo E. Patalinghug from Mt. St. Mary's Seminary in Emmitsburg, Maryland, is getting more well known. His ministry, Grace Before Meals, now includes speaking engagements, a cook book, podcasts, and a TV pilot.

Through www.gracebeforemeals.com's blog and weekly newsletter, Fr. Leo says, "You'll all have a chance to get to know me better, to get to know each other better, and most importantly, get to know better the One Who invites us to His Table ... where the Food is an 'eternal banquet.'"

It all wouldn't have happened if not for 9/11. When his planned trip to France was cancelled, he and a few other priests got together for an impromptu retreat. Fr. Leo's cooking and the fellowship prompted one priest to suggest a cooking show. Fr. Leo claims he responded, "That is the dumbest idea I have ever heard!"

The idea would not go away, however. As Fr. Leo explains, he now understands "It's time to try something new to engage people and their faith. It is part of a movement among traditional Catholics who are pushing what Pope John Paul II called 'the new evangelization,' an effort to use mass communication to draw people to the Church."

His Grace Before Meals: Recipes for Family Life not only gives recipes for two meals a month centered around feast days, holidays, and family events, but includes Bible passages for reflection and conversation starter questions, such as, "What qualities do you expect out of an ideal friend?" "What is your most memorable meal?" "If you had a chance to bring one person back from the dead, who would it be and why?"

There's even a Fr. Leo grace: "Loving Father, we thank You for the family gathered around the table, the friends who extend your goodness, the food which nourishes our bodies, and the Faith that strengthens our souls. Keep us ever mindful of these blessings, and may this food inspire us to bring these blessings to those who go without family, friends, food, and faith. We ask all of this through Christ our Lord. Amen."

On fast food he comments, "Our culture has become too busy. We are too busy to prepare food for each other. We are too busy to spend time together. We are too busy to make this effort for people we love," says Fr. Leo.

"It's the mentality behind it that makes us not slow down, not come together as a family, not develop the relationships that are fostered at the home," he said. "I have no trouble with people bringing fast food, just eat it together, slowly, and say prayer beforehand."

Cincinnati-native James Boric, at the seminary, took part in some of Fr. Leo's fraternal dinners in Westminister, and was impressed by how he went out of his way to make dishes especially for him without seafood or red meat, like breaded portabello mushroom salad. "I like to think that I have forced him to become a better chef," he says.

Priests and seminarians are not the only ones included in this project. Many members of his family have also been on the show. Archived episodes of his show include pasta carbonara with his sister Angelique and his sister-in-law Angelica, zucchini frittata with older brother Carlos, mandarin Asian chicken salad with his nieces Alyssa, Angelique, and Christiania, and peanut butter and banana hot dogs with his nephews C. J., Manjo, Gabriel, Jared, and Chad.

Fr. Leo also visited the family of Thomas H. Powell, president of Mount St. Mary's University, for creamy coconut curry chicken.

His own mentor, however, is his spiritual mother, the Blessed Mother. "Life was not easy for her," he says. "She suffered." Yet he can picture her providing the Child Jesus and Joseph with their meals. "She is the model of calm generosity. She feeds all of us with the fruit of her womb, Jesus."

Fr. Leo gained a bit more notoriety when he beat chef Bobby Flay in a Fusion Fajita cook-off on the Food Network, which Fr. Leo calls "sometimes the safest thing to watch on TV."

He has been recently interviewed on "PBS" Religion and Ethics Newsweekly" and our local Sacred Heart Radio's "Son Rise Morning Show." "Grace Before Meals" won a People's Choice Podcast Award in the Food and Drink category.

Leo McWatkins Films is currently in development of a thirteen-part television series based on the *Grace Before Meals* book.

"The fact is we're all hungering for something." Fr. Leo concludes, "Let's not overlook the blessings! The food on the table and the people gathered around it. That's my hope: to come a little closer to our table as a family and to The Table as God's Family!"

In November Fr. Leo will be taping a show at Steubenville University called "Franciscan University Presents" which airs on EWTN.

A study by the National Center on Substance and Addiction at Colombia University confirms the Grace Before Meals philosophy. It compared families who eat dinner together less than three times a week with those who do so at least five times per week. Adolescents who eat with their families more frequently were forty percent more likely to talk to their parents about a problem. Their academic performance was better. They were significantly less likely to smoke, to drink, or use drugs. The traditional two-parent family was much more likely to have dinner as a family than a single-parent household.

[In 2017 Fr. Leo founded Plating Grace and the Table Foundation, hosts "Savoring Our Faith" on EWTN and co-hosts "Entertaining Truth" on Sirius Radio.]

Pro-Life Decisions Have Great Impact (October 2009)

Jim Caviezel, who played Jesus in Mel Gibson's "The Passion of the Christ", certainly has lived up to his professed pro-life convictions when challenged by a friend who was not pro-life to adopt a disabled child. He and his wife, Kerri, have now adopted two orphans with brain tumors from China.

The Caviezels' son, Bo, had been abandoned on a train, grew up in an orphanage until five, when he was diagnosed with a brain tumor. When they went to adopt a second child, they were first offered a healthy baby girl, but chose instead a five-year-old girl also with a brain tumor.

"We took the harder road," Caviezel says. "That is what faith is to me; it's action. It's the Samaritan. It's not the one who says he is; it's the one who does -- and does without bringing attention to himself. I'm saying this because I want to encourage other people." "You do feel scared," he tells couples thinking about adopting, "but you have no idea the blessings that you have coming to you if you just take a chance on faith."

Being one of the few faithful Catholics in Hollywood is "part of the cross you take up when you choose to believe in Him ... we all have this desire to want to be liked ... but what we should be asking God is the desire for humility."

On the other hand, Kourtney Kardashian, star of the reality show, "Khloe and Kourtney Take Miami," says she is still pro-choice, but has chosen not to abort her and her boyfriend Scott Disick's baby. Ironically, after a highly-divided discussion of this moral issue older than she is, she still can say, "I don't think it's talked through enough."

Faced with her own challenge, Kourtney did talk about it. She did not want to give her baby up for adoption and so had to choose between aborting or keeping the baby.

"I can't even tell you how many people just say, 'Oh, get an abortion,' like it's not a big deal," she said.

But when she called her doctor, he told her, "There is nothing you will ever regret about having the baby, but you may regret not having the baby."

Sitting on her bed hysterically crying, she read stories on-line of women who felt so guilty from having an abortion," she says. Finally she told herself, "I can't do that."

"For me, all the reasons why I wouldn't keep the baby were so selfish," she says. "I felt in my body, 'This is meant to be. God does things for a reason.' I just felt like it was the right thing that was happening in my life."

She's not telling exactly which websites that she visited. If Kourtney may have read testimonies from the older, unmarried women at the Priests for Life's site, or others very similar to "My body knew it had been robbed."

"I was twenty years old," this mother writes, "separated from a marriage that hadn't lasted three months. I bled heavily for a whole month. No one ever told me what to do or expect after.

"I was a mess. I hated men, was really trying to hurt them and me, and I was on an emotional roller coaster. My body knew it had been robbed and my head couldn't face up to it.

"One year later I became a Christian. A lady helped me go through steps of healing and God's forgiveness. Even so, I took about five years to really look at the whole situation and come to terms with it.

"I realize now that this was all Satan's lies and that doctors are only human. The one and only thing that has really given me comfort over the years is to know that that baby will never suffer and that it is in the arms of Jesus. Life is so precious -- we can't take it for granted."

She acted upon those feelings and happily the baby's father supports her decision, even though many other friends and relatives don't. "I really wanted to think it through for myself, and not hear what my sisters were saying, or what Scott was saying. Even though I took it all in, I wanted it to be my decision," she says.

When she finally did make the decision, the choice for life, she says, "I got so excited, and when I told Scott he was so excited."

Jim also gets excited. The strength of Christian faith, he says, is "in just giving it up and saying I'm going to be a servant of Jesus Christ, and my Father in Heaven. We were not awarded any Oscars for "The Passion", but do you think that's the important thing for God? Certainly if we received ten Oscars, it would not bring any more peace into the world.

"When the world looks at us, in complete and utter dismay, and asks why would you choose to suffer like this? But in that, that's where the great strength is when God starts to work."

[Caviezel has more recently played St. Luke in "Paul, Apostle of Christ" and is said to be playing Jesus again in "Passion of Christ: Resurrection" to be released in 2019 or 2020.]

Battle The Culture Of Death (September 2009)

If you are asking yourself, "What can one person do against the overwhelming culture of death?" there are many things. The Lord has raised up warriors on many fronts in this battle for life.

"Leave room for the Holy Spirit to work." Amarillo's Pro-life director, Rita Diller, says, "Empty yourself and be God's humble instrument so that His work may be accomplished."

Her bishop, Bishop John W. Yanta, initiated a campaign against the Planned Parenthood centers in his diocese and all nineteen were gone in twelve years. It was basically just following Jesus' command to be clever as serpents and gentle as doves. It included both spiritual and political activism.

Catholics in Amarillo prayed at a weekly diocesan pro-life Mass, held prayer vigils at the Planned Parenthood centers and events, displayed Our Lady of Guadalupe's image and Jesus' message of forgiveness.

Diller included such visible witnesses as the Knights of Columbus and post-abortive women. They kept the police and newspapers informed while building a reputation with them of peaceful protest. They even confronted the Girl Scouts on their support of Planned Parenthood.

They went inside the abortion facilities to learn exactly what was going on in each one, attended Planned Parenthood events, got on their mailing lists. They could then speak specifically to the men and women thinking of having an abortion.

The pro-life, however, involves other life issues as well. Leslie Kuhlman is involved with the new Theology of the Body Teaching Center which opened just last January. Already this ministry has reached adults, teens, teachers, and engaged couples, spreading the truth about marriage. "God gave us the Theology of the Body because we need it," she says. Even in this culture of death everyone craves Love. They just need to know where to find Him.

Located in suburban Cincinnati, it combines a pastoral setting and the power of the Holy Spirit. Its website, www.ruahwoods.org, expresses this.

Although Joe Brinck is one of the co-founders of the center, he says, "There is no one silver bullet." He recommends everyone get and watch "Maafa21" by Mark Crutcher at Life Dynamics Inc. out of Denton, Texas. It is the most informative presentation of the workings of this century-old devilish conspiracy. Their motto is, "We're not here just to put up a good fight. We're here to win, because winning is how the killing stops."

Brinck also suggests that all Catholics visit the National Catholic Bioethics Center (www.ncbcenter.org) to keep informed, write informed letters to their congressmen and senators, and discuss the life issues with friends and co-workers.

The fight is not only for the rights of the unborn or the sanctity of marriage, but increasingly for the rights of the chronically or terminally ill, for all of us as we grow older.

"Human life is an inviolable gift from God." The NCBC website says, "Our love of God and His creation should cause us to shun any thought of violating this great gift through suicide or euthanasia." It quotes Wisdom 1:13, "God did not make death, nor does He rejoice in the destruction of the living. For He fashioned all things that they may have being."

He also recommends Missionaries of the Gospel of Life, based on Fr. Frank Pavone's Priests for Life (www.priestsforlife.org/missionary/), but expanded for the laity.

The Coalition for Life recently led another Forty Days for Life in 144 cities in 44 states. The Cenacles of Life emphasize fasting one day a week on bread and water and praying ten decades of the rosary "to transform the face of the earth -- and to defeat this war on life."

Although some of these initiatives have grown to national and international outreaches, Brinck recommends fighting the fight locally in what ever way God calls you to do. This is what is called the principle of subsidiarity, working on the lowest necessary level, for even the least in the Kingdom of God is vital.

Miss California USA Defends Marriage (June 2009)

"It's not about me," the 21-year-old Miss USA runner-up Carrie Prejean says, "it's about the future of marriage. But I'm honored to do my part."

Miss California USA defended one-man-one-woman, traditional marriage during the USA beauty pageant and has been persecuted then and since. It was not apparently such a popular opinion among some residents of the Left Coast.

The crowd booed her, while judge Perez Hilton frowned. He later called her a "dumb b -- -- " but apologized for that remark. Keith Lewis, director of the pageant, said, "I support Carrie's right to express her personal beliefs, even if they do not coincide with my own. I believe the subject of gay marriage deserves a great deal more conversation in order to heal the divide it has created."

There seems, however, to be almost irreconcilable differences between the two sides. Prejean said she was raised to believe that marriage is between a man and a woman and the bloggers called her "a bigot," "self-righteous," and worse.

Carrie took a semester off her junior year at San Diego Christian College to participate in the contest. She has also modeled for Bliss Magazine, been featured on the cover of PJ Salvage Fall Catalog 2008, for Target, Saks Fifth Avenue, Bloomingdales, and Nordstrom, and was on "Deal or No Deal" model finalist. She has volunteered with Best Buddies, Special Olympics, and Voices for Children, preparing to work in special education.

"I was raised in a way that you can never compromise your beliefs and your opinions for anything." She does this by living life by the verse, Philippians 4:13, "I can do all things through Christ Who strengthens me."

Since doing so in the national spotlight, she has been interviewed by World Magazine, World Net Daily, One News Now, and Townhall, among others.

"I'm grateful for all the prayers and well-wishes I've received," she says, "from all different kinds of Americans who believe as I do that America is a place where people should stand up for our values, for what we think is right.'" Fox News talk show host Sean Hannity told

Prejean, "There's a lot of people cheering you tonight that you stood on your principles, that you put the principles above winning."

National Organization for Marriage (NOM) President Maggie Gallagher praised in National Review, "I would like to nominate Miss California as the new face of the marriage movement. Much better than mine!" Miss Prejean has now begun working with NOM on their new ad campaign, "No Offense," that tries to warn Americans that legalizing same-sex marriage in fact "will create widespread and unnecessary legal conflict" for individuals, small businesses, and religious groups.

It follows an earlier NOM ad, "Gathering Storm," that warned Americans that the push to legalize same-sex marriage has significant implications for religious liberty. In response, a heterophobic representative of the Human Rights Campaign denounced NOM and supporters of marriage on "Hardball" as "outright bigots."

"Many backers of same-sex marriage simply do not want to debate the consequences on society of this profound proposed change to redefine marriage," said Brian Brown, executive director of NOM. "They want to browbeat and silence opposition. But no matter how loudly they yell, their attacks on supporters of marriage will fail because people of integrity will speak the truth -- whether they are in pulpits, law schools, or even beauty pageants."

Besides the ad campaigns (viewable on YouTube), the NOM Advocacy Center provides updates on important issues related to marriage and an easy on-line way to contact elected officials on them. You can personalize your own e-mail from a sample and they will automatically identify your representatives and send them copies based on your nine-digit zip code.

One current project is writing to advocate protecting the already passed Defense of Marriage Act (DomaDefenseFund.com). It's only DOMA that currently prevents a few judges from imposing same-sex marriage on all the other states.

Screenwriter Shares Conversion Experience (May 2009)

Crossbearer: A Memoir of Faith by Joe Eszterhas has become a bestseller at Amazon.com. Reviewer G. Grant sums it up well at their website, "He is still the same, raw guy, telling it like it is in his brusque, humorous style. His life turns around, due to three incidents; he comes down with diagnosed incurable throat cancer; has a miraculous cure, and he experiences a religious, curbside enlightenment when his life is at the bottom ebb."

Eszterhas has already told much of his life story in *Hollywood Animal* and *The Devil's Guide to Hollywood*. Then it was about the Hollywood lifestyle and the challenges of being a screenwriter. Now his story is more a story about faith, Catholic faith.

Jerry Felty writes, "One part that stands out is his love of his mother who suffered from mental illness much of her life and died with her rosary. As horrible as life must have been for her, she never relinquished the comfort of her belief in Our Blessed Mother."

It is also the story of how he came from post-World War II refugee camps and grew up poor in Cleveland, Ohio. That Eszterhaus' parents made little effort to learn English or assimilate into American culture didn't help. He clawed his way to the top to become the highest paid screenwriter, getting three million dollars for "Basic Instinct." "I'm sorry for some things I did and said," he confesses.

He begins raising four sons with his second wife on the beach. "We didn't want them to become surfers," he says, so the family went back home to Ohio, to Holy Angels Church, Bainbridge township.

Predictably, since he had been smoking since the age of 12, he was diagnosed with cancer and, in the process of recovery, he stopped drinking and smoking when God came to him. "I've discovered that fighting cancer is a breeze compared to fighting certain directors." Now he has to learn to deal with hard-to-deal-with neighbors and kids' coaches.

Dennis Doverspike wrote at Amazon, "What Eszterhas does well is describe how the Church makes it difficult these days to be Catholic," the narrow way, "while at the same time describing the sense of community the Church provides."

Victor G. Kakavas wrote, "Often we forget the power of faith and prayer, only to go back to it when we really need it. We are all guilty of that -- that is why this book is a must-read. If anything, this book will make you re-examine your own life and hopefully bring you closer to your faith."

When asked what his next project is, Joe says simply, "I'm going to raise our boys and love my wife forever."

Debt Continues To Enslave (March 2009)

Debt slavery is nothing new. Proverbs 22:7 says, "The rich rule over the poor, and the borrower is the slave of the lender." Saint Paul advised, "Owe no debt to anyone except the debt that binds us to love one another." (Romans 13:8)

However, most debtors today don't even realize how enslaved they are. Credit Cards.com found more than 90 percent of those surveyed thought themselves as having the same -- or less -- debt as the average American.

The average college graduate is now $20,000 in debt and the average principal amount owed on a mortgage, before bailouts, was about $70,000. Myvesta.org figures the average American spends $1.22 for every dollar they earn.

According to the latest consumer debt statistics by the Federal Reserve Bank, U.S. consumers are indebted to the tune of over $2.5 trillion. Of that, almost $1 trillion is revolving consumer (credit card) debt. According to the U.S. Federal Reserve, however, 25% have no credit cards, and slightly more pay off their entire balance every month. Less than half owe all the credit card debt.

Besides this private debt, we all have a huge national debt. To keep track of the national debt Seymour Durst put up a debt clock in New York in 1989, when it was about 2.7 trillion dollars. When it passed ten trillion late in 2008, the dollar sign was replaced with a one. A re-design is underway, with enough space for a quadrillion dollars, which might last more than another twenty years. Right now it figures to be over $37,000 per capita.

As Neal Boortz explains it, "A politician cannot spend one dime on any spending project without first taking that dime from the person who earned it. So, when a politician votes for a spending bill, he is saying that he believes the government should spend that particular dollar rather than the individual who worked for it."

National Defense accounts for most of the national debt. The country was born in debt from the Revolutionary War, but on January 8, 1835, President Andrew Jackson paid it off. It soon returned, however, skyrocketing from $65 million to $16,569 million with the Civil War. After World War II it was $260 billion. Adjusted for inflation, that would be about three trillion 1835 dollars.

Income redistribution programs such as the Departments of Health and Human Services, HUD, and Agriculture (food stamps) account for the second largest portion of the debt. The Congressional Budget Office (CBO) has written that: "Future growth in spending per beneficiary for Medicare and Medicaid -- the federal government's major health care programs -- will be the most important determinant of long-term trends in federal spending." The interest on the debt is the third largest portion of the debt.

It is no wonder, therefore, that Andrew L. Yarrow, author of *Forgive Us Our Debts*, writes, "Americans feel like they are paying a lot on April 15, only to see highways clogged and deteriorating, workers' livelihoods not being protected, global warming going unaddressed, schools failing, and sundry other failing public services."

Defaulting on the debt, however, is not considered a viable solution. It would do great damage to many pension funds, life insurance companies, banks, state, county, and municipal governments, and foreign governments, securities, 22 percent of those are to China, 19 to Japan, and 12 to the United Kingdom.

All is not hopeless, however, at least for some of the most indebted countries. Rev. Bob Edgar in "Ending Debt Slavery" says, "Thanks to debt relief commitments in 1999 and 2005, now more than 20 countries have seen 100% debt cancellation from the IMF, World Bank, and African Development Bank.

Mary Continues To Call For Conversions (January 2009)

With the recent rekindling of the genocidal violence between the Tutsis and the Hutus in the Congo, we ought to remember the message of Our Lady of Rwanda, or as she called herself, Nyina wa Jambo (Mother of the Word). Archbishop Augustin Misago of Gikongoro, Rwanda, and the Vatican gave official approval to her appearances in 2001. She has appeared from 1981 to 1989 to at least three, possibly seven, visionaries in Kibeho, Rwanda, just a year after Pope John Paul II's visit to Rwanda.

Her first apparition occurred in Kibeho, Rwanda, on November 28, 1981. She called to Alphonsine Mumureke as the girl was serving lunch in the school cafeteria. When she entered the corridor "a very beautiful woman" identified herself with, "I am Mother of the Word. I have heard your prayers. I would like you and your companions to have more faith. Some do not believe enough."

Witnesses tell of Alphonsine speaking in several languages and then remaining motionless and unresponsive for a quarter hour. A second apparition occurred in the dormitory the evening of the next day. Mary continued to give advice and encouragements, make remarks to bring the school, both teachers and students, to come to believe and listen to her important message. There were even signs such as twinkling lights which all could see.

Alphonsine's companions, the other visionaries, were Agnes Kamagaju, Vestine Saima, the doubter Marie-Claire Mukangang, the pagan Emanuel Segatashya, and Stephanie Mukamurenzi, as in other apparitions, young people just twenty-one to thirteen-years-old. Alphonsine continued to receive apparitions every year on November 28 until 1989.

The thousands of pilgrims to Kibeho also witnessed several extraordinary phenomena: the dance of the sun like that in Lourdes, the sun's replacement by a greenish moon, a dance of the stars, and luminous crosses in the sky. The greatest miracle, however, was this wave of conversions and prayers, especially among the youth.

Mary revealed to the visionaries the bloodbath that could be stopped by prayer. To Alphonsine she revealed heaven, hell, and purgatory. In a private revelation in February 1994 Agnes is said to have foreseen her parents being killed. She was told, "Do not lose time in doing good and praying. There is not much time and Jesus will come."

The genocide started in April and by June 800,000 had been killed, mostly brutally with machetes and clubs. Included were Marie-Claire who was killed in Byumba and Emanuel while fleeing Kigali. The broader war from 1998 to 2003 killed another estimated 4 million people.

Our Lady emphasized beforehand and as she had several times before the need for repentance and prayer. "I have come to prepare the way for my Son," she told the visionaries and us, "for your good, and you do not want to understand. The time remaining is short and you are absent-minded. You are distracted by the goods of this world which are passing. I have seen many of my children getting lost and I have come to show them the true way."

"If I am now turning to the parish of Kibeho," she explained, "it does not mean I am concerned only for Kibeho or for the diocese of Butare or for Rwanda, or for the whole of Africa. I am concerned with and turning to the whole world."

Anathalie and Marie-Claire got similar urgent messages, "We must dedicate ourselves to prayer, we must develop in us the virtues of charity, availability, and humility," and "we must recite the Rosary and the beads of the Seven Sorrows of Our Lady to obtain the grace of repentance."

Jesus Himself told Emanuel, "Too many people treat their neighbors dishonestly. The world is full of hatred. You will know my Second Coming is at hand when you see the outbreak of religious wars. Then, know that I am on the way."

Not unexpectedly the name given to the Marian sanctuary at Kibeho is dedicated to Our Lady of Sorrows. It had been a place of pilgrimage since 1988, with the unofficial approval of Bishop Jean Baptiste Gahamanyi, of the Butare Diocese, of which Kibeho was at that time a part.

Books with further information on the apparitions include *Meetings with Mary* by Janice T. Connell, *The Day Will Come* and *The Final Hour* by Michael H. Brown, *The Woman And The Dragon* by David Michael Lindsey, and *The Thunder of Justice* by Ted and Maureen Flynn. There is also the video "Kibeho, Africa: Mary Speaks to the World."

Books Focus On God (November 2008)

Several recent books seem to be dealing in different ways with the same questions, "If God exists, what does that mean to me?" Anthony Flew, Newt Gingrich, Paul Davies, and Francis Collins come at God from four different directions.

After decades of insisting belief was a mistake, "A super-intelligence is the only good explanation for the origin of life and the complexity of Nature," Flew now says. "I'm thinking of a God very different from the God of the Christian and far and away from the God of Islam, because both are depicted as omnipotent." He now believes that such evidence has, and his book, *There Is A God* tells his journey from staunch atheism to deism.

His *Theology and Falsification* has become the most widely reprinted philosophical publication of the last 50 years. Flew earned his fame by arguing that one should presuppose atheism until evidence of a God surfaces.

Newt Gingrich too has written a book *Rediscovering God in America*. "There is no attack on American culture," he writes, "more destructive and more historically dishonest than the secular Left's relentless effort to drive God out of America's public square."

"I believe deeply that people fall short and that people have to recognize that they have to turn to God for forgiveness and to seek mercy," Gingrich said. "I don't know how you could live with yourself and not end up breaking down if you didn't find, try to find, some way to deal with your own weaknesses and to go to God about them."

Gingrich quotes many deist Founding Fathers, including George Washington, John Adams, Alexander Hamilton, and others, who all believed that a republican form of government could not succeed without (in Adams' words) "a moral and religious people."

He takes his reader on a virtual tour of the most important monuments, buildings, and landmarks in Washington, D. C. Starting with the National Archives, and its Declaration of Independence and Constitution, he continues on to the Washington Monument and the Jefferson, Lincoln, and Roosevelt Memorials. Then come the Vietnam Veterans Memorial, the Capitol and Supreme Court buildings, the White House, the Library of Congress, the Ronald Reagan Building, the World War II Memorial, and Arlington National Cemetery.

He emphasizes the relevance of faith in all this concrete history and in the lives they commemorate. He criticizes the courts' distortion of the meaning of the First Amendment with the mythical separation of church and state. He uses America to rediscover the faith of her fathers.

In *The Goldilocks Engima* Paul Davies claims that new scientific discoveries have brought us to the brink of comprehending the underlying structure of nature. The title "enigma" is why "the universe seems 'just right' for life."

Davies contends that life and consciousness are essential components, not merely interesting bonus features of the universe.

His previous books include *The Mind of God,* which won the Templeton Prize for progress in religion, worth more than half a million pounds.

He gives the example of stars, hot gas held together by gravity, which if the force of gravity were stronger than it is, stars would burn far more quickly and expire sooner. If, on the other hand, gravity were weaker, they would burn too dimly, and their energy output would not be enough to support life. It seems that the strength of gravity, and seeming countless other constants of nature, are all "just right." Even given this so-called anthropic principle, Davies says, we are left wondering why Nature (or God) chose the particular rules it did.

Although coming from a natural scientist's perspective, he does praise the insights of St. Augustine, Leibniz, and others, who approached the problem from a theistic perspective. Davies, however, cannot believe in an Intelligent Designer. Neither can he accept that the universe is just an accident in an infinite multiverse of possible universes. Causality, he argues, could work backwards, so that the real cause of our universe is its endpoint. Our conclusions, as Davies himself admits, are a matter of personal faith.

In *The Language of God: A Scientist Presents Evidence for Belief* geneticist Francis Collins explains why faith and reason can and do co-exist peacefully, and how they can actually complement each other. As director of the National Human Genome Research Project, he has seen how intricately life seems to have been crafted. He does not think, however, that the question of when life began is "the place for a thoughtful person to wager his faith."

Collins does admit he rejects deism because of its moral law, which seemed to represent God's personal involvement with His creatures. He proposes instead that God did intelligently design His creation with such precision that Humans would be the result, but that He did all but start it naturally. About a hundred thousand years ago God supernaturally created the first hominid soul, but so it would be indistinguishable from naturalism. His concept of "BioLogos is not intended as a scientific theory. Its truth can be tested only by the spiritual logic of the heart, the mind, and the soul."

Conversions Continue (October 2008)

Much has happened since "Protestant Pastors on the Road to Rome" by Elizabeth Altham appeared in the Spring 1996 issue of *Sursum Corda!* (www.ewtn.com/library/answers/ protpast.htm). The converted pastors continue to minister to and convert others by the thousands. They are ministering to singles, families, priests, teachers, Catholics, and non-Catholics.

Included among the graduates of Gordon-Conwell Theological Seminary, South Hamilton, Mass., mentioned in Altham's article, have been such evangelical Catholics as Marcus Grodi, Scott Hahn, Steve Wood, Bill Bales, and Gerald Matatics.

"Without sounding super-spiritual," says Steve Wood, "I think it's a sovereign move of God. I think I can tell you why it happened at my seminary. Our seminary was bought by Pew of Sun Oil, a very wealthy evangelical, and Billy Graham."

As part of the story he also tells about his meeting Fr. Schevers:

"He asked, 'Where did you do your theological studies?'

"I said, 'Oh, it's a place you'd never have heard of, Gordon-Conwell.'

"He looked at me and smiled. 'I taught there,' he said. You see, it had been a Carmelite boys' school with the purpose of producing vocations for the Church. They were praying and praying, but there weren't vocations coming and in great agony they put the property up for sale. To add double insult to injury, here came Billy Graham and bought the campus. I'm convinced that for us it was the prayers of those Carmelites."

Since his conversion, Marcus Grodi has founded the Coming Home Network International (chnetwork.org) which includes Deep in History conferences, Deep in Scripture radio, and Deep in Christ regional gatherings.

The goal of the CHNetwork is "to assist the Catholic Church in fulfilling its mission of evangelization and its call for Christian unity, as proclaimed by Pope John Paul II in his encyclical, *That They May Be One* (*Ut Unum Sint*)." They do this especially by ministering to other converts to the Catholic Church and their families.

Scott Hahn, besides being a professor at the Franciscan University of Steubenville, OH, and popular author and speaker, is the founder of St. Paul Center for Biblical Theology. Its website, salvationhistory.com, describes it as a non-profit research and educational institute that promotes life-transforming Scripture study in the Catholic tradition. Their goal is "to be a teacher of teachers. We want to raise up a new generation of priests who are fluent in the Bible and lay people who are biblically literate."

Their *Letter and Spirit Journal* began in 2005 and their monthly newsletter *Breaking the Bread* includes short Bible studies on the readings for each of that month's Sunday Masses.

Steve Wood founded Family Life Center International (http://www.familylifecenter.net/) which deals with many aspects of family life. As Wood describes it, "Whether it's strengthening your Catholic marriage, building the Catholic family, tackling the terrible two's, passing on the Faith, or parenting teens, you'll find the practical help you need."

His ministry is not only in strengthening marriages yet to be but saving those in trouble and aiding those which have broken. This includes the monthly Dads.org e-news and the Faith & Family Circle newsletters.

Bill Bales is now president of National Association of Catholic Home Educators, a Professor of Sacred Scripture, Mount St. Mary's Seminary, and a senior fellow of the St. Paul Center for Biblical Theology. He and his wife, Lisanne, have six children.

Gerald Matatics is currently a full-time staff apologist for Catholic Answers in San Diego, CA. Matatics is also the founder of Biblical Foundations International (see http.//www.gerrymatatics.org/), a non-profit organization committed to proclaiming historic, Biblical Christianity. Part of their mission is to Australia, Brazil, Cambodia, Canada, Korea, Macedonia, Malawi, and New Zealand. He recently gave a speaking tour of New Zealand and Australia (before, during, and after World Youth Day). It was part of his 200-city, 7-year Mega-tour.

Chinese Church Built On Martyrs (July 2008)

As the victims of the Chinese earthquake and the Olympics in China attract the media's attention and our prayers, the Chinese martyrs will also be remembered. Their feast day is July 9. The Chinese Martyrs Catholic Church in Toronto, Ontario, is named for them.

It was no mere coincidence that Pope John Paul II canonized the Chinese martyrs on October 1, the feast of St. Therese of the Child Jesus, patroness of the missions. Since it was also the anniversary of the founding of the Communist state in China in 1949, the People's Republic of China took offense.

The first Catholic mission in Beijing was by Italian Franciscan Giovanni de Montecorvino in 1234, who baptized thousands and founded three churches. By 1300 Chinese Catholics numbered about 30,000.

One of the first martyrs was forty-six-year-old Peter Wu Guosheng, a lay catechist, martyred in 1814. Fr. Augustine Zhao Rong and Joseph Zhang Dapeng, another lay catechist, were strangled to death in 1815. Fr. Joseph Yuan Zaide was strangled in 1817 and Fr. Paul Liu Hanzuo was martyred in 1819.

A typical story would be that of eighteen-year-old Chi Zhuzi, who cried out to those who had just cut off his right arm and were preparing to flay him alive: "Every piece of my flesh, every drop of my blood will tell you that I am Christian."

As Catholic Culture puts it on their website, www.catholicculture.org, "The fact that this considerable number of Chinese lay faithful offered their lives for Christ together with the missionaries who had proclaimed the Gospel to them and had been so devoted to them is evidence of the depth of the link that faith in Christ establishes. It gathers into a single family people of various races and cultures, strongly uniting them not for political motives but in virtue of a religion that preaches love, brotherhood, peace, and justice."

Priests and lay catechists continued to be persecuted and martyred. Fr. Thaddeus Liu Ruiting was strangled in 1823. Lay catechist Peter Liu Wenyuan was exiled to Tartary for almost twenty years. Joachim Ho was baptized at about twenty before becoming a lay catechist. When forty he was arrested, tortured, and finally exiled to Tartary, where he also remained for almost twenty years. When they returned, they were both arrested and strangled in 1834 and 1839, respectively.

By 1844 Catholics were permitted to practice their faith and by 1846 the old penalties were abolished. By 1856, however, the persecutions returned. Lawrence Bai Xiaoman was beheaded. Agnes Cao Guiying, a thirty-five-year-old widow, born into an old Christian family, was arrested for instructing young girls.

In 1858 three catechists, Jerome Lu Tingmei, Lawrence Wang Bing, Agatha Lin Zao, known as the Martyrs of MaoKou, were beheaded.

The Martyrs of Qingyanzhen, two seminarians, Joseph Zhang Wenlan and Paul Chen Changpin, a layman John Baptist Luo Tingying and their cook Martha Wang-Luo were martyred on the same day in 1861. Four lay catechists were martyred in 1862, Martin Wu Xuesheng, John Zhang Tianshen, John Chen Xianheng, and Lucy Yi Zhenmei.

An estimated 20,000 Christians were killed during China's Boxer Uprising in 1900. Among them were the Franciscan seminarians John Zhang Huan, John Wang Rui, John Zhang Jingguang, and the secular Franciscans Patrick Dong Bodi, Philip Zhang Zhihe, Peter Wu Anbang, and Matthew Feng De.

Franciscan lay catechist Simon Chen Ximan was martyred as were catechumens Zhang Huailu and Lang-Yang.

They came from all walks of life – farmers Francis Zhang Rong and James Yan Guodong, laborer Peter Zhang Banniu, manservants Thomas Shen Jihe and James Zhao Quanxin, cook Peter Wang Erman, and virgin Rose Fan Hui.

Others we know even less about, from seventy-nine-year-old Paul Liu Jinde and seven-year-old Paul Lang Fu.

The Eastern Orthodox Church has recognized 222 Albazinians who also died during the Boxer Rebellion as "Holy Martyrs of China" since 1903.

Faith-Building DVDs Are Increasing (April 2008)

There are growing numbers of faith-building DVDs available now with just a little searching. Among the Bible stories are the New Testament classics, "Jesus of Nazareth", "The Passion of the Christ", "The Gospel of John", and "A.D." previously on video. There are also lesser known ones as well, like "The Final Inquiry" which takes place three years after the crucifixion as a Roman is sent to investigate the continuing rumors of Jesus of Nazareth.

There are, however, programs on the earliest saints, "The Story of the Twelve Apostles and Mary". "Our Lady of Guadalupe, Mother of Hope" tells the story of Mary's appearance to St. Juan Diego, including stories of miracles and conversations since, and her continuing pro-life message. "The Miracle of Our Lady of Fatima", "The Events at Garabandal", "and "Marian Apparitions of the Twentieth Century" tell of other appearances.

There are many faith-building non-Biblical stories now on DVD too. "The Keys to the Kingdom", "A Time to Remember", "The Bells of St. Mary's", "The Scarlet and the Black", "The Small Miracle", "The Fourth Wise Man", "The Miracle of Marccelino", "The Staircase", and "The Inn of the Sixth Happiness" are but a few of them.

There are several excellently done lives of the saints lovingly made in their countries of origin. The Italian-made "Maria Goretti" includes a 16-page study booklet. Also from Italy comes "St. Anthony" with subtitles rather than dubbing.

From France comes "Bernadette", recommended by the Vatican as a "sensitive portrayal of a very moving story that deserves a wide audience," which is shown daily at Lourdes. The sequel, "The Passion of Bernadette" tells the rest of the story, what happened after Mary's appearances.

"Becket" is now on DVD with the usual extras, commentary, interviews, and more. Then there is also "Xavier, Missionary and Saint".

Holy women are not excluded. We now have "Thérése" and "The Miracle of St. Thérése", as well as "Rita". The Theresa of Avila miniseries has been converted to a three-disc DVD set. "Theresa of Avila: Personality and Prayer" on the other hand is a practical how-to presentation.

"Saint Francis" was filmed on location in Assisi. Both it and "Padre Pio: Miracle Man" come in both a subtitled and dubbed version, both with a 16-page booklet. "Don Bosco" is on the same DVD as "Monsieur Vincent, St. Vincent de Paul". The three saintly Poles, Sts. Faustina, Maximilian Kolbe, and Pope John Paul II, are on one DVD, "Ocean of Mercy".

Also available are documentaries on newer saints, "Padre Pio: Sanctus", "The Healing Prophet: Solanus Casey", and "Mother Teresa: The Legacy". "The Life of Sr. Faustina" tells her story based on her writings, including her beatification miracles. "Two Suitcases" tells the story of St. Josephine Bakhita, the Sudanese slave who became a Catholic, a nun, and a saint.

Among animated DVDs for children are "Bernadette: The Princess of Lourdes", "Francis: The Knight of Assisi", "Francis Xavier: The Samurai's Lost Treasure", "Patrick", "The Day the Sun Danced: The True Story of Fatima", "Juan Diego: Messenger of Guadalupe", and "Nicholas: The Boy Who Was Santa Claus".

Besides the popular Veggie tales series teaching basic morality and Bible stories, others deal with such varied things as guardian angels, "My Secret Friend", or a child-sized "Ben Hur: The Race to Glory". Still others help parents teach about the Church and their Friend Jesus, "The Mass Unveiled", "The Way of the Cross for Children", and "Children's Adoration". "Champions of Faith: The Baseball Edition" even brings together faith and baseball.

Further information can be found about these and future DVDs at the Leaflet Missal Company (www.leafletonline.com), Catholic Child (www.catholicchild,com) and Ignatius Press (www.ignatius.com). They are three of the companies who have branched out from Catholic publications to videos and now to DVDs.

Iraqi Refugees Need Assistance (October 2007)

Speaking of Iraqi refugees, Jack Connolly says, "More, much more, needs to be done in terms of assisting and protecting this population." There are several non-governmental organizations (NGOs) which are trying to help.

Connolly himself represents Catholic Relief Services (CRS) in the Middle East, which is providing assistance to Iraqi refugees in Syria and Lebanon. Nearly two million dollars is coming from the US Bureau of Population, Refugees, and Migration, and more than half a million from private funds. The United Nations estimates two million Iraqis have become refugees in neighboring countries, Jordan and Syria primarily, but also Lebanon, Egypt and Turkey. Another two million are displace within Iraq. The UN estimates 50,000 Iraqis flee their homes per month.

"When you look at the numbers affected, more than four million people uprooted, the response is still not sufficient," Connolly adds.

The first influx of refugees into Jordan was about eight years ago. A million refugees have come in that last two years, 50,000 of them Christian.

"Usually the first thing they do is come to the Church. It is the first contact they have with other people and with relatives," said Ra'ed Bahou, the director of the Pontifical Mission for Palestine.

"People know they now have to come a half-hour earlier to get a seat," he said.

While some professionals are working illegally, he explains, most end up as a day laborers.

"Organizations like us can give them the basics, but we can't support whole families. We can give them money for one or two months. It is very difficult emotionally," he said. The Iraqis have been accepted by the Jordanian population, he said, and are slowly becoming part of the ethnic makeup of the country.

In Syria, CRS is working with the local Caritas/Syria and St. Vincent de Paul Society. Bishop Antoine Audo, of the Chaldean Catholic diocese of Aleppo, said that some 25,000 Iraqis refugees are in Syria. He said that the refugees had packed into Damascus because the authorities had allowed them in without visas and supported the aid efforts of the Church.

"There is a big need to help the people in Damascus. We cannot provide a solution for all the problems but we are doing whatever we can. We are very grateful to Aid to the Church in Need, (ACN)."

Many gave gone on to Lebanon, which is almost one third Christian. Up to 40,000, at the al-Farad's Assyrian Church of St. George, Iraqi refugees now make up almost one-third of the congregation. "It was bad in Iraq under the old regime," says James Isho. "Now it's even worse."

"Every day five or six more families come here," says Bishop Michael Kisargi. "Everyone can tell me a story about persecution by Muslims."

Lebanon already has 400,000 Palestinian refugees, some of whom have lived there for almost 60 years without citizenship. The newly arriving Iraqi refugees therefore aren't legally allowed to work in Lebanon.

"I can't go on like this," he says. "We are a poor church and the situation is getting worse."

"More information on these and other of our needy Christian brothers and sisters can be found by contacting the organizations mentioned above. CRS can be found at www.crs.org or 228 W. Lexington Street Baltimore, MD 21201-3413.

The Pontifical Mission for Palestine is one of the local organizations under the Catholic Near East Welfare Association (www.cnewa.org, 1011 First Ave., New York, NY 10022-4195).

Caritas Internationales is out of the Vatican itself (www.caritas.va, Palazzo San Calisto, 00120 Vatican City). The ACN is also international (www.aidtothechurchinneed.org, 725 Leonard Street, PO Box 220384, NY 11222).

TV Show Is Modern Morality Play (April 2007)

"Heroes" is proving to be this season's most popular new TV show. It has already received several award nominations. More important than its popularity or critical acclaim as mere entertainment, however is its role as a modern morality play.

As writers Joe Polaski and Aron Coleite explain at 9thwonder.com: "We all make good and bad choices. Selfish and selfless. These characters are no different. Every action has a consequence. People will be forgiven, seek redemption, and be punished."

The idea for "Heroes" isn't so much about people with superpowers. It's more, as Joseph Campbell wrote, about our universal need for the heroic. "The hero's journey crosses all cultures, so to find something similar in a different culture is not surprising."

The characters have had to deal with some pretty serious decisions. Isaac chose not to go back to his habitual drug abuse. Niki turned herself in trying to protect her family from her deadly alter ego. Claire repented of revenging her attempted rapist, and forgave her lying foster father. Matt forgave his unfaithful wife, and she in turn encouraged him to return diamonds that didn't belong to him.

They have saved lives and grown spiritually by using their newly discovered powers, identified explicitly as gifts from God. Some have misused their gift and taken lives.

With the unusually large number of regular characters and built-in mystery, the internet discussions are part of the whole phenomenon. Missed shows can be downloaded to computer or other player; so can a companion graphic novel.

The official site even has a do-it-yourself Heroes test to see if you have the makings of being a Hero. They mention three characteristics: a mysterious guidance for the creating of what isn't or recreating what was, a longing for the extraordinary and a dissatisfaction with present underachievement, and an attunement to the collective unconscious with longing to more deeply belong. More simply, these might be called a hero's faithful soul, hopeful spirit, and loving heart.

In describing how they're relating the struggle to be more heroic, the writers say, "We're dropping into scenes at the most critical moments and we're jumping from scene to scene knowing our audience is smart to enough to keep track. And that keeps it fresh – for the audience and for us."

The seeking to do better seems to apply for the people involved in the show as well. Tim Kring is the one behind the idea, the one they call OFL (Our Fearless Leader), although all the writers contribute to every episode. He was the executive producer under whom Polaski and Coleite wrote for "Cross Jordan."

Masi Oka, while playing the time-stopping and time-traveling Hiro, still works part-time on special effects for George Lucas. He's worked on "Star Wars" I, II and III, "The Perfect Storm", "Terminator III" and "Pirates of the Caribbean II". Oka was already on a *Time* cover as a whiz kid at 12 for his 180 IQ. He got the role of Hiro partially by translating and performing his screen test script in Japanese. So far Hiro has warned of a disastrous future, found and lost love in the past, quested for the sword of legendary samurai Kensei (sword-saint) Takezo, and faced off his demanding father, played by George Takei. Takei, of course, played Sulu on "Star Trek" and won the role with the same trick as his "son," in Japanese.

Just as Oka actually was born in Japan, Sendi Ramamurthy, who plays the Hero-hunting Dr. Mohindar Suresh, was born in India. He has appeared in "Numbers," "Gray's Anatomy," and "Guiding Light."

Several others of the cast have humble soap opera backgrounds. Jack Coleman, who plays Bennet, started with "Days of Our Lives" and has more recently acted on "Without A Trace" and "CSI: Miami." Tawny "Simone Devereau" Cypress was in "All My Children." Hayden Panettiere, who is now the indestructible cheerleader Claire Bennet, started on "One Life To Live" at 5.

Ali Larter, who was a model at 13, plays the double role of the vastly different Niki and Jessica Sanders, not so unlike her very different film credits, Legally Blonde and House on Haunted Hill. Noah Gray-Cabey, 9, plays her computer-commanding son, Micah. He started on "CSI: Miami" at 7.

Besides the Asians, the cast also includes the British Christopher Eccelston, formerly the ninth Dr. Who, Chilean Santiago Cabera, and Haitian Jimmy Jean-Lewis as "the Haitian." Leonard Roberts played Joe Lewis in Joe and Max, and Milo Ventimiglia played Rocky Jr. in Rocky Balboa.

The show has even featured cameos by people as Stan Lee, the creator of the Hulk and Spiderman.

Finding the answer to "Who among the characters will make the right choices and become Heroes?" keeps fans blogging and tuning in. When they ask the writers questions like "Who is Uluru?" they are evasively told to look up the mythology of Ayoro Rook. "We did lots of research in crafting our stories – some of which came from Hindu and Indian mythology. Remember how we've said the number 9 is important? When they ask 'Does the Haitian have other powers than mind-wiping?', they are told 'Our minds are blank.'"

Passion Play Continues To Proclaim Jesus (March 2007)

The St. John Passion Play began in 1918 at St. John the Baptist Church in Over-the-Rhine in Cincinnati, Ohio. Like America's oldest in Union City, New Jersey, it was originally meant as a prayer offering, especially for our soldiers and a response to Pope Benedict XV's plea for prayers for peace (World War I). Both were modeled after the much more elaborate and much older passion play of Oberammergau, Bavaria.

Ommerammergau's began in 1634 after its survival through the bubonic plague. It now involves thousands of villagers, but it only performed once a decade. Union City's began at Holy Family Church in 1915 and is annual, but has for some time been out of the Park Performing Arts Center, using 1980's style music and charging admission. In 1997 it gained fame and infamy with an African-American Jesus. Greater Cincinnati's however still remains all volunteer and completely free.

In the Fifties, after the Oberammergau production was reported associated with Nazi anti-Semitism, the script was changed. In 1969 St. John's was closed and the players had to incorporate. The play has had to relocate many times since, including Mt. Notre Dame High School, Emery auditorium, Westwood Town Hall, and Pleasant Ridge Presbyterian.

In 1991 it was edited again this time to better conform with the guidelines of the U.S. Conference of Catholic Bishops (USCCB) and the advice of Rev. Ronald Kettler, Thomas More College professor of theology.

Richard Parker explains the play's message by saying, "It's not a play about what 'they' did to our Lord. It's about what our Lord did for us." And as we still have wars to deal with, what He still is doing.

Over the years changes have been made in the script such as better distinguishing between the Seder (the Jewish Passover meal) and the Last Supper, or giving all, not just a few, of the apostles lines.

Pontius Pilate "He has changed from a man who caves to the will of the people to one who is in control and manipulative of the crowd," Don Schlosser says. The words of Jesus however continue to all be taken directly from the Bible.

The hundred-plus members of the cast and crew come from different walks of life. They have many different style of worship. All however strive to make come alive the Scripture, "For God so loved the world that He gave His only begotten Son, that whosoever believes in Him should not perish but have everlasting life" (john 3:16).

"That's why this play's just a relevant as ever." Don Schlosser says. "It's a Cincinnati tradition," Judy Hughes says. If you saw it with your parents or grandparents, she urges, share it with your own children or grandchildren. "It's a good preparation for Easter and is never the same. We always make it better!"

"There's an intense dependence on one another, a trust." Parker explains. "And sometimes the trust is compromised, when someone shows up late or intoxicated or not at all," which have all happened.

It has become not just a Lenten tradition to view the play as a family, but many take part in the play as family, for two or three generations of some families. Children who have been literally raised in the wings often know every word of dialogue and wait years to get on stage. The cast and crew are family.

After the play it has also become traditional for them all to approach the cross. "Some genuflect. Some touch the cross of crowns. Some cry," Parker says. "I can tell that they're touched. They go from, 'Now we're playing the parts to now we're approaching the cross as ourselves.' They go from 2,000 years ago to present day."

Singer Evangelizes With New Lyrics To Old Songs (February 2007)

Catholic recording artist Nick Alexander's new album, *I Wanna Be Debated*, contains the title song, new lyrics put to the tune of "I Wanna Be Sedated" by The Ramones. It therefore follows the pattern of his previous two in being new lyrics put to familiar tunes.

"I attempted," he explains, "to make this album as relatable to the average Joe as I possibly could, grounding this project in today's current issues. As a topical album, I address issues as vast as abstinence, the obesity crisis, Catholic guilt, depression, and the priestly scandal over the last few years."

His songs may deal with serious topics, but by contrasting the Catholic perspective with the original tunes' secular ones, he does it in an entertaining way. He converted to Catholicism in 1993 because of a gift book on Marian apparitions. In 1999 he was encouraged to record his "silly songs." Since then he's gotten married and performed for World Youth Day in Toronto and Proud 2 B Catholic.

"It is my opinion," Nick says at his website, "that this album is both my funniest release yet, but also my most encouraging."

To those who question his mixing of the sacred and secular, he asks, "Is there anything so wrong with taking what is so precious and trying to convey it in such a way that others can understand it?" There is precedent. This is just the sort of thing that St. Ephrem, "the Lyre of the Holy Spirit," did back in the 4th Century.

Oldies fans – though not quite that old – will recognize the tune of "Suicide Hotline" as "I Am the Walrus" by The Beatles, "Love That Someone Right" as "Summer Nights" by John Travolta and Olivia Newton-John, and "Holy Thursday" as "Monday", Monday by The Mamas and Papas.

The new album also contains "ΙΧΘΥΣ" (that's the Greek word for fish, the famous acronym for "Jesus Christ, Son of God, Savior") to "Footloose" by Kenny Loggins. There's also "Salad Bowl" to "Centerfold" by The J. Geils Band, "This Time of Forty Days" to "King of Pain" by The Police, "Careless Blunder" to "Careless Whisper" by George Michael/Wham!, "Nicene Creed" to "Dancing Queen" by ABBA, "Priest" to "Superman (It's Not Easy)" by Five For Fighting, and "Internet Bloggers" to "Radio Ga Ga" by Queen. Just as with his other two albums he finishes this one with a wholly original worship song, "Holy God, We Praise Your Great Name".

Podcaster Susan Bailey said in *Grapevine News Minute*, "I love this album and here's why – it's crackling with excitement from the vocals to the last guitar and drum beat."

Youth director Maria Elena Ponce praises not only the presentation but the content: "I especially liked the emphasis you placed on encouraging the youth to have a greater appreciation for the Eucharist."

His first album, *A Time to Laugh* contained: "Old Time Gregorian Chant" to "Old Time Rock and Roll" by Bob Seger, "Repent" to "Respect" by Aretha Franklin, "Transubstantiation" to "Revolution" by The Beatles, "I Got You Saved" to "I Got You Babe" by Sonny and Cher, "Tradition (500 Years)" to "I'm Gonna Be 500 Miles" by The Proclaimers, "Should I Stand or Should I Kneel" to "Should I Stay Or Should I Go" by The Clash, "Our Mass" to "Our House" by Madness, "Tithe After Tithe" to "Time After Time" by Cyndi Lauper, "Confession" to "Pressure" by Billy Joel, and "R. C. I. A." to "Y. M. C. A." by The Village People. It too concluded on a serious note with the worship song, "Father".

Eternal Life: The Party Album began with "Get Canonized A Saint" to "Fly Away" by Lenny Kravitz, and continued with "Don't Take That Crown" to "Don't Bring Me Down" by ELO,

"Nahum, Zephaniah, Malachi" to "Jenny (867-5309)" by Tommy Tutone, "These Beads" to "These Dreams" by Heart, "Evangelize" to "I Will Survive" by Gloria Gaynor, "Monastery Trip" to "White Room" by Cream, "Melt Me" to "Pinch Me" by BNL, "Therese of Lisieux" to "Electric Avenue" by Eddy Grant, "Teaching Them to Read" to "Turning Japanese" by The Vapors, and "We Want to Stand United" to "We Didn't Start the Fire" by Billy Joel. It ended with "Too Late Have I Loved You", based on St. Augustine's *Confessions*.

Nick does not just perform in the recording studio, however. To schedule "the Alexander experience," as he calls it, at your parish or youth group, he asks that he be contacted by e-mail at nickalexander.com. You can listen to, buy, and download his CDs there as well. He promises you will "be entertained, uplifted, and tickled silly while being affirmed of orthodox Catholic teaching."

Experience The Nativity Story (January 2007)

The release of "The Nativity Story" is the first time in nearly half a century that any major studio has released a religious film. Even more surprisingly it premiered at the Vatican, at the request of those who had seen the preview. This time it came from New Line Cinema, made a major studio by their very successful "Lord of the Rings" trilogy. Also a factor has to be the box office success of Mel Gibson's "The Passion of the Christ", which told of the end of Jesus' life. Moviemakers seem to be beginning to notice what kind of films the public will support.

"(This film) isn't something that most people know pretty well," Oscar Isaac, who plays Joseph, explains. "It's something that was really trying to find a deeper truth about what these people went through and what they're really feeling."

The reviewer at the Internet Movie Database (IMDb) wrote enthusiastically that the film "depicts the emotion, the hope, the awesomeness of God and much more that you don't really think about when thinking about the Nativity. This is what Christmas is all about!"

Screenwriter Mike Rich is known for his Radio and Rookie. He says that his inspiration, however, came in December two years ago from the cover stories on the historical Jesus in *Time* and *Newsweek* – and, of course, the original sources. After nearly a year's research, he finished the first draft in five weeks of writing – with intercession from his parish.

He tried to put himself – and so the audience – into the hard life of a couple of faithful young Jewish newlyweds under Roman oppression. They then find God changing the whole world in ways they never expected – through them.

The film opens with the climax of the massacre of the Holy Innocents and then portrays the rest of the story as a flashback. The annunciation scene is not given the emphasis that the Catholic Church gives it.

Director Catherine Hardwicke says that she was intrigued by how Rich "had gotten right inside the heart and soul of these characters." Both her previous films, "Thirteen" and "Lords of Dogtown" also dealt with teens facing crises, so she felt she had to do it.

At one point in the filming, when the donkey was most uncooperative, she asked that the cast and crew pray in all of their seven languages. They did and the donkey did as he was directed to until the sun set that day.

Keisha Castle-Hughes was an Oscar nominee five years ago at eleven when she starred in "Whale Rider" and has had some exposure to Mary in having gone to Mass with her grandparents. Taking the role of Mary, however, forced her to take a closer look at this teen-in-crisis role.

"She was just a girl," she says, "and she was just, like, playing with her friends. and then she's married to a guy that's totally older than her, and then the next minute she's got the hugest responsibility and becomes, like, the mother of the world."

Isaac, who is ten years older than Keisha, tells how playing the role of Joseph in the film encouraged him to get deeper into the Scriptures. He not only read and mediated on the nativity narratives in Luke and Matthew, but also the Song of Solomon and 1 Corinthians 13.

"I think what surprised me was how full of love he is," Isaac says, "and really, love for her. No matter how angry he is, no matter how he is tempted to (humiliate her), or even with the desire to scream and yell, and throw her out into the street, because he loves her so much, he doesn't do that."

This seems to come through as indicated by the reactions of many of those who have seen it. Women are saying, "I want a husband like Joseph!" and men, "I want to be a husband like Joseph!"

Keisha had to learn to press olives and grapes, milk a goat, make cheese, and ride a donkey on a dusty road in the midday heat. Isaac had to learn carpentry, and learned to like it. Viewers have a chance to experience, at least vicariously, the everyday life and the extraordinary challenges that this holy couple faced in their first journey together.

The perhaps too human portrayal of the birth of Jesus, the Sinless One born of the Immaculate, might also not be as viewers had envisioned it. It very well may not have looked very out of the ordinary, as extraordinary as it may have been.

Like their Son, Joseph and Mary were fully human. We, like them, are also called to change the world by the grace of God.

Family Theater Lives (November 2006)

After 60 years the ministry that Father Peyton started on the Mutual Broadcasting Company network with a free half-hour program has changed a bit but continues to pray for and support families. It began Mother's Day, May 13, 1945, which had been declared a national day of prayer by President Eisenhower. The first show had a talk by Bing Crosby and a decade of the rosary by the parents and sister of the famous five brothers who died on the same ship during World War II.

Over the years the show broadcast radio – and television – dramas offering "inspiring insights into how to build unity within your family." It now offers videos, DVDs, and CDs as well at www.familytheater.org.

Volume 1 contains "A Daddy for Christmas," (hosted by Shirley Temple and starring Pat O'Brien and Bobby Driscoll), and "God and a Red Scooter," (hosted by Gregory Peck, starring Robert Mitchum). Volume 2 has "Robert of Sicily" (hosted by Irene Dunne, starring Raymond Burr) and "Ozzie and Harriet" (hosted by Barry Fitzgerald, starring Ozzie and Harriet Nelson).

The other volumes feature "Footsteps in the Night," (hosted by Kate Smith); "Journey Home"; "The Windbag," (hosted by Bing Crosby); "The Prayer That Won the West," (hosted by Henry Fonda); "Mother's Halo Was Too Tight," (hosted by Gene Kelly), "Life's a Circus" (hosted by Fred Allen, starring Margaret O'Brien and Pat O'Brien); "The Bishop's Candlesticks"; and "Hound of Heaven" (hosted by Jack Benny).

Audio tapes offered are "Mystical Rose Music and Meditation," including "Ave Maria," "Gentle Mother," "O Holy Mary," "Holy is His Name" or "Pray the Rosary with Father Patrick Peyton, CSC" available on CD or Playaway self-playing digital audio player. "The Apostle of the Rosary: Servant of God Patrick Peyton, CSC" CD tells the story of "the rosary priest."

The site also offers "15 Mysteries of the Rosary" on DVD as well as others, such as, "A Dedicated Man," a tour of his homeland of County Mayo, Ireland; "A Most Unusual Man," featuring Bob Newhart, Ann Blyth, and Macdonald Carey; and "A World at Prayer," which examines the effect this one man had – and still has – by promoting the rosary.

"The Face: Jesus in Art" did win an Emmy. It examines 2,000 years of artistic renderings of Jesus Christ by tracing the dramatically different ways in which Jesus has been represented in art throughout history from ancient Rome to 20th century America, from Europe to the Middle East.

The Family Theater Classic Television series has "A Star Shall Rise," telling of the journey of the Three Wise Men; "Hill Number One," a modern day war story, related to Christ's crucifixion; "Hound of Heaven," a pictorial presentation of the classic poem by Francis Thompson; "Joyful Hour," the Christmas story; "Our Lady of Fatima"; "That I May See," a story of Bartimeus; "Trial at Tara," St. Patrick's story; "Triumphant Hour," the Easter story to the coronation of Mary; and her own story in "World's Greatest Mother."

Other videos show the lives of other inspiring priests. "Glidepath to Recovery" tells the story of Fr. Peter Young, who spent more than 35 years with men and women struggling to free themselves from addictions. "God, Country, Notre Dame" tells of Fr. Ted Hesburgh, C.S.C," and "Henri Nouwen's Passion & Spirituality" of Fr. Henri Nouwen.

The Manifest Mysteries series is available in both English and Spanish, all contemporary stories based on the mysteries of the rosary. "Haunted Heart" is, for example, inspired by the Crowning with Thorns, "Taylor's Well" by the Ascension, "The Eggplant Lady" by the Agony in the Garden, and "The Hero" by the Crucifixion.

"The Journey" is a modern retelling of the Christmas story. "The Search" interweaves a runaway's story with the Finding of Jesus in the Temple. "The Secret of the Horse" relates martial arts to the sacrificial love of the Scourging. "The Visit" deals with AIDS and the Visitation.

The Mysteries of Life series comes with downloadable study and discussion guides. "Grieving to Grace" tells of a California lawyer's Way of the Cross. "Journey to Joy" and "Shadows to Sunlight" dramatize the Joyful and Glorious Mysteries.

Then there's "Pray the Rosary with Father Peyton and the Stars!"; "The Fifth Gospel: The Land and Sea of Galilee," based on the book by Benedictine priest-archaeologist Bargil Pixner; and "A Journey with Mary: The Rosary Wake Service."

There are also many publications on Fr. Peyton and the rosary available, such as *All For Her* by Fr. Peyton; *American Apostle of the Family Rosary* by Fr. Richard Gribble, CSC; *Fr. Peyton's Rosary Prayer Book*, which has been updated to include the Mysteries of Light; *Learning the Rosary, Minute Meditations on the Mysteries of the Rosary* by Fr. Thomas Feeley; *Praying the Rosary* with prayers and testimonies; *The History and Devotion of the Rosary* by Richard Gribble, CSC; and *Your Own Mysteries* by Br. Philip Armstrong, CSC.

[All 528 family theater radio programs are now available on one flashdrive from AffordableOTR.]

Holy Families Are Possible With God (October 2006)

Every marriage between a baptized Christian man and woman is meant to be holy, set apart as representing the union of Christ and His Church (*Catechism of the Catholic Church*, 1661). Some marriages have been especially holy, being between canonized and/or beatified saints.

In *Married Saints and Blesseds Through the Centuries* Ferdinand Holbock notes several canonized or beatified couples. Mary and Joseph of the Holy Family are, of course, the model par excellence for all other holy families.

Hildulf (died 707) and Aya (died 708), after many years together in a childless marriage, retired in their old age to the monastery and convent. Holy Roman Emperor Henry II (973-1024) and Cunegund (died 1033) may have had a Josephite marriage without exercise of marital rights. Elzear (died 1323) and Blessed Delphina (died 1360), both Franciscan tertiaries, certainly did.

What little information there is on Ann and Joachim, Jesus' grandparents, Holbock notes, comes from apocryphal texts, like the Protoevangelium of James. There can be no doubt that Mary's parents, whatever their names, must have been holy to have such a holy daughter. According to their legend Ann was barren for twenty years before their prayers were answered after Joachim withdrew for a while into the desert. She was told and indeed did conceive the day he returned. Holbock quotes John Damascene's exhortation beginning, "Ann and Joachim, how blessed a couple! All creation is indebted to you. For at your hands the Creator was offered a gift excelling all other gifts: a chaste mother, who alone was worthy of Him."

Elizabeth and Zechariah, the parents of John the Baptist, also prayed long for a child and so are also a good example for other childless couples. Elizabeth recognized the mother of her Savior and Zechariah repented of his doubt. Their feast day is November 5.

Basil (died before 349) was a lawyer and professor of rhetoric and a grandson of St. Macrina the Elder. Together he and his wife Emmelia (died 372) ministered to the poor while raising ten children, including four saints, Basil the Great (died 379), Gregory of Nyssa (died about 395), Macrina the Younger (330-379), and Peter of Sabaste (died 391), two doctors of the Church, an abbess, and a bishop. Gregory was married to Theosebeia (died about 385), described as "genuinely holy and a true wife of a priest." The other six died young. It is therefore no wonder the monks of Calabria celebrate the feast of the Relatives of Gregory the Great on May 30.

Nonna (died 374) converted her Zeus-worshipping husband Gregory Nazianzen (died 374) and with him raised three children. Gregory the Younger (died 390) reluctantly accepted the call to be a bishop and a saint. Caesarius (died 369) was a medical doctor, baptized only after surviving an earthquake. Gorgonia (died 370) was such an exemplary wife and mother of three that she too was canonized.

Senator Hilarius (died 420) and Quieta (died 467) lived in Burgundy and were the parents of three children, including St. John of Réome. So close were they in life that Hilarius is said by St. Gregory of Tours to have reached over and pulled Quieta to himself when she was entombed with him.

Vincent Madelgarius (died 677) and Waldetrudis (died 688) were from Belgium and had four children, Adeltrudis, Landerics, Dentelinus, and Madelberta, all who were also canonized saints, as was Waldetrudis's sister, Aldegundis. After their children were grown, by mutual consent, he entered the monastery and she entered the convent. The two girls succeeded their aunt as abbess and Ladericus served in the military and then succeeded his father as abbot. Dentelinus died at seven, but all in this holy family had many miracles attributed to them.

Isidore the Farmer (died about 1130) and Blessed Marie de la Cabeza (died 1135) were Spanish peasants and had only one son. Isidore and Marie both attended Mass daily and gave generously to the poor and patiently endured false accusations against them for it.

Blessed Erkenbert (died 1132) and Blessed Richlinde (1150) had two sons. After recovering from a serious illness Erkenbert's already strong faith turned to full-time ministry to the poor. He died with the odor of sanctity.

St. Stephan of Hungary (died 1038) and Blessed Gisela (died 1060) were the parents of St. Emeric. Stephan, who had been born Vaik, was baptized with his father prince Géza. He married Gisela of Bavaria, sister of future emperor St. Henry II. Prince Emeric married a Greek princess but was killed by a wild boar in 1031. After Stephan died, Gisela was imprisoned and disinherited as a foreigner, but was finally freed and returned home by her nephew, Henry III.

God Cares About Your Finances (September 2006)

Perhaps the most interesting of all the marvelous chapters in *Mysteries, Marvels and Miracles in the Lives of the Saints* by Joan Carroll Cruz, given today's high personal and public debts, is the one on money miracles. She has authored many faith-building books based on signs and wonders: *The Incorruptibles, Eucharistic Miracles, Miraculous Images of Our Lady, Miraculous Images of Our Lord*, and *Relics*.

Just in *Mysteries, Marvels and Miracles* she has collected stories of saints' preternatural gifts of bilocation (being in two places at once), levitation, the odor of sanctity, miraculous transport, invisibility, knowledge or being understood, commanding animals or nature.

All of these, but especially the financial miracles, are explained by St. Therese's quoted words to Mother Carmela, "The power of God takes away or gives the same ease in matters temporal as in matters spiritual." He will, these seem to be demonstrating, provide for our every need, but not our every want.

In 1911 the Sisters of Carmel of Gallipoli were so impoverished, they had to pray rather than eat. On the third day of fasting and praying, January 16, Mother Carmela had a vision in the night. At first she thought "the brilliant Carmelite nun" was Theresa of Avila, but the saintly nun told her humbly, "I am the servant of God, Soeur Therese of Lisieux." St. Therese had died only fourteen years earlier.

She gave Mother Carmela five hundred francs, two hundred more than they needed to pay what they owed. The money continued to multiply over the following months, finally ending exactly a year later. The bishop, acknowledging the miracles, sent the convent a commemorative contribution. When opened on the anniversary of the first miracle, it too had been added to in the sealed envelope.

This sort of thing is nothing new, but has been happening for those who trust in God and when it's truly needed. Cruz retells the story in *The Very Rev. Fr. Paul of Molli* by Edward van Speybrouck. A friend who had known him before he died in 1896 put a picture of him in her safe and prayed. Two days later she says, I found more money than I had ever had at my disposal."

Jean Vianney, the Cure d'Ars, (died 1859) prayed to Our Lady of LaSalette and found the money needed for a mission.

St. Joseph Benedict Cottolengo (died 1842) showed his dubious creditor his empty pockets and then several gold coins appeared in them.

St. Gaspar del Bufalo (died 1837) advised Fr. Velentini to bless stones into money. He didn't, but did bless the little money he had and it became the amount needed to save the monastery.

Bl. Francis Xavier Bianchi (died 1815) had money in a drawer multiply. Gerard Majella (died 1755) prayed all night before the Blessed Sacrament to save his monastery and two bags of money were outside the door in the morning.

The mother superior of Rita Cascia (died 1457) found, as she'd told her she would, the exact amount needed in the alms box.

St. Lydwin of Schiedam (died 1433) had to sell off a family heirloom to pay off her brother's debt when he died. When her nephew returned the empty purse, it still contained the original amount. She named it "the purse of Jesus" and it never was without money for good works.

When Bl. Gonsalvo of Amarante (died 1259) begged from a certain rich man, the man gave him a note to give to his wife. On the note he had told her to give the man "as much gold as would balance this note." It took "a considerable amount of gold" to do so.

St. Benedict (died 543) prayed for the money to pay off Peregrinus' debt and after three days directed his brothers to a particular chest of grain, and they found the needed twelve coins and one extra for good works.

My own most memorable experience with Providence would be a lesson I learned when I had newly joined what would become Presentation Ministries. I had lost my contact lenses and needed glasses, but did not have the money to pay for them. In faith I went to the clinic and had my eyes examined. Just before the glasses were ready, just the amount needed came. It came from the most unexpected source, my missionary cousin, who has never sent me money before or since. He just said, "I thought you needed it more."

Bishops Decode Jesus (July 2006)

The U. S. Catholic bishop's new documentary, "Jesus Decoded", has been shown by many stations over the past few months. The DVD will soon be available and may be preordered at jesusdecoded.com.

Msgr. Francis J. Maniscalco, who contributed "What's Missing from *The Da Vinci Code?*," begins his introduction at jesusdecoded.com with: "Causing people to see something they never saw before in a five-hundred-year-old work of art which is among the most famous and reproduced of all time is an accomplishment of genius, if that 'something' is a valid new insight. If it is not, then this kind of achievement usually goes by other names."

He is, of course, referring to Dan Brown's book, *The Da Vinci Code*, and Ron Howard's movie based on it, which claim that the beloved disciple in John's Gospel and in Leonardo's mural, "The Last Supper", is actually Mary Magdalene. It also claims Emperor Constantine deified the otherwise unnoteworthy Jewish rabbi, Jesus of Nazareth.

"This claim," Maniscalco writes, "cannot be sustained on the basis of the existing evidence which demonstrates that Constantine did no such thing. It also highlights the schizophrenia in *The Da Vinci Code* about Jesus Christ. Only if Jesus is divine would we have any interest in the possibility that His descendant might walk the earth today."

"Jesus Decoded" was shot on location in Israel, Turkey, and Italy, and features international scholars versed in art, history, and Scripture. Its purpose is to present "clear and accurate information about the person of Jesus, His disciples, and the formation of the books included in the official canon of the Bible."

The most important question the documentary answers may be: "Is the movie as bad as the book?" The answer is "Yes."

In both, the character Sir Leigh Teabing makes the incredible statement, "Until that moment in history [the Council of Nicaea, AD 325], Jesus was viewed by His followers as a mortal prophet ... a great and powerful man, but a man nonetheless. A Mortal."

Records clearly show that the question decided at Nicaea was not "Is Jesus divine?" but "Is Jesus equal to or subordinate to God the Father?" The bishops, then as now, overwhelmingly affirmed as the faith of the Church from the beginning, that Jesus is "true God from true God, one in being with the Father."

Teabing continues with "... the early Church needed to convince the world that the mortal prophet Jesus was a divine being. Therefore, any gospels that described earthly aspects of Jesus' life had to be omitted from the Bible ... More specifically, [Mary Magdalene's] marriage to Jesus Christ."

Even the Gnostic writings he refers to do not make any claims about a sexual relationship between Jesus and Mary Magdalene, the website article explains. The Gnostics were not enthusiastic about the material world, but they were enthusiastic about secret spiritual knowledge. If the so-called *Gospel of Philip*, the website says, "has Jesus kissing Mary, that is meant to be a symbol of a spiritual communication, not sexual. The apostles' reaction makes that clear. They are portrayed as being jealous of this alleged fondness for Mary. If it were the affection of a husband for a wife, there is no reason for jealousy. But the fact is the *Gospel of Philip* is no more a reliable source for knowing about Jesus and His relationships than the script of 'Jesus Christ Superstar'. Both use the name of Jesus and His followers for reasons other than proclaiming the gospel as it came from Jesus Himself."

Other questions answered are: "How reliable is the text of the New Testament that we have today?", "Does it reflect what was originally written?", "Didn't copyists introduce many variations either deliberately or by mistake?", "Is there a woman in Leonardo's Last Supper?", "Wasn't Jesus a rabbi and didn't rabbis have to be married?", "Is belief in the divinity of Christ found in the New Testament?", and "Did Jesus remain unmarried?"

Visitors to the website are also invited to submit questions in the Question box.

There are not many left unanswered by the website's contributors. Amy Welborn answers "What do you say to a Da Vinci Code Believer?" and Fr. John Wauck "What's Wrong with *The Da Vinci Code*?"

Elizabeth Lev has articles on the historical Leonardo and other depictions of the Last Supper. Peter Feuerherd has one on secret societies and Kate Blain on killing witches.

It also has "The origin of the 'Holy Grail' " by John Gehring and "The real Opus Dei" by Peter Bancroft. There is also one on the early councils by Alan Schreck, Ph.D. and another on Ignatius of Antioch by Rev. Thomas G. Weinandy.

The Military Tells Their Side (May 2006)

The website Milblogging.com describes itself as "the world's largest index of military blogs." It currently has links to 1,290 blogs or web logs by 1,354 registered members. Many are just men and women in the military and their families trying to tell each other how much they miss each other. Technically it is much faster, much better than previous wars' letters, but it is still hard. The following are a few which were called up by a search for the word "God."

Sgt. Chancy Humphries writes, "I have been a soldier in the National Guard for eight years. I never thought I would be in Iraq, but here I am. God knew what He was doing when He put me here. For more reasons than one. I am a proud soldier and a proud man. I miss my family and wife, and will be home soon."

Sgt. David Francis of the Iowa National Guard in his blog, "Freedom Was Never Free," writes, "I am among the most fortunate men of all time. If you disagree, you are wrong. I know because I have been chosen as a son of God Most High." He also tells of "Hank," Shiite Gulf War veteran who went AWOL and survived to become a translator. "I've read the Bible five times," Hank told Francis proudly, and he said, "Wow! That's five times more than most Christians."

He got quite angry, however, right there in mess hall once when he shouted out, "There are weapons of mass destruction here! I know! I've seen them!"

"He got choked up and his lip quivered as he continued, I just don't know what they did with them. I'm afraid the people who know are already dead," Sgt. Francis writes. "This is a big desert. Not even America has enough time or money to look everywhere."

Francis added that he knows for a fact that a number of MiG 29's – which would be classified as WMD's – were buried, because some of these have been dug up and are now on display at Al Taqqadum Air Base.

Navy Seaman Yem Sophat, a hospital corpsman from Pomona, Calif., says, "Besides combat, we help a lot of unfortunate people in this country. I wish we could do more." With Marines from his company he delivered a brand new pediatric wheelchair to the family of a disabled little girl in the town of Al Hasa. She had her back broken in a traffic accident.

Rob Meehl's blog is mostly photographic. "These pictures," he explains, "are of regular soldiers interacting with regular kids. These kinds of scenes happen a thousand times a day around here. We are here to help give these kids a future."

Millman, on the other hand, is concerned about the children back home and not just his own. "I want the Governor of N.D. to run for President. This is what he said. 'In the history of the world, the true test of a civilization is how well people treat the most vulnerable and most helpless in their society. The sponsors and supporters of this bill believe that abortion is wrong because unborn children are the most vulnerable and most helpless persons in our society. I agree with them."

On another one called simply "Greg's blog," SFC Greg writes of the Iraqis, "They see that they CAN make changes and have a say in the government. I believe that the overall process will take up to three generations to be where it should be, but it is such a huge start. I have said in the past, that I am not here for the adults, but it is the children which will make the mindset change. After evaluating the last year, I recant that statement. Yes, it will still take three generations; however, the adults are changing. I have seen it."

He expresses the opinion of perhaps everyone in the military when he writes, "As I reflect on my life and I look around me, I realize what we as Americans have, yet we take so much for granted. The peoples we are aiding know nothing of the changes which are happening. They have nothing to compare it to. They have lived in total fear and oppression for over 35 years of hard rule. This makes the average Iraqi who has memories of pre-Saddam, at least 50 years old."

"Yes, we are the world police," he continues, "I am so proud to be one. I swore an oath of allegiance when I joined the military. I was not drafted, but joined on my own accord. The following words have become my life and are forever etched into who I am: 'I will support and defend the constitution of the United States, I will guard against all enemies, foreign and domestic, and will bear true faith and allegiance to the same so help me god!!'" (his emphasis).

Decent Films Do Exist (February 2006)
The Decent Films Guide is a handy tool for evaluating current films, but among its list of most recommended films, many are "oldies." Those few rated both A+ and Four Stars do have a variety of moral/spiritual values and audience ranges.

Listed first, as the site states purely as a personal opinion, is "Star Wars: A New Hope" (1977), rated between +2 and -1 on a scale from +4 to -4 for kids and up. Second in the list is the second Star Wars film, "The Empire Strikes Back" (1980), rated slightly lower at +2 to -2.

The next, '[The Ninth Day" (2004), however, has a higher moral/spiritual rating, the maximum in fact, +4. It is not for "kids" since it tells the story of Dachau prisoner Fr. Jean Bernard.

Next come the family-friendly classics, "The Wizard of Oz" (1939), "Bambi" (1942) and the relatively new "The Incredibles" (2004), all rated at +2.

Another with a perfect +4 rating is "The Life and Passion of Jesus Christ" (1905). It was, the reviewer writes, "a remarkably in-depth presentation of the Gospel story, running about thirty minutes at its original length and nearly three-quarters of an hour in the expanded version – one of the first long films ever."

In rating "The Prince of Egypt" (1998), at +4, the reviewer points out what are to him important details, "the astonishing animation of scale at work in capturing the towering monuments of Egypt, or the host of departing Hebrews," the scene where "the infant Moses, caught up in the Queen's arms, eclipses the toddler Ramses in her line of vision," "those quiet numinous moments: the pebbles rolling back at Moses' feet at the burning bush; the halo of clear water around his ankles as the Nile turns to blood; the horror of an Egyptian servant as the surface of the water bubbles and the first frogs begin to flop out of the river onto the palace stairs; an extinguished candle flame or an off-screen sound of a jar crashing as the destroying angel swirls in and out among the Egyptians."

"The Miracle Maker" (2000) is called an "astoundingly lifelike stop-motion animation, supplemented with traditional hand-drawn animation for flashbacks and other special sequences, and digital effects." Another +4 is "Miracle of Saint Thérése" (1952).

"The Lord of the Rings: The Return of the King" (2003) is not for kids and is not a +4, but only a +3. Even so the reviewer describes this film as a "soaring achievement" and "the grandest spectacle ever filmed" and "the most satisfying third act of any film trilogy, completing what can now be regarded as possibly the best realized cinematic trilogy of all time."

"Diary of a Country Priest" (1951) and "Andrei Rublev" (1969) are both +4s. The second film is also compared to and rated better – because of its better ending – than the classic "The Seventh Seal" (1957).

On the list are even a few recommended films with a moral/spiritual neutral rating, "the zaniest, most delightful, most romantic screwball comedy of them all, "Bringing Up Baby" (1942), but also Buster Keaton's "The General" (1927), Danny Kaye's "The Court Jester" (1956), Fred Astair's "Singin' in the Rain" (1952), the Marx Brothers' "A Night at the Opera" (1935), and "Duck Soup" (1933), and Wallace and Gromit's shorts (1993).

Others with +4s are worth looking for would be "Faustina" (1995), "The Son" (2002), "A Man for All Seasons" (1966), "The Passion of Joan of Arc" (1928), "Chariots of Fire" (1981), "The Gospel According to St. Matthew" (1964), "The Flowers of St. Francis" (1950), "Ordet" (1955), "Babette's Feast" (1987), and "Monsieur Vincent" (1947).

Other most recommended films with positive moral/spiritual ratings are: "Babe" (1995), "The Pianist" (2002), "Fantasia" (1940), "Toy Story 2" (1999), "Raiders of the Lost Ark" (1981), "Citizen Kane" (1941), "It's A Wonderful Life" (1946), "The Kid Brother" (1927), "Open City" (1947), "Grand Illusion" (1937), "The Adventures of Robin Hood" (1938), "Casablanca" (1948), "Holiday" (1938), and "City Lights" (1931).

The Chronicles of Narnia Movies Begin (December 2005)

This December the first of a projected series of the high-budget adaptations of C. S. Lewis' classic *The Chronicles of Narnia* will begin. The first film, "The Narnia Chronicles: The Lion, the Witch and the Wardrobe", will premiere in New Zealand where it was made (as were the films of Lewis' friend J. R. R. Tolkien's *Lord of the Ring* trilogy). It premiers on December 8th, the feast of the Immaculate Conception, there as well as simultaneously in Germany, Switzerland, and the United Kingdom, and the next day in the United States.

The rights to adapt all seven books in Lewis' series has been granted by his stepson Douglas Gresham. MovieFone calls it "sheer cinematic gold," not only because of the first film, but because of the promise. As it puts it, there is in the popular series "enough to fill movie screens for the next decade – at least."

Unlike the Harry Potter series of books and films, they depict witchcraft as evil and family as good. As Lewis quoted Wisdom as saying in his *The Pilgrim's Regress*, "For this end I made your senses and for this end your imagination, that you might see my face and live." This brings to mind Pope John Paul II's admonition to look upon His face.

Tilda Swinton, who plays the evil White Witch, says that "This is not a religious film." Pastor Jarvis Ward, who watched a preview, however says, "It has a gospel message." Like Jesus' parables, believers can see and unbelievers cannot, but might yet.

In Lewis' own words from the book, "Perhaps it has sometimes happened to you in a dream that someone says something which you don't understand but in the dream it feels as if it had some enormous meaning ... which makes the dream so beautiful that you remember it all your life and are always wishing you could get into that dream again."

This is just what Andrew Adamson, the film's director, noted for "Shrek" and "Shrek 2", says he was trying to do. "I really wanted to bring the world of Narnia to life how I imagined it as a child.

"To me," he says, "the main messages are that of family, sacrifice, and forgiveness. I can't think of more relevant messages for today."

The basic plot elements cannot be denied that Aslan, who created and maintains the existence of Narnia, dies and rises from the dead to save it, that the leader of Narnia is Peter, Aslan's representative, that Narnia – and our own world that we think we know – is just a shadow of the Real World.

Governor Jeb Bush has promoted a reading contest before the movie comes out though ninety million have already read *The Chronicles*. There are already posters, costumes, and companion storybooks available for Christmas presents. SermonCentral.com has a Narnia-based sermon contest whose prize is a trip for two to London. The multi-hundred -million-dollar film is being marketed by Motive Marketing, which also marketed Mel Gibson's record-breaking "The Passion of the Christ" and distributed by Disney.

Walter Hooper, Lewis' biographer, now a convert to the Catholic Church, recently shared on Eternal Word Television (EWTN) of his own visit to Narnia. The Italian town of Narni on the river Nar, formerly called Narnia, is home to Bl. Lucia of Narnia. "Coincidentally" this is the same as the name of Lewis' goddaughter, Lucy Barfield, to whom he dedicated the book, and his heroine, Lucy Eve's-Daughter.

There has been an Emmy-winning animated version of "The Lion, the Witch and the Wardrobe" and a BBC version of four of the books, including "Prince Caspian, The Voyage of the Dawn Treader, and The Silver Chair". Until the high-quality film versions of "The Horse and His Boy", "The Magician's Nephew", the prequel to The Lion, the Witch, and the Wardrobe and the climactic "The Last Battle" come out in the theaters, you can always read and re-read the books. Generations of visitors to Narnia, sons of Adam and daughters of Eve, have encountered giants and dragons. Talking Animals and mythic creatures, even new ones like marshwiggles, had great adventures and fought and won just wars, and ultimately arrived at the unimaginably glorious Land of Aslan.

As Lewis concluded, "All their life in this world and all their adventures in Narnia had only been the cover and the title page: now at last they were beginning Chapter One of the Great Story, which no one on earth has read: which goes on forever: in which every chapter is better than the one before."

Successful Marriage "Secrets" Revealed (October 2005)

Many at Catholic Match say the reason they stay in the group is not so much that they are expecting to find a match, though almost all are open to God so working out their vocations. A large number say they do because of the forums available where they can discuss issues important to single Catholics. One popular discussion tried to answer "What makes a successful marriage?," begun by Debra who had already had nine thousand postings in the forums.

Malinda thought thoughtfulness was most important. Referring to her own parents' successful marriage, she wrote, "Neither one would ever do anything without first asking themselves how it would affect the life or happiness of their partner.

"They were kind, thoughtful, and considerate to each other. They grew together over the thirty-plus years they were married and truly became 'one.'"

Megan shared, "My mom and dad have been married for almost forty years and from what they've told me, the glue that has kept their marriage going is their tremendous faith in God." When her older brother was killed in a car accident, her father saw how her mom's faith sustained her and shortly before she was born, he became Catholic, and a very faithful and active one.

Many of the singles from successful marriages had comments similar to hers, "I can't wait to have a marriage just like theirs!"

Christy answered "communication," based on her parents' thirty-eight-year marriage. "If you have someone you can like to talk to ... then you are more likely to stay together." Her parents, she wrote, "tell each other virtually everything and are loving and respectful to each other daily." Non-verbal communication is also important. "They hold hands and kiss playfully," she said.

Andrew shared that he saw his father "taking care of us and the house without complaint (and disciplining us)." He saw his mother always deferring to his father because he "is a humble and wise man and knows what is right." Another important factor, he notes, is "my parents did not doubt themselves and did not let outside influences erode their beliefs."

Dan gave the simple, though he admits hard-to-practice advice, to decide each day to love the other person. Ivan credits prayer for saving his parents' marriage, when his father decided "he was not going to let anything happen to" his wife.

Carla, among others, offered "commitment" as the "secret" to a successful marriage. "The most successful and healthy marriage are," she wrote, "ones where both parties have the same attitude about marriage, that it's until death, and divorce is not an option. That way, they are forced to work on their problems, sacrifice to each other, and forgive when necessary."

Heidi shared about the mutual respect of a Southern Baptist couple she knew. "The wife," she wrote, "practices respecting her husband, no matter what. When he doesn't treat her lovingly or cherish her, she still strives to treat him respectfully. This couple seeks to be mutually submissive and respectful to each other, but the husband is definitely the head of the house here; the wife is definitely the heart of this home."

If, she concludes, each spouse strives "to do that which is the most difficult for him/her to do: husband – to cherish and love as Christ loves the Church, and wife – to respect, honor and obey, then marriages can succeed." "When we put the vows back into the Scriptural context from whence they originate, then it is much, much easier to begin to have a godly, Christ-centered, God-honoring marriage of mutual love and respect."

Susanne agreed, and added, "You have to be friends first." Ann quoted Ephesians' "The two shall become one flesh. If we can all truly understand with great wisdom this passage," she said, "we can all have successful marriages."

The most common factors mentioned by participants in the forum, Debra noted, were: practicing the Faith together, mutual respect, stick together through the trials, communication, selflessness, being good examples for each other. "These refer to 'successful marriages,'" she concluded, "but I think most of these make successful relationships too."

Interest In Papal Prophecies Increases (July 2005)

Since the transition from Pope John Paul II to Pope Benedict XVI, there has been an increased interest in the so-called *Prophecy of St. Malachi*. It is a list found in the 16th century, attributed to the 12th-century saint, with a short description of future popes -- the list ends with just one more pope after Benedict XVI.

Some think this means the end of the papacy, others an anti-pope, still others that the hierarchy will be forced into exile and secrecy by persecution. The only sure thing, as Jesus told us, is "only the Father knows."

Some of the list's descriptions, however, do seem to fit. Benedict XV, the pope during the first world war, was described with the phrase, "Religio Depopulata" ("Christendom depopulated"). Pius X was "Fides Intrepida" ("Fearless Faith"); Pius XII, "Pastor Angelicus" ("Angelic Shepherd"); John XXIII was from Venice and launched the Church into aggiornamento with Vatican II, "Pastor et Nauta" ("Shepherd and Sailor"). Paul VI, who completed the council, was "Flos Florum" ("Flower of Flowers"). John Paul I, who was only pope a month, was "De Mediatate Lunae" ("From the Midst of the Moon"). John Paul II, the most prolific and most well-known pope ever, was "De Labore Solis" ("Of the Labor of the Sun").

The new pope is "De Gloria Olivae" ("Of the Glory of the Olive Tree"), which may refer to the olive branch of peace, anointing olive oil, or the agony of the olive garden. The last pope, in the list at least, is "Petrus Romanus" ("Peter of Rome"), commonly called Peter II.

We have many other prophecies yet to be fulfilled -- or not, some more recent and with better credentials than that already mentioned. They seem to say it's going to get worse before it gets better, unless the world repents first.

Abbot Joachin Merlin wrote in the 13th century, "After many long sufferings endured by Christians, and after too great an effusion of innocent blood, the Lord shall give peace and happiness to the desolate nations." That certainly sounds like the 20th century.

He, and many others, write of a Great Pope who will reunite the Eastern and Western churches. Louis-Marie de Montfort (18th century) wrote that by the power of Mary the kingdom of her Son will extend to idolaters and Moslems as well. Telesphorus of Cozensa (16th century) said this will be a French pope. An 18th century Capuchin says he will be descended from the Carolingians. Bartholomew Holzhauser calls this the sixth period of the

Church, marked by "the greatest of all councils," a peaceful period, which will last until the coming of the anti-christ.

The nursing nun of Bellay (c. 1820) wrote that what she saw of this future was "so wonderful that I am unable to express it."

Before this, however, comes the end of the current, not-so-peaceful period of Church history, marked possibly by an exiled pope. St. Pius X wrote, "I saw one of my successors taking to flight over the bodies of his brethren. He will take refuge in disguise somewhere and after a short retirement will die a cruel death."

Even Michel Nostradamus wrote rather clearly, for him, "For seven days the great star shall be seen, As if two suns in the sky should appear, The big Mastiff shall be howling all night, When the Pontiff shall go into exile."

John of the Cleft Rock (14th century) said this pope will flee to a place he is unknown. Helen Wallraff (19th century) says to Cologne with four trusted cardinals and Premol (5th century) says "to other shores." John of Vatiguerro (13th century) wrote that after the pope's exile of twenty-five months or more, a new pope will be elected from those who survive the persecutions. After, an 18th century Fransican friar says, a German, Italian, and a Greek vie for the papacy. Bl. Anna-Maria Taigi (19th century) wrote that France will then fall into anarchy, according to many prophecies, until the restoration of the monarchy.

Through it all we have Jesus', "The gates of hell shall not prevail against [My Church]."

The DaVinci Code Turned To Good (June 2005)

Dan Brown's book has triggered a great outpouring of counterbooks for various readerships. We now have more edifying offerings like Breaking the DaVinci Code, Cracking the DaVinci Code, The DaVinci Code: Fact or Fiction, The DaVinci Deception, De-Coding the DaVinci Code, Dismantling the DaVinci Code, The Gospel Code, and The Truth about the DaVinci Code.

CBS's "Dateline" story, "Secrets of the Code," did not reveal many secrets of The DaVinci Code by Dan Brown. At least not secrets for anyone with long enough memories. It also did not seem to bear much resemblance to Secrets of the Code by Dan Burstein.

It was better done than ABC's piece on the book "Jesus, Mary, and DaVinci" back in 2003. The planned movie has rekindled interest – and confusion.

Stone Phillips interviewed many experts on art, history, and Church history who all agreed that there is absolutely no evidence that Mary Magdalene and Jesus were married. It seems to be a "controversy" that reappears about every twenty years, "fact" based on fiction and now fiction based on "fact."

Phillips also went back to the authors of the 1982 "non-fiction" book Holy Blood, Holy Grail, Richard Leigh and Henry Lincoln, who are suing Brown – as are others. They told about their primary source, Pierre Plantard. Plantard himself was on tape explaining about the Priory of Sion and his 1967 book L'Or de Rennes. Both books go back to the medieval notion that the Holy Grail was actually the royal bloodline of France going back to Jesus and Mary Magdalene – based on the medieval pun of san greal (holy grail) being read as sang real (blood royal).

The Catholic Encyclopedia explains that Mary Magdalene seems to have gotten to France by a confusion of the relics of Mary of Aix (and later Vézzelay) and Lazarus of Aix with Mary and Lazarus of Bethany. The relics of the latter are pretty well documented as having been moved to Ephesus and then in 886 to Constantinople. One Lazarus was the fourth century bishop of Aix who returned after a pilgrimage to the Holy Land and the other was the first century friend Jesus raised from the dead.

It also notes that the traditional equating of Mary Magdalene, the delivered demoniac, with the forgiven adulterous and Mary of Bethany is not contrary to Scripture, even if not explicitly stated.

Carl E. Olson, co-author of The DaVinci Hoax, has said, "Frankly, The DaVinci Code is an attempt to slap the face of our mother the Church," Jesus' actual spouse.

Brown references several Gnostic sources, as if Scripture, such as the apocryphal Gospel of Philip, which calls Mary Magdalene Jesus' companion. It is obvious from the text that this is merely to distinguish her from Jesus' two kinswomen, Mary, Jesus' mother, and Mary, Jesus' aunt. Brown even fills in the gaps in the text with his own words, adding "on the lips" to "Jesus often kissed the beloved disciple."

Art professor David Nolta pointed out that any number of "secret" messages could be found in the silhouettes of Leonardo's "Last Supper," including the much more plausible "DaVinci."

Not only does Brown invent "facts," he gets many facts wrong, making the fiction almost unreadable. The DaVinci Hoax calls it "the poorest scholarship one will find between two covers."

He is so wrong in his facts in so many areas that it seems he must be doing it for humorous effect. He has Leonardo's "Madonna of the Rocks" the wrong size, St. Peter's basilica in the wrong direction, the Louvre with a security gate and without cameras, not the other way around. His key murder victim would have had only a 5% chance of dying from the wound described. The Nag Hammadi documents are codices, not scrolls. Tarot decks have 78, not 22 cards. Opus Dei is a lay association and has no monks.

This is not surprising considering the way he wrote his prequel book, Angels and Demons. He had Michelangelo designing the Swiss Guards' uniforms; Holy Communion coming from Aztec god-eating, Buddhism before hatha yoga; Galileo supporting Kepler; Copernicus murdered by the Church; the Hiroshima A-bomb at 20 kilotons, not 13; the Hasshashin destroyed by the Christians, not the Mongols; "The Serenity Prayer" of Alcoholics Anonymous attributed to St. Francis of Assisi; and Tim Berners inventing the internet rather than the world-wide web.

Eucharistic Congress Builds Faith (April 2005)

Cincinnati's Archbishop Pilarczyk concluded the Eucharistic Congress at Good Shepherd, Cincinnati, on February 26 with, "If you liked today, you'll love New Bremen." The congress' third and final session will be held there at Holy Redeemer April 16.

Entitled "Do This in Remembrance of Me," the congress brings together 18 workshops on various aspects of the Eucharist, exhibits by local religious goods stores, and, of course, Jesus in the Eucharist Himself. "This is," the archbishop says, "an opportunity for the entire Church to grow in their love and understanding of the Eucharist and its importance in our lives."

"Getting the Most Out of Mass" was presented in Dayton by Rev. Jerry Chinchar, S. M., and will be presented again in New Bremen by Karen Kane. It is described as "practical suggestions for getting more out of the Mass through personal preparation beforehand," like reading the Scriptures with Presentation Ministries' own One Bread, One Body, "and practical explanations of how to participate more fully during Mass."

Among the workshops offered at all three locations, many focus on the Mass: "Eucharistic Spirituality for Sundays and All Days," "The Mass: Why We Do What We Do," "The

Eucharistic Prayer: Praise of the Whole Assembly," "The Communion Rite: Dining in the Kingdom of God," "The Lay Person at Mass," "Setting the Table and Giving Thanks," "Becoming Welcoming Communities Amidst Diversity," and "Preparing Children to Participate in the Mass."

A couple are aimed specifically at teens: "Shake Off Those 'Boring Mass' Blues!" and "What's It All About, Jesus?"

Other workshops addressed: "Sacramental Speech: The Liturgy of the Word as an Encounter with the Lord," "Praying in the Presence of the Blessed Sacrament," "The Liturgy in the World: How the Eucharist Compels Us to Clothe the Naked, Feed the Hungry, Liberate the Oppressed, and 'Ask Why!,'" and "Looking Toward the Future: The Dilemma of Fewer Priests."

Additional topics included: "Adoration and Its Connection to Sunday Eucharist" and "Preparing for and Living the Eucharist: Why and How We Are Eucharistic People" (only offered at the Cincinnati location).

In the second of these workshops Joyce Ann Zimmermann, C. P. P. S., tried to impart some of what she has learned about the Eucharist. As she explained, even with a doctorate and postdoctorate work specifically on the Eucharist, "there is always more."

Although the Word of God and the Church's prayerful response to God are important, "we need to hear God through other things than words," she says. The gestures such as opening and closing the Mass with the sign of the cross are full of food for meditation. The traditional design of the church with the altar at the East end and the exit at the West brings to mind Easter, sunrise, the Son's rising, the Son's return, and the mission out into the world that still does not know the Light.

Receiving the Eucharist in Communion, individually and communally, is another whole area for reflection. In this we are called, Sr. Joyce pointed out, to both action and passion. Catholics are invited by an altar call daily, invited to give ourselves unreservedly to He Who gave His all for us. We celebrate the Eucharist as a Church community and live it out in the secular community. We are also called to express our passion for and with the Eucharist in praise, thanksgiving, and adoration in and after Mass. God's gift to us is to be – not merely receive – the Eucharistic Christ.

To whom much has been given, however, much will be expected. She is not surprised, she says, that some are hesitant to say "Amen" to such a Gift. "It is not healthy," she warns, "if you want to hang on to your current lifestyle."

By our baptisms we were made a priestly people, a Eucharistic people. We are mediators between God and others, offering Him ourselves, our joys and sufferings, our prayers and those of our friends, family, and the world. By surrendering our lives so God can live in and through us, we can go ever deeper and deeper, be ever more truly who we already are.

We can do this, Sr. Joyce suggests, by examining ourselves every evening, asking, "How have I been Eucharist today?" Every Friday we can ask ourselves, "Did I do penance today?"

We can prepare for the Sunday liturgy by reading and praying the readings beforehand, by wearing our Sunday best, by making Sunday special (perhaps sharing a sundae?).

Anything we can do to enhance our understanding and living out the Eucharist will be good, because unlike the prodigal son who asked for half his inheritance, we have been given everything, the whole body, blood, soul, and divinity of Jesus Christ, far more than we had any right to, far more than we can ever know.

The Holy Eucharist Is Still Miraculous (March 2005)

If you expect a miracle during Holy Week or Easter in this Year of the Eucharist, you are likely not to be disappointed. There have been many such miracles as precedent. But then, every Eucharist is a miracle.

On Holy Thursday, 1255, while Fr. Dompfarrer Ulrich von Dornberg was taking the Eucharist to the sick, he slipped and fell in the stream called Bachgrasse near Ratisbon, Germany. He collected the ciborium and hosts with some difficulty, but that was not the end but just the beginning of the story. Parishioners erected a wooden chapel on the site and finished it three days later on Easter. It was two years later when a priest doubting the Real Presence of Christ in the Eucharist celebrated Mass there. The corpus of the crucifix behind him took the chalice from his hands. The chalice was returned to him when he repented of his lack of faith. By 1260 St. Saviour's chapel was rebuilt and expanded because of the many pilgrims there, becoming Kreuzkapelle (Cross Chapel).

On another Holy Thursday, this time in 1384, something miraculous happened at St. Oswald's in Seefeld in Tyrol provence, Austria. Sir Oswald Milser drew his sword and demanded that the priest give him the large Host rather than a small Host. When the frightened priest did so, the floor under the knight's feet is said to have opened up under him and he sank down to his knees – and then the miracle happened. He grabbed the altar, begged the priest to take back the large Host, and repented of his pride.

The Host, which had turned blood red, has been venerated in a Gothic style reliquary ever since. The hollow into which Sir Oswald sunk and the impression on the stone altar left by his hands can still be seen.

On Easter, 1171, at Saint Maria del Vado, Ferrara, Italy, Padre Pietro de Verona broke the Holy Eucharist as usual, but not as usual this time the Host flowed with blood. It was witnessed by his concelebrants, Padre Bono, Padre Leonardo, and Padre Aimone. The blood even sprinkled the semi-circular vault behind and above the altar. The Host had turned to flesh. The bishop, Amato, and the Archbishop, Gherardo, both came and witnessed the miracle.

When Pope Pius IX visited in 1857 the still venerated altar where the miracle had happened, he said, "These drops are like the ones on the corporal in Orvieto!" Since 1930 the basilica has been appropriately in the care of the Missionaries of the Most Precious Blood.

Again on Easter, this time in Blanot, France, in 1331 vicar Hugues de la Baume did not notice that the Eucharist had fallen from the mouth of Jacquette d'Effour to land, his servers told him, on the Communion railing cloth. When he went back to retrieve the Host, however, he found a blood stain. When he tried to wash the blood stain out of the cloth, it only grew larger and darker. An investigation was held 15 days later by Cure de Lucenay, a monsignor from Autun and an apostalic notary.

The unused Hosts from that Mass were still in good condition during a five-hour procession in 1706. Although placed in safekeeping during the French Revolution, the blood-stained cloth has traditionally been solemnly exposed every Easter Monday.

On the third Sunday of Easter, 1560, in Morrovale, Italy, a fire destroyed the Church of St. Francis. Among the ashes and broken marble, however, Padre Girolama and the others helping him found an intact Host, even though the tabernacle and the sacred vessels in it had been completely destroyed. It was the judgement of the investigation commissioned by Pope Pius IV that the event was "undoubtedly miraculous." He granted a plenary indulgence to any pilgrim who visits the church on the anniversary of the miracle, April 16.

These and many other well-documented accounts of such stories are collected in *Eucharistic Miracles* by Joan Carroll Cruz (Tan Books, 1987). "There have also been many other such miracles," Cruz writes in her prefix, "but research would be endless if an attempt were made to include every single one. It is hoped that the reader, after reflecting on the contents of this volume, will be blessed with a deeper reverence for this Holy Sacrament."

Men Called to Fight for Freedom (May 2004)

The 4,000-plus men attending the 2004 Answer the Call conference were greeted by patriotic sounds of the Hamilton County Sheriff Department bagpipers, a prayer and taps for "men and women who have given their lives for our country" by the ROTC, the pledge of allegiance (with "in God we trust") and "God Bless America." The call was, however, not just a call to join in the fight for freedom from terrorism, but freedom from sin, particularly sexual sin.

Jesse Romero, a former kickboxing champion and L.A. policeman, now a lay evangelist, pointed out that Satan kicks us men right between the legs. With pithy one-liners like "At the center of SIN is I," or "Make your home a no-sin zone," and references from Scripture, particularly the rise and fall and raising up again of King David, Romero taught how to fight for freedom.

"Even the Lone Ranger had Tonto," he says, emphasizing the need for other men. Just as David needed Nathan to be brought to repentance and find the awesome mercy of God, we need each other. Even Al Capone, so a Chicago priest told Romero, knew how important repentance was, giving victims he liked a chance to confess before he killed them. Those he did not like he gave a prostitute.

There is no excuse not to turn to God for forgiveness and sanctification, he concluded, not Abraham's old age, Timothy's youth, Jacob's lying, David's and Moses' murders, Job's poor health or poverty, the Samaritan woman's divorces, or even Lazarus' dying! We all have the chance to repent and be changed.

The Rev. Dr. Jerry Kirk, better known as Scott Hahn's father-in-law, spoke on his special call as chairman of the Religious Alliance Against Pornography. Rev. Kirk put much of the blame for the sexualization of our culture on MTV and the Internet. He quoted the statistics that one-fourth of our young people are sexually active, that four million per year are getting sexually-transmitted diseases, that one-third are pregnant before age 20. The key to changing those statistics, Kirk says, is showing them how they should treat others and expect to be treated – as the children of God that they are. They – and we – need to know that purity is always smart and impurity is always stupid. We need to show them that purity doesn't come because we try harder, but because we come to Christ. This is the Christ Who suffered infinitely greater because of our sins than the physical suffering portrayed in Mel Gibson's The Passion of the Christ.

Denis Beausejour, president of Answers for Life, continued the freedom fighter training. He shared about his own 10-year addiction to porn. It took an earthquake back when he was selling Tide and Crest to China before God got his attention. "God is going to change your life," he says, "Try to stay out of His way." He tried and God moved his wife to forgive him, because she had been forgiven. God strengthened their marriage which would be tried by her getting breast cancer. "Freedom is not free," Beausejour says, "but Jesus paid the price."

Fr. Mark Burger needed to spend over three months as a hermit before God showed him how shallow his spirituality was. We need, he says, to invite our secular activities into our prayer life, not prayer into our secular lives. He defined spirituality as learning to truly see and prayer as learning to truly hear. His deepening spirituality was confirmed by a dying man he anointed who told Fr. Burger that his mother was right when she promised, if he remained faithful, a good and holy priest would be there when he died. When we have a problem bigger than we can handle, he says, we need to remember God is bigger than any problem, and so far bigger than us.

Fr. Richard Neuhaus pointed out that the gift of the Holy Spirit we were given in Baptism must be given to others. He encouraged praying every morning that we will go to bed every night without having discouraged the Holy Spirit.

Archbishop Pilarczyk emphasized humility, the best weapon against pride, the root of every other sin. We must recognize that we are like everyone else, a sinner in need of repentance. Only then can we be truly free.

The Greatest Gift: The Incarnation (December 2003)

The understanding is growing of what an incredible Gift is Jesus beciming a human. Much of the interest is undoubtedly because of Pope John Paul II's Theology of the Body, a series of 129 of his weekly talks, 1979 to 1984 and its enthusiastic promotion by Christopher West.

West has taught on it atSt. John Vianney Theological Seminary in Denver and at the John Paul II Institute for Studies on Marriage and Family. For his speaking schedule and available tapes, CDs and books, see christopherwest.com. He recently visted Cincinnati in October.

As he puts our mission for the new century and millennium, "Satan has put hios name on sexuality and the body and we are here to take it back! If we don't, it is an illusion to think we can build a culture of life. We must proclaim the Love that everyone is looking for."

He has a more-to-earth and colorful style than the Holy Father as he states, for example, the obvious consequences of sin, "if you comb your hair with a chainsaw, there are going to be traces that you shouldn't have done that."

How can we discern between life-giving and deadly choices? West simply says, "All questions of sexually morality come down to this: 'Does it image God's free, true, faithful and fruitful love?"

This is, of course, the love that prompted the Father to give us His Son, Love incarnate. It is a message that is spreading around the world.

Anastasia Northrop, president of Theology of the Body International Alliance (TOBIA) says, "We are a support network providing resources for those striving to evangelize the world by means of Pope John Paul II's understanding of the human person, explained in his works, Love and Responsibility and The Theology of the Body. Our aim is to lead every person to an encounter with Jesus Christ." The alliance's current projects are a quarterly newsletter, yearly forum, building the website and attending World Youth Day 2005.

The website, theologyofthebody.net lists Theology of the Body study groups in the United States: Atlanta, GA; Bellingham, WA; Boston, MA; Camden, NJ; Dallas, TX; Denver, CO; Kansas City, MO; Laurel, MD; Minneapolis/St. Paul, MN; New Orleans, LA, and New York, NY. Many are held at universities, but more are being started in parishes.

People meet for obe or two hour discussions one to four timec per month. They cover not only The Theology of the Body, but also other of John Paul II's teachings and related Vatican II documents.

Northrop says, "I've been leading a study group in Denver for the last two years -- an incredibly enriching experience -- and am currently writing a study guide for te test of The Theology of the Body." She has also given talks about the movement of similar groups around the world who are on fire with this messag! "It is certainly exciting," she says, "to se what God is doing!"

Beth Daly holds Atlanta's study of The Theology of the Body in her own home. "It is getting to be a tight squeeze," she says, "with 20-plus people in my living room." She has also written a book study of *Love and Responsibility* and related Vatican II documents and encyclicals. This is because, she says, "The truth is so attractive!"

Many who who are so attracted "have either bought into Satan's lies at some point or have, after reaching professional and financial goals, questioned true happiness and the deeper goals in life. Most are in love with the Catholic Church, the Holy Father and are seeking to grow spiritually" to develop "a greater understanding of the meaning of being created male and female, the gift of self and the gift of sexuality."

Msarty Meyers of the Kansas City group says, "Our group actually goes back to 1987 when it was formed as a men's study group. We opened it to women about five years ago." Then in 2000 their assistant pastor, Fr. Steve Cook, insisted they study The Theology of the Body.

"Over the years," Meyers explains, "we had people dropout because they feltbthe were not up to the task of studying the Holy Father's writings and I certainly understood the problem." They have anywhere from four to 12 show up.

Sometimes "they are intimidated by the complexity of this teaching," he says, "but are also fascinated by it and drawn to it. Most have never heard any of this. You can almost see wheels turning in the heads of those who are not making an honest efort to live out the Chgurch's teaching on sexuality. They are both drawn to the beauty of God's plan for love and marriage and frightened aboutv the implications of opening their lives to its power."

As for himself Meyers says, "The concepts I havebcome tio understandbmore fully from Teologybof the Body have become vthe framework through which I try to approach every aspect and everybrelationship in my life -- bself-gift, persons as subjects not objects, communion of persons, the difference between sexual attraction and lust tempation vs. sin, self-possession, the battlefieldbof the heart, etc."

God Stars in New Series (November 2003)

Around 13.2 million viewers heard God speak in the "Joan of Arcadia" pilot. He gives the title character and the viewers a little theology lesson: "I've know you since beforebyou were born.", "I don't bargain; that would be cruel.", "I don't answer the question 'Why?'" and He reminds her about her prayer that her brother Kevin live after his automobile accident.

He explains I don't look like anything you would recognize. You can't see Me. I don't sound like anything you would recognize. You see, I AM beyond your experience. I take this form because you're comfortable with it. It makes sense to you. If I'm snippy it's because you understand snippy.I AM not really snippy. I've got a great personality."

When Joan asks Him to work a miracle, He points to a tree, alluding to Alfred Joyce Kilmer's famous "only God can make a tree."

God is more concerned about how the members of the Girardi family dealwith the consequences of her brother Kevin's accident. The Girardis are more-or-less functional and large for a TV family, but still in need of a little help from their Friend,. whether they know it or not.

Joan Girardi is playued by Amber Tamblyn, for seven years Emily Quartermaine in the daytime drama, "General Hospital" and more recently in "The Ring". Joan had promised to improve her life, "even go to church," if Kevin lived. God isn't holding her to it, just inviting her to take a step in faith.

Tony award winner Joe Mantegna, the voice of Fat Tony on "The Simpsons", plays Joan's father, new police chief Will Girardi. He is labeled "funny" for taking time to be with his family. He reveals his true feelings with a Freudian slip, that he had his own hope's dashed along with his son's. Yet he admits he gives thanks every day that he lived.

Academy Awardbwinner Mary Steenburgen play's Joan's mother, Helen. who also works at Joan's school. Leonard Maltin's Movie Encyclopedia calls Mary Steenburgen "one of the screen's most compulsively watchable actresses." Helen confronts a poor priest in a parking lot with the Problem of Suffering, but literally turns her back on the suggestion to come to church. She yeilds to her husband's unexpected assertion of authority with "I kind of miss the Fifties.', a subtle reference to the classic family show, "Father Knows Best."

Joan asks her younger brother, played by Michael Welch, for help dealing with God. In front of a poster of Stephen Hawking, Luke's answer surprisingly is a quote from Michael Faraday, "Nothing is too wonderful to be true." (It is found on refrigerator magnets.)

The show's creator, Barbara Hall, says she's commited to showing how "God exists within the physical laws of the universe" and she won't lean on special effects for depicting the Deity.

Joan's older brother, Kevin, is played by Jason Ritter, son of recently deceased John Ritter. He playfully pretends that Joan has hurt his unfeeling legs. After Joan attempts to get a job at a bookstore, he feels the need to get a job himself. Another effect of Joan's obedience was her learning to discern evil in the rapist-murderer. Because of her encounter, her father reached out to her and promised, "I will not lose you." Because God let it rain, the serial killer's boots left recognizable prints, thus saving their lives.

The adventures continue in "The Fire and the Wood". Joan heeds advice to enroll in an advance-placement class, where she's partnered with her school's biggest underachievers. Meanwhile Will is frustrated when another murder trail goes cold due to an arson investigator's overly thorough examination of the crime scene and Helen is eager for Kevin to get a car now that he has passed his driver's ed test.

Songs enhanse the show. Joan Osborne's 1995 hit, "One of Us" ("What if God was one of us, ... just a stranger on the bus ...") is the show's theme. "Kryptonite" by 3 Doors Down ("If I go crazy then will you still call me Superman?") was another appropriate song.

Many critics praise the show. Megan Walsh Boyle, in TV Guide, called it a "warm and intriguing mysterious series, perhaps the best new one of the season, an intelligently written and performed series."

Laura Urbani in the Pittsburgh Tribune-Review called it "a humorous and thoughtful look at religious perceptions and the effect people have on one another." Sausan Young of the Almeda Times-Star wrote that "'Joan of Arcadia' stands head and shoulders above the competition as a compassionate, thought-provoking series that presents us with an average family facing some severe challenges", "a series that should not be missed."

David Zurawik of the Baltimore Sun wrote "Viewers searching for a promising new drama will do no better." Alan Sepinwall of the Star-Ledger wrote, "In a season full of shows about people who converse with the dead, inanimate objects and various spiritual entities, 'Joan' is at the head of the Sunday school class, a drama that manages to tackle weighty issues with respect and irreverence at the same time."

Year of Rosary Ends, But Rosary Power Continues (October 2003)

Although the October-to-October Year of the Rosary proclaimed by Pope John Paul II is ending, the rosary has been associated with answered prayers for seven centuries. Pope

Pius IX proclaimed, "Among all the devotions apprpoved by the Church, none has been favored by so many miracles as the devotion to the Most Holy Rosary."

101 Inspirational Stories of the Rosary (Franciscan Monastery of St. Clare, Spokane, WA) compiled by St. Patricia Proctor, OSC, omly touches the surface. It does, however, demonstrate a statement of the surviving Fatima visionary. Sr. Lucia said, "There is no problem however difficult it is, whether temporal or above all spiritual ... that cannot be solved by the rosary." It went into its second primting in only three weeks and has its own website, www.rosary101.com.

Among the temporal miracles Sr. Patricia shares are miracle involving actual rosaries. Laurelle T. Guck felt a urgency to pray the rosary when she came upon the rosary her aunt had given her as a girl. She came back to the Church after 13 years after crying all day the next day, September 11, 2001.

After suffering six cardiac arrests while visiting Niagara Falls, Patrick Barlow was anointed by a priest. When he got out of the hospital, he wanted to go to Mass and pray the rosary -- for the first time in 40 years. His wife Barbara says, " Sometimes our Lord has to hit us over the head to get our attention."

Tom Danforth's life changed because of the rosary. He earned the nickname Preacher Man in drug rehab because he made rosaries from loose mop string. He spoke out against drug abuse, violence and abortion and for marriage and family.He died in an automobile accident at 17 and the judge who had sentenced him wrote, "If I can accomplish just a small part of the good that Tom did in his short life, I will be a happy man."

Dorothy J. Donohue's father prayed a rosary a day during World War II for her two brothers-in-law, cousin and future husband to come backbsafely. All did, even her future husband who had been taken as a POW.

Mariella G. LeBeaus's father also credits the rosary his mother gave him for getting him safely though action in N. Africa and his own time in prison camp. He was buried with the rosary he had prayed with for 70 years.

Veronica M. Hairgrove prayed a rosary with Monsignor Rabroker for her son during Desert Storm. She learned later that at that very time, with bullets flying over his head, he too was praying and hear a voice from the sky say, "You are going tobe all right."

Kathryn M. Hillier learned of the rosary through the Eternal Word Television Network. While listening to Mother Angelica, she heard "Make rosaries." After making a hundred and praying for nine days, without knowing what a novena was, she was healed. Both her she and her husband have become Catholics.

Rosemary J. Hanley's doctor refused to treat her when she refused to abort her baby diagnosed with an enlarged head. She prayed the rosary and saw Mary standing behind the replacement doctor. Mary smiled and nodded with her hands on the doctor's shoulders. The doctor patted her on the hand and thanked her for coming without turning around. Rosemary's son was born without an enlarged head.

Sheila D. Dowdell converted after praying the rosary for 12 years. After praying the rosary as her mother lay comatose and dying, she felt Mary's touch and heard, "Sheila, it is time." and "Sheila, she is at peace and will join your father. She is so happy." That was Valentine's Day 2002.

Nok N. Napaatalung of Thailand was surfing the internet for the occult and discovered a rosary website. She began praying the rosary and was slowly delivered from idol worship and witchcraft.

The rosaries themselves seem to be powerful channels of grace. Carol Pettis's rosary has been slowly turning gold link by link as she prayed about her husband's dealing with the marriage tribunal. "It would happen," she wrote, "when I started getting depressed about the annulment process, when I would sometimes think "Oh, God, I must be a very bad person to not be able to receive Communion or be absolved of my sins."

Karen S. Peterson repairs rosaries and once had an especially difficult job. "The repair involved replacing one stone that was missing. However, this missing bead was so unusual," she writes, "that I was having trouble finding a replacement." She prayed for Mary's help to find a suitable bead, but after several month decided to return it to the owner. "I had counted many times and there were only 58 stones before I asked for Mary's help. Instead of guiding me to a store where I could find a matching stone, our Blessed Mother gave me a wonderful gift of a miracle by placing an extra stone with the broken rosary.

Carmel R. Gillogly tells of when her daughter Julie's rosary, a gift from her grandmother, was broken. Julie's father looked at it and said it had too many parts missing to fix. The family prayed the rosary together after dinner, Julie reluctantly using another rosary. When they took another look at the rosary it was whole. The greater miracle, however, was that Carmel's family was made whole when her husband was led into the Church by the next Easter.

Scott Robinson's drug deal was going bad. When he reached into his pocket, he found no money, just his rosary. When he pulled it out, the leader of the gang threatening him paled and backed away, saying, "You leave him alone!" "The power of Mary and that rosary," he writes, "has left an impression I will never forget."

Besides many more inspiring stories, the book includes appendices with the history of the rosary, the encyclical *Rosarium Virginis Marirae*, as well as instructions on praying, making and finding out more about the rosary.

Men Challenged to Change the World (May 2003)

Fr. Stan Fortuna is co-founder of the Francisca Friars of Renewal and author of U Got 2 Believe, but was introduced as "an everyday Catholic rappin' priest". He called the men assembled for thge Answer the Call men's conference in Cincinnati in March to take a risk with their hearts for Christ. "Open, open, open up your heart," he sang, "You gotta live in love."

He based his analysis iof the crisis in modern society by quoting "Brother Webster", Daniel Webster's particular definition of "man" as "a man especially devoted to a particular thing as a garbage man or fireman". A Catholic man would therefore be one especially devoted to Jesus' Catholic Church.

"Catholic or not," he added, including the non-Catholics in the audience, "put your own twist on it and together we'll make a fabric that can last. We have to. "If we don'tnstand up yo the culture, the culture will make you impotent, that is, without spiritual power. It's a type of castration."

He interpreted the common male excuse, "I can't", as meaning "I'm afraid, afraid to suffer" and then sang, "D'you think that you're the only one gotta suffer?" If you answer the call, he elaborated, you're going to have to carry the cross and if your going to carry your cross, you're going to suffer.

If taking on the seemingly unstoppable culture of death seems too much, he encourages, "All the stupid things you've done, all added together and multiplied by infinity cannot match the power of the Almighty."

Although Episcopalian Gen. Charles Duke, one of only twelve men who have walked on the moon, had much the same message. Marital love, like Christ's love, must be sacruificial, 100% giving love. It wasn't uuntil six years after his visit to the moon that he began to humble himself and pray and communicate with his wife that their marriage was healed. "We were headed for the divorce court," he sums it up, "and the Lord said, 'This is the way.'"

The Lord did not stop there. "God is still in the miracle-working business," Duke proclaimed. He was convicted of the damage that his unloving tongue had inflicted on his children and began blessinbg themrather than cursing them. His son's video games, which he had called useless, turned out to have prepared him to become a jet pilot. His dad accepted the Lord two weeks before he died. Duke himself was moved to approach a drunk in San Antonio and tell him "Jesus loves you," When he did, he says, "I didn't see a drunk. I saw a soul that Jesus died for."

Jim Crosby was a "cradle Catholic", but marks the turning point of his life a Confession in 1991 when he finally admitted to embezzling from the non-profit he worked for and all the lying that went along with it. During a prayer service one week before his sentencing, he felt a hand on his shoulder. When he turned around "no one" was there. Thoughout the experience God sent the right people at the right time in the right place. He told of a fellow firefighter who accepted the apology and the asked Jim for his forgiveness. He knew that the ordeal was not entirely due to Jim's weakness, but also his own abandoning their friendship. They had trusted each other with their physical lives and ought to have with their infinitely more vital spiritual lives as well.

"I lost everything that I thought was important," he says. Now he knows that "we, as Catholics, have great gifts which we take for granted; I speak of the sacraments, guaranteed opportunities to meet God," Soon hundreds of men were lining up in the Cintas Center to go to Confession.

Frank Keating was governor of Oklahoma at the time of the Oklahoma City bombing. He is now chairman of the National Catholic Review Board. He received flak for boldly identifying Oklahoma's problems on immorality -- premarital sex, alcohol and drug abuse and divorce. Now a thousand churches have covenanted to require marriage preparation courses.

Fr. Richard Ho Lung converted from Buddhism to Catholicism at age 8 because of a devoted nun in his native Jamaica. Now he ministers there -- and in four other countries -- as superior general of Missionaries of the Poor. "We are called to be Christ,"he says, "and we must not stop until we have accomplished this, This is the only way we can become truly ourselves."

"We have a big, big job," he says because the media's target is no longer just the Church, but life itself. "There is an insidious paganism that is getting into American culture."

"Men are called to be heroes," he says. "Under all circumstances we must speak the truth even if we must die for the Truth. There is no other Truth thjan Jesus Christ. We must lay down our lives if we are to save this world from death."

Ethic Saints Enrich Universal Church (April 2003)

Talking Eagle is now the first canonized Native American saint.That is the English translation of his Indian name, Cuatitloatzin. Perhaps you know him by his more familiar Spanish baptismal name, Juan Diego.

Some saints have become more easily distinguished by their surnames, such as Aquinas, Becket, Bellarmine, Goretti, Jogues, Kolbe, Seton, Stein, Xavier. All such names are legitimate baptismal names. Many are quite ethic like Talking Eagle.

From the Japanese we have Bizzocca (Frances, August 17), one of the martyrs of Japan. A Dominican tertiary and the wife of Bl. Leo Bizzocca, Frances sheltered missionaries in her home, an act that brought about her arrest. She was burned alive in Nagasaki in 1827. Then there is Ishida (Anthony, September 3), Juruke (Gabriel, February 6), Miki (Paul, February 6) and Shamada (Dominic and Clare, September 10).

From the Korean comes Chong, Hasang, Kim, Ryou and Taegon. Paul Chong Hasang (May 28) was a convert who later fell away from the faith and became a member of an outlaw band. Captured by the government, he proclaimed his faith and was thus singled out for especially cruel treatment and finally beheaded in 1859. Fr. Kim Kim Taego and his father Ignatius Kim were martyred in 1839 as were Columba and Agnes Kim and Peter Ryou, 13, and Peter Chong.

The Polish name Zorard refers to Andrew (July 17). He lived as a hermit on Mt. Zobar Hungary. Benedictines resided nearby and Andrew trained St. Benedict of Szkalka. He died in 1010 and was canonized in 1083.

The Portuguese saint Alvarez (Bartholomew, January 12) was a Jesuit martyr born near Braganza. Sent to Tonking, he was arrested in 1736 and beheaded the following year. More Portuguese names would be de Silva (Beatrix, August 16), Garcia and Pacheco (both Gundisalvus, both February 6).

The Russian Nevski comes from Alexander Nevski, the son of Grand Prince Yaroslav II. He heroically defended Russia against the Swedes at the confluence of the Ithra and Neva Rivers in 1240 and from this victory earned the name "Nevski". Alexander was also victorious over the Lithuanians and the Finns. He died in 1263 in Gorodets.

Spanish names include Galvez (Francis, December 4), martyr of Japan. He was born in New Castile, Spain, and became a Franciscan in 1591. Assigned to Manila, PHilippines, he worked there for 12 years and entered Japan in 1612. When the persecutions started, Francis went to Macau, where he had his skin dyed to make him appear Japanese. He entered Japan again in 1618 but was arrested and burned alive in Edo in 1623.

Others are Alonso (Luke, September 28), Blanco (Francis, February 6), Ferrer (Vincent, April 5), Flores (Isabel Rose Flores y del Oliva, August 23), Garcia (Gonclaco, February 6), Henares (Dominic, June 25), Rodriguez (Alphonsus, October 30), Solano (Francis, July 13) and Xavier (Francis, December 3).

The Ukrainian Pechersky comes from Anthony Pechersky (July 10), one of the fathers of Ukrainian monasticism. Born in 983 in Ljibeck, Anthony went to the famed monastic community on Mt. Athos in Greece to become a hermit, remaining there for several years He returned to Ukraine and built a hermitage in Kiev on land given to him by a local prince. He founded another monastery in Chernagov, but died in the caves of Kiev in 1307.

The Ugandan martyrs include Bauzabaliawo (James). When Mwanga ordered ordered him to be killed with the rest, James said, "Goodbye. Why are you so sad? This is nothing to the joys you have taught us to look forward to."

His companions included Badzekuketta (Athanasius), Gonza (Gonzaga), Kagwa (Andrew), Kalemba (or Murumba, Matthias), Kewannuka (Achilleus), Kibuka (Ambrose), Kiriggwajjo (Anatole), Kizito, Ludigo-Mkasa (Adolphus), Lwanga (Charles), Mbaga (Joseph), Mulumba (Mathaias), Ngondwe (Pontian), Sebuggwawo (Dionysius or Denis) and Seronkuma (Bruno).

Buong (Paul Tong, October 23) was a Vietnamese martyr. A native of Vietnam, he served in the bodyguard of the king. A convert, he gave his assistance to the Paris Foreign Missions and so helped to advance the Catholic cause in the country. Arreseted by authoritues for being a Christian, he was tortured, humiliated and beheaded in 1833. Pope John Paul II canonized him in 1988.

Others include Can (Francis, November 20), Dat (Dominic Nicholas, July 18), Dich (Anthony Peter, August 12), Diem (Vincent, November 24), Dieu (Dominic Van Hohn, August 1), Dung Lac (December 21), Duong (Peter, December 10), Hien (Joseph, June 27), Hieu (Peter, April 28), Hsanh (Paul, May 28), Khang (Joseph, November 6), Loc (Paul, February 13), Luu (Joseph, May 2), Mau (Francis Xavier, December 19), Moi (Augustine, December 19), My (Paul, December 18), Nam-Thuong (Andrew, July 15), Nam-Quynh (Anthony, November 24), Ngan (Paul, November 8), Nghi (Joseph, November 8), Phuong (Matthew, May 26), Phung (Emmanuel, July 31), Thanh (John Baptist, April 28), Trach (Dominic, September 18), Trach (Dominic, September 18), Trieu (Emmanuel, September 17), Trong (Andrew, November 28), Trung (Francis, October 6), Tuoc (Dominic, April 2), Uy (Dominic, December 19), Uyen (Joseph Peter, July 3), Vien (Joseph Nien, August 21) and Xuyen (Dominic Doan, November 29).

Year of the Rosary Begins (December 2002)

pope John Paul II, now the fifth-longest serving pope, began the twenty-fifth year of his pontificate by designating it a Year of the Rosary (October 2002 to October 2003) and adding five mysteries, significant events in the life of Jesus upon which to meditate during the traditional prayers in "The Rosary of the Virgin Mary" (Apostolic letter *Rosarium Virginis Mariae*). The pope proposes meditating on five Luminous mysteries, mysteries of light: the baptism of the Lord, the miracle at Cana, the proclamation of the Kingdom, the Transfiguration and climaxing with the institution of the Eucharist on Holy Thursday. The weekly cycle, for those unable to pray all twenty mysteries per day, would then be the Glorious mysteries on Sunday and Wednesday, the Joyful on Monday and Saturday, the Sorrowful on Tuesday and Friday and the Luminous on Thursday.

"In continuity with my reflection in the Apostolic Letter Novo Muilrnnio Ineunte," he writes, "I have felt drawn to offer a reflection on the rosary, as a kind of Marian complement to that letter and an exortation to comtemplate the face of Christ in union with, and in the school of, His Holy Mother. To recite the rosary is nothing other than to contemplate with Mary the face of Christ."

He explained that it was "so that I can carry out to the end the mission that has been given to me." That mission apparently means continuing to promote world peace and family values through devotion to Mary and the sacraments of Baptism, Marriage and the Eucharist.

The rosary has had other additional mysteries over its history. The Ecumenical Mystery rosary, for example, includes the miracle at Cana and the Transfiguration. It also includes Jesus' healings of the centurian's servant, the woman who touched His garment, the blind man by putting mud in his eyes, the raising of Lazarus, the ten lepers, calming of the storm, feeding the 5,000, walking on the water, withering the fig tree and His appearane to Mary Magdalene, Thomas and Peter. The Franciscan rosary includes the visitation by the Magi and the appearance to Mary.

Pope Pius V officially fixed the Joyful, Sorrowful and Glorious mysteries in 1569, but their origins go back to Mary's Psalter, a simple 150 Ave Marias in imitationof the 150 Psalms. It was promoted by St. Dominic to win bak the heretics of 13th Century France. Pope John Paul II mentions the efforts of opes Leo XIII, John XXIII and Paul VI in prompting the rosary as a weapon in spiritual warfare and a tool in evangelization.

St. Bernard of Clairvaux (1090-1153) contributed the prayer, "Hail Holy Queen, mother of mercy, our life, our sweetness and our hope, to thee we come, before we we stand sinful and sorrowful. O mother of the Word incarnate, despise not our petition, but hear and answer us." Our Lady of Fatima (1917) requested the prayer, "O my Jesus, forgive us our sins and gave us from the fires of hell and lead all souls into heaven, especially those who most need Thy mercy."

The pope lamented that the practice of praying the rosary had diminished. According to a national poll in the United States in 2001 by the Center for Applied Research for the Apostolate at Georgetown University, 39% never say it, 33% say it only a few times a year and 27% say it several times a month.

Author and Prof. Scott Hahn of Franciscan University, Steubenville, OH, comments, "When I announced [the change] to students, it blew their minds. They think it's awesome because it connects Jesus and Mary even more than before. Sixty percent of the student there pray the rosary daily already.

A person who prays the rosary gains some rather persuasive, if little known, practical benefits. If a priest has blessed the rosary, each bead carries with it an indulgence, the rmission of the temporal punishment suffered for sins either on Earth or in Purgatory. There are the promises of Mary that anyone who faithfully prays the rosary will be able to resist the attacks of Satan. According to St. Theresa of Avila in an appearance shortly after her death, a life of suffering until the end of time would not merit the degree of glory which God rewards one devoutly recited Hail Mary.

There are other testimonies like those from the Ukrainians who survived Communist persecution who maintained their faith by using tiny rosaries made from bits of dried bread on a single tread. Luis Cruz attributed his survival in a Californiacanyon for eleven days with a broken back last August to his praying the rosary.

Men In Black Delivers Message With Humor (September 2002)
Remember who you are is the message of the Men In Black sequel and a good one for life. There is a lot of fun in the way the film delivers it. Reviewers who expressed disappointment seem to have missed the deeper humor in this movie.

As Terry Lawson put it in the Detroit *Free Press*, "MIB prefers gags that take asecond or two to absorb but stick around the cerebrum a lot longer." Paul Clinto of CNN called it smart and witty. Mary F. Pols of Contra Costra Times called it "solid, contemporary American humor, which is to say, cynical on topics from global warming to the vagaries of the postal system."

J finds his newest partner disappointing when he makes the nearly fatal mistake of trying to pick a "flower" out of a grating. His next partner, agent F, may look good in a custom-made black suit, but cannot seem to control his mouth.

K, who had his mind wiped at the end of "MIB 1" has found his new life disappointing. He describes it as "sleeping late on his weekends and watching the weather channel". His long-lost love did not love him long and he is now playing badly the role of a Truro, Mass., postal worker. The contrast between the Man In Black K we remember and the man in gray short, Kevin, is humourous, yet we know he is destined for much greater things, just as we know that we know that there must be some other than the obvious explanation for the coming from the mail-sorting machine.

Some inside jokes can be found on the official website, which like J has its own alien identifier. The large-headed Cerebrans are, for example, the ones who gave us the Afro wig. "Joey", the thick-lipped, hairless Xysian, was formerly with the Standing Stones rock band. AS

Steve Rhode advises on his review website, "Let the good times roll as aliens of all shapes and sizes entertain you," like the alien that operates an upper torso tentacle-puppet.

Serleena the Kylothian's spaceship bears a more than coincidental resemblance to that described by Joseph Blumeridge in the UFO classic *Ezekiel's Spaceship*, based on Ezekiel chapter 1. She assumes a persona as different as conceivable from the Edgar suit used by the giant cockroach that ate K. She does so, not insignificantly from the bottom up, however so that just before being fully transformed she resembles Medusa, the snake-headed Gorgon killed by Perseus in Greek mythology.

K has an accident at MIB headquarters that reminds one of the accidental discovery of flubber in the original "Absent Minded Professor" J and K escape the takeover of the headquarters via Flushing, N. Y., but agent M is helpful to Zed.

Some of the alien criminals that Serleena recruits are interesting, if comic-bookish. Shark Mouth the Crolaxian, for example, was arrested for threatening New Englanders by impersonating a shark, Dog Poop the Gurgean for just stinking in public.

The plot thickens when Rita, the woman J decided NOT to neuralize, is threstened and taken to the Worm Guys' not-so-safe house. Their cell phone commericial line, "That's going to smart," make a lot more sense after the events that take place there.

The clues lead eventually to Newton morgue attendant turned video store owner the climax line, "It was raining", that restores K's memory -- and heartbreak.

Looking up in the sky, K and Rita gaze on the three stars of Orion's Belt, the cryptic key to the first movie, just as J recognizes the key to the second. Lady Liberty plays a part again as she did in the Ghostbuster's sequel's ending.

The new New York City skyline itself, filled with Fourth-of-July premeir fireworks, has to move every American, every freedom-loving person in the world. Knowing that they shot the World Trade Center scene after the tragedy of 9/11 makes it ever so much more meaningful.

Mike LaSalle wrote in the San Francisco Chronicle that it was "in every way an improvement on the original" and Mike McGranaghan of Aisle Seat called it "the rare sequel that makes me yearn for a part III".

Victoria Alexander of filmsinreview.com most valued what she called the "philosophical visual coming right at the end." It was completely missed by many reviewers just as they had missed the first film's galactic game of marbles. We are warriors against extraterrestrial, superhuman evil in a war vaster than we can imagine -- and yet love, true self-sacrificial love, not only survives but triumphs, always has and always will.

Miracles Are Happening In Mexico (August 2002)

St. Juan Diego, Our Lady of Guadalupe and the Holy Spirit are still working miracles in Juarez, Mexico and El Paso, Texas, through Fr. Richard Thomas, S. J. and his flock. Signs and wonders continue over twenty years since the healing and food multiplication miracles documented in the book *Viva Christo Rey* by Rene Laurentin and the video of the same name.

The Juarez city dump in which the poorest of the poor once scrounged for a living is now the location of a clinic, a school and a daycare center, in buildings that had been intended to become a toetilla factory. The city finally released the land to a co-operative when six hundred people blockaded the dump. The daycare now cares for 60 children whose mothers work in maquilladoras, the low-wage border assembly plants.

The Lord's Ranch in the Chihuahua Desert near Vado, NM, no longer raises crops or catfish, but does still have horses and chickens. The Ranchers do, however, help feed 350 families a week by letting them work off some of the already lowered cost. Food and precious water are delivered to those who cannot make it to the distribution center or who do not have anyone to fetch water. This isnecessary because the water pressure is not strong enough to reach up the steep hillsides.

Some of the youth who were ministered to by Our Lady's Youth Center decades ago are now discipling others and leading ministries.

It was taken as a sign that theyshould concentrate on delivering basic needs and the good news rather than producing it themselves when the crops and catfish died at the same time.

The Ranch's main ministry now, besides discipleship and community building, is its shortwave radio station, KJES, frequency 11750. The station simply broadcasts Scripture in both English and Spanish and has thus reached every continent but Antarctica with the good news. There is even a story told of the man who wrote from 130 miles away to request moreripture in Spanish, since his friend had become instantly healed of an incurable ailment while listening to it. The Rachers had to try to rxplain to the man that they had not been able to transmit anything for the past three weeks, though they had continued to play the tapes in the station, solely for their own edification they thought.

"Executing the word" is what they call it. Those who can read the Scriptures read it aloud. Those who cannot memorize verses. All believe that the Wordof God does not go forth without having an effect. The sacraments, holy water and blessed salt are also much used with good effect.

When discerning on whether to start a jail ministry, Fr. Thomas asked for a sign in water. The pool dug but not yet hooked to the pipes filled to overflowing overnight. On his first visit he was not at all welcome, so he executed, "Every knee shall bow and every tongue confess that Jesus Christ is Lord," for a half hour. Then every prisoner and guard was slain in the Spirit. Another jail would not let him come until they arrested a coven of Satanists. Now holy water and rosaries are welcome. Much remains to be done, however, with two police captains and hundreds of young women tortured and murdered in Juarez over the past nine years.

Food multiplication continues to happen from time to time. Sandwiches for waiting mother at the clinic were multiplied. Bread for the prisoners was turned into sandwiches.

In June Fr. Thomas bravely became a pro-life delegate to the Texas Democratic convention. He acted upon his "Whom shall we fear" homily that day. When his sign got torn in two, a Democrat motorcyclist unexpectantly defended his right to free speech. From then on security just turned away and allowed free access to pro-lifers to the conference. The protest did not, of course, make the local news, but Fr. Thomas declared it a great victory because we had proclaimed the truth and at least some hearts were changed.

A very important factor in the pro-life message proclaimed as it was at the convention, and of all the ministries, was the intercession going on back at the Los Alas ministry center. Several small groups continuously executed Scripture or prayed the rosary, the Stations of the Cross or the Chaplet of Mercy.

The week before the convention testimonies came in of healings of the mother of a five-year-old daughter healed of cancer and of a heart attack victim's twisted mouth. A former witch who was reveal to have been dedicated to Satan as a child had her husband and four-year-old son lead her in prayer.

Such life-changing miracles and ministry have drawn Ranchers from near and far. They have come from Italy and England, from both coasts and the Midwest, even to the middke of the desert from Hawaii, and from either side of the border. The Harvest Master is sending workers for the harvest, but the harvest is still very great, "Long live Christ the King!"

Jesus Is the Light (July 2002)

Philip Boatwright, www.moviereporter.com, makes some good points in his review of "Star Wars: Episode 2: The Clone War", connecting it with concerns not so far, far away.

His advice to parents is "If you are allowing your younger children to attend, you should view this film with them. Make sure they understand the difference between the film's 'Force' and the real Force, Jesus Christ."

"I don't think 'Star Wars' is going to lead a great many people to follow Eastern religions," he says, "But it does subtly cultivate such philosophies. My suggestion ... is that if parents know the teachings of God's Word, they can help their children spot and resist beliefs in films. 'Train a child in the way he should go and when he is old, he will not turn from it,' as Proverbs 22:6 puts it."

"The mysticism is played down, as the filmmakers put the emphasis on battle action; we see Anakin giving in to the darker side when, out of vengeance, he kills an entire village he considers responsible for his mother's death and the death of a mother may trouble little ones." As the fall of the democratic Republic begins with rebel attacks, Anakin, rebellious disciple of Obiwan Kenobi, accepts a mission as Jedi bodyguard to princess-turned-senator Amidala.

"True we are discovering how Anakin became Darth Vader, but it was unnerving having this guy as the film's hero. It's difficult to like the main character, knowing he will become an evil being. It's like feeling sympathy for the devil."

This is especiall difficult when Jedi leadership explicitly states in the film that their goal is to balance the two sides of the Force, rather like Lucifer wanting to balance out the "too good" heavenly host.

Marcia Montenegro, ex-astrologer, however puts it even stronger. "Anakin, the future Darth Vader, is accepted as a Jedi apprentice in order to 'balance the Force.' In recalling the [previous] movie where Luke Skywalker discovers his father is Darth Vader, the message is that Darth Vader has gone over to the 'dark side', not that he is evil. As Luke faces his father, together they represent the polarity of dark and light."

Montenegro explains on her website, cana.userworld.com, where CANA stands for Christian Answers for the New Age. "In occult philosophies, evil is usually expressed in one or more ways, which overlap: (1) the dark sideis just another aspect of the good, (2) both good and evil are needed for the balancing of energy and life (polarity), (3) good and evil are part of the whole and therefore are ultimatelynthe same thing and finally (4) good and evil are transcended and combined in the One."

All these, of course, contradict the apparently not so obvious truth that good is good and evil is evil, that light is light and dark is dark.

In Deepak Chopra's resent best-selling book, *How to Know God*, she goes on, Chopra claims that in the sixth of seven stages of knowing god, good and evil to the visionary "are two sides of the same force. God created both because both are needed; god is in the evil as much as in the good." This is certainly not the All-good God Jews and Christians, children of the Light, believe in.

The quintessential illustration of this philosophy, in her opinion, is the yin-yang symbol. One side is black with a white dot and the other side is white with a black dot. The dark and ligt sides are polarities that need to be balanced. Each has a dot of the other color in it because though they appear to be opposites, in accuality the are constantly changing and merging with one another, thus becoming one another. The dark becomes light and the light becomes dark. The symbol therefore means there is no absolute dark or absolute light.

The Kabbalah, a Gnostic spin-off, teaches that good and evil each "has the spark of the other," according to Rabbi David Cooper. "The basis for polarity is not good against evil and good cannot exist without evil, or as they are called gevurot (restrictive powers) and chasidim (expansive powers), and these "forces of the universe are constantly tugging and pushing."

That is very different from the Bible's absolute, "Whoever loves his brother remains in the Light and there is nothing in him to cause a fall. Whoever hates his brother is in darkness; he walks in darkness and does not know where he is going because the darkness has blinded his eyes."

Authors Make Case for Marriage (June 2002)

Linda J. Waite and Maggie Gallagher begin their new book, *The Case for Marriage: Why Married People Are Happier, Healthier, And Better Off Financially*, by noting that for several decades this once holy institution has been under attack. It has been called "slavery", "legalized rape", "dependancy", "a trap", and too many have become casualties. Waite and Gallagher bombard the opposition with copious statistics.

The overwhelming majority of Americans (93%) still hold being married in a happy marriage as the ideal, but few believe it is possible any more. The authors describe "America as a society on the verge of becoming a postmarriage culture," in which marrying is optional.

They debunk five stubborn myths: (1) Divorce is better for the kids than a troubled marriage, (2) If you don't have kids, you don't need marriage, (3) Marriage is bad for women, (4) Married women risk violence and the worst (5) Marriage is just between two people.

They point out: "On the average, divorce causes a child's standard of living to drop by about a third." It cuts the amount of parental attention by more than half, because the custodial parent has to try to fo double duty. They are 50% more likely to have health problems, ones that persist into adulthood, over 30% more likely for mental illness. It doubles the probabilities they will drop out of school or have sex before fourteen.

The mortality rate for non-marrieds over 45, compared to those married, is 50% higher for women and 250% higher for men. They even write, "Being unmarried can actually be a greater risk to one's life than having heart disease or cancer." Thiry percent of men who lose their wives, in whatever way, also soon lose their lives.

Gwtting married improves a woman's mental health more than her physical health, resulting in declines in problem drinking and depression. "The strong positive impact of getting married remained even when the researchers took into account initial levels of depression and alcohoo abuse." they note. "Even single adults who lived with others were more depressed than the married."

The never-married and the no-longer married both show more hostility and depression, lower levels of happiness, personal and environmental mastery, sense of purpose and self-acceptance and fewer positive relationships than the married. Only 2% of husbands and 4% of wives say their marriage is "not too happy", compared to 61% and 59% who said they were "very happy".

A study of the median net worth of various groups yeilded the stark contrast: married families, $26,000; single-father households, $22,930; remarried families, $22,000; unmarried couples $1,000; single-mother household, $0.

"Marriage seems to help men desist not just from domestic violence, but all forms of lawbreaking," they conclude after quoting much data. It "can change the way even hardened criminals behave." "The victimization rate for women separated from their husbands was about ... 25 times higher than that of married women."

It was the prolific Pope John Paul II who made a case 20 years agi in *Familiaris Consortio* against the last myth. "The mission of married couples and Christian families by virtue of the grace received in this sacrament," he told us, "must be placed in the service of building up the Church, the establishing of the kingdom of God in history." Then he wisely invoked the aid of the Holy Family.

Men Answer the Call Again (May 2002)

Bob Paraza witnessed at the 2002 Answer the Call men's conference. He lost a son who had been on the 104th floor of the World Trade Center on September 11th. He gave thanks to his local men's group for helping him get through it and said the worst was the website that falsely reported that his son survived. He quoted the passengers of the thwarted hijacking, "Let's roll!"

Senator Rick Santorum referred to his wife's *Letters to Gabriel*, a collection of letters to their son who lived two hours. That was back in 1996 when he was in debate over the partial-birth abortion ban. He sensed the promise "Be a beacon and God will reward you" and said for the record, "It's a baby." Immediately after he did so, a door to the Senate chambers opened momentarily and a baby was heard crying in the hallway outside.

Two weeks later they discovered the defect in Gabriel Michael. Soon after that he died in his arms.

Santorum considers his vocation as father much higher than that of senator. When he visited the Holy Father two-and-a-half years ago, so did the pope, so he called him "an important man", a father.

He usedstatistics to emphasize just how important fathers are, now more than ever. One third of our children are now born outside of marriage. One half are in broken marriages. Seventy persent of male prisoners had no fathers in their homes. The average age of a grandfather is now only 51 years old.

It happened to be Xavier University president Fr. Michael Graham's birthday. He pointed out that creation points to a Creator unlike us and that we need to be a Church to learn wht we could not otherwise know.

Alex Jones gave a very condensed version of his story of conversion from Pentecostal pastor to Pentecostal Catholic. The book will, he says, "hopefully be out before 2030." [see *No Price Too High: A Pentecostal Preacher Becomes Catholic* (2006)]

He is often asked why he gave up what he had worked so hard to build for twenty-five years, giving up long-time friendships, causing relatives to stop speaking to him. His answer is simple, "What I found is so much more valuable. There is a move of the Holy Spirit in the Catholic Church."

The Holy Spirit was acting in his life when at 16 he fell to the floor of his father's church and made the sign of the cross. It was the Holy Spirit that prompted him to read the early Church Fathers. "I didn't know," he explains, "apostolic is Catholic." His studies showed him that Christ's Church has always been hierarchical, liturgical, and Eucharistic, but he knew that if he taught that to his congregation it would break the church up.

He let them vote on it and they let him share what he now believed. Half left; holy people, he calls them, but unwilling to change. Most of thosewho stayed, including his own family, came into the Catholic Church with him -- nearly overwhelming the local RCIA.

"I was going to retire at 60. Well, I am60 and I'm starting all over again. I'm not ashamed of the Catholic Church because it is the sanctified, redeemed Church of Christ."

Fr. Larry Richards said, "Since both my parents were cops, I thought I would be -- and in a way I am." Confirmation of his vocation came in the form of a newborn black bull with a white spot on its neck -- like a Roman collar.

He emphasized a few vital truths: "God's will is whatever happens.", "Loving is more important than understanding.", "Sins of omission are much greater than sins of commission." The most vital of all was simply, "Tell the ones you love you love them."

The Gates of Hell Do Not Prevail (April 2002)

Fr. Gabriele Amorth's second book *An Exorcist Tells More Stories* has just been released by Ignatius Press. In his previous book, *An Exorcist Tells His Tale*, the exorcist of Rome pointed outthat more powerful and frightening to demons than an exorcism is adoration, and more powerful than adoration is a good Confession.

Fr. James LeBar, technical advisor to the film "Lost Souls" and New York exorcist, when asked if exorcism ever fails, answered, "No, but sometimes it takes a long time."

Diabolic possession, with which exorcism deals, is the graves form of demonic activity, a continuing though not necessarily continuous, presence of a demon in a human body.

"Possession implies intervals of temporary suspension of mental, intellectual, affective and volitive faculties," Amorth writes. "Symptoms can include the knowledge of languages unknown to the victim, superhuman strength and the ability to know the occult or someone else's thoughts. Typically, the possessed also shows an aversion to anything sacred, often in conjunction with blasphemy."

On the other hand, under diabolical obsession's symptoms he includes unexplainable rages and a tendency to complete isolation. Oppression can affect both individuals or even very large groups. "Clearly, nothing happens without divine permission, but God never wills evil, suffering or temptation. He gave us freedom and allows the existence of evil, but know how to turn it into good. When He gives the demon His permission to torment us, He does so tostrengthen us in virtue, as in the biblical example of Job, as well as many blesseds and saints. We must keep in mind that diabolic harassment in itself has nothing to do with the state of grace of its victims."

The many individuals who abandon themselves to sexual perversions, violence and drugs fall into his category of being hardened to sin, Judas Iscariot, for example.

The terrible repercussions of abortion are clearly seen during exorcisms, because to liberate a possession victim guilty of abortion usually requires a very long period of time. "Due to the current devastation of the family and the laxity of morals," Amorth writes, "the repercussions that stem from the scourge of abortion are much more common than in the past. When we take all these factors into account, we can understand why the number of individuals stricken by evil ailments has multiplied."

He attributes possession to proximity to evil places or persons. In this category he includes attending spiritualistic sessions, dabbling in magic or consulting magicins, witch doctors and some card readers, practicing the occult arts or belonging to satanic sects. All these put the dabbler at great risk.

To this category he fearlessly adds the mass media -- pornographic shows, violent horror movies, even satanic rock. He says, "We should not be surprised that, today, there is an explosion of these activities; a decline in faith life is directly connected to an increase in superstitions."

This last category, he says, has greatly contributed to the increase in evil ailments in the last decades, especially among the young.

Alois Weisinger in his classic *Occult Phenomena* writes, "It is admittedly difficult to distinguish possession from many other morbid condin particular that "psychology and medical science know no such prompt cure effected by the simple speaking of a single word." itions of an occult kind, since the symptoms are very often similar, but there are certain things that enable us to distinguish", in particular that "psychology and medical science know of no such prompt cure effected by the simple speaking of a single word." That is as Jesus' recorded exorcisms. Documented, non-biblical cases seem to take somewhat longer but less than 'normal' psychological 'cures'."

Before her final exorcism in 1928 Emma Schnidt of Earling, Iowa, broke her restaints, climbed the walls, ate only unblessed food and Exorcist-like vomited 30 time per day. Michelle Smith reported satanic child abuse in Vancouver, B. C., in 1958.

The cure can sometimes be worse than the illness as when Anneliese Michel, a student at University of Würtenberg, Germany, was apparently the victim of a botched exorcism, dying of malnutrition and dehydration in 1976.

"Sr. Rosa" of Rome, besides having been associated with poltergeistic noises, apports and obscenities, levitated *through* the ceiling in 1977.

"By and large, however," Weisinger says, "one should see the picture as a whole and judge from the totality of the symptoms." Fr. LeBar recommended especially praying the "Hail Mary", because devils hate Mary.

The St. John Passion Play: A Cincinnati Tradition (March 2002)

The St. John Passion Play began with a promise by then pastor Fr. Richard Wurth and the parishioners of St. John Church, Cincinnati, in 1917. As then and for every one of the 86 years since, it has been primarily presented as a thanksgiving for what Jesus did and continues to do for us and more particularly for our loved ones at war. As director Don Schlosser notes, "That's why this play's just as relevant as ever."

It is the second-oldest continuous passion play in the country, but with the closing of St. John Church in 1969, it almost ended. A charitable nonprofit organization, St. John Passion Play, Inc., was formed to continue the tradition. Since then the play has been performed in numerous locations in the Cincinnati area, Mt. Note Dame High School, Emery auditorium and Westwood Town Hall. Most recently it is being performed at Pleasant Ridge Presbyterian (5950 Montgomery Road, Cincinnati, OH) and St. Angustine (1839 Euclid Avenue, Covington, KY) Churches, beginning this year on Leap Day, Sunday, February 29th.

"It's a Cincinnati tradition," producer Judy Hughes says. If you saw it with your parents or grandparents, she urges, share it with your own children or grandchildren. "It's a good preparation for Easter and is never the same – we always make it better!"

This year's production has made an effort to address the needs of the harder-of-hearing. More youth have been encourage to participate as well, since it is not just a tradition to view the play as a family but many players participate in the play as a family.

The cast and crew come from different walks of life with different ways of worship, but all strive to authentically bring alive in a dramatic and moving way John 3:16, "For God so loved the world that He gave His only begotten Son, that whosoever believes in Him should not perish but have everlasting life."

The script itself has been changed somewhat from recently years in adding a new beginning to the garden of Gethsemani scene and a better distinguishing between the Seder (Jewish Passover meal) and the Last Supper. All the apostles will now have at least some speaking part.

Many of the actors are veterans, having lovingly participated in the play for many years. Some are moving up to more challenging roles. There will, for example, be a new Pilate this year.

As for Mel Gibson's film, "The Passion" to be released at nearly the same time on Ash Wednesday, Don Schlosser says he will reserve judgment until he has seen it. He does point out however that there are guidelines for passion plays and that The St. John Passion Play does conform to them. A play is much more up-front-and-personal than a big-screen movie. The post-crucifix epilogue with the whole cast singing "And Can It Be" with the resurrected Jesus will certainly bring tears to the eyes of young and old again this year. The victory over death and evil has already been won!

This Christmas Is Different (December 2001)

Nat Freedman says he used to play Santa at the firehouse every Christmas. "They were like my children." This Christmas, more than ever since the tragic events of September 11, the New York firefighters "embody what we feel is best in this country, putting service to others before their own personal safety," he says. His shop, next door to the Ladder 20 fire station, has been selling many more FDNY caps, shirts and coats. "There's been a massive leap in sales," he says, "but this is certainly not the way we wanted the business to grow." He decided to take the phone off the hook, though partly because of the overwhelming number calling the shop, not to place orders, but to express their grief and anger at the hundreds of deaths.

Camille Tokerud, who lives across the street from the shop and firehouse, says her two young sons have always idolized the firefighters here. They want to be firemen when they grow up.

September 11th brought the world together. Typical of countless others around the globe, Alun Griffiths of Jersey, Channel Islands, told the BBC's "Talking Points", "My sympathy goes to all those who will have suffered loss as a result of this terrible act of terrorism. With the grace of God those responsible will be brought to account for their actions."

Sam in Hong Kong said, "I pray to God for everyone ... this is an act of evilwhich shocked me." From the Ukraine, Nataliya wrote, "I want to express my condolence to all peple in the U. S. It's the most terrible thing I have every heard. God helpusbto live through all these stupid acts."

Many Americans were reminded to value those precious moments with our family members and friends. Stephen Packard of Evanston, IL, thanks God his niece Nora survived and prays for those families whose relatives did not. "We were very fortunate not to have lost her," he says. "Her normal stop on the subway is the World Trade Center. AS she came out, the second plane hit. She says the walk from the subway to her office was stunned bewilderment, but not panic."

There she met her boyfriend Ted. "They went to her office and watched the Trade Center burn through her windows. She turned away for maybe eight seconds and when she looked again, the first tower was gone and then watched as the second tower fell. After the towers fell, she and Ted decided to go home and the came outinto another world, one of panic and chaos -- people running and screaming, covered with a thick layer of dust and debris falling everywhere."

United Airlines flight attendant CeeCee Lyles was among those on the doomed jets who used their last minutes wisely. She called her husband at home in Ft. Myers, FL, on her cell phone and let him know how much she loved him and their boys. Mark Bigham, on the same plane, called his mother, Alice Hoglan, in San Francisco, to say "Hi, Mom, ... I love you very much."

Many others have seen the hand of a loving Providence at work. Chef Siby Sekou should have been at Windows on the World, then New York's highest restaurant on the 106th and 107th floors of Trade Tower One. He had filled in for a colleague on the Sunday before the attack which left him off on his normal Tuesday workday.

His relief at having escaped is tempered only by the nearly overwhelming grief for his lost colleagues, many of whom were his friends and one of whom was his cousin. Siby was at home in the Bronx when he first heard about the attack. His cousin's wife called him, frantically worried for the safety of her husband. Siby called the restaurant, but all the lines were busy. He got no answer at his cousin's cell phone. "I didn't have anything more to do. I just had to wait and pray. But I never in a million years thought the building would collapse."

Ian Robb should have been at his desk at Marsh on the 99th floor 30 minutes before the jet struck. He "happened" to arrive late -- in spite of running into the lobby -- just in time to miss the elevator going up. When he did manage to get one, it stopped seconds after the doors shut because of the impact of many stories above from the plane hitting. Mr. Robb and his fellow passengers were trapped for about an hour before they pried open the doors and escaped. The other elevator -- the one he had missed -- had come crashing back down the shaft and left nothing but charred remains.

Matthew Corenelous found himself trapped on the 65th floor as the attacks began. "We made it pretty fast down to the 40th floor and from there, the smoke got a little thick and it was a lot slower,;; he says. "We made it about a floor every two minutes. It was packed. It was a virtual traffic jam in the staircase. Up and down it was very full.

"Everyone maintained calm really well; I was impressed with that. I was amazed really. We got into the stairway. We were moving down. The fire department, when we were coming out, said 'Move to the left, move to the left.' Everyone complied."

"'We moved out the back toward Broadway. The police were saying, ';Don't look back! Don't look back!" and, of course, we made it about a half a block and I saw the othert tower on fire and I couldn't believe it. I'm very lucky. I thank God very much."

[At the 9/11 Memorial Museum website, 911memorial.org, is a podcast series called "Our City. Our Story".]

The Net Is Being Mended (October 2001)

The Godless holes of pornography and gambling and violence that have marked much of the Internet are being mended by the linking of good Catholic sites. The Church is preparing to cast into the deep for a great catch. Starting just with the links now listed at the Sacred Heart Radio (WNOP, P. O. Box 20253, Cincinnati, OH 45230) website, we find something for Catholics.

The American Catholic Youth's well-stocked site has on-line editions of *St. Anthony Messenger, Catholic* and *Youth Updates* and *Scripture from Scratch* as well as Catholic greeting e-cards and Sisters United News' Pledge for Peace aiming for a thousand years

(8,765,940 man-hours) of peacemaking. There too are links to "Fr. Jack's E-spirations" newsletter, *Every Day Catholic* and for lapsed Catholics and their families, *Once Catholic.*

Angeles Media Distribution Group (AMDG, P. O. Box 3311, Sea Bright, NJ, 00760) offers "everything Catholic", audio rosaries, devotions, books, etc. There's a handy Catechism of the Catholic Church search engine and the Couple to Couple League (P. O. Box 1111184, Cincinnati, OH 45211-1184) and the One More Soul Center (3020 Erie Ave., Hyde Park) information sites on Natural Family Planning (NFP) with sterilization reversal stories.

There is a comprehensive Decent Film Guide by Steven D. Greydanus, as well as St. Faustina Kowalska's "Revelation of the Day" among other blessings at the National Shrine of Divine Mercy and Association of Marian Helpers site (Eden Hill, Stockbridge, MA 01263).

Generation Christ, Mater Institute, connected with St. Gertrude's, aims to reach Christians in their 20s and 30s, while Paraclete Xtreme Sports links being extreme faith and extreme multi-sport athletes. From tere is a link to the Columbine martyr, Cassie Bernalis, memorial site, named for her famous last words, "Yes, I believe." National Catholic Register columnist Dr. Ray Guarendi has a site reaching out to help parents and children.

The hierarchy is represented by Priest for Life with Fr. Frank Pavone, the National Conference of Bishops, the Diocese of Covington, KY, the diocese of Cincinnati, OH, and the Vatican's treasure of a site, in English among other languages.

The Eternal Word Television and Radio Network (EWTN, 5817 Old Leeds Rd., Irondale, AL 35210) has schedules and links and news with "Catholic Answers" (2020 Gillespie Way, El Cajon, CA 92020) having its own link.

Last but certainly not least is listed True Presence, the site of the Apostolate for the Eucharistic Life (P. O. Box 413, Ann Arbor, MI 48106-0413) hosted by director Tim DiLaura.

Men Called to Change (May 2001)

Bishop Carl K. Moeddel summed up this year's "Answer the Call" men's conference at Xavier University, Cincinnati, by challenging some eight thousand men "to conversion, to change, to better relationships, better parishes" and "to live as children of the Light, to give testimony to the wonderful works of Jesus in our lives."

"We are blessed with so many spiritual enrichment groups," he noted, but asked, "Do they motivate their participants to be more active in their parish?"

Senator Connie Mack, grandson of the Philadelphia Athletics' owner, told of the changes worked in his life. Speaking before such a large crowd was not something that came naturally to him, but was the result of experiences over the last several years.

Through the Senate prayer breakfast, he realized that in seventeen years he had never expressed joy, ever since his brother Michael had died from cancer. Now he, his wife and his daughter are all cancer survivors. "Each day now," he says, "I give thanks for the fruits of the Holy Spirit and pray that I will be an instrument of the Holy Spirit."

One of the fruits of his prayer was a relationship with Butch whom he was with when he died in the hospital. The experience taught him the important lesson that "it makes no difference to God whether you're a U. S. senator or a U. S. Senate dining room busboy."

Another lesson was learning: "If I take one step at a time, I will eventually get where He wants me to be."

Fr. Dan Coughlin, the first Catholic priest to become chaplain, gave an update of his experiences from last year's conference. He tells members of both parties that "God is in every transition," He gives -- after much prayer -- wise counsel. "We need to know how to connect better ... Until we get over the liking and into the loving, ... we need to listen." Fr. Coughlin advised all men, "When you're tempted to pull away from family, be careful, talk with someone, deal with it."

One thought that has helped him much personally is the question, "Why are we so insecure when Jesus said, 'I AM always with you.'?"

Maurice Blumberg, executive director of the National Resource Center for Catholic Men, also spoke on how his life changed. Six months after his father disappeared in Florida, he read a Gideon Bible, gave himself to Jesus and found his father in New York. He told how he tried to grow in faith by himself and it didn't work and how he kept the faith through the death of his first wife.

David Kauffman exchanged his successful business career to minister full-time through song. He has sung for the pope and at the World Youth Day in Paris. At the conference he shared how parenting his five-year-old daughter Cameron teaches him about our heavenly Father.

Tim Philpot won his seat the Kentucky legislature by only two votes, so he figured God wanted him there. Now he is the president of the Christian Businessmen's Committee International. Like Blumberg, he says, "I can't make it by myself." Like migrating birds, we can get where we need to only by working together in formation.

Like Fr. Coughlin, he too asks questions:"Where are you going to be a hundred years from now?" "If God's not worried about the storms in your life, why should you be?"

He concluded from the story of Jesus calming the sea (Mark 4) that "there is safety in Jesus' ship." -- friendship, fellowship, discipleship and leadership; and "when you follow Jesus, life becomes an adventure."

Fr. Bruce Neill, C. S. P., put it bluntly as well he should as Director of Evangelization for the National Conference of Catholic Bishops. "The greatest gift that God has given me is being a Catholic ... It is Christianity that will bring about the changes in society that we are looking for." If you follow Jesus, he notes, as the world said of Him, they "will marvel at the gracious words that come from your lips."

[CBCI started in Chicago in 1930.]

Christ Came at Christmas (February 2001)

Yes, Christ did come to Christmas in 2000 and you may very well have missed it. He came to television, not His long-awaited second coming. According to Dr. D. James Kennedy of Coral Ridge Media, "There has been extensive criticism and concern over programs such as ABC's 'The Search for Jesus', which presented extremely questionable and controversial information as well-established facts." In response came "Who Is This Jesus?"

This two million dollar faith-building presentation which he calls "one of the definitive television projects of Jesus" was turned down by the networks, so Dr. Kennedy had to go station to station to get it aired. Of the top 38 CBS and FOX stations, 28 or almost three-quarters accepted the offer, and on PAX an additional 61 did. Although it therefore reached a potential 110 million viewers, it was missed by many more in the smaller markets.

The co-host to this program was not a skeptical news anchor, but Dean Jones. Best known as a star in the family comedy "The Love Bug" and 35 other films, he has a much more serious side. He is also president of the Christian Rescue Committee, author of Under Running Laughter and producer of the adaptation of Frank Peretti's supernatural thriller This Present Darkness. He has also done a one-man show "St. John in Exile."

Other participants in the program were Dr. John Dominic Crossan, co-founder of the Jesus Seminar and Fr. Jerome Neyrey of Notre Dame.

Jerry Newcombe, senior producer, notes, "Regardless of one's spiritual beliefs, we can all agree that Jesus is one of the most influential persons in all history,"

At the same time, PBS was presenting its four-part series, "From Jesus to Christ", produced by Marilyn Mellowes. It, in contrast, includes such uncanonical sources as the Q hypothesis' "lost gospel", the apocryphal *Gospel of Thomas* and the Gnostic "gospels". The evengelists are covered in the segment "The Story of the Storytellers", without the greatness of *The Greatest Story Ever Told*.

Some of the points covered may demythologized some people's misconceptions about early and present-day Christians. Sociologist Rodney Stark, author of *The Rise of Christianity*, sees the Gospel as an answer to "a world saturated with cruelty," an alternative to failed paganism.

Wayne A. Meeks notes that Erastus was Corinth's city treasurer and that Gaius, Stephanos and Lydia all had homes large enough to assemble the Corinthian church in. Eric Meyers noted the very Romanized city of Sepphoris near Nazareth. L. Michael White of the University of Texas pointed out, "The worship of the early Christian house church probably centered around the dinner table."

The PBS website features comments from viewers more educational than the series itself. Sr. Mabel Mariotti wrote, "For those who feel threatened in their faith by this scholarly work, I suggest to relax, pray and open their minds. This may be a call to a deeper faith, a faith that is alive."

John Mark Ockerbloom wrote, "What I would really love to see is a program brave enough to tackle head-on the debates over who Jesus and the early Christians were, rather than just presenting a single 'iconoclastic' point of view."

Robert Krcelic wrote, "My conclusion is that it is truly a miracle that Christianity is a religion today."

2000 Was A Year of God's Favor (January 2001)

In his apostolic letter, *Tertio Millenio Adveniente*, Pope John Paul II identified last year, the last year of the second millennium since Christ's incarnation, as a jubilee year, "the year of the Lord's favor" (Isaiah 61:1-2), that favor which "characterizes all the activities of Jesus." "For the Church," he wrote, it is "a year of the remission of sins and of the punishments due to them, a year of manfold conversions and of sacramental and extra-sacramental penance."

For readers of *My People* the year 2000 was when "Gus" Morgan reminded us "Love Will Aways Be There" and to "Praise the Lord" and of Iwo Jima. Fred Summe reminded us that in this turning point in American history, slow progress against the culture of death is still progress. Michael Halm told us about the "Answer the Call" men's conference in "The Signs of the Times Are Hopeful" and that "God Works Miracles" even on television. The Light to the Natures column told us that the Philippines declared a death penalty moratorium. We read Joan Paul II speak out on peace and justice, youth and elderly, solidarity, the Eucharist, vocations, evangelizing the media, the Holy Spirit and forgiveness.

We also read about the youth conference in Paris: "Youth celebrate and share their faith" and the Third World Meeting with Families: "Children bring a message of life and hope." We learned how with respect to Ecuador Oil indigenous groups scored gains, and at the World Day of Prayer for Vocations how the Eucharist is the source of all vocations.

Fr. Al Lauer continued to tell all how "The Truth Will Set You Free" and Sue Seta about how God has made, and continues to make us, new creations. We continue to pray the news and give glory to God in the Scripture greetings.

Considering what others had foretold would happen -- that did not -- we have been most favored. We certainly are a year closer to the long awaited return of Jesus, the Savior of the world.

Many predicted worldwide depression with millions jobless, homeless and starving because of the millennium bug. Since 1994, Martha Raemer's Mary statue was reported to have bled and wept and said, "The world will end January 1, 2000."

Dr. Hong Yeun Park prophesied that North Korea would be violently overthrown early in the year and Kim Jong-II assassinated. Dr. Julian Salt predicted "mile-high waves, hurrican-like winds and volcanic explosions worldwide" in May when the planets aligned.

Dr. Renzo Cavotta claimed Jesus would return in the Fall having allegedly examined secret passages of the Dead Sea scrolls. Rabbi Herzl Rosenblum, author of *Interpreting the Dead Sea Scrolls; A Reconstructionist Approach*, based on his prophesy on Daniel 8:14, naming 300 days into the year or October 27 as Doomsday.

Rev. Connor Barlow predicted a great earthquake on the West Coast and a killer meteor shower in the Southwest and a 700-mile-per-hour supercane in the Southeast. Patience Dereign prophesied a total collapse of the Russian economy triggering a civil war. Rev. Roger Claypoole, Anglican Institute for Bible Interpretation, said, "Doomsday will occur at the end of the second millennium -- the year 2000."

Prof. Brian Kingsley, author of *A Comprehensive History of the Church of Latter-Day Saints*, said: "New translations [of Joseph Smith's golden tablets] will reveal a prediction that 'in 2000 A. D. all the world will be consumed." Prof. and Seventh Day Adventist minister Joan Merchen bases her year 2000 prediction on the 67 years since the Antichrist Adolf Hitler rose to power.

The Bethlehem Scroll Conference's prophesies for the year 2000 come from their imaginative interpretation of the so-called Bethlehem scrolls alleged to have been written by the Wise Men. They have annually met since the scrolls discovery in Cologne in 1991. They say Pope John Paul II "is almost certainly the emissary and ambassador "vaporized by a nuclear missile" ball of fire while visiting N. Korea, "the East".

An accidental release of germs and nerve gas would kill millions of Iraqis including Saddam Hussain. Adolf Hitler would rise from the dead and imprison or murder 666,000 Christians in one day. The predicted 200,000 dead in race riots in New York on Easter, half the world killed in the aftereffects of a comet tail and almost all the rest in a pandemic with only one hundred raptured away.

Christmas Is Miraculous (December 2000)

Some miraculous stories have been collected that have taken place during "the mosr wonderful time of the year" -- Christmas time.

Christmas Miracles: Magical True Stories of Modern-Day Miracles by Jamie C. Miller, Laura Lewis and Jennifer Basye Sander collects some thirty-two of them. Sander's own story is called "Homeless Santa". She tells how she nearly took PamAm 103 flight back to California for Christmas in 1988, the plane that exploded over Lockerbee, Scotland. She'd been gone for three months trying to deal with "the breakup of a long-term romance". On Christmas Eve she and her roommate went out for burritos and encountered an old, white-bearded man with a sack who gave them unexpected gifts. To her roommate he gave an apple and to Jennifer a

Snickers. "The spirit of giving is all around us and can come upon us so unexpectedly," she continues. "We need to be able to give back what we can to those who need it most."

From Rabbi Abie Ingber of Cincinnati came "Christmas Saved My Mother's Life". His mother, Fania Paszt, had been a teenager in Lutsk, Poland, in August, 1942. She alone left with a Ukrainian peasant who offered to help her family escape, but before she could return for them, the ghetto had been sealed off. Over the next two days, 17,000 Jews were massacred including her whole family. She hid in the Ukrainian's flue for four months, as long as he dared keep her. After being attacked by guard dogs, the county warden refused her plea that he shoot her and she was passed from Christian to Christian until liberation. Many years later she learned of the Polish proverb, "On Christmas Eve, even a stray cat is allowed to live."

Nora Lynn tells in "Bologna from Heaven" how as a student, divorced, broke and yet with two Pekinese to care for, she stooped to write a check that wouldn't be covered until her student loan came. When she got home, she discovered five pounds of bologna she hadn't put in the sack. It reminded her of the fried bologna sandwiches her grandmother had made for her as a girl. Her grandmother had died the year she got married. She cried for joy and has enjoyed fried bologna sandwiches every Christmas since.

Sandi Schureman tells of how her family taught he "Christmas Doesn't Come from a Store". Her husband, a fireman, wanted to do something for the mother and children he'd just visited when she and the children had gone to visit him at the station. They had fled an abusive situation and now one of the boys was ill. When they learned all the stores were closed, Sandi's children offered their own Christmas gifts, baseball mitts. One son gave up home-run baseball to go with them.

Arnie Giers, editor of Heroes of the Holocaust, tells of when his family was trying to flee to Holland from the Nazis. It was on the last day of Hanukkah when just before the border there was a power failure on the train. Arnie's father seized the opportunity to light his Hanukkah candles and incredibly the Gestapo used the light to process all the passengers' papers. When they had finished, the lights came back on and they even thanks Arnie's father for the use of his "travel candles". Even after they had gone on from Holland to America, Arnie never forgot his father's "Like in the days of the Maccabees, a great miracle has happened here."

The PAX network series, "It's A Miracle", has dramatized many others, such as Nancy Bayless' "The Quicker Picker-upper". In it she tells of her hopelessness when trying to deal with all the consequences of her husband's Lynn's bone marrow cancer. At midnight on Christmas Eve she went to get a roll of paper towels and became even more depressed when she found they were not white as she thought she had bought, but had printing on them. Finally she read the paper towels' messages, such as "Friendship is a special gift", "Love is sharing", and "No act of love no matter how small is ever wasted" and received peace. The next morning she discovered that the towels were plain white after all. Her husband lived another seven years.

Gwen Ellis of Idaho City, ID, tells another Christmas story, "Little Treasures". When Gwen and her daughter, Jamie and Kristen, were low on money after the youngest had had pneumonia, she says, "I did a lot of praying. The Lord showed me "One day at a time", you know, we will receive our gifts and the gift from Him was the love we had for each other. What matters is giving the love from yourself to someone else. That's the most important thing."

The Lord also gave them a little thing, too, though. On December 1 the girls found a gold nugget on the playground worth $300. "I knew it wouldn't changeeverything," Gwen admits. "It meant more knowing that our prayers were answered."

Monica Dradi was on her way to her father's beach house during Christmas week. She was only seven-and-a-half months pregnant, but suddenly she got several sharp pains and her water broke. "I kept praying and praying that someone would please help me." She explains, "I wasn't praying for myself. I was praying that my baby would be okay."

She drove off into a residential neighborhood in Upper Marborough, MD, but found herself in a dead-end street. She saw a fully-lit house, but she adds, "Something told me to go to the house on the other side." It was the house of Joyce Ware, whose daughter, a nurse with delivery experience, and a son-in-law, an emergency medical technician, "happened" to be there for the holidays!

Nurse Diane Minter says, "I told myself God did not send her here for this baby to die. It's just not going to happen. " The baby was sideways, but moved when they put Monica on the stretcher. The baby came, but he was blue and limp with the cord around his neck, but loose enough for Diane to remove it.

[Miller and Laura Lewis also wrote *Heavenly Miracles: Magical True Stories of Guardian Angels and Answered Prayers* and Miller and Sander wrote *The Miracle of Sons: Celebrating The Boys in Our Lives.*]

God Works Miracles (November 2000)

Richard "John Boy Walton" Thomas hosts "It's A Miracle", possibly one of the best things on television. It airs on PAX, a cable channel, and has been shown on UPN. The show not only has re-enactments of the testimonies sent in by viewers but interviews with eyewitnesses.

In "Double Angel", Don and Carol Colenda told of how when they had trouble adopting a second child from Korea, they went out to a cabin to get away and decided what to do about it. Carol got a bit upset when she saw her husband talking with another woman, but when he told her he had been alone praying, she believed him. They did what his prayer had led him to decide, to seek help from the international adoption agency over the local one. The person they contacted, Judy, straightened out the situation and they soon got a baby daughter, Jackie, but when they tried to thank the one who had helped them, the agency said there has never been anyone by that name working there.

"I think it all happened," Carol says, "because we were at thepoint where we could not fix this problem. God was aware of the problem and I think He answered our prayer in the form of an angel that told Don what to do. Then when we did call the agency, she was able to find out what the problem was and get it solved. But the biggesr miracle was just having Jackie for a daughter.

In "Tooth Fairy", Joyce Brown, once a model, had suffered for years with a debilitating condition the doctors could not identity. She got respiratory infections, crippling rheumatoid arthritis, low white blood count and had reactions to the antibiotics. Finally she prayed, like Sarah and Tobit, for God to end her life. Instead she says, "I saw a beautiful white light, I saw a life review. Oh, it was very enlightening what I saw. I saw this world belonged to all of us. I saw how precious life is and how much time I had wasted. We all have many more miracles around us than what we realize we have."

Joyce also saw a gold-crowned tooth. When she finally convinced her dentist, he found a hidden but massive infection underneath. In three weeks even here arthritis was gone.

In "Thank You Note", Diana Gonzalez, a Miami medical reporter, managed to connect Frank Lamberti with the doctor who could save his cancerous leg, having gotten his letterjust before her interview with the doctor. The real miracle, though, didn't happen unti; six years later when she got the same rate thigh tumor. "What this experience has taught me," Diana says, "is that little acts of kindness can really make a huge difference in someone's life."

Jan and Greg Gregaro experienced a "Hurricane Andrew Miracle". They survived the storm and Jan's father had even managed to get a generation, so they had air conditioning to cope with the heat after the storm. A week later they saw a man working on the phone lines, tried the phone and were able to take in Uncle Charlie and Aunt Maggie too. That right, though, they were all overcome with carbon monoxide from the badly-ventilated generator. Only the ability to call 911 had saved them.

It wasn't until full powerwas restored two months later that they learned that no one from the phone company could have fixed the phone lines that night. "I believe what happened was a miracle," Jan says. "I thought about it and realized we had a guardian angel looking over us and that's why we had a phone just for that night. I get peace of mind knowing that I'm never alone and that I always have an angel with me."

In "Angels Among Us", teenager Robbie Mendonzes was declared three-quarters dead by his doctor, Dr. Bass, after both his liver and heart failed. His parents, Robert and Nancy, say they "prayed to our heavenly Father that He not take our son, to give us strength, to help the doctors so they would know what to do to save his life." When morning came, they found Robbie had regained consciousness but became concerned when he asked, "Is there anyone else in the room with you?", when there was no one else.

He said he could barely see and hear them, but thought some other people were in the room and had been all morning. Robbie's parents finally realized that they were not angels there to take their son away, but to help him recover. After five weeks of prayers by his family and many friends at Salinas High, he came home. In three months he was well enough to have his name taken off the transplant list.

Nick Tassoni tells in "Message from Ted" how the death of his son Ted after a head-on collision nearly killed him as well. He had already lost a daughter in another lost a daughter in another traffic accident. Ted's organ donations saved six others, but that could not console his father. Finally he and his friend, Fr. Paco, visited yet another accident victim in the very University of Massachusetts hospital hospital room his son had died in. Ties Morace woke and after asking, "Are you Nick?", Fr. Paco says, "She was the one who comforted us!" She told them that a voice had told her that if she chose to come back, she should tell Nick that his son was fine and not to worry.

["It's A Miracle" aired nearly two hundred episodes before ending in 2004. On DVD are *It's A Miracle*: 44 Real Llife Stories and *It's a Miracle: 50 New Stories*.]

The Signs of the Times Are Hopeful (May 2000)

Signs of hope, and of challenge, for the new millennium were the hallmarks of the recent "Answer the Call" men's conference. The first such conference five years ago had four hundred men; the April one in Cincinnati drew nine thousand. Two publications that helped are the weekly discussion guide, *Signposts: How To Be A Catholic Man in the World Today* by Bill Bawden and Tim Sullivan and the family magazine, *Togethor in Christ*.

Australian speaker Matthew Kelly has written his own best-seller *A Call To Joy* and now *Rhythm Of Life*. He opened his talk with hope in action saying that when he prayed, he usually praised, adding, "It's been a long time since I asked for anything, but I pray for healing for my friend, Fr. Jim Willig." Fr. Willig, whose Scripture teachings on tape were also acvailable at the conference, has been diagnosed with terminal cancer.

Kelly then put his audience in place by reminding them that only thirty-two percent of the people in the world are literate, only thirty percent Christian and only one percent college-educated. Literate, educated Christians are indeed blessed. All, however, are called to answer God's challenge to change, to break out of the day-to-day drudgery that life can become without God. Quoting John 10:10 "The thief comes only to steal and slaughter and destroy; I came that they might have life and have it to the full," he said. "There is only one immutable fact in life: life takes courage. The courageous are answering the call and the abundant life of Christ described in the Scriptures takes courage too."

As youth director at St. Frances Cabrini Church in Littleton, Colorado, Jim Beckman shared some of what other media haven't reported. Columbine students tried to sort out what had happened after the school shootings, more things than just the shootings. Some told of running and then the next thing they knew they were on the other side of the street without remembering how they got there. Others told of running without feeling their feet touch the ground. One told of running into one of the killers, being shot at pointblank range and hearing the bullets hit the wall behind. Still others ran through the four-inch deep water that had accumulated from the sprinklers and came out with dry feet. Beckman's conclusion is: "There were thousand of angels in that school that day!"

Beckman told of an experience of his own earlier, during their trip to the World Youth Day in Paris, on a side trip to Assisi. Because the main chapel was so crowded they were allowed down to a simple, cave-like one below. When he felt a wind after Communion, he knew it was the Holy Spirit and felt that saints were with him, like the saints who had celebrated Mass here in secret before. One was Val Schnurr, who was shot in the chest, abdomen and arm just because she had a Bible.

Columbine student Ben Schumann told of the challenge Bishop Jacobs had given them just five months before the shootings, when the question of dying for one's faith seemed so hypothetical. He credited his father with helping their family keep the faith, his father who had just come into the Catholic faith that Easter, three weeks before the shootings.

Chuck Colson, author of How Now Shall We Live?, referred quite extensively to Pope Paul II. "This is a great moment to be a Christian." (The Threshold of Hope) "The signs are beginning to shiow a trend," he said. Crime levels, though appalling, are the lowest since 1973; sexual promiscuity is down for three years in a row; abortions too are down to 1990 levels.

"There is a change too," he notes, "in public attitude taking place before our eyes that's just what John Paul II is talking about. Society collapsed when everyone did what was right in their own eyes. The media and the public are waking up, searching for something better. That something better is the Biblical way of living."

"We've got to come together," he challenged. "We've got to love one another and stand together. That's the kind of love the world hungers for."

Fr. Benedict Groeschel, author of The Journey Toward God, told how this might not be as difficult as we might think. In his study of Church history, he learned that the Puritans had devotion to the Sacred Heart, Wesley believed in the Eucharist, Calvin in the Immaculate Conception and Luther had a life-long devotion to the Blessed Virgin Mother.

Fr. Groeschel identified the pope's recent Great Jubilee pilgrimage to the Holy Land as another sign of Hope. He identifies the beginnings of his hope, however in the prayer groups started by the woman honored by the Protestants as Catherine Adorno and by Catholics as St. Catherine of Genoa. They led to the familiar old lay associations such as the St. Vincent de Paul Society and third orders. He also notes newer signs in the communities forming in

Britain, France and Italy, all deeply Catholic, Pro-life and called via mystical experiences to evangelize the world-weary. Another turning point, he notes, was when Cardinal Joseph Ratzinger, so associated with the new *Catechism of the Catholic Church*, led the Second Vatican Council to address not the old Christendom but the world.

Even if the culture as we know it does not survive, the Franciscan priest said, "Know your faith; live your faith, because with the grace of God, the future will be yours."

[Matthew Kelly has also written *The Four Signs of a Dynamic Catholic, Rediscover Jesus, Rediscover Catholicism* and *Resisting Happiness*; Jim Beckman *God Help Me: How to Grow in Prayer*; Chuck Colson *The Sky Is Not Falling: Living Fearlessly in These Turbulent Times*; Fr. Groeschel *The Saints in My Life* and *Jesus and Mary: In Praise of their Glorious Names*, etc.]

Hanoi Jane Finds Prince of Peace (April 2000)

Jane Fonda was born into celebrity as a daughter of actor Henry Fonda. She is probably best known, however for her visit to Hanoi, the capital of the enemy, North Vietnam, during the controversial Vietnam War. For the visit and the things she said there, she earned the name "Hanoi Jane" and was called a traitor before Congress. "Traitor" is the first Internet linkage listed after her name.

She won an Oscar in that very same year for her portrayal of a call girl in the murder mystery "Klute", but stopped making films since marrying media billionaire Ted Turner. Since this is the third marriage for both of them, it was not surprising when they announced they were separating. The less reported story behind it, however is.

It started with her chauffeur witnessing to her. Over two years she began to put her faith not in fame or fortune, but in Him. She objected to her husband's proposed bid in this year's presidential race and he obliged. She is regularly attending Bible studies and church services and those close to her say her faith is maturing.

Ted Turner would certainly need time to adjust to this since he once called Christianity "a religion for losers". "While we continue to be committed to the long-term success of our marriage," they explained, "we find ourselves at a juncture where we must each take some personal time for ourselves."

Jane admits to being a loser, having lost her virginity young and having made many mistakes over the years, most regrettably as a mother. "It seems," she said, "that talking about sex requires more intimacy than actually doing it." She supports programs that encourage refraining from premarital sexual activity, but also critcizes so-called Christians who seem unconcerned about those who have already been sexually active or those of a different social or economic class.

"We have to be on a crusade," she has said, "and be just as passionate on behalf of our children, but not use the same tactics -- not lies, not use misinformation and scare tactics."

At an environmentalist conference she demonstrated just what tactics she now uses. She suggested that rather than the planned period of meditation, the attendees would better use the time to "pray to Jesus Christ."

Now Hollywood is taking of rewriting a '00s version of her campy '60s "Barbarella", more like the French "comic". Her critics are writing: "She is getting old and is obviously losing what little grip on reality she may have had," "rather vacant between the ears", "terribly wrong and cannot be forgiven".

Fortunately her chauffeur knew differently.

[Jane and Turner divorced in 2001 and she was a student at the Interdenominational Theological Seminary, but did not continue.]

Sherlock Holmes Finds God (January 2000)

In His book, *Holy Clues: The Gospel According to Sherlock Holmes*, Unitarian minister Stephen Kendrick acknowledges that "In the grand scheme of things, reading detective fiction ranks pretty low on the list of spiritual disciplines, but simply by reminding us of, and returning us to, a proper sense of the realities of our true nature, it certainly redeems itself."

That the world's most well-known fictional character can illuminate God, the world's most real Creator, that mysteries and Mystery can overlap is what he proposes. He begins by reminding his readers of the Biblical origins of the detective story. In the deuterological books, "Bel and the Dragon" and "Susannah", Daniel finds clues and cross-examines witnesses in typical detective story fashion.

He notes several indirect references to the Bible in Holmes, most not from the Gospels. In "The Speckled Band" Holmes refers to the schemer falling into his own pit (Eccl 10:8), in "The Copper Beeches" to making bricks without straw (Ex 5:7), and in "The Illustrious Client" to the wages of sin (Rom 6:23).

Holy Clues is written especially for those for whom "God has become not just the riddle in the middle of the greatest mystery of all, but much like the corpse at the start of a mystery story, a corpse that has mysteriously disappeared, as if it had never existed at all," "a God Who hides Himself." (Isa 45:15), Whom the seeker is promised to find (Mt 7:7). It is Kendricks explains, for "those who look closely for signs that are still scattered everywhere that point to the presence as having indeed been there -- evocative and tantalizing clues to God's existence that defy our despair, our bewilderment."

He describes it as "a book that finds parables where other have not noticed them before, "in the "revelation of the triumph of friendship over isolation," as when in "The Empty House" Wtson fainted for the first and last time in his life upon finding Holmes, whom he had presumed dead for the past three years alive or when in "The Hound of the Baskervilles" Watson find Holmes unexpectedly on the eerie moor.

It's revealed also in the triumph of mercy over justice and compassion over judgment as in the Christmas story, "The Blue Carbuncle", when Holmes, having recovered the stolen jewel, lets the first-time offender escape. Of the 60 felons mentioned in the Holmes stories, the Geat Detective has mercy on fourteen, 23%.

"We love mystery tales," Kendrick writes, "because we can tell ourselves that we are safely in the corner of goodness, truth and right, along with our hero."

"Most spiritual pilgrims, and I count myself among them, possess both a deep hunger for a fresh and creative faith and and equally strong need not to be fooled or manipulated. We want a faith that is not being propped up with rickety tales of miracles and tinseled visions. We want a faith a little closer to the ground, something that seems threaded into the realm of everyday and the ordinary, not the grand and the glittering."

Including in the book, too, are lessons from Sir Arthur Conan Doyle's and Kendrick's own stories. Doyle's boyhood faith was severely damaged by a fierce Irish priest whom he remembered damning all who were not Roman Catholic. In turning away from this heresy, he lost his way in beliefs (later called "New Age"), in spiritualism, mediums and fairy photos. Kendrick take half-seriously the joke that claims Unitarians pray "to Whom it may concern."

Still he warns, quoting Luke 21:8, "Take heed that you are not led astray," the 'supernatural' tales of Holmes were meant to help us, besides showing us a rattling good time, to be utterly cautious and clear when facing the ineffable. It is in the ordinary that the holy dwells and it is not so much hiding as it is constantly being overlooked and neglected." For example, there are "ordinary" bread and wine, water, oil, wood, the touch of a hand, the spoken word. It is truly looking for, not overlooking, the clues to the holy that is "the gospel of Sherlock Holmes."

Jubilee Means Debtfree (December 1999)

Inspired by the definition of Jubilee in Leviticus, the once-in-fifty-years year when slaves were freed, land returned to the original owners and debts canceled, Jubilee 2000 seeks to free the world's poorest from debt slavery.

The worldwide movement includes national campaigns in developed countries of Australia, Austria, Canada, England, Germany, Ireland, the Philippines, Scotland, South Africa, Sweden and the Unites States. It includes prayer, discussion group and letter writing to government and financial leaders.

To make Washington aware of the debt crisis, David Dancombe fasted for 45 days to show legislators what a hungry person looked like. Brian Baird (WA), Tony Hall (OH) and Spencer Bachus (AL) also fasted.

The world produces 4.3 pounds of food per capita per day, yet in that same day 300,000 children starve. Seventy-eight percent of the starving children under five are in countries who export food to pay interest on their debts. The local external debt of developing nations was $2.2 trillion in 1997, with $269 billion for "debt services". That of the 41 poorest nations is over 5200 billion.

President Clinton, saying "The pope has asked us to do it for the millennium," pledged $970 million -- a mere 1/7% of the $665,951 million (as of 1997) demanded by the backs from nations unable to pay.

The U. S. bishops wrote, "The debt crisis should be measured in term of its human costs and moral consequences," in "A Jubilee Call for Debt Forgiveness". They call for more than debt relief. They demand morality in banking, an end to the unjust practices that all but forces nations to cut primary health and education, child labor or trafficking in illegal drugs and buying and selling debts. They ask for accountability to churches, philanthropic organizations and other nongovernmental organizations, if not from the banks or national leaders themselves.

The third world's farmland waters and forests are being overdepleted. Brazil owes a hundred ninety-three billion dollars and is cutting fifty thousand square kilometers of forest per year. Forty percent of Bolivia's workforce depends on drug trade.

Half the world's six billion people live on two dollars per day. The number of Indonesians averaging just one dollar per day has increased threefold in the last two years. Because of a two hundred ten million dollar default on its loan, its "poverty alleviation" loan, which would increase its indebtedness by another six hundred million dollars, was delayed until 2002.

In Bangladesh it's only two hundred seventy dollars per year per capita which translates into an eighty-two percent infant mortality rate and a fifty-eight year life expectancy. Eighty percent of Thais have no secondary education; the average is about five years.

Africa contains thirty-three of the forty-one heavily-indebted poor counties (HIPCs). Zambia cannot farm nnety percent of its land because the World Bank and the International Monetary Fund have denied farmers loans. Uganda sends seven dollars per capital on debt repayment and only three on health and education.

In 1997, before Hurricane Mitch devastated the country, Honduras paid over eleven percent of its GNP toward "debt service". Côte d'Ivoire over fourteen, Jamaica sixteen, Nicaragua seventeen and Angola over nineteen.

The Holy Father has designated a number of "Jubilee Days" in the Jubilee year to honor and remember particular groups for what they have contributed to the life of the Church and society and as an opportunity for deeper reflection on the challenges to be faced in living the gospel in society. Some of these which seem particularly relevant players in the issue of debt forgiveness are: the children (January 2), the sick and those who care for them (February 11), scientists (May 25), the media (June 5) and seniors (September 17).

Among the Jubilee year activities the U. S. bishops invite participation in the Pledge for Justice and Charity, making a pilgrimage and/or joining a small Christian community, such as those of Presentation Communities.

[Jubilee 2000 later became less international and more nation as Jubilee South, Jubilee Debt Campaign, Jubilee Scotland, Jubilee Research, Jubilee USA, etc.]

Blessed Are the Persecuted (September 1999)
Enter "persecution" on any search engine on the internet and you'll find the Voice of the Martyrs site, www.persecution.com. It has ministered to and reported on the persecuted Church since 1967. It reported much much just in the first half of this year.

On January 24 near Manoharpur, Orissa, India, Graham Staines and his two sons, Philip, nine, and Timothy, seven, were burned to death while sleeping in their station wagon by a mob of a hundred Hindus who poured gasoline on the car and set it on fire. Staines had ministered to lepers in Mayurbhanj since 1965. Word is that this was in reaction to area Hindus burning their idols because of his example. His widow Gladys is continuing the work with her thirteen-year-old daughter Esther. A few days afterward, Dr. P. P. Job challenged the record hundred eighty thousand Indians at an outdoor crusade and tens of thousands said they would also be willing to die for Christ.

In Indonesia, Pastor Thyessen on the island of Ambon was carrying materials to his church when he was attacked by radical Moslems, who cut off his head and arms and threw his body into his burning house. His widow says, "We surrender everything to God no matter what happens. Whatever happens to us, we Christian should depend on and be faithful to God, our Savior."

Rachel Scott died in the Columbine High School shooting in Aporil after professing she believed in God. She wrote in her journal, "I am not going to hide the light that God has put in me. If I have to sacrifice everything, I will. I will take it. If my friends have to become my enemies for me to be with my best friend Jesus, then that's fine with me. I always knew being a Christian is having enemies, but I never thought that my 'friends' were going to be those enemies."

In Afghanistan last January, mosque loudspeakers announced that any man no attending the five-time-a-day Muslim prayers would be punished, businesses must close during prayer times and the ultra-Moslem Taliban government made it the legal responsibility of the oldest son to kill any family member for apostasy, that is, believing Jesus is Lord.

Algiers, Algeria, is the most restricted part of the country when Christians must meet secretly in small groups; in the mountainous Kabili region there is more freedom, but even in the southeast one imam still preaches in the mosque, but now about Jesus.

After being arrested and having his house church gutted, Hua Du officials began handing out beer and playing loud rock music over loudspeakers whenever Pastor Li De Xian would begin to preach. Another church home leader, Sze, now seventy-one, was imprisoned from 1958 to 1979. "Before prison we heard about God," he says, "but in prison we experienced God." In January he had all his belongings confiscated from his home and questioned eight times over the next several months because he refused to register with the Three-Self Patriotic Movement, like eighty percent of the churches in China. Also in April, police raided an underground church in Sui county, confiscating Bibles and arresting twenty-five Christians. In Henan province twenty were arrested and the next day in Wuhai, Inner Mongolia, four more were. In June, thirteen of the forty arrested in Shangqiu were still being held after six months for "holding illegal religious services".

On February third in Cuba, thousands of Bibles were burned at Arroyo Naranjo, Managua, as "subversive books".

Christians in That Dam Prison, Vientiane, Laos, still have over nine months left to serve for holding a service in a home, but one of them, Bounleuth, says prisoners are coming to Christ by witnessing the joy and courage of the believers.

In March the Chin tribe of Myanmar celebrated the centennial of their introduction to Christianity under coercion from the military government to convert to Buddhism in violation of its own law. No new church buildings have been allowed to be building three years. Buddhists force Christians to build houses for them and even pay a temple tax.

Last Easter in Nepal, Christians gathered in a football field in Katmandu. They had written for permission, but police came and beatmen, women and children with clubs.

Newly elected Nigerian president Obasanjo says, "Prison isn't such a bad place; I found God there." He was imprisoned in 1995 under Gen. Abacha where many of his fellow political prisoners died. "Thank God for saving my life from the hands of death." A Nigerian youth choir returned to their church burned by Moslems "because of Jesus, Jesus Christ."

Pakistani teenager Saleema was arrested for leading one of her young friends to Christ and was accused of being responsible for her friend's death when the friend's family killed her. In January, she was unable to make a court appearance because of injuries received from abuse while in custody.

Ghulam Masih, a Christian in Shekhupura, was arrested of murdering an elderly woman by four Moslem men identified as his seven-year-old daughter's rapists. Police inspector Mushtaq Ahmed, who had released the rapists "for lack of evidence," commended, "My first duty is to Islam. The courts will take a similar view and Ghulam Masih will be hanged."

After last Christmas, the Vietnamese authorities' persecution of the Hmong tribe, more than fifty percent Christian, intensified and they fled south to the forest highlands.

[Voice of the Martyrs was founded in 1967 by Pastor Richard Wurmbrand, imprisoned for fourteen years in Communist Romania for his faith in Christ.]

Pope Challenges Youth, World (March 1999)

"You think 'He's an old man' until he gets around those young kids," comments Vivian Jansen, on the pope's recent visit to St. Louis. Seventy-eight-year old Pope John Paul II, suffering with Parkinson's, walked with a shuffle, and occasionally his voice became unsteady, but brightened when the crowd there, mostly young people cheered. Each encouraged the other. As Vivian put it, "The kids were just marvelous. There was such reverence and such good news."

Elizabeth Egan, a youthful member of Presentation Ministries, Cincinnati, was delighted when the pope pretended his cane was a hockey stick. Wearing a commemorative T-shirt, shevremembers, "We were ten to twenty feet away standing on chairs close to yje partitiomn when he went by."

More than a hundred thousand attended the one Mass the pope said during his visit, concelebrating with a thousand [riests and more than two hundred bishops and cardinals, believed to be the largest indoor gathering in the United States.

Jerry Kohlbrand, who took all his older children, ages eight to sixteen, says they saw more on television while there than by going into the crowd. "It was remarkably well organized and prayerful," he said, Security, however, was very tight, even to lifting up manhole covers and checking the sewers -- and closing the restrooms for for forty-five minutes.

"The Lord just opened the way," Vivian Jansen explains. She was given a ticket the day vefore. Someone cancelled and she got a ride there and she got a room after she got there. "God is so good. I just want to thank Him, because He'll never let you down. I went and was blessed, blessed abundantly."

The rally emphasized 1 Timothy 4:12, "Let no one have contempt for your yout, but set an example for those who believe, in speech, conduct, love, faith and purity." and Matthew 5:14, 16, "You are the light of the world ... Your light must shine before others, that they may see your good deeds and glorify your heavenly Father." These Scripture passages were suggested by young people themselves.

"The light shines in the darkness and the darkness does not overcome it." (John 1:5) the pope reminded them. "Young friends, in the days and weeks and years ahead, for as long as you rember this evening, remember that the pope came to the United States, to the city of St. Louis, to call the young people of America to Christ, to invite you to follow Him. He came to challenge you to be the light of the world! With the help of Mary, the mother of Jesus, the young people of America will do this magnificently. Be light to the world, as only young people can be light. It is time to let your light shine!"

He noted as a sign of hope for America's future the increasing recognition that the dignity of human life must never be taken away, even in the case of someone who has done great evil. He taught by example. At his urging triple-murderer Darrell Mease, whose execution had been postponed because of the papal visit, was given life.

He urged "Catholic throughout the United States and wherever my words may reach -- especially to those who for one reason or another are separated from the practice of their faith" to "a special emphasis on the family and renewal of Christian marriage, call for followers of Christ who are unconditionally pro-life, who will proclaim, celebrate and serve te gospel of life in every situation and to put an end to every form of racism." His words reached many broadcasts live over the internet by the St. Louis-based Digital Broadcast Network.

The pope told Americans that we now face a time of trial similar to that of St. Louis' Dred Scott case which opposed slavery. He urged Americans to reaffirm the truths and values summed up in the phrase, "The Spirit of St. Louis", referring to the plane which took Charles Lindbergh solo to France, its saintly king and St. Louis' own St. Philippine Duchesne.

Coming to St. Louis from Mexico, the site of the first of his eighty-five papal vists over twenty years, the pope was "creating a sort of bridge between the two parts of te continent," Msgr. Timothy Dolan said. This continues the theme of last year's Special Assembly for America of the Synod of Bishops and the apostolic exhortation *Ecclesia in America*, which he signed when he was in Mexico.

The pope met, of course, with St. Louis' Archbishop Justin Rigali, who had invited him, who he had known during the twenty years when Rigali had worked in the Roman Curia. He met with Rosa Paks, eighty-six, a heroine of the civilrights movement and withbMark McGwire, the home-run king.

Pope John Paul II also challenged President Clinton. It was the fourth time the pope and the president had met. In their twenty-minute private conversation, aides say they talked about the sanctions against Iraq and Cuba which the pope opposes as harming the poor. They talked about the Middle East peace talks. Although both are against assisted suicide, now legal in Oregon, they continued to disagree on abortion which the pope also calls "a terrible rejection of God's gift of life and love."

George Weigel, his biographer, says, "We are witnessing a man giving himself to the end. For the first time, the world will watch a pope die." He is giving his life to save many lives for He Who is Life.

Another trip to Poland is planned for later this year. Trips to Ur, Abraham's homeland, in Iraq and to Mt. Sinai are planned as part of the millennial celebrations.

During a recent briefing on the next five years of bishops' synods at the Vatican, the pope stopped the recitation at the year 2001, explaining that the first year of the new millennium is for someone else." Since he has appointed but sixteen of the cardinal electors who will choose that "someone else", the next pope will kost likely continue to emphasize these same positions on these same issues, though Prof. Avery Dulles of Fordham University notes, he "will be a very hard act to follow."

[Pope John Paul II lived another five years and was canonized in 2014.]

Persecution Both Dealt With and Ignored (February 1999)

Last year in *The Lion's Den* by Nina Shea and *Their Blood Cries Out* by Paul Marshall were published, signs of the growing awareness of religious persecution as the century draws to a close. Scholars call persecution a "complex brew of racial, economic, political, tribal and religious rivalries", but the problem is basically spiritual. Now, however, it seems that some Christians who once opposed one another on the issues of abortion or homosexuality are uniting against persecution of Christians.

Last May the Christian Coalition backed the House bill to punish countries that persecute people for their religious beliefs. It included such reactions to persecution as diplomatic protests and economic sanctions such as cutting off non-humanitarian aid and restricting loans and exports.

By October, however when the Senate voted unanimously ninety-eight-to-nothing for the bill, it had been watered down to include a waiver in cases of "importanrt national interest". like profitable Chinese trade or the Pakistani atomic bomb threat

Gary L. Bauer of the Los Angeles *Times* identified it as "trading our moral leverage for business interests." Ambassador James R. Sasser on the other hand declared, "Constructive engagement is bearing fruit." Senator Rothenthal's comment was that American Christians do not seem very much concerned about the issue because persecution is taking place mostly in countries where American money and technology bolsters the persecutions. "A man cannot love both God and money "

It was also in May that Bishop John Joseph allegedly shot himself in protest over the death sentence of Ayub Masah, who had made a remark supporting Rushdie's book *The Satanic Verses*. In Mexico a priest denied Communion in the continuing war between the PRI (Institutional Revolutionary Party) and the Zapatista National Liberation Army.

In that same month Apple Computer, Inc., changed its ad featuring the Dalai Lama for the Asian market and substituted Amelia Earhart, presumably so as not to offend the Tibetanpersecuting Chinese. In June Bishop Zeng Jingmu, seventy-eight, was put under house arrest after serving thirty-two years in prison. William Donahue of the Catholic League for Religion and Civil Rights, called anti-Catholicism "the newest respectable form of bigotry".

In July altar wine sparked dispute among Indians who want Christian churches removed from the list of official places of worship. One person was injured and three hundred Bibles were burned. Christians make up only two percent of people in India.

Wuille Ruiz Figueroa was released from a Peruvian prison after serving five years for allegedly possessing "subversive material", and in Saudi Arabia twenty were deported for distributing Christian material and worshiping together as Christians. In Ireland there were three thousand parades commemorating the defeat in 1690 of the Irish Catholics by the English Orangemen.

In September noted Bangladesh writer Taslima Nasrim returned from exile to visit her dying mother. In Indonesia three million ethic Chinese Christians rioted. In Iran Ruhollah Rowhani was hanged for the crime of converting a Moslem to Baha'i.

On November 15, sixty thousand United States churches prayed for the estimated two hundred million suffering religious persecution on the International Day of Prayer for the Persecuted.

[The International Day of Prayer for the Persecuted Church started in 1996 and continues to this day.]

Holidays Not Only Happy, But Holy (December 1998)

Ann Perle has noted, not in any religious publication, but in *Workforce* that it is at this time of year that people are most involved in the exchange of goodwill, both by exchange of tangible goods and by messages of peace and good tidings. Some employees, she writes, even mention the intangibles, saying they want to give integrity and understanding and receive fairness and respect.

The holidays do bring families together for at least the possibility for such exchanges. Almost seventy-five percent visit their families at Christmas, sixty-five percent do so at Thanksgiving and fifty-nine percent on New Year's Day. Seventy-eight percent of those visiting stay with the family at Christmas, nearly as many, seventy-two percent, do so at Thanksgiving and sixty-four on New Year's.

Keeping Christ in Christmas and the holidays holy days is not without its struggles. Last year, the U. S. Court of appeals in Jersey City, NJ, sided with the American Civil Liberties Union to allow the removal of all religious symbols from public grounds against the objections of the Jersey City Religious Liberty Defense Fund.

Mayor Bret Schundler, who may seek the Republican nomination for governorbin 2001, spoke out strongly on the continuing struggle. "While we won in District Court in '96, the Court of Appeals reversed the earlier ruling ... and in so doing, the judge took a swipe at Supreme Court Justice Sandra Day O'Connor's ruling in the Pawtucket case. This si the height of judicial activism, where judges are so radical, they not only toss out precedents of a generation ago, but rulings made only a few years ago."

According to the Supreme Court, the U. S. Constitution requires employers to accommodate all their employees' religious practices, not just those of the majority. That would include: the all-American holiday Thanksgiving (fourth Thursday in November), the pagan Solstice (December 21), the Christian Christmas (December 25 to January 6), the Jewish Hannukkah (Kislev 25 to Tevet 2 or 3), the African-American Kwanza (December 26 to January 1) and New Year's Eve and Day (December 31 and January 1).

This goes far beyond the demographic shifts forcing many groups and organizations to greater understanding and respect. The Foodservice and Hospitality Alliance is dealing with more African-American and Hispanic employees. The Tourism and Economic Summit and Trade Show has had to address problems of non-American travelers.

Metropolitan Life figures that by 2050, forty-seven percent of the United States will be non-white, that is, Native American, Asian, African-American or Hispanic. Most of the cultural diversity, however is concentrated in a few gateway cities. Los Angeles, for example, accounts for twenty percent of U. S. Hispanics.

Last year Castro granted limited public celebrations of Cristmas after the Pope's first-ever visit to Communist Cuba; Clinton extended the Christmas holiday to Friday, December 26, making it a four-day celebration, a situation which will occur again in 2003. This year, Christmas and New Year's are part of three-day weekends.

Even in Taiwan, December 25, has been declared a holiday, albeit as Constitution Day. That's in addition to the second Saturday in the month Lien Chan has already given workers off.

The *Wall St. Journal* has published the not-so-frivolous solution to the over-commercial-ization of Christmas proposal separating the religious holiday of Christmas from the secular holiday, "excessmas". This is a proposal quite workable at a grassroots, individual and family level.

Cross-cultural understanding and respect, particularly during this holiday season, can spread as never before because of the internet, telecommunications, the global marketplace. In the next census in the year 2000, multiple racial categories will be allowed, reflecting a truer image of America, diverse yet united states. The Los Angeles diocese already celebrates Christmas with a church family including a hundred two ethnic groups -- a great opportunity to be truly catholic.

[At the 2017 Christmas Vigil Mass Pope Francis proclaimed, "The faith we proclaim tonight makes us see God present in all those situations where we think he is absent."]

Christians Bear One Another's Burdens (September 1998)

Alternatives to insurance are springing up. Many are getting tired of supporting the secular insurance system which they believe subsidizes ungodly and unhealthy life-styles.

Rev. Bruce Hawthorn tells how in one week in 1980 his four-year-old daughter broke her arm, his seven-year-old son had appendicitis, his fourteen-year-old son cracked his cheekbone in a playground accident and his nineteen-year-old daughter wrecked the car! When he first tried to organize a cooperative for medical expenses, the lawyer told him it was legal in Ohio, but that he thought all the people would get sick at the same time and not follow through by sending gifts.

In the next year, his wife and little girl were killed in a van accident. When supporters of his home for recovering alcoholics heard of his need, Rev. Hawthorn learned it could work. The fifty-four thousand dollar hospital bill was paid in forty-five days and he says was "bathed with emotional and spiritual support from people across the nation who had never met me." It reminds one of the first Century Gentile Christians' aid to the Jewish Christians.

The first newsletter had a response rate of ninety-three percent of two hundred twelve subscribers. It is now up to seventy thousand.

Subscribers to Christian Brotherhood Newsletter receive the newsletter which reports on current evens around the Christian world, gives the name of a Christian in need and are encouraged to pray and respond to a Christian in need. The subscriber might pray for the person, send a card or letter of encouragement or a financial gift. There is also a provision for needs above the hundred twenty-five thousand dollar limit, the Brother's Keeper program.

Subscribers in need are encouraged to pay their medical bills as much as they can and trust that God will provide for the rest.

The most significant difference from the secular insurance system (aside from the encouragement to pray) is the final statement on the form which a subscriber signs: "I attest that all participating adults are Christians living by Biblical principles, attend church regularly and totally abstain from alcohol, tobacco, illegal drugs and a homosexual life-style."

The Christian Care Medical Ministry is identical in its basic purpose, expressed in Galatians 6:2, "Bear ye one another's burdens." It is a ministry of the American Evangelistic Association and has a fifty-five member Board of Overseers (many of whom are doctors) to oversee the members' stewardship. For catastrophic bills above fifty thousand dollars, it has a back-up carrier. It has a twenty-four-hour prayer chain, publishes a health newsletter and encourages use of life-style centers. It claims a ninety-eight percent participation ratye from its hundreds of member families.

On their form the applicant must affirm the statement: "All persons listed on this form believe that the body is the temple of the Holy Spirit, to be kept pure. They do not practice a homosexual life-style. They do not use tobacco or illegal drugs, nor do they abuse alcohol, abiding by the rules of the local church to which they belong and have confirmation from their pastor."

[Christian Brotherhood Newsletter, now Christian Healthshare Ministries, was sued for fifteen million dollars in 2001 for misuse of funds. Only those cooperatives active before 1999 are exempt from government mandated penalties and some have been shut down by other judges.]

Men Are Answering the Call (August 1998)

At the Answer the Call men's conference in April, Fr. Jim Willig described the end of the millennium as "decades of crisis of manhood", yet said, "God is doing something here not to change this city, this state or even this country, but the whole world through men who are meeting in Cincinnati." He backed up this claim with the fact that this area has more small men's groups than any other in which the Answer the Call conferences have been held, fifty in two dioceses.

There were eleven thousand men, more than a hundred priests and the Knights of Columbus on the floor and in the air swallows who nested near the altar.

Jerry Faust, former Notre Dame football coach, said that winning the championship there in the Crown arena eleven years ago wasn't nearly as important as winning with the men there that day.

Admiral Jeremiah Denton confessed, "I've learned more here than I'm going to teach." Yet he promised that just as God had done for him through his more than seven years as a P. O. W., "He's going to answer beyond your questioning."

Brown spoke on a call to true success. He'd looked up the definition of "successful" in the 1806 Webster dictionary and compared it to the modern edition. Then it meant fortunate, happy, kind, prosperous; now fame and wealth.

Among other stories Brown told of Paul Anderson, who believed he could do all things through God Who strengthens. From a little schoolboy whose pencils were broken by a bully, he became the world's strongest man, shattering an 1896 record by lifting, carrying and holding six thousand, two hundred seventy pounds.

Scott Hahn, author of many books, including *A Father Who Keeps His Promises*, referred to the Paul Anderson story by declaring, "My older Brother Jesus, is the strongest man in the world. He carried more than six thousand pounds on His; He carried the weight of the world's sins."

Hahn explained that the Father's love is not in spite of our weakness, but through it. We are only strong when we admit our weakness. He shared how he was taught to forgive by his father being someone who needed to be forgiven, yet it is still a daily struggle. He also advised five ways to strengthen the bonds of family: "I love you.", "Thank you.", "Forgive me. I'm sorry.", "Tell me about your day." and the hardest, "I'd be glad to!"

Fr. Tom Forrest, founder of Evangelization 2000, taught on the call to discipleship, noting that all the movie portrayals of Jesus and the apostles make the mistake of having them walk beside him. Disciples always followed their master. They were were almost indistinguishable from slaves and their master.

We should not, he said, be ashamed to make the sign of the cross in public. It says, "I am a disciple of the Man of the cross." Jesus is the greatest success the world will ever know. When Jesus told His disciples to come follow Him, it meant live His life, share His life, learning to eat, talk, forgive, love like He did, like Elisha did with Elijah.

Like John the Baptist we understandably do not feel worthy even to be a slave, let alone a disciple, yet Jesus washed His disciples' feet. We too must "Go, do it!", he says.

Admiral Denton, author of *When Hell Was in Session*, says we face a more hideous challenge than communism in the moral corruption he saw upon returning to the "one nation under God" he had sworn allegiance to. His Coalition for Decency couldn't get the denominations to work together. Judges overturned the law they managed to get passed to help inform young pregnant women.

The memorized prayers of the Catholic Church, the only ones he could manage during his imprisonment, to the Sacred Heart, to Mary, the rosary, the morning offering, aspirations, were what he'd prayed and he testified, "They work." His survival through this ordeal, he believes, "proves the total validity of the Catholic Church. It is the one, holy, catholic and apostolic Church. This is the Faith and the gates of hell shall not prevail against it no matter what."

[In 2009 the name of Evangelization 2000 was changed to Evangelization2033, to prepare for that Jubilee.]

Book Prepares for End of Millennium (March 1998)

The title of Fr. Richard Foley's book, *Mary and the Eucharist*, is an obvious reference to John Bosco's well-known prophetic dream of the Two Columns In the Sea. To quote Fr. Foley, it "is closely relevant to the present-day crisis of faith in the Church. The prophecy is most reassuring, because it indicates that the Church will be dramatically delivered from the present crisis and its deliverance will come about through a twin devotion to the Blessed Sacrament and Mary."

We face this crisis because "hatred of the faith -- particularly Eucharistic faith -- burns and rages in Lucifer, head of the fallen angels, and he kindles it in every willing instrument he can find on Earth." Atrocities in Bosnia or Rwanda or Sudan are more visible examples, but countless sacrilegious Communions every week and the continuing disunity of Christ's Body are worse. "If anyone eats this cup unworthily, he will be held to account. Unless we eat His Flesh and drink His Blood, we will not have life in ourselves."

Fr. Foley goes on, however to tell another John Bosco story about the Basilica of Our Lady, Help of Christians in Turin, that is even more relevant to our time. John Bosco arranged that two large metal banners be placed on his façade. One the victory of Lepanto with a "1571" and the other "19" followed by two dots. As Fr. Foley points out, the only reasonable conclusion to be drawn from this is that Mary's next major victory will take place in one of the few years remaining to our Twentieth Century.

To further prove his conclusion, Fr. Foley makes use of many sources. He quotes the Scriptures a hundred twenty-six times in a hundred ninety-eight pages. He references the Catechism of the Catholic Church, the Vatican II documents, several popes (John XXIII, John Paul II, Leo the Great, Leo XIII, Pius IX, Pius X, Pius XII, Paul VI) and others including Archbishop Fulton J. Sheen, Sr. Faustina Kowalska, Mother Theresa, Padre Pio, Sr. Briege McKenna, the Medjugorje visionaries and even Sergei Bulgakov, the Russian Orthodox theologian.

Bulgakov, for example, wrote in his *Le Paraclet*, "The Holy Spirit ... abides in the ever-virgin Mary as in a holy temple, while her human personality seems to become transparent to Him and provide Him with a human counterpart." If so, then so too must any believing Communicant.

The book is not all dry theology however. Fr. Foley also quotes from several Christian poets: Christina Rosetti, David Gascoyne, Edith Sitwell, Gerard Manley Hopkins, John Donne, Richard Crashaw and Robert Southwell. The last such excerpt comes from Hopkins, "In the gardens of God, in the daylight divine, Show me thy Son, mother of mine. In the gardens of God, in the daylight divine, I shall worship His wounds with thee, mother of mine."

[Fr. Foley has also written *The Drama of Medjugorje, God 2000, Mary Calls to Holiness and St. Joseph, Patron of Triumph*.]

Play Together, Stay Together (December 1997)

"Jingle All the Way" is out this year in video to remind everyone, as if anyone needed reminding, how hectic finding that one particular gift can be. An alternative might be to get a board game the whole family could play together.

In *A Rhyme in Time*, up to sixteen players create four-line poems based on words taken from a playing card, recite popular rhymes or challenge their rhyming vocabulary. In *A to Z* players try to cover as many initial letters as possible on the board.

Articulation Family has bridges, traps, and pits that test players' knowledge of slang, jargon, vocabulary and spelling using multiple choice cards. *Ancient Board Games* includes "Hounds and Jackals", "Menet", "Senet" and the "Roual Game of Ur" that the Israelites might have played in Egypt or Babylon.

At Whit's End is a game based on the popular radio in which players try to find Mr. Whittaker by spelling WHIT with game cards earned by answering Bible questions or playing charades. The circular board game *Baliwick* earned Parent's Choice award. Players move toward the center on colored spaces, backward on white ones and up on stepping vstones without getting bumped off.

Many boldly promote Scripture. *Bible Battle* can be played by up to twelve players, testing Bible knowledge. *Bible Baseball* plays and scores like baseball with teams earning runs by combining other "hits". *Bible Bingo* is for youngsters, teaching them colors, letters, numbers and Scripture. *Bible Charades* has two hundred category cards and a timer. In *Bible Land Adventure* the goal is to reach Heaven by moving through the Bible. Heaven's also the goal in *Bible Trivia* for older players. *Family Bible Challenge* is on CD ROM.

Bibleopoly, as might be guessed, is somewhat similar to *Monopoly* but players build churches and draw cards such as "Go meditate! Lose one turn." *The Good Steward Game* is another *Monopoly* variation.

Card Caper uses a board which gives instructions regarding players' dealt hands, all in an attempt to discover one's opponents' cards. *Illusions*, for up to six players, builds a new board game each game and then uses illusion interpretation to determine moves. *In Other Words* challenges players to paraphrase Scripture passages, hymn titles and books of the Bible.

Kit & Caboodle, for up to three players, requires logic and perception of science and nature. *Knowledge* is called "the educational game for children and their parents". *Life Stories -- Christian Version* makes witnessing fun. *Origins* does not deal with evolution but with eord and phrase origins. *Pilgrim's Progress* is based on John Bunyan's allegory, the quest for the Celestial City.

Quadwrangle, for up to four players, uses die and strategy. *Quickword* mixes logic, strategy and word skills and the catch that only a players unique words score. *Redemption: The City of Bondage* requires players to free Lost Souls in a city overrun by evil cults using Faith, Wisom and Deed. *Rhymation* gives clues answered by amusing rhymes, such as "obese feline" giving "fat cat".

Sequence combines cards and board game for up to twelve players. *Swoggle* is a *Scrabble* variant for four players that uses dice. *The Ten Commandments Bible Game* requires cooperation from up to six players. *The New Kid's Choices* game is about young people applying Bible principles to everyday life, for up to ten players. *The Tower of Babble* uses "acting out" to bridge the language gap and build the tower. When it is everyone, up to six players, are winners. *Tribond* asks such questions as "What do Hilary Clinton, a duck and Congress have in common? (The answer: bills)

The Ungame -- Christian version probes the players, up to six, lightheartedly and seriously. *Ultimate Stratego* simulates battle between four sides, not just two, as in the original *Stratego*. Players of *Words from Words* do just that, make smaller words from a larger word, determined by game cards, timer and dice. *Words War III* combines chess, word games and handicapping. *Zypher* combines time-limited anagrams and board play.

Ex-homosexuals Persecuted (August 1997)

Cincinnati's own *Everybody's News* recently bashed Jerry Armelli's local ministry to homosexuals, Prodigal Ministries, but only by resorting to attacks on his character and appearance. A reporter, he says, came in for two private counseling sessions, but did not participate in the group meetings where everyone must sign an agreement to abide by rulkes like confidentiality.

Meanwhile on the Internet Doug Upchurch is developing an "ex-ex" site. After trying for over twelve years to overcome his own homosexual addiction, he's promoting the idea that "gays" cannot change. Of ex-homosexuals, he says, "Either they're greatly in denial and the a living a life to satisfy the perceived demands of a harsh God or they are bisexusal, which is really a rare possibility, or they were really never gay in the first place."

The Catechism of the Catholic Church, on the other hand, says, "By the virtues of self-mastery that teach [homosexuals] inner freedom, at times by the support of disinterested friendship, by prayer and sacramental graces, they can and should gradually and resolutely approach Christian perfection." Based on Ron Brassgalla'a survey of other Exodus agencies, it is being misreported that Exodus agencies have had a hundred forty-seven or seventy percent that have failed, implying this was because the ministries' leaders had failed to so master their selves.

The truth is that that number was actually built up with twenty-five who were never associated with Exodus, twenty-seven still active though no longer an Exodus referral, eleven which just changed their address, five which just changed their names and thirty-seven because of reasons unrelated to any kind of sexuality, such as deaths, illness, etc. Only thirteen actually failed because of a return to active homosexuality and five of those were in the first three years, 1976 to 1979. Since then only five percent, not seventy percent, have failed because an "ex-gay" became "gay" again.

The Gay and Lesbian Alliance Against Defamation (GLAAD) included Exodus as a "Hate Wb Site" along with Knights of the Ku Klux Klan and Skinheads USA's, but its testimpnies speak rather of God's saving love.

Perry Desmond tells in "The Final Transformation" of his quitting the university at eighteen to work as a waiter at a "gay" bar, then as a male prostitute. He joined the Navy, was married and divorced, discharged, but then returned to his old life as a prostitute and drag queen. When his lover Wayne left, he attempted suicide. Three days later Wayne called, saying, "I'm saved. I got Jesus in my heart!" They went to church frequently and he began wearing men's clothes for the first time in six years.

When John Paulk was only five years old, his parents divorced. His first sexual experience was with the school psychiatrist at ten and his first drink at fourteen. When he asked Jesus into his heart at fifteen, he "backslid" six months later for lack of support. Paulk, like Desmond dropped out of college, drank, had a "gay" relationship that only lasted a short time, tried suicide, then became an eighty dollar per hour prostitute and drag queen. As "Candi", he even fooled his parents.

Making the spiritual steps of AA helped John realize there was no person in the shell and he could say, "Candi, I don't need you anymore." He writes in "Taking Off the Mask", "It felt like ten tons were being lifted off my back." He started reading the Bible again, threw away his homosexual paraphernalia and porn. "I had a difficult time accepting the reality of His total love and acceptance of me" and the love of and from Anne also an ex-homosexual. His father and mother accepted the Lord the night of their wedding. "In the past, there were many masks I hid behind to protect myself from being hurt again, But now I see that they only stood in the way of God's love reaching through to me."

Sinclair "Sy" Rogers in "Man in the Mirror" tells how he was sexually molested at three by a "friend" of the family. His mother was killed in an auto accident when he was five. As an adult he became a crossdressing member of Metropolitan Community Church, Honolulu.

He didn't believe it when two friends, a "married" "gay" couple, wrote they hadturned away from the life-style. He continued to live and work as a woman. After eighteen months, three days after reading Jeremiah 29:13, John Hopkins stopped doing Sexual Reassignment Surgery. After he received the Holy Spirit, he "established healthy relationships with men and homosexual yearnings began dissolving." After three years he married his prayer partner. He founded Exodus International and now directs Choices. He sums it all up with Proverbs 14:12, "There is a way that seems right to a man, but the end leads to death," but Jesus is the Way, the Truth and the Life." (John 14:6)

[When Exodus International shut down in 2013, the organization's president Alan Chambers said, "We're not negating the ways God used Exodus to positively affect thousands of people, but ... For quite some time, we've been imprisoned in a worldview that's neither honoring toward our fellow human beings, nor biblical." It was reborn as WeSpeakLove.org, but not soon enough to prevent Rogers from abandoning Christianity.]

In God We Still Trust (May 1997)

The theme for this year's National Day of Prayer, May 1, is "In God We Trust", words inscribed in both the House and Senate chambers. On November 26, 1789, President Washington called all citizens to "unite in most humbly offering our prayers and supplications to the great Lord and Ruler of Nations, and beseech Him to pardon our national and other transgressions," He called for prayer days again on January 1 and February 19, 1795.

President John Adams called for April 25, 1799, to "be observed throughout the United States of America as a day of solemn humiliation, fasting and prayer, that the citizen ... call to mind our numerous offenses against the most high God, confess them before Him with sincere penance, implore His pardoning mercy, through the Great Mediator and Redeemer." President James Madison issued four such proclamations.

In 1814 the people of New Orleans filled their churches and prayed for God's help against the twenty thousand invading British troops. The Ursuline nuns promised Our Lady of Prompt Succor that if the Americans won the battle, a solemn high Mass would be offered every January 8 and in just twenty-five minutes General Andrew Jackson's poorly armed, poorly trained six thousand militiamen won. Afterward Jackson visited the sisters and acknowledged his victory was due to God's help.

In 1862 many people began to request that our coinage make reference to God. At the request of the Senate. President Lincoln proclaimed April 30, 1863, "a day of national humiliation, fasting and prayer" saying, "It is the duty of nations as well as of men to owe their dependence upon the overruling power of God, to confess their sins and transgressions in humble sorrow yet with assured hope that genuine repentance will lead to mercy and pardon and to recognize the sublime truth, announced in the Holy Scriptures and proven by all history: that those nations only are blessed whose God is the Lord."

Dr. Phineas Gurley, Lincoln's pastor at the New York Avenue Presbyterian Church "claimed that the death of Willie Lincoln in 1862 and the visit to the Gettysburg battlefield in 1863 finally led Lincoln to personal faith in Christ. Gurley also indicated that Lincoln planned to make a public profession of his faith at some time in the near future -- a future which never came."

"God our Trust" and "God and our Country" were other mottos proposed before "in God We Trust" first appeared in 1864 and was formally approved in 1865. Tho motto was dropped in 1907 on American sculptor Augustus Saint-Gaudens' new coin design. President Theodore Roosevelt mistakenly answered an objecting minister that was "no legal warrant for putting the motto on the coins." In 1908 Congress restored the motto.

In April 1917 America entered World War I. On May 5, Pope Benedict XV ordered a message sent to the world's bishops, of "our ardent desire that recourse be made to the Heart of Jesus, Throne of grace, and that to the Throne recourse be made through Mary ... and the peace we asked for be obtained for our agitated world." Eight days later Mary appeared at Fatima asking for prayers and repentance and promising, "If my requests are granted, Russia will be converted and there will be peace," a promise still to be fulfilled.

On the site of America's bombing of Hiroshima that ended World War II was Our Lady's Memorial Shrine for World Peace. In the Marian Year, 1954, it was dedicated and since then cloistered nuns pray there continuously night and day.

In that same year, both houses passed a resolution to build a prayer room in the U. S. Capitol building. In the next year Congress extended the act to include paper money and mad it the official national motto in 1956. In all seven pre-1981 editions of The Capitol the prayer room's strain glass window was described as bearing the prayer from Psalm 16:1; "Preserve me, O God, for in Thee do I put my trust," and the scene of George Washington kneeling in prayer.

[Every president since 1952 has signed a National Day of Prayer proclamation. The theme for 2018 was Ephesians 4:3, "Making every effort to keep the unity of the Spirit through the bond of peace."]

Jesus Is Alive (March 1997)

Easter's much more than a parade; it's the occasion for the greatest story ever told -- and still disbelieved. Irving Berlin's "Easter Parade" (1948) with Fred Astaire and Judy Garland -- and most Easter parades -- have little, if anything, to do with Mary Magdalene's message: "Jesus is alive!"

A more truly Easter musical would be "Easter: A Play for Singers" by John Masefield (1929) or even "The Easter Promise", the fictional quest of Jeremy for the King. Another more serious, animated video is "The Easter Story" in the Greatest Adventure series by Hannah-Barbera. Books like *Miracle in Jerusalem: An Easter Story* by Ross Yockey also try to retell to children this greatest story ever told.

The ending of Cecil B. DeMille's lavish, yet reverent, "The King of Kings" (1927) or last hour of the 1961 "talkie" remake remain inspirational even on a small screen because of the story. It's a story that has been told with still pictures too as in *Last Hours With Jesus: The Passion Play* photos by Max and Hilda Jocoby, text by Lawrence F. Michlon (1982), *the Easter Story* from the National Gallery of Art, *And the Third Day, a Record of Hope and Fulfillment* pictures chosen by John Rolhenstein (1948) or simply the children's book *The Easter Story* by Carol Heyer.

Since "The Dialogue of the Three Maries and the Angels" (925), many plays have retold the Gospels' story in many ways: *Easter Wings, a Play in One Act* by Dorothy C. Allen (1944), *The Redemption Easter Play* translated from Low German by A. E. Zucker (1941), *As Easter Dawns, a Religious Play in Two Episodes* by Mary Bennet Harrison (1936), *The Glowing Cross, a Miracle Play for Easter* by Ethel Bain (1932) and *Darkness and Dawn: the Easter Evening* by Frederica Le Fevre Bellamy (1925).

Some books combine drama and meditation: *The Cross and Our Witness: Dramas and Meditations for Lent and Easter* by Harlan F. Heier (1990), *What Did Jesus Do? Meditations and Dramas for Lent* by W. A. Poovey (1968), *He Is Not Here! He Is Risen! A Dramatic Service for Easter Containing the Ritual of the Kindling of the Holy Fire and a Service for the Dedication of an Easter Garden* by Paul Nagy (1946).

Others include collections such as *Song of the Morning, Stories and Poems for Easter by E. B. White, Angela Elwell Hunt, C. S. Lewis and other favorite authors* compiled by Pat Alexander or *He Is Risen, a Heartworming Collection of Easter Traditions, Stories, Prayers, Poetry, Recipes and More* by Bonnie Harvey.

This Easter 1997 is the earliest until 2005. The date of Easter was defined in 325 by the first Council of Nicaea as the first Sunday after the pascal or first spring moon. So it was somewhat removed from from the pagan dawn goddesses' feasts, Eostre's in April, Austron's at the equinox. It is also different from the Orthodox Easter date. All Eastertide is, however connected to spring, new life, new light, pilgrimages, the first Passover.

Decorated Easter eggs, symbolizing new life, came into use in A. D. 700. There are said to still be ten missing bejeweled Easter eggs of the Tsars worth a million dollars each.

Easter water ws the water blessed on Holy Saturday in connection with the blessing of the Baptismal Font and set aside for use in the home before the special baptismal water blessing and different from "ordinary" holy water.

The Easter lilies, with their trumpet-shaped flowers, are not the only flowers associated with the feast. Other spring-blooming flowers are the Easter anemone or pasqueflowee, the Easter bell or greater stitchwort and the white rosette Easter daisy. There is also an Easter cactus and even an Easter mackerel. Easter Island or Rapa Nul was so called because it was discovered by Dutch explorers on Easter 1722.

[In 2004 "The Passion of the Christ" came out and in 2016 "Risen".]

Christmas Time Is Storytime (December 1996)

Christmas is the time for sharing good old stories, the first Christmas story in Luke or Matthew's accounts or later ones in books or fills. Such stories are timeless.

The family-friendly 1937 "Heidi" starting Shirley Temple, is now colorized. The 1952 version with Elizabeth Sigurd was filmed on location in Switzerland. Then, too, there's the 1986 made-for-television version Earl Hammer, Jr., scripted. All retell Johanna Spyri's tale of faith and the reunion of a loving granddaughter and grandfather.

"A Christmas to Remember" (1978) is based on Glendon Swartout's generation gap crossing *The Melodeon;* in "Christmas Eve" (1986), a not-so-young Loretta Young tries to reunite her long-estranged family. "Christmas Lilies of the Field" (1979) reunites an older Mother Marie and Homer Smith.

The colorized "Meet John Doe" (1941) by Frank Capra with Gary Cooper and Barbara Stanwyck puts corrupt politics and lost idealism, still as relevant now, into perspective with the climactic scene as Christmas church bells ring. Thje special midnight Christ's Mass (Christmas) reminds, in and outside the film, of the One Who came as Light in thedarkness, as the Psalmist says, when the night was half spent.

There are several film versions of Charles Dicken's 1843 "A Christmas Carol;; in which all the action takes place on the eve before. The best may be the 1951 British "Scrooge" with Alastair Sims. There are also American versions, the colorized 1938 one with Reginald Owen and the 1984 made-for-television on with George C. Scott.

"Penny Serenade" (1941) with Irene Dunne and Cary Grant, now also colorized, tells of a couple's struggles with the death of one child and the adoption of another, including a Christmas play. The idea of playing out the first Christmas goes back to Saint Fracis, who in 1223 with the approval of Pope Honorius III, staged the first manger scene.

"The Gift of the Magi", one of the stories in the 1952 "O. Henry's Full House", is based on the story of true love and gift-giving from The Four Million (1906). The practice of gift giving had become more widespread, not just for or especially for children, when in 1844 W. W. Dobson sent a card illustrated in the spirit of the feast, the first Christmas card. The now colorized "It's A Wonderful Life" (1939) by Frank Capra again, with James Stewart and Donna Reed, is about friendship and family, life and death. It was based on Philip Van Stern's short story, "The Greatest Gift", originally written as a Christmas card.

The association of Christmas with Saint Nicholas (Dutch "Santa Claus") and children began, not with his life of early veneration in the Forth Century, but in the stories of his appearances during the Middle Ages. His popularity was further promoted by the 1823 poem "The Night Before Christmas or A Visit from Saint Nicholas" by Clement Clarke Moore and the famous New York Sun editorial ninety-nine years ago. The custom of giving gifts to children on their patron's feast, December 6, continues though much replaced by the December 25 date.

The traditional date in the West of December 25 for Jesus' birth was promoted by Saint John Chrystostom ("The Golden-Tongued"), based on Zechariah, John the Baptism's father, entering the temple on the gay of atonement, which in A. d. 386 fell on September 25. In the East it is traditionally celebrated on "Little Christmas", Epiphany, January 6, based on the Furius Dionysius Filocalus' earlier chronicle from A. D. 354.

[In 2005 Andrew Adamson's adaptation of "The Lion, the Witch and the Wardrobe" came out at Christmas.]

Vitamins Are Pro-Life (August 1996)

Vitamins were discovered exactly one hundred years ago, but on;ly gained public attention when they were proven essential to good health in 1911 and renamed vitamins, from "vita" for life.

Vitamin A, carotene, the carrot vitamin, is also called the anti-infection vitamin since it helps resist infection. It is also essential for night vision. Vitamin A deficiency can lead to diaper rash, stunted growth or prematurely aged skin. On the other hand, an overdose can lead to fatigue, hair loss, insomnia or vitamin B deficiency. The body, by God's design, uses vitamins together in the proportions naturally found in foods. Vitamin A is stored in the liver so daily intake is not necessary as with many other vitamins. You can get it in dark green vegetables (especially kale and parsley), fish liver oil, egg yolk and milk.

The B complex vitamins (and C) are water soluble and so can be lost into cooking water. B-1 or thiamin deficiency may lead to fatigue, nerve pain or numbness, even beriberi. You can get it in brown, not white, rice, wheat germ, brewer's yeast, sunflower seeds, legumes (beans, peas) and oranges. Five centuries ago English peasants consumed more than twice what Americans do now.

B-2, formerly called G, also called riboflavin, is the yellowish, florescent green pigment in milk, You can also find it in lean meat, almonds, mushrooms and turnip greens. Deficiency may lead to a sore mouth, itchy or light-sensitiv eyes. It too is sensitive to sunlight and rapidlybdestroyed by exposure.

B-6 or pyridoxine helps form antibodies and red blood cells. Deficiency may lead to muscular weakness, depression, even convulsions or anemia. You can find it in meat, blackstrap molasses, whole grains, nuts and brewer's yeast.

B-12 or cobalamin is used by all cells, but especially in bone marrow, the gastrointestinal tract, the nervous system and red blood cells. It can be found in meats, fish, eggs and soybeans. Most is synthesized however by intestinal bacteria. B-15 or pangamic acid is found in brewer's yeast and seeds. B-17, the laetrile cancer treatment, contains cyanide and is found in apricot pits.

C or ascorbic acid helpsheal wounds, prevents bleeding and scurvy and propotes iron absorption. More is required with hot weather, air pollution (including smoking) or aspirin and, like the B complex, during stress. It is however found in most fruits and vegetables.

D regulates calcium and phosphorus and prevents rickets. Sunlight can change skin cholesterol into D, but you can also get it in fish, liver oil, egg yolks, organ meats and milk.

E or tocopherol prevents the breakdown of A and red blood cells and aids in healing. Deficiency may lead to premature births, infrequent ovulation or other reproductive problems.

You can find it in wheat germ, whole grains, organ meats, rice, fruits, peanuts, eggs and green leafy vegetables.

H or biotin aids in formation and burning up of fatty acids and is blocked by raw egg white. K prevents bleeding by aiding clotting. It is destroyed by mineral oil, alcohol, alkali and light and blocked by sulfa drugs and antibiotics. You can find it in green leafy vegetables, alfalfa sprouts, fats, oats, wheat, rye, nuts and seeds.

P, a bioflavonoid that prevents bleeding, is water soluble and found in citrus juices. PP, the pellagra preventative, niacin, is found in lean meat, fish, legumes, whole grains and peanuts. Q too aids clotting and is found in organ meats, green leafy vegetables and seeds. T, which aids blood coagulation, was originally found in termites, yeast and molds and later also in sesame seeds and egg yolks. U helps treat ulcers and is found in cabbage and alfalfa.

Last, but certainly not least, is "vitamin L", Love of which there has never been an overdose.

Film List Aids Viewers (July 1996)

The recent Vatican movie list was compiled after consultation with film experts. Factors included opinion polls and availability. The committee divided the films into three categories: art, religion and values, all of which have suffered in too many recent films. This review does not cover all the firlm on the list, but the following fifty-three hours worth may be useful when selecting video tapes.

"A Man for All Seasons" (1966 British, 120 minutes) is based on the play about Thomas More's conflict with Henry VIII that led to his martyrdom. It's six Oscars included best actor, cinematography, costumes, director, picture and screenplay.

"Andrei Rublev" (1966 Russian, 185 minutes) was not released by the Soviet authorities until 1971. The historical drama focuses on the famous Fifteenth Century icon painter's choice between reflecting or affecting social and political change.

"Babette's Feast" (1987 Danish, 102 minutes), based on a short story published in Ladies Home Journal, won a Best Foreign Film Oscar. The tale of two ministers' daughters and the Parisian refugee they take in is told with subtlty, wonder and humor.

"Ben Hur" (1959 American, 212 minutes) is, of course, based on the play and had been filmed before in 1943, telling of the long journey of a Jewish family to Christ.

"Chariots of Fire" (1081 British, 123 minutes) is based on the true story of two runners in the 1924 Olympics, Eric Liddell, a devoted Scot, and Harold Abrahams, a driven Jewish Cambridge student. It won Oscars for best costumes, poicture, score and script.

"Ghandi" (1982 British-Indian, 188 minutes), Mohandas K. Ghandi's peaceful fight for freedom, won eight Oscars including best actor, director, picture and screenplay.

"Intolerance" (1916 American, 208 minutes), a landmark epic, interweaves four stories of intolerance from ancient Babylon to the present.

"It's A Wonderful Life" (1946 American, 129 minutes) shows the changes in a would-be suicide's world had he never been born. It was based on the short story, "The Greatest Gift", written on a Christmas card.

"Nazarin" (1958 Spanish, 92 minutes) tells of a saintly priest's efforts to instruct and his rejection by hypocritical peasants. It was filmed in Mexico.

"On the Waterfront" (1954 American, 108 minutes) honestly tells of the New York harbor workers. It won eight Oscars (best actor, art and set decoration, cinematography, director, editing, music, screenplay, story and supporting actress). It debuted Martin Balsam, Fred Gwynn, Pat Hingle and Eva Marie Saint.

"Open City" (1945 Italian, 105 minutes) tells of the underground during the Nazi occupation of Rome.

"Ordet" (1955 Danish, 125 minutes) was based on a play and had been filmed before in 1943. It tells this inspiring story of love and hatred, true and false religion in two rural families and ends in what has been called "a never-to-be-forgotten climactic scene".

"The Bicycle Thief" (1949 Italian, 90 minutes) simply and honestly tells how the bicycle theft of a working man's bicycle affects him and his son. It earned a special Oscar before there was a foreign film category.

"The Burmese Harp" (1956 Japanese, 116 minutes) tells of a Japanese private who takes on burying war casualties in 1945 Burma after a religious experience.

"The Gospel According to St. Matthew" (1966 Italian-French, 135 minutes), as the title implies, is based upon just the one Gospel. This and its all-amateur cast, including the Marxist director's mother, give it a quiet dignity not found in most other such films.

"The Mission" (1966 British, 125 minutes) tells of the Jesuits' struggle to live and preach the gospel in Brazil in the late Eighteenth Century, threatened by forces inside and out. Called literate, high-minded and finely performed, its cinematography won an Oscar.

"The Passion of Joan of Arc" (1928 French, 77 minutes) is based on the transcript of Joan's trial. Its use of close-ups was "groundbreaking".

"The Sacrifice" (1989 Swedish-French, 145 minutes) tells of an intellectual's sudden realization of his spiritual needs and his quest for faith.

"The Seventh Seal" (1957 Swedish, 96 minutes) tells of the unique tale of a disillusioned crusader who plays chess with Death. It made Ingmar Bergman known internationally.

"The Tree of the Wooden Clogs" (1978 Italian, 185 minutes)simply and beautifully tell of a year in the life of a peasant community about 1900.

"Therese" (1986 French, 91 minutes) tells of a young girl's intense desire to become wedded to Christ as a Carmelite nun.

[Both video tapes and DVDs are now less available with the advance of media technology, but these are worth hunting up.].

Astronomical Discoveries Glorify God (April 1996)

Early this year the *Galileo* probe sent back surprising discoveries from under the planet Jupiter's cloud cover. Over the last few years new planetoids have been found far away from the sun. New planets have also recently been discovered orbiting other stars. "The heavens declare the glory of God and the firmament proclaims His handiwork." (Psalm 19:1)

"There's always a sense of humility when the data come in," said *Galileo's* chief project scientist, Torrance Johnson. Jupiter's atmosphere proved more like the sun's than the astronomers had expected, with more hydrogen, few organic chemicals and no water. Water had been indicated by the *Voyager* and Shoemaker-Levy 9 data.

The planners had picked the probe site as typical. Yet *Galileo* found it denser, windier and with a hidden radiation belt. The belt's at least ten times as strong as Earth's. At the last measurement it was up to the pressure seven hundred fifty feet deep in our water oceans (twenty times surface normal) with three hundred thirty-five mile per hour winds and a temperature of three hundred degrees Fahrenheit. "We don't know," says Harald Fischer of University of Kiel, Germany, "where these high-energy particles come from." Meanwhile Richard Young, Ames Research Center, can only speculate, "Jupiter's winds appear to originate in the heat from the deep interior."

There will undoubtedly be more revelations as the orbiter that launched the probe continues to study Jupiter and its moons this year and next.

Four years ago an object orbiting beyond Pluto, forty-four times as far from the sun as Earth, was discovered by Jane Luu and David Jewitt of the University of Hawaii. Officially called 1992QB, they nicknamed the little planet "Smiley". The have now twenty more large objects out there and another eight other objects, "The things that astronomers are learning about the Kuiper belt are beyond what we had dreamt," Luu says. "What we thought of as a planet is probably just the biggest member of a rather large population of objects," up to ten billion.

Since 1993 five other objects have been discovered which cross the outer planet's orbits like Chiron (discovered in 1977) and red Pholus. They're now called Centaurs -- part planet, part frozen comet.

51 Pegasi B, 70 Virginis B and 47 Ursae Majoris B are the first planets discovering orbiting other stars. Michel Mayor and Didier Qureloz, Geneva Observatory, announced the first las October. Then in January Geoff Marcy, San Francisco State, and Paul Butler, University of California at Berkeley, announced the other two. Only the third one of the three is not surprising in some way. "It's the first planet that kind of looks like it would fit into our solar system," Butler says. Still it's three and a half times Jupiter's mass and only twice Earth's distance from the star. The second planet has been nicknamed "Goldilocks" because it, unlike Jupiter, may have liquid water. Its temperature is "just right" at a "lukewarm" hundred eighty-five degrees Fahrenheit.

Butler predicts that within a year more extrasolar planets will be known than there are in our solar system. With Pluto no longer countered as one, that'd be eight. "I'm confident that many new planets will be discovered in the coming years," Mayor agrees, since they've only analyzed half their data so far. Yet he adds, "The theorists are just now beginning to recognize that they need to invoke much more physics that had not been anticipated. It's time to pull back and realize that we've been too cocky."

[The largest of an estimated 44,000, Charikло is the largest known Centaur at about 250 kilometers in diameter. As this is written http://exoplanet.eu/catalog/ lists 3,824 planets in 2,859 planetary systems, all very different.]

Only Jesus Is The True Light (December 1995)

As we near winter solstice, we once again against remember Jesus, the Light of the Nations. The subject of light has been receiving much attention of late.

It seems to have begun with *Closer to the Light*. It and its sequel, *Transformed by the Light*, by Melvin More are rather sober collections of NDE (Near Death Experience) stories. It was followed by the more bizarre *Embraced by the Light* by Betty Jean Eadie with Curtis Taylor. It stayed five weeks as number one best seller. Bantam paid one and a half million dollars and the audio book rights went for a hundred thousand dollars, although the medical records which would document Eadie's alleged near death experience have not been made public.

Doug Grouthuis writes in his recently published *Deceived by the Light* of Alison Birman committing suicide six months after reading *Embraced by the Light*, days after her boyfriend had committed suicide. She wrote "God willing, I live." She apparently believed that she would live happily ever after even after suicide, the Mormon doctrine of eternal progression. He points out that according to the view given by Edie, everyone chooses their manner of death before birth, even the Holocaust victims.

Dick Baer, founder of the Ex-Mormon and Christian Alliance, called it a carefully crafted book of deception". Richard Abanes said the "Jesus" Betty Jean Eadie encountered was NOT the crucified Savior by a "happy tour guide".

As if to top Eadie came *Saved by the Light* by Dannion Brinkley with Paul Perry which told of his alleged experiences after dying twice after being struck by lightning through a telephone. He has predicted, among other things, a nuclear catastrophe in Norway before this year ends. *Beyond the Light* goes beyond Brinkley with three deaths. It's by Phyllis M. H. Atwater, a professional psychic (at two dollars ninety-five cents per minute). She describes hell, not heaven, with skulls and zombi-like people.

Light seems to be sought by everyone everywhere. *Traveling into the Light* by Martha Brooks tells stories of teens growing into adulthood, *I've Got the Light* by Charles M. Payne of the struggle for freedom by Blacks in Mississippi. *Standing in the Light* by Severt Yoing Bear and R. D. Theisz describes "the Lakota way of seeing", while *Coming to Light* edited by Brian Swann collects a selection of Native American literature.

"Blinded by the Light, Burnt by the Sun" is a film by Nikita Mikhalkov, *Walking for the Dark, Waiting for the Light* a novel of Czech black humor by Ivan Kl'ima. Messengers of the Light by Paul Maynlim is about Chinese Buddhists in India, while the same title by Terry Lynn Taylor is a guide to spiritual growth said to be from another source, angels. Sally A. Paulsell offers *Color and Light: Huxley's Pathway to Spiritual Reality* and Arthur Zajonc *Catching the Light: The Entwined History of Light and Mind.*

"Not only books but music reflect the search with "Looking for the Light", a country song by Rick Trevino, "Shine the Light" one by The Main Squeeze, while Hanoi's heavybmetal band is "The Light".

[Grouthuis has also written *Christian Apologetics: A Comprehensive Case for Biblical Faith*.]

The Truth About Pocahontas (October 1995)

Pocahontas, the animated heroine of Disney's "Pocahontas" does not bear much resemblance to Lady Rebbeca Matoaka Rolfe on whom the character is said to be based. Yet God turns all things to the good for those who love Him. All the hype has led Andy Holmes to write *Pocahontas and the True Story of An American Hero and Her Christian Faith*. He says this is an opportunity for parents to teach their children the truth when the children ask about Pocahontas whether they have seen the film or not. He advises that they should not see it so they won't have the misinformation to unlearn.

Little is known about this true Native American heroine. She did have the childhood nickname Pocahontas, "the playful one", but then so did other daughters of her father, Powhatan. Some doubt the legend that she saved the life of Captain John Smith of the Jamestown colony. The tale was not included in his own General History of Virginia. Others think that, if it did happen, it might have been a sort of initiation into the tribe rite and not an execution. In any case, in 1608 when it was supposed to have happened, she would have only been about twelve and Captain Smith at least twenty-eight.

The film annihilates this age difference and makes no mention of her conversion to Christianity or of her love and marriage to John Rolfe. It does not mention her visit to London, the first by an Indian, their documented plans to return to America as missionaries or her tragic death at twenty-two.

Disney's revisionist history prompted Michael Lind of New Republic to write "Dishonest Injun: Pocahontas Exposed" and Mike Clark of USA Today "A Low-key Romance That Ends

Too Soon". Joyce Purnick of the New York Times called the Disney character a "Barbie glamour girl", not much like the "robust" and "not pretty", but "adaptable and charming" Rebecca. Actually the films star's looks blend fifteen white, black and oriental models, but not any kind of Indian. Robert Eaglestaff objects to the animism exemplified in the Grandmother Willow character.

Disney has spent a hundred twenty-five million dollars on marketing this imaginary character and her neopagans, in picture and activity books, stuffed animals and games. There have also been free mall showings with hands-on animation effects and stage shows at Disney World and Disneyland. In New York, they have a new suerstore on Fifth Avenue and a hotel, entertainment and rental complex on Forty-second Street.

Co-promoters, such as Burger King, Chrysler, General Mills, Hallmark, Nestle, OPayless Shoes and Pizza Hut, have spent another fifty million dollars on cups, toys, cards, moccasins, etc., etc. The Woodstock-like premiere on the Great Lawn in New York City's Central Park, complete with jugglers, musicians and face painters, drew a hundred thousand people and a half million requests for free tickets to watch the ninety-two-foot screen. Policing a public park for gatecrashers drew criticism from ex-mayor Edward Koch.

[Andy Holmes has since written the *Bible for Me* series, *Night Light Tales, Building God's Kingdom, My Princess Bible, My Great Big God, God Moments for Men* and *Growing with Jesus.*]

Stars Should Lead Us To Jesus (December 1994)

In this season of the year we remember one particular star, the star of Bethlehem and the three Magi who followed it. The term magi originally meant a Persian castle of royal advisers. From it comes our word magic, magi-like. By the time of Jesus' birth it meant any wise man or a man with more than human knowledge, an astrologer or diviner of some sort.

Most newspapers and many newsstands carry horoscopes and astrological forecasts. Studies have found that most readers of such "literature" are female, either under thirty or over fifty. Astrology began in Mesopotamia about the time of the Babylonian exile. The Magi may have been some still exiled Jews, though tradition identifies them as representing the Gentiles because of their seemingly fulfilling the prophecies of Psalms 72:10-15 and Isaiah 60:6 when they prostrated before and gave gifts to the newborn King.

Since the earliest times, the stars have been thought to signal the great people and events of history. The sun, the moon and the stars have certainly indicated the cycles of the days, the weeks, the seasons.

Johannes Kepler, an astronomer not an astrologer, suggested that the star of Bethlehem was perhaps the triple conjunction of the planets Jupiter and Saturn in 7 B. C. Such a conjunction has a period of eight hundred five years on the average. The Jewish rabbis, according to Abrabanel in the Fifteenth Century, held that just such a conjunction took place -- also in the constellation Pisces -- three years before the birth of Moses and that another was anticipated before the birth of the Messiah.

Pisces was significant as the national constellation of the Jews as well as then marking the vernal equinox. Since then the precession of the equinox has shifted the signs of the zodiac again so that we are now in the so-called Age of Aquarius. The constellations of the zodiac are now two months off from what astrologers originally had them.

The 7 B. C. conjunction progressed across the sky from May to December from East to West, just the direction the Magi traveled. Because it is said by Matthew to have stopped over the place where Jesus was, some identify it not as a conjunction of the two brightest outer plants, but an actual new star, a nova. Others think it a completely miraculous and personal vision of the Magi, perhaps their less clear sighting of the angels of the shepherds.

In recent times astrology has been important, even if not true science. During World War II the Allies had a refugee German astrologer predict what Hitler's astrologers were telling him, such as the best date for the invasion of Sicily. There now is the legitimate science of astrometeorolgy which predicts the occurrence of solar storms from the planetary positions. The combined total tidal effects do have an effect on the sun and the sun's radio waves on communications.

Such "predictions" as Arcandus' that anyone born under Sagittarius in 1542 would have three marriages, be fond of vegetables, have three special illnesses and die at the age of eighty are too much to take seriously. So too is the prediction of the polar shift May 5, 1995. The planetary alignments may affect the sun somewhat, may be an interesting sight, but we ought to look to the Morning Star, Jesus Christ.

[*Exciting New Millennium Prophesies* predicted that President Bush would be assassinated, Dick Cheney would become president and Castro would be overthrown in 2001, Hillary would become the first woman U. S. president in 2008 and the papacy would end in 2010.]

Praise God For Jupiter's Comet (September 1994)

Long ago Edward Young wrote, "An undevout astronomer is mad." The Shoemaker-Levy 9 crash into the planet Jupiter brought out both the devout and the not so devout."

Arthur C. Clarke, author of *The Hammer of God*, about a comet nearly colliding with Earth in the near future, said, "I think the universe is a machine constructed for the amusement of astronomers."Also via picture phone from his home in Sri Lanka, he said it "is more incredible than even we crazy science fiction writers dreamed."

David Levy, one of the three discoverers of the comet, called the ciollision "the most fabulous thing I've seen in my life". After the first fragment fell, he said, "I am absolutely flabbergasted about this." Carolyn Shoemaker, who with her husband also is a co-discoverer, said in a similarly amazed state: "I didn't really expect to see that sort of thing."

Before the collision of fragment A, Michael Allison of NASA says the talk was that they might miss it. The Galileo space probe due to arrive near Jupiter next year could only make images a hundred forty times per minute. It might not be quick enough. It lasted ten minutes. Later in the week came the large fragment G. It too was brighter than expected, as bright as Jupiter. It was larger than expected, only slightly smaller than Earth. It too lasted long.

Heidi Hammel of the Space Telescope Science Institute spoke with awe of the amazing structure, the absolutely incredible streaks, the huge plume. "We're going to be thinking for years," she said, "trying to figure what that one's all about."

Dr. Neil Tyson seemed no so awestruck. "If we couldn't measure it as we are," he said, "it would be less of an event." Another astronomer did admit, "Most of what we 'know' is top-of-the-head speculation."

The numbers are impressive, however. As Paul Nohr of U. C. Observatory observed, "When you say 'hundred million megaton bomb,' those things tend to get people's attention." Some reporters got attention misreporting "facts" such as energy is being created and planets are colliding. Hiro Yukazumi was quoted in the tabloids under headlines warning, "Comet Crash Will Start U. S. Ice Age."

Analogies helped somewhat to appreciate the numbers. Fragment G's estimated two hundred million megatons of energy is six hundred times that of the world's nuclear arsenal, over three million times the most powerful man-made explosion. As much bigger as a nuclear explosion is to a Fourth of July sparkler was the come crash to the bomb's.

But the comparisons could have gone on. The energy of G's impact to the sun's output for one second is as the sun's is to the Crab Nebula supernova explosion. Visible to the Chinese in A. D. 1054, its smoke cloud is still expanding after nearly seven thousand years.

The Crab supernova is to the sun as the S Andromedae supernova is to it, In 1885 Reverend S. H. Saxby discovered the new star, as bright as the Andromeda galaxy, said to be over a million light-years away. It must have put out as much energy as a hundred trillion fragment G's. Professional astronomers then thought it was a comet until it reached its brightest August 31.

With this summer's cosmic show some spoke about the source of comets, the still hypothetical Oort cloud. They spoke of the comet only seen for the first time last year as billions of years old. They declared the dinosaur-killing comet "not a theory any longer, but a fact". This is just the sort of unscientific hastiness that got Galileo in trouble when he look at Jupiter.

Michael Allison explains, "Deep down there is a romance and a poetry to our subject," the devotion Young wrote of. Robert Browning might have fit right in with the new enthusiasts: "Whoso turns as I, this evening, turns to God to praise and pray while Jove's planet rises yonder ..."

"We can't understand what happened on Jupiter," says Hal Weaver, Hubble astronomer, "until we really understand what plunged into Jupiter." The mystery is still there. Asthe spectacle ended Keith Noll, STSI, said, "We still haven't seen anything we can say for sure is debris from a comet and that's quite interesting."

Whether it was a comet or not, it was a sign in the heavens. Perhaps the best observation of all was made by non-astronomer Fred Schnieder: "Don't start fighting with your neighbors over petty things because it could all end tomorrow."

[Just hours before Clarke's death on March 19, 2008, the light from most powerful gamma ray burst ever seen by the naked eye reached Earth after traveling 7.5 billion years!]

Christians Produce Alternative Comics (February 1994)
Jim Borgman's Christmas cartoon in the Cincinnati *Enquirer* pointed out the situation well. It showed a boy with a puzzled expression on his face. The boy had opened the box marked "Superhero action figure" to find the Christ Child.

An alternative to the increasingly unchristian themes and characters in comic books is making in-ways. More and more of these alternatives appear each year. *Brothers* creator Nate Butler says, "The nations great distributors won't touch them and even some Christian bookstores haven't fully accepted them." An artist for Heathcliff and the Muppets, Butler in his comic book tells of two brothers who fight street crime and bring hope to the hopeless. In *Aida-Zee* the Eterna Teens fight crime.

John Celestri's *Christian Crusader* was inspired by Ephesians 6:11's encouragement to put on the armor of God. Comic books have lost the goodness they had in the days of Captain Marvel, Superman, Tarzan and the Lone Ranger. "The stood for a code of conduct that is Christian whether it was stated or implied," Celestri said. Billy atson, if you remember, gained among other powers the wisdom of Solomon when he said "Shazam" and became Captain Marvel. Clark Kent's meekness carried over into his alter ego Superman. The Lone Ranger used relatively harmless silver bullets.

The Christian Crusader, Sir David, bears a resemblance to other superheroes, too. Like the Bible's David hid foe is a giant, the evil emperor Za-Tin. Like Rocketman he flies through the air with a rocketpack. Like Buck Rogers he was trapped in a cave. Like Batman his fights are full of bongs, zooms, crunches and fwooshes. His weapons, however are a sleepraygun and prayer. Celestri gives explicitly the code of conduct for would-be Knight of Christ: (1) keep the Commandments, (2) don't abuse your body, don't take drugs, (3) never take advanage of others, (4) help the less fortunate, and (5) ask Jesus to empower you to do your best every day.

Probably the best comment on these comics comes from readers. Joey Madden, ten, says, "I like Christian Crusader. It taught me not to fight my enemies, but to be nice." Roy Anderson, eleven, says, "He teaches me about Jesus and how to pray." Paula Donemuth says her six-year-old boy begged her to read more and Mrs. McDowell wrote, "It's encouraging to see children reading such as your CC Comics instead of the trash and filth of today's publishing."

Many of today's so-called comics devalue human life. Many "heroes" are not even human -- X-men, Toxic Crusaders, Ninja Turtles. Although not legally pornography, many certainly encourage indecent and unchaste behavior. Al Hartley lost his job with Marvel for refusing to do "adult" themes before getting an offer from Archie comics. Now his uncompromisingly Christian comics have sold over forty million copies.

[L. Nathan Butler organized the first International Christian Comics Competition (ICCC) in 2005 and took part in the Spirituality in Comics panel with Marv Wolfman at Supernova 2007 in Australia. He co-scripted and art directed a graphic novel about entitled *Yun: The Illustrated Story of the Heavenly Man.* Until 2010, Butler assisted Shinsei Senkyodan (New Life Ministries) with their Bible manga series: *Manga Messiah* (Four Gospels), *Manga Metamorphosis* (Acts/Letters), *Manga Mutiny* (Genesis to early Exodus), *Manga Melech* (Exodus to King David), and *Manga Messengers* (Solomon to the Prophets). His COMIX35 also published Christian comics for English- and French-speaking Africa.

John Celestri has animated not only "Animated Stories from the New Testament", "Animated Stories from the Bible" and "Animated Hero Classics", including Maccabees and Joan of Arc, but also "Animated Stories from the Book of Mormon" and "X-Men: Evolution", and the "Bloodwing Angel Chronicles" webcomic.

Henry Allen Hartley with Spire Christian Comics animated at least nineteen Archie titles with six Bible stories, twelve biography adaptations, four other book or movie adaptations and Kiddie Christian Comics with Barney Bear. He died in 2003 after sixty-one years of marriage.]

Angels Impact People's Lives (December 1993)

"When Christmas carols fill the air ... everyone believes in angels," Joan Wester Anderson writes. "But it's harder to accept the likelihood that the 'multitude of heavenly hosts' on that long-ago Bethlehem hillside has relevance in our lives too."

She opens her second collection of angel stories, "Where Angels Walk, with her son Tim's encounter with an angel just ten years ago. He had just dropped off a friend at his home and had four more hours driving to reach his own home for Christmas when the car quit. He and his companion only then realized they had been foolish to ignore the warnings about the extreme cold that silent night.

"Well, God," he prayed. "You're the only one who can help us now." and Joan adds that she too was praying for them. A tow truck suddenly appeared and towed thier car back to their friend's home. It seemed a fortunate coincidence. They realized it was more when their friend told them he had not seen the tow truck pull them up and they could find no tracks left by it in the snow, only their own.

In the same year as the publication of Anderson's *A Book of Angels* (1990), Frank Paretti's *Piercing the Darkness* and Godwin Malcolm's *Angels: An Endangered Species* also came out. Since then the interest in angels has grown rapidly. In '91 came Sophy Burnham's *Angel Letters*. In '92 *The Angel Book* and *How to Find Your Angels* by Karen Goldman and *Ask Your Angels* by Alma Daniel. Now in '93 comes *The Angels Within Us* by John Randolph Pierce.

A recent CBS poll reported nearly seventy percent of Americans beliee in angels now, as compared to the fifty percent quoted in Malcolm's book. Another study reports an even higher percentage among teens.

Fr. Andrew Greeley, priest, sociologist and novelist, puts it, "Some of it is real faith. Some of it is real kookiness. And sometimes it's hard to tell where the dividing line is between the two."

Films like "It's a Wonderful Life" and the television series like "Highway to Heaven" have contributed to the confusion. The media continually confuses the helpful disembodied spirit and the true angel. The New Agers have shifted their talk from God or Christ within to the angel within. Goldman writes, "To become an angel you must discover your inner light for yourself and let it shine. Just recognize that you already are somebody perfect and heavenly. Then just be yourself." Malcolm redefines angel to mean "one of our inner and most magical aspects."

The Opus Sanctorum Angelorum (Work of the Holy Angels) explains true devotion to angels.

Alma Daniel hosts angel workshops for learning to appreciate and contact your angel. In Angel Fire, NM, recently was the first Angel and Nature Spirit Conference. A hundred attended the eight-day program for a thousand dollars each.

Burnham's book has been translated into five languages and optioned for a Broadway play. Tony Kushner's "Angels in America" is already there. Ellen McLaughlin who plays the angel describes it as "playing the whole culture's dream". She relates it to our feelings of helplessness and vulnerability and the need for powerful helpers.

The angel storytellers describe angels as completely other, as he puts it, coming when they are told to or want to, not when we call them. Johnny Cash tells of the angel of death coming to him at twelve when his brother died and later again when his friend Johnny Horton died.

Vladimir Solevev, Oleg Atkov and Leonid Kiaim, cosmonauts on Soyuz 7, reported seeing seven giant figures with wings and halos. Malcolm Muggeridge tells of his documentary on Mother Teresa in which the dimly lit inner scenes photographs bright than those in the sunny courtyard, lit by a supernatural light.

Mother Mary Angelica, founder of the Eternal World Television Network, tells of her angelic encounter as a child. At eleven Rita Rizzo had been lifted by invisible hands from in front of aeeding car to safety. It changed her life. Padre Pio, the famous stigmatic, had had a initimate relationship with his angel since childhood. When he died, several American tourists in Italy saw angels in the night sky, who disappeared with the dawn.

[The opussanctorumangelorum,com website answers quoction, shares stories about angels and hosts retreats in fourteen language. In 1961 the first association of the faithful in the Work of the Holy Angels, the Confraternity of the Holy Guardian Angels, began in Innsbruck. In 2003 OA was incorporated into the Constitutions of the Order of Canons Regular of the Holy Cross in 2003. Padre Pio, fka Francesco Forgione, became St. Pius of Pietrelcina in 2002.]

Oldest Scripture Is Discovered (March 1992)

Amid the excitement of Hebrew Union College's unauthorized release of the Dead Sea Scrolls, another significant discovery has been neglected. Between 1975 and 1980 Dr. Gariel Barkay made three excavations in the Valley of Ben-Hinnom, just north of St. Andrew's Church in south Jerusalem. In 1979 he found one unplundered tomb dating back to the pre-exilic era, about 600 B. C., several centuries earlier than the oldest Dead Sea texts.

In this tomb, a large family burial place, he found the skeletal remains of nearly a hundred bodies, hundreds of pieces of pottery and jewelry, carvings in ivory and iron and bronze arrowheads. Among the jewelry were two small silver scrolls, one by one-half inch and one-half by one-fifth inch.

The difficult task of unrolling these extremely thin scroll of corroded silver was given to the experienced restorers at the University of Leeds, Great Britain. When they refuse to take the chance, they were sent to Germany with the same reaction. The Israelis finally dis it themselves by inventing a new method of handling the old metal.

They found inscribed within the scrolls the priestly blessing given in full in Numbers 6:24-26; "May Yahweh bless you and keep you; may Yahweh let His face shine upon you ... and give you peace!"

These are not only the earliest known inscriptions of the Bible yet discovered, they prove that the Old Testament predates the Exile. They are as relevant a prayer for peace now as twenty-six centuries ago. These remarkable scrolls are now on display, under magnification, at the Israel Museum in Jerusalem.

[In 2016 Yosef Porath used X-rays to "virtually unwrap" a charred scroll of Leviticus discovered in 1970 at Ein Gedi.]

Share Jesus This Christmas (December 1990)

Remember last Christmas? Remember the excitement of the Berlin Wall coming down? East and West embracing? Remember giving pieces of the Wall as Christmas presents, as symbols of liberty for all? Do you remember the fake pieces sold for purely personal gain?

Gorby did not bring about the change in the hold of communism in Europe; God did. Last Christmas the Orthodox Patriarch Maksim of Bulgaria appeared on television with his Christmas message of hope. In Romania the exiled Josef Tron's return was televised.

What do the newly-freed Iron Curtain peoples want this Christmas? The same thing that they have asked for before freedom, our prayers. With the new freedoms in speech, publications and worship come the troubles of Western materialism, the prosperity gospel, the cults and Muslim and Buddhist evangelism.

Ralph Man of Missions Possible says, "We're dabbling in one of the world's most important areas with one of the greatest opportunities of our lifetime." He is concerned about the lack of follow-up that may follow the initial rush of Bibles and evangelizers from the Free World.

Last October a thousand pastors and lay leaders met in Moscow representing a hundred-fifty ministries. They are trying to deal with the as yet uncoordinated effort to help our Christian brothers and sisters. They ask for more than money; they ask for our prayers.

In Romania the Lord's Army has been legalized, but so has abortion as well. Private worship, seminaries and open pentecostalism are now allowed in Czechoslovakia, but they need teachers and leaders.

The United Bible Societies estimate thirty million Bibles are needed in the former Soviet Union in the next four years. Teachers and evangelists are also needed. As the Ethiopian eunuch asked Philip, "How can I grasp what is read unless someone explains it to me?" (Acts 8:31)

Open Doors reports an increase in contributions. The Word of Life Fellowship is working with drug addicts, the Campus Crusade for Christ and Youth for Christ with the youth. Most of the efforts, however remain in the best-known churches in the largest cities. The Missions Research Group says the people of the country are still inreached, prey to the wolves in sheep's clothing.

Hank Paulson, director of the Eastern European Bible Mission, points to the division between Christians as a major problem. "If we as Western missions cannot work together, we really have very little to say to the church in Eastern Europe."

Peter Deyneka, Jr., of the Slavic Gospel Association, says the many changes over the past year have him "wondering how the landscape of Central Europe and the [former] Soviet Union will look not only next year, but next month."

Other communist nations -- China, South East Asia, Africa -- and the Americas are watching as well. the effect that the underground Romanian Church had in its overthrow of their government especially has them watching carefully.

Dr. Jonathan Chao, director of China Ministries International, has noted "the triumph of the non-institutional church", Christians, actual and potential, throughout the world need the support of both the institutional and nob-institutional Church. This Christmas give a heavenly treasure, change history, change lives. Thank God for your freedom to do so and pray.

[Since 1974, Mission Possible (mp.org) has operated through five sister organizations in the West (in the United States, Finland, Sweden, the United Kingdom, and the Netherlands), and ten local organizations in Eastern Europe (Russia, Ukraine, Bulgaria, Albania).

Fr. Iosif Trifa founded the Lord's Army to evangelize Orthodox Christians in Romania in the 1930s.

Founded in 1946 United Bible Societies (unitedbiblesocieties.org) now provides twenty percent of its thirty-two million Bibles per year on-line to over two hundred countries.

Open Doors (opendoors.org) provides Bibles, prayer and support "to believers in most danger".

Since 2012 Campus Crusade for Christ has been known by the nickname Cru (cru.org) apparently to avoid using the three words its been know by since 1951; Youth for Christ (yfc.org) started in 1944.

Originally named the Russian Gospel Association in 1934, the Slavic Gospel Association (sga.org) does the same in former Soviet countries. Eastern European Bible Mission (eem.org), founded in 1962, now provides Bibles to thirty countries in twenty languages.]

Celebrate A True Christmas: Adore Jesus (December 1989)

How do you celebrate Christmas? Since the so-called reindeer rule (Pawtucket, RI, 1984), public displays during the season of this national holiday have been a source of controversy and confusion. A creche or manger scene may be put up in a public (if allowed at all) if subsumed by a larger secular display. To celebrate publicly the birth of the God-man, we must snowmen (even snowpersons) more than equal time.

Alleheny County attorney George Jancsko says such cases "are elevating trifling details and making them matters of constitutional significance." One reaction to this public trivialization of Christmas is to bring back the season's meaning privately. The Father so loved the world He gave us the Gift of His own Son, the Light of the world.

"Holiday customs' psychologist John Rosemand says, referring to both Christmas and Hanukkah, "help develop family unity by establishing a sense of belonging, especially in children." Since the end of World War II, he says, many factors, including divorce, working mothers and the changing economy, have divided families. He warns, "Don't let the material aspects of the holidays overwhelm the spiritual."

Some families separated by distance bridge the gap by lighting candles at a particular agreed upon time, such as the Sabbaths or Sundays of December. Through lighting up at different places and at different times of days, everyone can take part in the celebration simultaneously. Still others have found the best way to celebrate is to the family by volunteering to serve at a Christmas dinner, either individually or as a whole family. This kind of outside activity has even been said to break through to teenage Scrooges.

Traditional ethnic treats can bring families together and also teach children about their roots or others'. Plum pudding, goose, fruitcakes, Scandinavian fruit, soup, mincemeat or pecan pies are but a few possibilities.

Some mothers get together every year for a "no-cal bake-off". The bakers combine their favorite cookies into packaged and wrapped assortments which they don't eat. They distribute them to seniors and shut-ins. Other mothers trade time babysitting others' children so that they can shop without children. Not only does this build the true Christian spirit of sharing, it also helps reduce the holiday hassle.

Just taking time to talk and listen to each other and to share with each other may be what most of all. One truly wanted gift received can make up for a lifetime of unwanted Christmas gifts of whatever cost. Taking the time to invite an acquaintance to church for Christmas or a Christmas Christian for the week after could change a life.

Making cards or decorations, making a display of past Christmases' photos could be "old family traditions" you could start this tear. Stuffing stockings with a list of the year's or the month's good and not-so-good memories could be another. Painting Christmasy scenes on the windows and countless more ways can help remind us of the true meaning of Christmas.

Whatever the outward circumstances, we can find Christmas within. We can find our own way to celebrate the King's birthday. "Come let us adore Him!" as a favorite carol urges.

[The Thomas More Society and the American Nativity Scene Committee have worked continuously to get Christian displays erected in public places across the country.]

Voyager Reveals Glory of God (September 1989)

The Grand Tour of *Voyager II* did not end with its fly-by Neptune, the now most distant known planet. Its cameras are planned to be shut off in the mid-1990s and its power will run down by about 2015, but it will continue to fly.

It began long before the launch in 1977 in the minds of scientists and engineers at the Jet Propulsion and Laboratory, Pasadena, CA. The providential spiral positioning of the outer planets in the '70s would not come again until 2159. "This was a rare opportunity that was seized," planning manager Charles Kohlhase says. "The public has gotten their money's worth out of this one."

In 1971 the project's promoters finally got a budget allotment, but only about a third of that requested. The project team had to make many hard decisions. Self-sacrifice, cooperation, discipline and submission to authority kept the project going. They decided to include a gold-plated copper phonograph recording greetings in fifty-three languages, ninety minutes of music -- from Bach to Chuck Berry -- the songs of birds and whales, the surf, a heartbeat and a baby's cry. It concluded with then President Jimmy Carter's proclamation, "This is a present from a small distant world, a token of our sounds., our science, our music, our thoughts and our feelings ... our hope and our determination and our goodwill in a vast and awesome universe."

Like David slinging a stone at Goliath, NASA threw a spacecraft at the giants. The mission could have failed at any point along the way, but for the grace of God. A totally new hydrozine steering system had to be invented, and new X-band radio tubes and a new plutonium power supply. New techniques and schedules had to be devised throughout the flight as man and machine worked together.

We lifted up our collective eyes, as Isaiah so long ago wrote, and began to see Who has created the heavens. We found unexpected sulfur volcanoes on Io and nitrogen ice ones on Triton. We found rings around all the giants and ten thousand around Saturn, with "shepherds" and "sheepdogs" ordering it all.

We got pictures of Mimas with its huge crater, a quarter of its whole surface area. We saw cratered Callisto, striped Europa, smooth Enceladus, potato-shaped Almathea and hamburger-shaped Hyperion. We found seven hundred miles per hour winds on Neptune and eleven hundred miles per hundred winds on Saturn, *Voyager* showed us sixty other worlds -- beautiful, complex and bewilderingly intricate -- all otherworldly.

"Each day it gets better," J. Eberhart said, "totally different from anything we've seen." Brad Smith said, "We are like students going into an exam thinking we know all the answers and then going blank. We just don't know to make of it, "God's ways are far beyond our ways, as far as the heavens are above the Earth.

Theorists will now try to explain the spokes and the braiding in Saturn's rings the five million ampere current between Jupiter and Io, the electroglow aurora of Uranus. The rest of us Earthlings will, hopefully remember our lessons. Creation is grandee than anything man can build or image. The Earth, and every living thing on Earth, is precious and unique. If we work together, we can accomplish grand things.

As then California governor Jerry Brown commented during the Jupiter fly-by, "As we spend more of our time in space, we will spend less of our time thinking about racial, linguistic and cultural differences ... that's a lot better than war. We'll gain an Earth view instead of a nationalistic view." Perhaps we'll learn to see ourselves as our Creator sees us.

[*Voyager II* proceeded on to explore Saturn in 1981, Uranus in 1986 and Neptune in 1989, is still communicating with the Deep Space Network after over forty years and not expected to run out of power until 2025.]

Jesus Cures "Holidaze" (December 1988)
Do you suffer from PHS -- Pre-Holiday Syndrome? Have you already had enough of the season to be jolly? Are you upset with the apathy, the greed, the short-tempered clerks and the long, unmoving lines? Do you go to parties to break through your depression? Or do you go into depression after going to parties?

The "holidaze" began before Halloween when Standard Time returned bringing evening darkness. It will continue into the new year, tht shows no indication of being any better than the old.

Experts talk of SAD, Seasonal Affective Disorder, and recommend spending more time in artificial light and changing sleeping patterns, or they call it holiday stress and advise slowing down, lowering expectations. The problem however is not so much too little light as no Light, not so much to much activity as the wrong activity.

It might be called XMS -- the X-mas Syndrome, trying to live out Christmas without Christ. X-mas has acquired its own traditions, its own meaning by borrowing and combining pagan and Christian rites. X-mas means exhaustion, expenses, exchanges. It means Santa and elves, Rudolph and Frosty, dying or artificial trees, football and food.

To some it means facing another winter without warm clothes or a roof or a bed. To some it means facing loneliness and the feeling that everyone else has someone who cares. Hospitals and nursing homes and prisons are filled with such unjolliness.

The cure for XMS is to remember the true meaning of Christmas: "He emptied Himself and took the form of a slave, being born in the likeness of men." (Philippians 2:7) Remember the young couple with no place to stay. Remember the shepherds who left their field and the travelers who left their gifts for Him Who was given to the world out of love. There are many ways of putting back meaning into your Christmas. You may even extend Christmas and celebrate a truly new year.

Linda Tabar, Alamogordo, NM, has become known as the Label Lady. She collects labels using them to send away for toy offers and then gives them to a local mission and to El Paso, TX, learning center. All year long now she receives coupons from people all over the country.

Michael Geenberg, Brooklyn, NY, gives gloves to individuals he sees in need of them in the Bowery, about two hundred a year. "The giver is the one who benefits," he says.

In Beaumont, CA, Sara O'Meara and Yvonne Fedderson got together and started the Village of Childhelp for abused children. Each Christmas the children put on plays for such celebrities as Cheryl Ladd, Bob Hope and Robert Young.

All year long volunteer senior citizens are knitting gifts for Christmas at Sea. This project for Seaman's Church Institute makes sure that none of the seaman who have passed through the ports of New York and New Jersey are forgotten at Christmas.

Ten branch banks in Athens, OH, have gotten together to collect coats, which they distribute through schools in Appalachia. Volunteers for Yule Collection, a Chicago hotline, help callers by listening, by referring them to where they can get other help.

Even those celebrating the season of Hanukkah can get into the spirit. Members of Temple Beth Israel, Phoenix, AZ, serve at the St. Vincent de Paul (SVDP) dining room to over a thousand so the Vincentians can spend Christmas with their families.

[After working for needy children in Japan, Vietnam and the U. S., in 1987 Pope John Paul II gave O'Meara and Fedderson citations for "recognition of the dedication to the loving care and commitment to protection of abused children in the world. In 2000 Merv Griffin donated his dude ranch to Childhelp. In 2004 they wrote *Silence Broken*, made into the film, "For the Love of a Child". They are still working for children at childcare.org.]

Jesus Victorious in La Victoire (July 1988)

Fr. Tim Atkin, the Missionhurst pastor of La Victoire, Haiti, wholeheartedly agreed with the Bishop'ss petition for a new election. There had been no one killed then in his parish, but everyone in the country had been a victim. Fear still ruled.

The soldier had only threatened with his gun. The rumors of what was happening elsewhere did the rest. Before the news blackout the stories of voters being shoot down in the streets had circulated. The attempt to hide the atrocities only made the fears hold stronger.

Attendance on Sundays had fallen off. Even if the government paid no attention to the petition, Fr. Tim felt glad to have a reason to go door-to-door visiting. As he did, he saw the fear in the eyes of his parishioners, "Is this truly any better than the days of 'Pa[a Doc' Duvalier's secret police?" Most of his congregation had someone in their family who had suddenly been arrested or simply disappeared. they did not want that past to return.

Although he had built a good relationship with the people, he knew they also feared Americans. They did not want that past of American military intervention either. What Haitians wanted and needed was the free and honestly elected government they had been promised.

Suddenly the local army post's private stepped up to him and arrested him. He had received orders from his superiors to stop anyone circulating such a petition. He escorted the priest off to jail, confiscated the petition and thought himself a pretty important fellow now.

As the crowd gathered outside, however he realized he had made a mistake -- a big mistake. He had made no friends since being stationed here. He was one of the many petty dictators that had sprung up since "Baby Doc's" ouster and the interim government's inaction.

Everyone had heard how his mother had come to set up housekeeping for him and how she had clubbed their landlady over the head. She had not asked for the rent they owed, only that they leave. Hundreds of people gathered about the post, some curious, some angry, some just enjoying the event.

"The little private has arrested the priest!"

"He cannot do that!"

"What is he going to do now?"

"Oh, look here comes the sergeant."

What the sergeant said does not translate easily into English. He expressed his displeasure.

Fr. Tim demanded the petition and the copy he had seen the private make. The sergeant finally agreed to forget the whole matter, promised to not take any action against those on the list and to see to it the private was transferred. He said getting his copy back would be no protection since there had been enough time to make many copies. Fr, Tim agreed and was released amid great rejoicing.

The best news however was yet to come. The sergeant kept all his promises. The people learned they could come together and change things. They began gathering for services at the church again. The fear had been routed. The new elections were not much freer that the first, but Love never loses hope.

[My cousin, Fr. Tim, was eventually transferred to serve many years in Rome. Missionhurst aka the Congregation of the Immaculate Heart of Mary (CICM) was founded in 1862 by Fr. Theophile Verbist of Belgium. Forty of their number have been martyred in the mission field. The website missionhurst.org includes current and past magazines published three time per year as well as blogs from the missionaries.]

"Colors" Deglorifies Gang Warfare (June 1988)

Dennis Hopper, who directed the new film "Colors" deglorifing gang warfare, knows what he's doing. He chose Los Angeles' Crips and Bloods, because he lives in the area. Having been set free from drug and alcohol addiction, he knows about that too.

L. A. last yearhad twelve thousand drug-related arrests and two hundred eighty-seven gang homicides, more than all homicides in Europe. The feuds are still over "turf" as in "West Side Story", but now that translates to "drug sales territory". As cocaine prices have dropped to one-sixth what they had been for four years ago, violence has risen just as dramatically.

The gangs include all races, blacks, whites, Hispanics, Americans illegals. They are spreading from the big coastal cities to the nations smallest towns. Chicago has its Cobras, Disciples, El Rakna, Latin Kings and Vice Lords; Miami its 34th Street Players and Untouchables. The so-called Jamaicans are found in many cities in the South and East.

The gangs -- as Hopper's film graphically tells -- have far greater manpower and fiorepower than the policemen, the peace officers trying to maintain peace. Assault rifles and semiautomatics have replaced chain and knives.

The gangs remain young however. An "O. G." or "old gangster" mean one who has prison experience, usually not yet thirty. Associated with the gangs too are the "wannabees", the youngsters who want to become members.

"Colors" portrays the problem well from the point of view of the police. It does not do so well with presenting the answer. there can be no victory without the Victor, Jesus Christ.

Kenneth Wheeler of the Community Youth Gang Services, L. A., says, "Someone has to tell them there's a better way." Last year the CYGS helped three hundred fifty ghetto families with food, education, housing, funeral arrangements, whatever they needed. They helped arrange forty-seven truces between rival gangs. The saw a hundred twenty gang members choose that better way and leave the gang. It's not a large number compared to the estimated seventy thousand gang members in L. A. It is however a step in the right direction.

[The Violence Prevention Coalition of Greater Los Angeles (VPC) includes members from a range of public and private organizations, including public health, the legal community, gun violence prevention, domestic violence prevention, victim support services, education, and arts organizations. CleanSlate began tattoo removals in 1997.]

Prodigals Meet the Father (February 1988)

Joe Miller, co-founder of Prodigal Ministries, has been helping recovering homosexuals full-time since July, 1987. Although few in number its staff is professional and also caring, leading them tonJesus and through Hom to the loving Father.

Miller was a prodigal son himself, a pastor who had left his family and his church for a homosexual life-style. It led him to the point of near suicide, when he had the knife to his throat, but God stayed his hand. He paced the floor for three hours and then was led to call the 700 Club" and ask for prayer for the prodigal.

Miller frankly admits he could return to practicing homosexuality, but asks himself, "Is it worth it? Not only the risk of disease, but the separation from God?" Now he has the greater desire not to grieve the Spirit; he wants to keep his truly loving relationship with Christ, with Christ in the person of a homosexual.

"It is our responsibility to love them, listen and offer hope in Jesus Christ. I know a lot of ministers who are actively homosexual, claiming to be Christian and a lot of Christians struggling with the problem. There is a difference. We do indeed live in the body, but we do not wage war with human resources. The weapons of our warfare are not merely human. They possess God's power for the destruction of strongholds. (2 Corinthians 10:3-4) This is what we teach. We do not compromise the Scriptures."

He speaks to mixed groups of both sexual orientations, explaining that homosexual behavior is sin, without neglecting to state that everyone's unmet love-needs are legitimate. What he visited the Forum at the University of Louisville, the Gay/Lesbian Coalition listened and respected him because he has been where they are.

"I see them every week. They need to work out their resentments. As long as it takes, I'll sit here. The process, changing from glory to glory in stages, really makes them strong. That strength helps us to deal with relational problems, rebellion."

H has no trouble, he says, with patience or empathy for those who come to him for help. But he does with the homophobia he encounters, based on ignorance and misinformation. Once people understand the problem, they become open to seeking the Answer.

Elizabeth Moberly has described the condition as "defensive detachment", a rejection of society's gender role for individual survival. "I get flack from the psychological associations who don't understand the redemption of Christ. But affirmation by a healthy adult, supported by heterosexual couples, is the only way to have a loving relationship. Healing of memories and spiritual healing is so important in recovery. I find joy in being a spiritual mentor, leading a person through the events of their childhood. I encourage them to picture Jesus touching their hurtful memories, to forgive the persons who molested or abandoned them. We go through the storm and wonder 'Where is God in all this?' When we stop and look, we see Jesus and realize Jesus was there. He does take us through the storm.

"From my own experience I know the healing process was excruciating, but through it I came back to the Hope of Christianity. Through it they come to realize they are a hundred percent totally dependent on God. That's the beautiful thing, when they can see God loves us right where we are and continues to love us. May the Lord strength and sustain all who serve the prodigals and demonstrate rue love to 'the elder brothers'."

[Prodigal Ministries (prodigal-ministries.com) which at first reached out exclusively to persons struggling with unwanted same gender attraction, now does so to five hundred per year of any age struggling in multiple forms of sexual brokenness, families and friends of those persons, persons with HIV/AIDS, individuals who struggle with gender identity disorder.]

Videos Tell the Good News (December 1987)

This year your family has the opportunity to travel back in time with Derek, Margo and Moki and witness the birth of Jesus, the vision of the angels to the shepherds, His exciting visit from the Wise Men and His lifesaving flight with Mary and Joseph to Egypt. "The Nsativity", the seventh video in Hannah-Barbera's The Greatest Adventure: Stories from the Bible series, is now available.

Hundreds of thousands have already passed through the time portal discovered by the three young adventurers and traveled with them to the times of Noah, Moses, Joshua, Samuel, David and Daniel. The thirty-minute tapes are aimed at children between two and twelve, but adults love them too.

Parents and teachers are enthusiastically giving thanks to Joseph Barbera -- and to God -- for the new translation of the Bible into the media children best understand, televion animation. The series has earned the Distinguished Service Award from the National Religious Broadcasters, the Golden Angel Award from Religion in Media and the Award of Excellence from the Film Advisory Board.

"The word 'enthusiasm' is derived from a Greek root meaning 'spirit'," Bruce Johnson, the executive in charge of production, notes. "And a number of people at Hannah-Barbera brought tremendous spirit to their work on the project. I think the results show it. You can get an idea of the amount of work involved if you think of the time we spend on each story. The stories are done concurrently, but scripting on each takes about two-and-a-half months, writing as fast as possible. Editing follows, then promotion -- each one is in production for nearly a year."

Hannah-Barbera's standards for the animation, Scripture scholarship and star-caliber casting remain high in "The Nativity". Helen Hunt does the voice of Mary, Jesus' mother, Gregory Harrison that of Joseph, His foster father and Vincent Price the voice of Herod. The three Magi are enacted by Roscoe Lee Browne, Richard Libertini and Alan Oppenheimer, while Brock Peters does the voice of the archangel Gabriel.

The number of sales even before distribution through video stores and B. Dalton bookstores were enough to win a platinum certificate by the International Tape/Disc Association (ITA). More than fifty thousand units of each title were sold just through direct marketing.

Other videos now in production are planned to be released next year, now through Magic Video Publishing: "The Creation Story", "Joseph and His Brothers", "Moses and the Ten Commandments", "Queen Esther" and "The Easter Story".

[The series had thirteen videos before ending in 1992. Five ("The Miracles of Jesus", "David and Goliath", "Noah's Ark", "The Easter Story" and "Moses") were released on DVD in 2006.]

Local Churches Fund Poverty Fight in Haiti (March 1987)

One year after the nearly three decades of Duvalier dictatorship in Haiti ended, have conditions there improved? Yes, they have by the grace of God working, not through the new military-civilian junta or U. S. government aid, but through dedicated laypeople working in base communities supported by such private groups as Harry Hosey's Adopt-a=parish program. Adopt-a-Parish provides money to individual parishes in Haiti, principally to train catechists and lay teachers in the Haitian bishops' literacy campain, Mission Alpha.

Rita George, translator of missionary correspondence for Adopt-a-Parish, describes it this way, "The first parish to be adopted was a rural-mountainous parish in the northwest called Beauchamp. It had nothing. "Now it has a dispensary, a very nice school, shelters for the old and abandoned, a nutrition center and trained catechists."

More than a hundred fifty U. S. Catholic churches have adopted Haitian parishes in the past nine years. Since last May when St. Mary's in Urbana, IL, adopted Cayle-Jacmel, a parish of seven thousand active members (and nine thousand inactive) with one central church and five mission chapels, Pastor Yves Favé has been able to set up kindergarten classes, training sessions for about seventy community leaders and help many families otherwise unable to participate. "It is really they," he writes, referring to these new parish helpers, "who are advancing the work of evangelization."

Reducing the fifty percent unemployment and eighty-five percent illiteracy rates that made a dictatorship like the Duvaliers' able to operate is the first step in pre-evangelization. "There is no lack of difficulties in this kind of work," Fr. Favé says. "Difficulties because people don't always see the need to read and write, to change their secular habits, difficulties because those who have already had the opportunity to be educated don't see any purpose in educating the masses."

Lt. Gen. Henri Namphy's interim government is made up of former Duvalierists who do not want tolose the privileges they had built up on exploitation, theft, lies and graft. During their long reign of terror every man able to lead the forces of change either joined with those in power, fled the country or was "eliminated". The secret police, the Tontons Macoutes, are still feared even though they have fled the country or remain in hiding. U. S. military intervention, like that from 1915 to 1934, is also feared.

"The only organization which today allows the people to hope for real change is the Church," Fr. Favé observes. "Which has taken to heart Pope John Paul II's appeal during his 1983 visit, "I'll tait que les choses changent icí." (Things have got to change here.)

Other missionaries, George says, report that recent constitutional elections showed a poor turnout or that there are over a hundred presidential candidates for an election set for February 1988 tyat may never take place.

Namphy has failed to address the "religious problem" which last year resulted in over a hundred murders by witch-hunting mobs, the unholy war between supposed Christians and Voodooists. The "problem" is that the Duvalierists continue to maintain Voodoo is not Satanic but "Haiti's cultural heritage".

Some investors have pulled out because of the instability, causing additional unemployment. The unemployment leads to an increased drain of manpower, particularly young men. "Under Duvalier there was a contract with the Dominican government," Fr. Favé explains. "It was a real slave trade. At this time, this contract has been denounced, but the slave trade has grown worse because those who go there go at their own peril, with no guarantee of salary or working conditions, totally at the mercy of their employers. It is poverty alone which causes them to leave under such conditions."

"We don't like to know about the poor," George says, "Knowing about the poor is a threat yto our own middle-class comfort. If we are somehow responsible for others, it will mean giving in and giving up." "It is time for the U. S. A. to take a good look. Haiti is next door; Haiti is starving."

The old Haiti is still there, but there is now a new hope. As Fr. Favé says, thanking his adoptive American church, "It is because of your help that we can help families who have problems. Now at least, even though we cannot meet all their needs, we can do something."

[The Parish Twinning Program of the Americas (PTPA at parishprogram.org) has been providing spiritual and material needs to Haitians since St. Henry's, Nashville, TN, in 1978. By 1999, the Program expanded to twinning with parishes in Central and South America, Mexico, the Philippines, and the Spanish-speaking Caribbean and the next year founder Hosey died.]